Developing Readers and Writers in the Content Areas
K–12

FIFTH EDITION

Developing Readers and Writers in the Content Areas K–12

David W. Moore
Arizona State University

Sharon Arthur Moore
Osborn (Arizona) Elementary School District

Patricia M. Cunningham
Wake Forest University

James W. Cunningham, Emeritus
University of North Carolina, Chapel Hill

PEARSON
and

Boston   New York   San Francisco
Mexico City   Montreal   Toronto   London   Madrid   Munich   Paris
Hong Kong   Singapore   Tokyo   Cape Town   Sydney

Executive Editor: Aurora Martínez Ramos
Editorial Assistant: Lynda Giles
Executive Marketing Manager: Krista Clark
Production Editor: Janet Domingo
Editorial Production Service: Modern Graphics, Inc.
Composition Buyer: Linda Cox
Manufacturing Buyer: Linda Morris
Electronic Composition: Modern Graphics, Inc.
Interior Design: Lisa Devenish
Cover Administrator: Joel Gendron

For related titles and support materials, visit our online catalog at www.ablongman.com.

Between the time website information is gathered and then published, it is not unusual for some sites to have closed. Also, the transcription of URLs can result in typographical errors. The publisher would appreciate notification where these errors occur so that they may be corrected in subsequent editions.

Library of Congress Cataloging-in-Publication Data

Developing readers and writers in the content areas K-12/David W. Moore ... [et al.].— 5th ed.
   p. cm.
 Includes bibliographical references and indexes.
 ISBN 0-205-49474-9
  1. Language arts—Correlation with content subjects. 2. Content area reading. I. Moore, David W.

LB1576.D455 2006
428'.43—dc22

2006042602

Printed in the United States of America
10 9 8 7 6 5 4 3 2 1   [RRD-VA]   10 09 08 07 06

Contents

Preface

Teaching students how to use reading and writing as tools for learning ranks near the top of the many responsibilities teachers assume. *Developing Readers and Writers in the Content Areas, K–12* introduces prospective and practicing teachers to this responsibility. Elementary- and secondary-school teachers alike will find this book to be a practical guide. Its engaging prose and numerous examples describe the principles underlying specific teaching practices.

 Developing Readers and Writers in the Content Areas, K–12 can be used in courses with titles such as *Literacy across the Curriculum* and *Content Area Reading*. Its attention to elementary and secondary teaching concerns makes it appropriate for courses aimed at either audience, as well as for courses with a mixture of upper-grade and lower-grade teachers. It is intended for use in undergraduate or post-baccalaureate teacher-preparation programs, during staff development activities, and in introductory graduate teacher education courses.

Shared Features of Earlier Editions and the Fifth Edition

This fifth edition of *Developing Readers and Writers in the Content Areas, K–12* retains features of the earlier editions that our students and colleagues found especially noteworthy. These features include the following.

General to Specific Progression

The first three chapters move from the general to the specific in order to show how overall instructional planning embeds content area literacy planning. Chapter 1 presents a rationale for content literacy instruction, describes thinking processes that can be promoted across all grades in all activities, and explains the role of academic identities in subject matter reading, writing, and learning. Chapter 2 sets a general stage for content literacy instruction by presenting professional practices, cycles of instruction, and settings that influence literacy and learning. Chapter 3 portrays the steps in planning units of instruction that contain reading and writing. The next eight chapters then concentrate on incorporating the major dimensions of literacy into classroom instruction. The final two chapters address reading assessments and policies, topics that are becoming increasingly important as content area reading becomes more visible and politicized.

Content Area Applications

Although the teaching practices described in the comprehension, vocabulary, writing, and studying chapters apply to all subject areas, the applications are not always obvious to newcomers. For instance, comprehension has many common properties, but comprehending poetry in English language arts class differs from comprehending explorers' journal entries in history, and both differ from comprehending directions in a technological work environment. Consequently, we describe specific content area applications at the end of Chapters 5 through 8. The content areas we address are English language arts, mathematics, science, second language, social studies, and activity, a term for hands-on courses.

Standards-Based Teaching and Learning

Educators in the United States continue teaching amid an unprecedented system of accountability. Mandated standards and high-stakes assessments currently affect teaching and learning in practically every classroom. Chapter 3, "Instructional Units," begins with a clear-headed view of how to design instruction that recognizes accountability systems. Remaining chapters then address this issue, showing how to make standards and assessments work for your students' best interests.

Multiple Possibilities

This book brings together multiple possible ideas and practices. First, it addresses the diversity of today's student populations. For instance, Chapter 4, "Reading Materials and Projects," illustrates the great variety of reading materials and projects appropriate for students' diverse cultural, linguistic, and cognitive settings. The "Vocabulary," "Comprehension" and "Writing" chapters set aside specific sections showing how to teach various strategies that remain aligned with basic principles of effective instruction. Each presentation at the end of Chapters 5 through 8 contains a special application for students who are learning English as a second language.

Second, even though separate chapters of this text highlight comprehension and writing, each chapter addresses literacy, the combination of reading and writing. Treating written language as a whole preserves the benefits that reading and writing have for each other and for the exploration of subject matter.

Finally, we address K–12 instruction in this book because teaching and learning processes across the grades are fundamentally similar. Students certainly become more sophisticated as they develop across the years, so their literacy instruction must keep pace, even though fundamental conditions such as meaningfulness and academic support remain unchanged. We show how literacy and subject matter instruction can be combined across the grades even as subject matter becomes more specialized.

Thorough Presentations of Key Concepts

Our goal is to allow ready implementation of specific teaching practices, and we assume that our audience does not already know them. So we present the practices clearly and completely. We use accessible terminology and concrete examples. Additionally, the learning aids in the text are included to enhance understanding and retention. The following aids are found either at the beginning or end of each chapter to help you think about the chapter contents:

- *Looking Ahead*, which appears at the beginning of each chapter, presents an overview of that chapter's contents.
- *Key Ideas* are listed in the introduction of each chapter, following the *Looking Ahead* section. They form the main headings for the chapters, indicating the major points within each chapter.
- *Looking Back* summaries occur at the end of each chapter.
- *Add to Your Journal* also appears at the end of each chapter. This learning aid suggests topics to consider and questions to answer when responding to this book in journal form.
- *Additional Readings*, the final section of each chapter, suggests books and articles that amplify the material presented in the chapter.

Along with the learning aids at the beginning and end of the chapters, we interspersed the following pedagogical features throughout these chapters to promote interaction with the ideas presented:

- *Do It Together* suggests group activities. Small-group collaborative effort can promote learning.
- *Listen, Look, and Learn* contains suggestions for checking out chapter contents with students and practicing teachers. It is a reality check for ideas and an opportunity to develop them.
- *Try It Out* encourages application. Learning occurs best when you do something with the ideas you encounter.

New Features in the Fifth Edition

Educators alter their practices when social and political changes affect school expectations and when research-based scholarship offers new professional knowledge. To keep pace with the changes in content area literacy instruction, we completely changed the final four chapters of the earlier edition, and we revised all the chapters that were retained. Especially noteworthy changes in this edition are as follows.

New Chapter Containing Cases of Instruction

Following our reviewers' suggestions, we reduced to one chapter the original final four chapters that contained narrative accounts of teaching. This new chapter now presents one case each of teachers presenting literacy-rich instructional units at the primary, intermediate, middle, and high-school levels. Readers are invited to form groups and evaluate each unit according to the dimensions of content area literacy instruction presented in the earlier chapters.

New Chapter on Differentiating Instruction

The U.S. commitment to all students becoming proficient with high levels of literacy means that all learners are expected to accomplish the same standards. Students who start out with different levels of academic preparedness, different approaches to learning, and different interests deserve multiple instructional pathways to accomplishing rigorous, uniform standards of achievement. A new chapter now highlights ways to address literacy-related accommodations for diverse groups of students.

New Chapter on Reading Proficiency

Current educational accountability systems for proficient reading, which typically direct readers toward only one particular type of reading, are at risk of limiting or devaluing students' competencies with other types of reading. In this era of accountability, educators require trustworthy information about the assessments being used for decision making. Consequently, we have dedicated an entire chapter to clarifying the issues involved in defining reading proficiency.

New Chapter on Reading Policy

The *No Child Left Behind* legislation is focusing attention on high levels of reading for everyone. The opportunity and the challenge that this legislation poses are to ensure that it serves all students well. The new, final chapter of this fifth edition examines these opportunities and challenges.

Clarification and Elaboration

Some portions of the earlier edition seemed to communicate better than others, so we clarified the language in a few spots and inserted new headings to better signal ideas in others. We also reconfigured some chapters according to new conceptual frameworks. For instance, the "Meaning Vocabulary" chapter now is arranged according to instructional practices that promote wide reading, teach sets of words directly, promote word consciousness, and teach word learning strategies. Additionally, we updated numerous examples, especially with regard to computer software and online sites.

The authors thank the following reviewers of the new edition: Mary Anne Bednar, La Salle University; Andrew B. Pachtman, William Paterson University; Gracie Porter, Middle Tennessee State University; Darlene Russell, William Paterson University; and Barbara N. Sherman, Liberty University.

Developing Readers and Writers
in the Content Areas
K–12

Content Area Reading and Writing

LOOKING AHEAD Elementary-, middle-, and high-school students acquire an incredible amount of knowledge while exploring content areas such as science, mathematics, and history. For instance, they learn that Confucius was a Chinese philosopher, that multiple natural forces produce land formations, that exponential growth explains many actions, that supply and demand underlies certain economic cycles, that yeast causes dough to rise, and that an isosceles triangle has two sides of equal length.

Because facts and ideas are accessible through print, effective teachers deliberately connect reading, writing, and content area instruction. They teach students how to use print to learn.

At this point, you might be wondering about your role in teaching reading and writing along with content area study. You might think something like, "Shouldn't reading and writing be taught during classes devoted exclusively to reading and writing?" If you are a middle- or secondary-school teacher, you might think literacy skills should be taught only by elementary teachers: "Shouldn't lower-grade teachers emphasize students' reading and writing so upper-grade teachers can present their content?" These questions and reactions are common when people first consider reading and writing in the content areas.

This book explains productive learning opportunities that occur when reading and writing are linked with subject matter. For instance, it shows how reading and writing about the solar system can improve students' understandings of the sun, planets, and moons. It also shows how literacy skills such as determining the meanings of unfamiliar words and creating effective compositions can be improved while studying something like the solar system.

The value of all teachers attending to literacy during subject matter instruction is well recognized by the many educational standards produced since the late 1980s. Moreover, the No Child Left Behind Act (NCLB), which the federal government enacted in 2002, holds states, school districts, and schools accountable for all U.S. students being proficient in reading (as well as math and science) by the 2013–2014 academic year. Among other things, NCLB focuses on eliminating racial and ethnic gaps in academic achievement (Strickland & Alvermann, 2004). All K–12 teachers, as never before, are responsible for all students attaining high levels of literacy. Fulfilling this responsibility involves reading and writing across the curriculum. (For a detailed examination of accountability, reading proficiency, and NCLB, see Chapter 13 of this book, "Reading Policy.")

This opening chapter lays a foundation for understanding how to meet current literacy achievement expectations. First, it details reasons for stressing literacy in all content areas, not just in reading or English language-arts classes. Then it describes thinking processes that underlie effective reading, writing, and learning. Finally, it explains how individuals' identities drive reading, writing, and learning. This foundational chapter contains three key ideas:

1. Compelling reasons support content area literacy instruction.
2. Thinking underlies reading, writing, and learning.
3. Identity drives reading, writing, and learning.

Compelling Reasons Support Content Area Literacy Instruction

Many educators have presented reasons for instruction that links literacy with subject matter (McKenna & Robinson, 1990; Moje, Young, Readence, & Moore, 2000; Moore, Readence, & Rickelman, 1983). Three of the most compelling reasons for linking students' reading and writing proficiencies with subject matter study are (1) reading and writing are tools for learning; (2) literacy requirements continually increase in school and society; and (3) content area teachers can teach content area reading and writing best.

Reading and Writing Are Tools for Learning

Because content areas consist of language, the study of content entails the study of language. Years ago, Postman (1979) presented the case this way:

> Biology is not plants and animals. It is language about plants and animals. History is not events. It is language describing and interpreting events. Astronomy is not planets and stars. It is a way of talking about planets and stars. (p. 165)

Biologists, historians, and astronomers work with words; they use language to construct and convey meaning. Consequently, thinking and acting like a biologist, historian, or astronomer means being proficient with magazine articles, textbooks, brochures, library books, and other printed materials. It also means being able to write observational notes, character sketches, reactions to experiences, reports, and other forms of expression.

Learning opportunities expand when teachers help students read and write about what they are studying. Individuals who struggle with reading and writing communicate largely through listening, viewing, and speaking; their opportunities grow tremendously when they gain proficiency with print. Indeed, reputable research syntheses consistently show that literacy learning is connected with subject-matter learning (Alvermann, Fitzgerald, & Simpson, in press; Biancarosa & Snow, 2004; Farstrup & Samuels, 2002; Jetton & Dole, 2004; National Reading Panel, 2000; RAND Reading Study Group, 2002). When youth increase their literacy abilities such as organizing ideas found in print, interpreting the meanings of unfamiliar vocabulary, composing reflective responses, recording study notes, and investigating topics independently, they increase their access to ideas and information.

Now that independent lifelong learning is an accepted requirement for staying abreast of our ever-changing worlds in the 2000s, access to print has become especially crucial. What happens when students leave their teachers? What will students do when they have no one to assist them with the print encountered in their personal, political, and occupational lives?

The role of literacy as a tool for learning is neatly encapsulated by the popular aphorism, "Give me a fish, and I eat for a day. Teach me to fish, and I eat for a lifetime." Teaching students to read and write well promotes learning in school and lasts a lifetime.

Literacy Requirements Continually Increase

Literacy requirements increase sharply as students become older and as our society continues moving from an industrial base to a technical/informational one. Teachers have the responsibility to help students with these increasing literacy demands.

Developmental Changes Living organisms that develop—including people—progress from relatively simple forms in the beginning to relatively complex forms later on. They elaborate, or expand in detail, from one state to another; they unfold in progressive stages. Through continued development, individuals express all their inherent possibilities. Development applies to reading and writing as much as other areas.

Consider the following well-known quote from Shakespeare's *Hamlet*:

To be, or not to be: that is the question.

Each of the words in this quote appears in books found in any primary-grade classroom, but great maturity and competence are needed to fully come to terms with what these simple words express. Students require instruction to grasp the message and appreciate the beauty of Shakespeare's writing. Novice readers and writers would require support in order to grow into proficient, well-developed readers and writers able to fully understand Shakespeare. The 1999 International Reading Association position statement on adolescent literacy referred to development this way:

> Public and educational attention long has been focused on the beginnings of literacy, planting seedlings and making sure they take root. But without careful cultivation and nurturing, seedlings may wither and their growth become stunted. (Moore et al., 1999, p. 9)

The ever-increasing difficulty of what students read unmistakably indicates the need for continual support across the subjects at all grade levels. Students read about neighborhood helpers in the primary grades, world geography in the middle grades, and comparative governments in the upper grades. As students progress through school, they read more and more expository material. Upper-grade students require help learning from their unfamiliar, complex, and abstract passage contents just as lower-grade students do with relatively familiar, simple, and concrete passage contents.

Technical/Informational Changes   Due to the rapid rate of change in our time, people require reading and writing abilities that are more sophisticated than those needed decades before. To illustrate, practically all occupations have been affected by revolutionary changes in technology. Office workers a generation ago relied on manual typewriters and filing cabinets; office workers today use online wireless information systems and computerized databases. Future office workers will need to master technology unheard of today and respond to the new demands it will bring. Jobs that call for predictable, simple, stable routines are giving way to work that requires complex procedures, problem solving, and decision making.

In brief, students require reading and writing instruction throughout their school careers and across the curriculum because it is necessary. Literacy instruction provided during only one part of the day for the first few years of school no longer suffices. Extended instruction in reading and writing is needed so that individuals can learn to handle the dramatic changes they will experience in school, in their future workplaces, in society, and in their personal lives.

Content Area Teachers Can Teach Content Area Reading and Writing Best

Primary-grade teachers directing the study of topics such as neighborhoods and animals' habitats can best present ways to read and write about these topics. Senior-high physics teachers presenting a unit on quantum mechanics can best teach strategies for exploring and learning about this topic and others. Those who regularly guide learners through content areas are in optimum positions to improve students' content area reading and writing competencies.

Multiple Literacies   Think how various specialists might perceive a large boulder they encounter during a walk in a meadow: a paleontologist might look for fossils

Students integrate reading and writing in order to learn content area information.

in order to learn about the prehistoric plant and animal life of the area; an anthropologist might look for pictographs to obtain greater insight about ancient cultures; a sculptor might search for the inspiration to compose an original piece; and a metallurgist might analyze the rock to determine what it revealed about the metallic elements in the surrounding area. Because each specialist would approach the boulder differently, each would read and write about it differently. Multiple perspectives require multiple literacies.

To further appreciate the different perspectives among content areas, consider the following brief samples of subject matter text:

Biology: Cells enclose protoplasm, the substance of life. Protoplasm consists of two parts. The nucleus is the more solid central part, and the cytoplasm is the softer, more liquid part. The bulk of protoplasm is made up of carbon, hydrogen, oxygen, and nitrogen.

History: In 1215, a group of barons forced King John of England to sign the Magna Carta. The barons wanted to restore their privileges; however, the Magna Carta grounded constitutional government in political institutions for all English-speaking people.

Mathematics: An angle is the union of two rays that do not lie on the same line. When the sum of the measure of two angles is 90°, the angles are complementary; when the sum of the measure is 180°, the angles are supplementary.

English:
To die, to sleep;
To sleep? Perchance to dream. Ay, there's the rub;

For in that sleep of death what dreams may come
When we have shuffled off this mortal coil,
Must give us pause.

The technical terms in these passages, such as *protoplasm, constitutional government, supplementary*, and *perchance*, refer to somewhat challenging concepts found in various disciplines. Other terms, such as *cell, grounded, angle, ray*, and *rub*, not only can be challenging by themselves, but they also have different meanings in different content areas. Among other things, *cell* can refer to a unit of protoplasm, a holding space in prison, or a receptacle for chemical reactions to generate electricity.

In addition, these passages, like the analyses of the boulder in the meadow described previously, present diverse perspectives on the world. The science passage describes the structure of a substance, the social studies piece explains the outcome of a human event, the math text presents measurements, and the English passage expresses an aspect of the human condition. Each has different ways with words.

Those with deep understandings of a discipline can best explain the reading and writing strategies required by that discipline. People who want help interpreting tax forms typically go to tax preparers rather than reading teachers. Tax preparers are the logical choice because these individuals know the mind-set of those who produced the material, the special vocabulary of taxation, the structure of the forms, and generally what it takes to make sense of the documents.

Teachable Moments   Along with being the best qualified to explain the demands of different materials, content area teachers also are in the best position to provide support when students are most receptive. Learners typically benefit most from instruction when they wish to accomplish something specific (Lave & Wenger, 1991). Teaching students to take notes about social studies concepts generally is most appropriate when they have the desire to understand and remember these concepts. Teaching students how to solve mathematics word problems is done best in math class when they want to solve such problems. Students who are taught how to take social studies notes or solve math word problems in a reading or an English class frequently lack motivation and have difficulty transferring what they were taught. Literacy learning occurs best when students have the need to know.

DO IT TOGETHER   The preceding section presented three reasons for promoting reading and writing during subject matter study. As a pair or a group, list these reasons and produce personal examples to illustrate each. For instance, how have you used reading and writing as a tool for learning? What experiences have you had with increased literacy requirements? What help with reading and writing have content area teachers provided you in the past? After producing your list, compare it with that of another pair or group. Do you understand each of these reasons for content area literacy instruction? Did your pair or group think of other reasons for content area literacy instruction?

Thinking Underlies Reading, Writing, and Learning

Thinking is the source of intellectual activity; it is the basis of reading, writing, and learning. People apply thinking processes in particular ways when they read, write, and accumulate knowledge. Having a firm grasp of the thinking processes that underlie reading, writing, and learning provides a solid base for planning appropriate content area literacy instruction. You can plan your teaching by asking and answering questions like, "What reading practice will best help my students connect what they already know with what they will be reading?" "How could my class best organize this passage?" and "Am I enabling all my learners to form images of what they are reading?"

Since antiquity, philosophers and learning theorists have attempted to identify the thinking processes that underlie reading, writing, and learning. Countless books and articles have been written on this subject, with countless thinking processes suggested. Some classic and contemporary references on thinking that we have found to be especially valuable include ones by Bransford, Brown, and Cocking (1999), Dewey (1910), Shearer (2004), James (1925), Marzano (2004), and Weinstein and Mayer (1985).

The following eight thinking processes account for a large share of the thinking involved in most reading, writing, and learning. These processes help educators plan productive learning experiences. Continually ask yourself how to provide opportunities for students to connect, predict, and so on, in order to enhance their reading, writing, and learning.

Eight Thinking Processes
1. Connect
2. Preview and predict
3. Organize
4. Generalize
5. Image
6. Self-monitor
7. Evaluate
8. Apply

Think back to your mid-teens when you were preparing for your driver's license test. You probably obtained a copy of your state's driving manual and set out to learn the driving rules, regulations, and suggested operating techniques. As the eight thinking processes are described in this section, think about the processes you went through to learn from the driving manual.

Connect

Learning involves *connections*. When you encounter a presentation of ideas organized around a topic with which you already have some experience, you connect the new input with what you already know. You call up previous knowledge and experience and either add to the information there or change the information to accommodate the new data. Connecting information is a matter of relating what is being presented to what is already known.

As a teenager studying the driver's manual, you began to call up all those insights and bits and pieces of information about driving that you had absorbed over the years. Without that background knowledge and experience on which to build, learning how to drive would have been nearly impossible to accomplish in the relatively short time you took. Calling up what you already knew about road signs, for example, would have allowed you to skim through that section because the information was so familiar. You probably needed to concentrate on just the few unusual signs that you had not yet learned.

You may never have considered that the road signs you had seen over the years were color-coded. You did know, however, that whenever drivers see a stop sign, they are required to come to a complete stop at the designated location. What you learned when reading your manual was that whenever you saw a red sign, no matter what shape it was or what message it contained, your basic thought should be to stop. DO NOT ENTER, WRONG WAY, and NO LEFT TURN signs are all red. While studying your manual, you might have called up your prior knowledge that a red light signals a stop and related that knowledge to the new fact that any red sign means movement is prohibited. Bridging old information with new information is connecting.

Preview and Predict

When you first obtained your copy of the manual and began to thumb through it, you were *previewing and predicting* what it had to teach you as well as what it contained that you already knew. You engaged in these combined processes automatically, without necessarily being aware of it. For instance, you might have thought there would be sections on starting the car and economizing on gas. In reality, however, you probably found practically no information on those topics. On previewing the manual headings about road signs, on the other hand, you probably expected to find information about their shapes and messages, and your examination of the manual no doubt verified that prediction.

Previewing is a way to get an advance showing of what is to come. The restricted view you receive gives you a head start when you carefully examine passage contents. Predicting involves thinking about what is to come, also giving you a head start on learning. Previewing and predicting tend to motivate you to get involved with the material. Why do movie theaters show previews of coming attractions?

Organize

To have made sense of the driver's manual, you needed to *organize* the information presented there. You analyzed the whole passage, breaking it down into ordered parts. You probably arranged the information according to some type of framework, perhaps according to the headings you found in the manual. Most manuals are divided into chapters with such headings as Parking, Turns, and Licenses. Within each chapter are headings that group the information into related subsets. A chapter on hazardous driving conditions might include topics such as driving at night, driving in adverse weather, and driving under the influence of alcohol and other drugs. Readers and writers who analyze information, grouping it into meaningful categories, go far in making sense of the world.

Generalize

Readers and writers *generalize* when they draw conclusions about information. They form a generalization by noting trends, commonalities, or patterns among specifics; they discover the rule or principle that unites various phenomena. They synthesize information. For instance, when you read the Right of Way section in the driver's manual, you probably found much information about yielding to oncoming vehicles when turning left, yielding to pedestrians whether or not they are in crosswalks, and yielding to emergency vehicles. After reading these laws, you might have concluded this: "The pattern in all this information about yielding right of way is 'Safety first.' Preventing accidents is the thread common to these laws." Coming to this conclusion helped you tie together all the right-of-way laws, which otherwise might have been a meaningless assortment of details to be memorized by rote.

Image

Engaging your senses internally and cognitively as you read and write adds to the learning experience and makes it more memorable. This process often results in an *image*. Visual images are used most frequently, although other sense images certainly come into play. Vicariously seeing, feeling, hearing, smelling, or tasting what is described in print can help you think deeply and richly about the ideas you are reading or writing about.

Imagery may have helped you with your driver's manual. Think about the part of the manual that discussed the appropriate distances to maintain between two vehicles in motion. Safe following distances vary according to how fast you are traveling. For instance, at 50 miles per hour, a safe following distance is 84 yards. You could easily have forgotten these figures if there had been no way to transform them. Thus, you might have imagined a 100-yard football field and then mentally placed a car at one goal line and your car 84 yards down the field. This visual image would have helped you remember the appropriate distance to keep between two vehicles traveling at 50 miles per hour.

Imagery also may have helped you deal with the information about turning at intersections. You probably studied the abstract diagrams and discussions about turning and visualized particular instances of those procedures. In your mind's eye you might have run a little motion picture of pulling up to a multiple-lane intersection and then executing the appropriate turn.

Self-Monitor

Throughout your study of the driver's manual, you needed to *monitor* how well you were doing with the information. Internally, and probably subconsciously, you asked yourself, "Am I understanding this? Am I getting what I need? Does this make sense?" Part of self-monitoring is checking internally to determine how well your learning or thinking is progressing.

The other part of self-monitoring involves repair work. If you sense a problem with what you are trying to learn, then you need to do something about it. If their understanding breaks down, good thinkers stop, identify the source of the difficulty, and try to get over it. For instance, when you got to the part in your driver's manual about different kinds of licenses, you might have plunged into information about chauffeur's license expirations, the minimum age for driving mopeds, and the cost of instruction permits. Eventually you realized that you were being overwhelmed, so you stopped and thought, "Now, what do I need from this section?" You might have determined that the renewal period and minimum age for a regular operator's license was all that was important, so you selected that particular information for careful study before moving on to the next section. Self-monitoring your learning by assessing its status and repairing breakdowns is a crucial thinking process.

Evaluate

The difference between self-monitoring and evaluating concerns processes, or strategies, and contents, or ideas. Whenever you assess the quality of your reading or writing process while you are actively engaged in it, you are self-monitoring. Whenever you assess the contents of what you are reading or writing, you are *evaluating*.

One of the hallmarks of proficient readers is deciding whether or not passages are believable, accurate, and appropriate. When you evaluate, you judge the content being presented. The root word of *evaluate* is *value*. Readers and writers who decide the value of information strengthen their grasp of it; those who simply accept information without examining it critically are at a disadvantage. As you read your driver's manual, you might have encountered a section on driving in unsafe conditions that caught your eye. "Does steering in the direction that a car is sliding on ice really help? It sure seems counterintuitive!" you might think. "Are there viable alternatives to what this passage says?"

Insights from critical literacy (see, for example, Fecho, 2004; Hagood, 2002; Rogers, 2002) have expanded notions of evaluation by concentrating on the links between print and power. Critical literacy educators have readers and writers evaluate the ways print maintains or transforms privilege. They critique media representations of events, looking for bias.

Critical literacy educators might lead students to question state authorities' linking of a driver's license with performance on a pencil-and-paper multiple-choice test. Why must potential drivers succeed in a traditional school-like task? Does this practice support or impede marginalized groups' access to full participation in society? Critical theorists lead investigations into whose interests are served when particular reading materials are selected. For instance, they call attention to books that predominantly portray scientists as male rather than female. They show how printed messages shape and are shaped by the power structures of society.

Apply

The eighth thinking process is *apply*. The reasons you plowed through the driver's manual were so that you could pass the driver's test, obtain a license, and get behind the wheel of a car. When you finally got behind the wheel, you were required to remember all the rules and regulations: how fast to go on various streets under various conditions, who has the right of way in different situations, and what the road signs mean. Applying is adapting what you learn to anticipated or actual situations.

When you apply knowledge, you select the most appropriate response from all the ones you have acquired. As was noted at the beginning of this chapter, this book is meant to help you teach students to read and write in the content areas. Our goal is to help you plan and actually use (i.e., apply) the thinking processes described here in classroom situations.

TRY IT OUT Take a passage with which you are quite comfortable, and sit with a classmate. Take turns reading a short section and then explaining how you used—or might use—a few of the thinking processes described previously. Do this until you explain how all eight of the processes were involved in your reading and learning.

Thinking Is Complex

The remaining chapters in this book explain how to generate learning activities that engage students in these thinking processes. When planning instruction, keep in mind several points about the eight thinking processes.

Overlap Our labels and descriptions overlap those presented by many other authors. Fostering thinking is a time-honored common goal among educators, and many types of thinking have been discussed. The professional literature about thinking contains such terms as *hypothesizing, speculating, inferring, extrapolating, elaborating, problem solving, synthesizing, analyzing, creating,* and *categorizing. Metacognition* frequently is used to denote a special constellation of thinking processes considered to be above the others.

Our list contains many of the cognitive behaviors presented in the 2001 revision of Bloom's classic taxonomy of educational objectives (Anderson & Krathwohl, 2001). The essential thinking processes presented in this chapter are listed in the following table alongside the ones presented by Anderson and Krathwohl. Our terms are often synonymous with several others, and ours share most of the characteristics of the others. Our list provides a solid basis for planning content area reading and writing instruction.

Essential Thinking Processes	*Taxonomy of Educational Objectives*
Connect	Remember
Preview and predict	Understand
Organize	Apply
Generalize	Analyze
Image	Evaluate
Self-monitor	Create
Evaluate	
Apply	

Flexibility   A second point about our essential thinking processes is that presenting them separately implies that each is isolated from the others. And listing them from *connect* to *apply* suggests that thinkers do first one, then another, then a third, and so on, in a prescribed sequence. But these thinking processes do not stand alone and are not used in a rigid order. Instead, each thinker integrates the processes flexibly according to the demands of each situation. Students might form images and predict upcoming information simultaneously; they might evaluate the first few sentences of what they read or write, organize their thoughts, and continue processing the information. Our point is that students flexibly combine thinking processes and emphasize certain ones at different times in order to conceptualize what they are reading or writing about.

Sophistication   Students at all grade levels can benefit from assistance with the thinking processes outlined previously. To paraphrase Bruner's famous quotation from *The Process of Education* (1977): We begin with the principle that any thinking process can be taught effectively in some intellectually honest form to any child at any stage of development.

This principle means that organizing, for example, can be presented in the primary- as well as the high-school grades. Primary-school children might categorize pictures of animals according to those that fly, those that walk, and those that swim; high-school students might classify one-celled life forms according to their kingdom, phylum, class, order, family, genus, and species. Similarly, very young children can learn to evaluate by thinking about questions like "Did a real boy named Jack climb a beanstalk and meet a giant?" and "Should Jack have climbed the beanstalk?" Older students can ponder how well *Lord of the Flies* portrays basic human nature. In brief, schoolchildren seem to share the same mental processes. Students from kindergarten through twelfth grade connect, preview and predict, organize, generalize, image, monitor, evaluate, and apply with varying degrees of sophistication.

LISTEN, LOOK, AND LEARN Visit a class during a subject matter lesson or tape-record a lesson that you present. Pretend that you are a student during this activity and list the chief thinking processes you would use. Which were used most frequently? Which were used least frequently? What could be done to elicit the thinking processes that were not tapped?

Academic Identities Drive Content Area Literacy and Learning

The eight thinking processes presented above are an effective starting point for content area literacy instruction, but an instructional focus only on thinking short-changes students. Instruction also needs to focus on students' identities as readers, writers, and learners of subject matter (McCarthey, 2002; Reeves, 2004). Realizing the importance of students' identities leads educators to approach learners as richly detailed human beings with predispositions, emotions, and motivations—as well as thinking processes—to be addressed.

Although scholars dispute the precise meaning of identity (Alvermann, 2001), it generally is linked with individuals' deep-seated understandings and beliefs about themselves. Identity answers "Who am I?" questions. It is found in the answers individuals compose to soul-searching questions about whether or not they are leaders, rebels, nerds, beauties, serious students, readers, and so on. Identities are established when individuals tell themselves and others who they are, act according to these words, and experience strong emotional ties with these words and actions. According to Holland, Lachicotte, Skinner, and Cain (1998), "People tell others who they are, but even more important, they tell themselves and then try to act as though they are who they say they are" (p. 3).

Academic Identities

Educators do well to recognize how youths' identities relative to academics affect their beliefs and actions in school as well as in particular classrooms (Moore, 2003). A positive academic identity means that individuals consider themselves insiders to education; they see themselves as members of scholarly learning communities (Davidson, 1996; Welch & Hodges, 1997). Students display positive academic identities when they present themselves as the kinds of people who embrace formal education, who take school seriously. These individuals align themselves with academic cultures, identifying with teachers and conscientious peers. They see themselves connected with academic ways of life. Students with positive academic identities seek to accomplish school-related goals through actions such as completing assignments, reading independently, and studying for tests (Jackson, 2003).

On the other hand, students who display negative academic identities in their classes tend to see themselves as lost in school, as educational outsiders, as unsuccessful learners who do not belong in academic settings (Colvin & Schlosser, 1997). Students who demonstrate negative academic identities often act out apathetic, foolish, or defiant behaviors as they resist school and school-related literacies. They put in little of the time and effort needed to excel academically.

Socially Situated Identities

An important distinction exists between individuals' core identities and their socially situated ones (Gee, 2001). Core identities are individuals' stable and continuous manifestations of the self. Core identities are revealed by peoples' words and actions that generally hold uniformly across situations. When people say, "That's just Pat being Pat," they are referring to Pat acting according to an identity that is relatively fixed, enduring across time and circumstance. Core identities express people's somewhat predictable responses to each and every situation. In contrast, socially situated identities shift across circumstances; they are to be found among particular group environments. Referring to such identities as *socially-situated* conveys the idea that individuals act somewhat differently as they move in and out of different social situations (McCarthy & Moje, 2002).

Outside of school many youth interact with community, family, peer group, and popular culture influences whose ways of thinking and communicating differ from mainstream academic ones (DeBlase, 2003; Jimenez, 2000; Moje, Ciechanowski, Kramer, Ellis, Carrillo, & Collazo, 2004). In order to be successful students, many youth shift their identities across situations. For instance, a culture that expects girls to regularly interact with the family at home presents different expectations from an academic culture that encourages girls to regularly read silently at home. A culture that regards school success as selling out to an oppressive, dominant establishment differs from an academic one that regards school success with pride. A culture that expects readers to obediently accept the written word holds different expectations from an academic one that expects readers to constantly question what they read. Cultures that endorse several individuals participating in story retellings differ from academic ones that expect one individual at a time to retell a story. To cope with social groups' particular cultures that differ from schools' academic cultures, youth adopt flexible identities, shifting what they say about themselves and how they act, according to the situation.

Not only do many youth alter their outside-of-school identities to fit inside-of-school requirements, they further adjust their identities from class to class. Students need to cope with different views of learning and ways of thinking and communicating that different teachers present across different content areas (Moje & Dillon, in press). For instance, students in a math class might be expected to act as problem solvers who calculate unambiguous data precisely and record their findings in meticulous order. These same students in literature class might be expected to act as problem solvers who form several possible interpretations of deliberately ambiguous text and present them in open-ended discussions. To do well, these students need to identify themselves as meticulous problem solvers in the math class, calling for meticulous problem solving, and adventurous problem solvers in the literature class, calling for adventurous problem solving. And in other classes, they may be expected to identify themselves not as problem solvers at all, but as bankers of information who accurately recover what is deposited during class lectures and seat work.

Implications of Socially Situated Identities

Youth shift their identities according to social situations, and they take up particular academic identities to succeed in school in general as well as in your class in particular. Realizing this has implications for your classroom instruction. Acknowledging youths' socially situated identities has implications to (a) put the person first, (b) adjust classroom instruction to accommodate students' identities, and (c) help students adjust their identities to accommodate classroom instruction.

Put the person first. To discern the value of putting the person first, form an image of four different individuals according to each of the following four descriptors:

1. a diligent student
2. a distracted learner
3. a willing researcher
4. a reluctant reader

Do you have an image of each? Note that these descriptors seem to apply to individuals as they participate in each and every situation. The descriptors seem to name peoples' core identities, their fixed traits, to be expected during all school and nonschool activities.

Now form an image of the same four individuals according to each of these descriptors:

1. a student who works diligently in history class but not in math
2. a learner who acts distracted only in Mr. Blanchard's class
3. a researcher who willingly conducts biology labs but avoids language arts projects
4. a reader who participates reluctantly during school time set aside for free reading but who avidly reads about music outside of school

Did the new sentences modify your view of the individuals? Did our putting the person first (e.g., *a learner*) and then characterizing him or her according to a specific situation (e.g., *who acts distracted in Mr. Blanchard's class*) refine your image of the person, pinpointing your view of him or her?

This demonstration shows how putting the person first then describing that person's actions in particular situations maintains his or her individuality. It guards against labeling students with negative descriptors such as *distracted* or *reluctant*, equating the person with the condition (*the distracted students, the reluctant readers*), then acting according to stereotypes associated with the label. It guards against overgeneralizing students' behavior to all situations and to forming misguided opinions.

Putting people first means initially thinking of each student as a human being who is subject to the power of situations rather than as a group member who always acts the same. Knowing that a student acts like a distracted learner in one class does not necessarily mean he or she should be classified as a member of a group of distractible people. This student might be an engaged learner in another class, so you might examine what the engaging class offers. Knowing that a student displays reluctant-reader behaviors inside of school does not mean he or she should be classified as a reluctant reader. This student might be an avid reader outside of school, so you might examine the circumstances of his or her reading outside of school (Alvermann, 2001; Knobel, 2001).

Adjust classroom instruction to accommodate students' identities. Teachers who recognize youths' multiple identities adjust classroom instruction to accommodate those identities. One way teachers make such adjustments is by linking their classrooms with what students bring to them, regularly inviting students to connect experiences and knowledge from their outside-of-school lives with their inside-of-school instruction. During the first day or two of school, many teachers have students record their outside-of-school interests and accomplishments on *getting to know you* cards. Teachers then refer to these cards when planning and delivering instruction, explicitly connecting parts of the class to students' lives. Math teachers might pose geometry problems associated with skateboarding ramps and halfpipes; science teachers might address the physical and chemical processes of cooking; literature teachers might highlight books they think certain students would appreciate; and social studies teachers might show how political and social issues affect people of different ethnicities.

In multicultural settings, teachers honor different patterns of speech and styles of conversation, knowing that cultural groups often differ along these lines. They address examples from students' different ethnic heritages when addressing topics like heroes, historical settlements, and popular literature. They provide culturally relevant materials such as ones presenting African-American, Native-American, and Hispanic groups' experiences with and perceptions of subject-matter topics. They adorn their classrooms with positive inclusive images. Teachers do all this so students can see themselves as members of a classroom community, as insiders to formal education.

Teachers also adjust their classroom instruction to accommodate students' identities by offering instructional voice and choice. These teachers offer a variety of print materials, realizing that students will find some materials more suitable than others. They present multimedia CDs, pamphlets, brochures, periodicals, alternative textbooks, and online encyclopedias. Finally, they provide multiple response options, enabling students to produce PowerPoint presentations, videos, and dramatic presentations, to name a few.

Help students adjust their identities to accommodate classroom instruction. Adjustments and accommodations are two-way streets: Teachers adjust to students, while students adjust to teachers. Instructional support is needed for the student adjustments to be most effective.

Teachers help students adjust their identities to accommodate classroom instruction by explicitly presenting the views of learning and ways of thinking and communicating that are needed for success in class. To return to earlier examples, if meticulous problem solving were expected, then teachers should inform students of this, explaining and demonstrating the processes and continually supporting students' identities as meticulous problem solvers. Teachers help youth adopt identities applicable to their classes.

The process of flexibly adapting identities to different situations can be considered a form of border crossing (Mehan, Hubbard & Villanueva, 1994). Think of youth regularly crossing community, family, peer group, popular culture, school, and subject-matter borders when they read, write, and learn. Youth might see themselves informally examining multiple texts while pursuing outside-of-school interests in folk dancing, cars, or music while they see themselves focusing on a few core texts in school. Border crossing permits students to maintain their culture and language in nonacademic settings while conforming to different views of learning and ways of thinking and communicating in academic settings. While maintaining stable core identities, youth can cross from one social situation to another, adapting their identities according to the circumstances.

LISTEN, LOOK, AND LEARN Observe a class for about three sessions. Single out a few students who typically enact positive academic identities in the class and a few who typically enact negative academic identities. Describe the students' actions that led you to your conclusions. Additionally, note the classroom actions that encouraged the students' display of their identities.

LOOKING BACK Developing students' reading and writing abilities in the content areas is one of the schools' major responsibilities, and content area teachers are the most effective agents in accomplishing this goal. Focusing on thinking processes enables teachers to plan and deliver learning activities that enhance content area literacy and content acquisition. Students who connect, organize, and apply, among other things, go far in bringing active and effective thought to their schooling. Additionally, youth who identify themselves as members of a community of learners, as insiders to schools and classrooms, have an advantage over those who see themselves as outsiders not fitting in academic settings. This chapter contained three key ideas: (1) Compelling reasons support content area literacy instruction; (2) thinking underlies reading, writing, and learning; and (3) identity drives reading, writing, and learning.

Additional Readings

To examine educational mandates and graduation requirements that each state requires relative to reading and writing, consult the following web site: Education Commission of the States [www.ecs.org].

The following sources examine how content area reading and writing instruction fits with teachers' backgrounds, beliefs, and practices. They provide a good overview of typical content reading practices.

BARRY, A. L. (2002). Reading strategies teachers say they use. *Journal of Adolescent and Adult Literacy, 46,* 132–141.

BEAN, T. (1997). Preservice teachers' selection and use of content area literacy strategies. *Journal of Educational Research, 90,* 154–163.

SCHUMM, J. S., VAUGHN, S., & SAUMELL, L. (1992). What teachers do when the textbook is tough: Students speak out. *Journal of Reading Behavior, 24,* 481–503.

SPOR, M. W., & SCHNEIDER, B. K. (2001). A quantitative description of the content reading practices of beginning teachers. *Reading Horizons, 41,* 257–268.

Descriptions of exemplary literacy teaching and learning that occur in actual classrooms offer future teachers excellent models. The following three books provide such descriptions:

ALLINGTON, R. L., & JOHNSTON, P. H. (Eds.) (2002). *Reading to learn: Lessons from exemplary fourth-grade classrooms.* New York: Guilford.

PRESSLEY, M., MORROW, L. M., BLOCK, C. C., WHARTON-MACDONALD, R., & ALLINGTON, R. L. (Eds.) (2001). *Learning to read: Lessons from exemplary first-grade classrooms.* New York: Guilford.

STURTEVANT, E. G., BOYD, F. B., BROZO, W. G., HINCHMAN, K. A., MOORE, D. W., & ALVERMANN, D. E. (Eds.) (in press). *Principled practices for adolescent literacy. A framework for instruction and policy.* Mahwah, NJ: Lawrence Erlbaum Associates.

The following six syntheses of research provide a solid base for the instructional recommendations presented in this first chapter and in succeeding ones. Although these syntheses are listed in this chapter's reference list, we reproduce them here to make them even more visible.

ALVERMANN, D. E., FITZGERALD, J., & SIMPSON, M. (in press). Teaching and learning in reading. In P. Alexander & P. Winne (Eds.), *Handbook of Educational Psychology I* (2nd ed.). New York: Simon & Schuster/Macmillan.

BIANCAROSA, F., & SNOW, C. E. (2004). *Reading next—A vision for action and research in middle and high school literacy: A report to Carnegie Corporation of New York.* Washington, DC: Alliance for Excellent Education. *www.all4ed.org/publications/ReadingNext/index.html.*

FARSTRUP, A. E., & SAMUELS, S. J. (2002). *What research has to say about reading instruction* (3rd ed.). Newark, DE: International Reading Association.

JETTON, T. L., & DOLE, J. A. (Eds.) (2004). *Adolescent literacy research and practice.* New York: The Guilford Press.

NATIONAL READING PANEL. (2000). *Teaching children to read: An evidence-based assessment of the scientific research literature on reading and its implications for reading instruction: Reports of the subgroups*. Bethesda, MD: National Institute of Child Health and Human Development, National Institutes of Health.

RAND READING STUDY GROUP. (2002). *Reading for understanding: Toward an R&D program in reading comprehension*. Santa Monica, CA: Science and Technology Policy Institute, RAND Education.

This book on content area reading and writing is based on the assumption that advantages occur when literacy and subject matter are integrated. The following reference presents subject-specific insights from mathematics, the arts, history, and science about such integration.

ALVERMANN, D. E., & REINKING, D. (Eds.) (2004). New direction in research: Cross-disciplinary collaborations [Special section]. *Reading Research Quarterly, 39*(3).

2

Setting the Stage

LOOKING AHEAD   Thinking like a content area specialist helps students read and write in the content area. Reading and writing about land formations, for instance, involves organizing them according to geological categories, connecting them with formations already known, and forming images of what shapes them. Classrooms that promote students' essential thinking processes and academic identities while reading and writing across the curriculum go far in promoting students' literacy.

But how do teachers promote literacy when they have so many other responsibilities? How do teachers organize instruction that promotes reading and writing along with subject matter learning? How does one set the instructional stage for developing readers and writers in the content areas? This chapter addresses these questions. It presents three key ideas:

1. Practices are a basic ingredient of literacy instruction.
2. Literacy instruction occurs in cycles.
3. Settings influence literacy teaching and learning.

Practices Are a Basic Ingredient of Literacy Instruction

Practices are a basic ingredient of any profession or craft. Practices consist of recurring actions, or routines, that enable practitioners to accomplish their goals. To illustrate, medical professionals follow certain practices in the course of their day. When a patient comes in for a physical exam or an ailment, doctors and nurses measure, record, and interpret body temperature, blood pressure, and so on, according to established procedures. Those in the legal profession base their actions on established practice, too. When representing clients, they exercise due diligence toward professional notices and documents.

Like other professionals, educators have access to established practices (Morrow, Gambrell, & Pressley, 2003; Stone, 2002; Zemelman, Daniels, & Hyde, 2005). This section introduces five general practices commonly used for developing literacy in content area classrooms. Only a brief overview of each is offered here; the remaining chapters of this book specify how you might implement them. The five professional practices applicable to content area literacy are as follows:

1. Providing access to reading and writing that students can and want to accomplish
2. Guiding readers through challenging passages
3. Providing explicit instruction in reading and writing strategies
4. Facilitating collaborative literacy efforts
5. Assessing literacy to inform teaching and learning

Providing Access to Reading and Writing That Students Can and Want to Accomplish

Students who read and write much tend to improve their reading and writing (Cunningham & Stanovich, 1998; Krashen, 2004). Time spent reading and writing connected text is associated with increased levels of word knowledge, fluency, and comprehension. Knowledge of the world and attitude toward literacy also tend to improve with opportunities to read and write each day. Content area teachers who provide students with access to literacy materials, time, and support go far in promoting literacy.

When students participate in units of instruction, they can locate and read appropriate materials by themselves. They can select topic-related books for sustained reading and response. Teachers often provide class time for students to read self-selected materials (Pilgreen, 2000; Fisher, 2004). One way to accomplish this in an era of crowded curriculums is to have students read on their own when they finish assigned tasks. However, many teachers provide reading opportunities by setting aside a certain time on certain days for reading.

Maintaining journals about what has been read is a powerful way for individuals to interact with materials. The reading materials could be selected for the whole class, small group, or the individual, but the journal entries would be produced only by individuals.

Listening to well-crafted English read well orally provides class members access to the magic of the spoken word (Trelease, 2003). Listening also presents subject matter that might remain inaccessible to students who struggle with reading. For instance, as someone skillfully reads *The Witch of Blackbird Pond*, students can vicariously experience Hannah's and Kit's adventures and learn about the Puritans' disdain for outsiders.

Most of the reading students do should be silent because it is most efficient; however, student oral reading has a place during content area instruction. Students might read aloud short sections to each other, and then examine what they

Younger students enjoy time to read a good book.

encountered. Oral interpretation is a good practice that allows students to prepare and present selections to a group.

In order to entice students to select and read materials, you can display posters, book jackets, and other attractions in the classroom. These displays change along with the units of study. You might invite members of the community to speak about their reading and writing preferences and habits.

Guiding Readers through Challenging Passages

Students deserve assistance and support with difficult passages. If your students are expected to learn from a demanding passage, then you are obliged to help them meet the expectations. For instance, you might prepare readers for a challenging text by connecting it with ideas encountered earlier, explaining the new ideas students will read about and presenting unfamiliar vocabulary. You might have students take notes or record questions while they are reading. And you might schedule after-reading activities in which students share what they understand and receive feedback. Chapter 5, entitled "Comprehension," is devoted to detailed steps for how to guide students through challenging passages.

Providing Explicit Instruction in Reading and Writing Strategies

If your instructional plans call for students to obtain information from the Internet, then you would show how to accomplish this, such as how to go online and record pertinent information, before having students do so on their own. You would provide students explicit instruction in how to accomplish what they are expected to accomplish now and in the future.

Students require well-developed repertoires of independent reading and writing strategies. Some of the more common ones teachers address during content area study include the following:

- Questioning oneself about what is read
- Reading with fluency and expression
- Synthesizing information from various sources
- Identifying, understanding, and remembering key vocabulary
- Recognizing how a text is organized and using that organization as a tool for learning
- Taking notes
- Searching resources such as the library and the Internet for information
- Keeping a learning log
- Generating questions to guide inquiry

These strategies enable individuals to understand difficult passages on their own, when no teacher or any other form of assistance is available. Effective teachers usually introduce such strategies when curriculum guides indicate (e.g., taking notes is introduced about the second week of a semester), and they frequently introduce the strategies with materials unrelated to the current unit of instruction. However, these teachers then revisit the strategies when ongoing coursework calls for them. They would integrate what was presented into current instruction (Langer, 2002).

Facilitating Collaborative Literacy Efforts

The photo on page 24 shows students studying in a group, having formed a community of readers. One youth begins a conversation about a passage and others join in. Those who have read something else question the reader and react to what they hear in order to learn what is new. Interaction is prized; students collectively think through the task at hand.

Collaborative literacy efforts bring students together to talk about and support each other's undertakings. Students hear what others have to say about possible interpretations and meaning-making strategies. Through dialogue, they generate new ideas and new ways with words. Small-group collaborative efforts in which students talk about the literature they are reading go by names such as *book clubs* (McMahon & Raphael, 1997) and *literature circles* (Daniels & Steineke, 2004).

Collaborative literacy efforts also might concentrate on reading strategies. For instance, students might participate in reciprocal teaching (Palincsar, 2002) by talking about their summaries of passage contents. Sometimes, individuals form pairs, or "study buddies," and take turns orally reading and summarizing passages.

Individuals often collaborate in groups to accomplish book projects. Along with the activities just described, they work together dramatizing what they read, gathering time-line information for a particular era, and completing inquiry projects, activity packets, or study guides. They brainstorm what individuals might say in a writing activity, and then react to the person's rough draft. They work as a team to plan compositions, although they generally produce compositions individually.

Another form of collaboration involves teacher–student conferences. During conferences, teachers assume the role of facilitator more than examiner. Teachers often schedule individual conferences with students to talk about what they are reading.

Assessing Literacy to Inform Teaching and Learning

Assessment is a regular part of instruction. Assessments measure what students have attained in order to monitor current actions and inform decisions for the future.

Literacy assessments promote learning in large part by maintaining focus. Setting aside time during initial teaching to show how reading and writing will be assessed clarifies expectations and signals what is important.

Youth in a book study group.

Literacy assessments also promote learning through self-reflection. Teachers and students determine how they are doing. Teachers find out what they need to reteach, and learners determine what they still need to learn.

Perhaps the most promising literacy assessments come from individuals' ongoing reading and writing amid daily practices (Shepard, Hammerness, Darling-Hammond, & Rust, 2005; Stiggins, 2005). Many opportunities exist during the school day to observe and document individual students' literacy strategies and subject learning. For instance, samples of individuals' writing plans, rough drafts, and polished work are gathered. Students reflect on their own literacy performances and preferences. The amount of reading accomplished in a certain time period is recorded. Completed study guides and worksheets are saved. Classroom, school, school district, and state level tests are administered, scored, and interpreted to determine students' performance relative to standards. All of this information can be stored in individuals' portfolios to chart progress.

LISTEN, LOOK, AND LEARN Visit a class and observe approximately three content area lessons. Describe the literacy practices that occurred and the organization of the class during each practice. Which literacy practices were most frequent? Which were least frequent? Should anything be done to balance the practices not utilized?

Literacy Instruction Occurs in Cycles

In classrooms that effectively promote reading and writing along with subject matter, students sense that they are improving as readers and writers, that they are getting somewhere. Progress is apparent. However, such movement is not in a straight line. Teachers and students build on the reading and writing that came before; they revisit prior experiences to add new layers of ideas and information (Good & McCaslin, 1992). This pattern of movement is a cycle.

Cycles consist of regularly recurring events. As Figure 2.1 shows, four events, or phases, make up cycles of instruction. Teachers repeatedly plan, introduce, guide, and culminate during content area reading and writing instruction.

Planning

In the planning phase you determine what you wish to accomplish and how you will approach it. Planning can be for different blocks of time (e.g., hour, day, week, grading period, semester, year) and for different blocks of content. If you are studying the solar system for three weeks, you decide what you want to accomplish relative to descriptions and distances of the planets; the sun, moon, comets, and asteroids; space exploration; and so on. You consider issues about linking subject

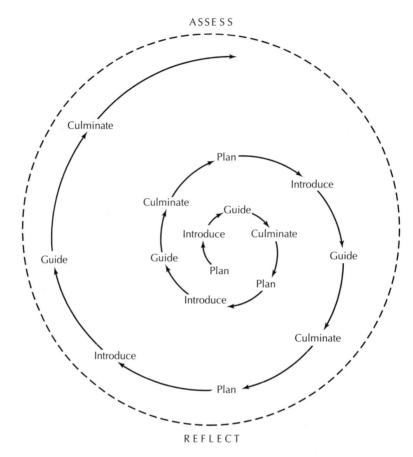

Figure 2.1 Cycles of Instruction

matter such as the solar system with learning processes such as image and apply. You devise teaching–learning situations that are authentic. You gather print and nonprint resources for your class. You decide on reading and writing options.

Introducing

As with planning, introducing applies to different blocks of time and subject matter. You might devise introductions that apply to general procedures for the entire year (e.g., how to gain the floor during class discussions, how to take notes) or to specific content being explored during the next hour (e.g., the distances between planets).

While the bulk of planning is done away from learners, introducing occurs in their presence. During this stage of instruction, you prepare learners for upcoming ideas and procedures. You share your plans with students, arousing their curiosity and interest and acquainting them with your expectations and available resources. You orient learners to the topics being addressed, the reasons for exploring them, and the procedures for accomplishing the learning activities. You show students—through modeling and explaining—how to do what they are expected to do.

Guiding

After planning and introducing learning activities, you continue your interactions with learners by offering guidance. You oversee the production. Learners get in on the act during this phase, exploring ideas on their own or practicing what has been modeled. This phase of the instructional cycle typically consumes the most time.

Guiding learners takes innumerable forms. If class members are discussing what they have read, you might facilitate the discussion. If everyone is writing, you might consult with individuals. If small groups are brainstorming generalizations about a passage, you might move from group to group, asking probing questions. If students are solving problems, you could contribute to their efforts. During this phase, you monitor learners' progress, offering feedback, encouragement, and praise where appropriate.

Culminating

Culminating activities bring events to a close. Effective culminations help learners reflect on their experiences, clarify what they have learned, review what is unclear, and celebrate accomplishments.

Culminating activities can last only a few minutes, such as when you review and summarize an hour's lesson, or they can last a week or more, such as when students exhibit science projects to different audiences. Assessing what students have learned through a quiz, test, or exam is a traditional way to culminate instruction. No matter what type of assessment you use, follow up the results and reteach what is needed either as part of the culmination or in the next cycle of instruction.

Cycles of Literacy Instruction Are Complex

It is important to realize that effective literacy instruction moves through phases of a cycle. But there is more to it than just moving through phases. Three points about cycles of instruction should be considered: scaffold and fade, spiral curriculum, and assess and reflect.

Scaffold and Fade   You might teach students how to take notes from a passage in your content area. To teach note taking through the cycle of instruction presented here, first select a passage that seems within the grasp of your students. Then demonstrate how you would take notes from the passage by actually producing notes and explaining how you decided to write what you did. Next, guide students as they practice note taking. Direct them to a portion of the passage, telling them to write notes about it like you just did. Compare your notes with some of the students' notes and have students compare their notes with one another's. Provide feedback about how they are doing. Eventually, in order to promote application, direct students to record their notes in a notebook and you check them occasionally.

Instructional cycles move from introducing to guiding to culminating as teachers fade out and students fade in. Indeed, the term *scaffolding and fading* capture the essence of this instructional progression. Teachers introduce students to subject-related literacy activities and then gradually fade back so the students can do them independently. Scaffolds are in place when they are needed, but then are gradually removed—or faded—when the learning can stand alone.

Scaffolds consist of the assistance, or support, teachers provide so that students can accomplish academic work. A common instructional scaffold is the dialogue among teachers and students as well as among students themselves when they are engaged in a learning activity. Another instructional scaffold consists of the relatively simple reading passages that teachers often provide when introducing complex strategies like critiquing an author's writing style. Again, the amount of dialogue and the simplicity of texts would be faded out as students gained independent control of their academic work.

Spiral Curriculum   As Figure 2.1 shows, instructional cycles move in a continuous spiral. One series of events merges into and builds on another. Although the culminating phase of the instructional cycle involves closure, it simultaneously is a beginning for the next round of instruction. Every door that is an exit also is an entrance. What students learned today about Jupiter leads into tomorrow's consideration of Saturn.

Dewey's (1938) time-honored notion of a spiral curriculum emphasized how ideas and insights obtained in one setting become the ground for ideas and insights in another. Procedures for solving two-step math word problems become the basis for solving three-, four-, and five-step problems later. Understanding characterization in a Brothers Grimm story leads to better understandings of Shakespeare's characters. Expert teachers routinely help students connect what they already know with what they are learning. Especially when planning instruction, think of a spiral and look for ways that students can build on earlier classroom experiences.

Assess and Reflect   The third point about instructional cycle decisions centers on the terms *assess* and *reflect* contained in Figure 2.1. Arrows do not connect these terms, because they refer to actions that occur during all phases of the cycle. The line separating *assess* and *reflect* from the others is broken to indicate fluidity; there is continual flow among these actions and the others. This means that teachers constantly gather data about instructional events to make informed decisions. Assessment occurs throughout instruction, not only during culminating activities.

Reflection also happens continually. Thinking about one's instructional practices informs decisions about future plans as well as daily on-the-spot actions (Schön, 1983). Students who regularly reflect on their academic performance enhance their opportunities to become independent students and lifelong learners.

Assessing and reflecting have assumed unprecedented urgency in our current educational era of standards-based accountability. Educators now emphasize test scores and codified state standards as never before. While these provide structure and direction for classroom instruction, they are at risk of leaving little room for creativity and individuality. This is a huge dilemma facing today's teachers.

DO IT TOGETHER Do you recall a class that explicitly layered ideas and information onto what had gone before? Gather in pairs and relate past teaching and learning that occurred in a spiral.

Settings Influence Literacy Teaching and Learning

Two classes with the identical title might be taught at the same time of day, have the same course outline and standards, employ the same materials for teaching and testing, and have the same teaching practices. Despite these identical circumstances, the students' reading and writing in the two classrooms probably would be affected differently. The differences would be due to classroom settings (Bean, 2000; Moore, 1996).

In this section, we present six dimensions of classroom settings to consider when planning reading, writing, and subject matter teaching. The six are literacy engagement, vision, authenticity, active participation, academic challenge and support, and social support.

Literacy Engagement

Literacy engagement refers to students' frequency and depth of involvement with reading and writing. Students who are engaged readers and writers actively use print for sustained periods of time. They frequently refer to print while interacting with their classmates and teachers. Multiple exposures to print and extended opportunities for reading and writing characterize classrooms with literacy engagement.

Teachers who demonstrate a deep-seated commitment to literacy offer classrooms with multiple reading materials and regular attention to literacy. Classroom interactions often center around print; classroom success depends on reading and writing. These teachers believe that formal education should result in highly literate graduates. They see the role of schools, the purpose of the subjects they teach, and the way students should be treated as naturally leading to a concentration on literacy.

Students who are engaged in literacy read and write because they expect personal satisfaction from the experience. They regularly use print to learn new ideas, perform tasks, and escape into imaginary literary worlds.

Vision

Along with a belief in literacy engagement, effective classroom settings are characterized by a clear *vision*, or purpose. Teachers and students know where they are going.

A statement of vision expresses where you see yourself and others in the future. It is a sign pointing in a certain direction. It articulates reasons for pursuing academics in your class.

Course visions are stated numerous ways. For instance, in one high-school literature classroom in which students read lengthy classics such as *Beowulf* and *Canterbury Tales*, the motto is, "If anything is odd, inappropriate, confusing, or boring, it's probably important" (Rex, 2001, p. 294). This somewhat sophisticated motto prompts students to invest energy in the tricky parts of texts they often overlook. It guides their close reading of novels throughout the year.

Another class devoted to general reading competencies centers about the statement, "It's cool to be confused" (Braunger, Donahue, Evans, & Galguera, 2005). This affirmation prompts students to regularly and confidently make public how they figure out text difficulties.

When you express your course vision, state it in such a way that it never can be mastered fully. For instance, statements like "Language gives us power," "Language gives us self-sufficiency," and "Language gives us opportunities" express goals that people never reach completely; power, self-sufficiency, and opportunities are ever expanding. They resemble balloons that continually touch new space as they expand. Being committed to such goals keeps everyone pressing forward. Such lofty, far-reaching, and enduring ideals can capture imagination and sustain action.

Authenticity

Authentic classroom settings are relevant to students' lives, engaging them at personal levels (Newmann & associates, 1996). Students learn information and strategies because they are seen as being useful. Students address important timely goals, such as making sense of a chaotic world, preparing for an occupation, and expressing a sense of self.

Linking learning activities to the world beyond the classroom promotes authenticity. When students' personal, societal, and occupational worlds are connected to the academic world, schooling can be seen as an authentic enterprise. For instance, smoking is an issue that upper-grade students face daily, so it has an intrinsic appeal that more academic topics, such as propaganda techniques and government controls, lack. Deciding whether to smoke is a personal value-based decision that individuals make. When studying golden ages of civilizations or literary styles, ask students to describe golden ages in their own lives. When examining the ATP cycle in biology, have students analyze the foods they're eating and digesting and figure out the caloric content.

Authentic activities also involve students in the range of thinking processes presented in the previous chapter. Learners in these situations transform information and make it their own. By predicting, connecting, organizing, generalizing, imaging, evaluating, and applying information, they use their minds fully to solve problems and construct significant ideas. They are involved in higher-order thinking about worthwhile ideas. Rather than participate in rote recitations about the contents of a driver's manual, students in authentic classroom settings would explain situations that exemplify driver's manual guidelines, participate in decision-making simulations, and demonstrate their knowledge while actually driving a car. Authentic letter writing occurs when students expect a response from real audiences, such as pen pals, sports figures, and newspaper editors. It moves students from relying on lifeless end-of-chapter textbook questions.

Active Participation

Active participation is another aspect of classroom contexts associated with effective literacy learning. Learners who are active participants do more than just passively receive information through lectures, assigned readings, and audiovisuals. They manipulate the ideas, paraphrasing them, reorganizing them in visual displays, identifying the most important points, asking questions about them, talking with others about them, and applying them to novel situations. They are animated in class, taking part in lively activities.

Classrooms with active participation exhibit flexible grouping practices. Students sometimes meet as a whole class for teachers to introduce something new, build common experiences, and review what has been presented. But for especially active participation, students also meet in small groups to collaborate on projects and share ideas, and they work on their own to pursue individual goals, apply strategies, and assess their learning. If a class were producing possible solutions to a community problem, the teacher's initial explanation and demonstration might occur before the whole class, the students might meet in small groups to brainstorm potential problems and solutions, and individuals might draft their own letters to community leaders.

Another way to enhance participation is to provide students with choices. When you choose the activities for students, offer them choices regarding which ones to perform and the order in which to complete them. Given two possible writing assignments, students could pick the one they are most interested in completing. Given certain vocabulary words, students could select their own ways of presenting the words' meanings. Given a set of short stories, students could decide the sequence in which to read them.

Along with choice, give students a voice in deciding their academic work. Students have the right to be heard, to get in on the act, relative to learning standards. If they are to retell a passage, have them suggest ways to do so. Will they use props? If so, which ones? Will they orally interpret selected portions? If so, which ones? Will they dramatize the retelling? If so, how?

Ensuring that every pupil responds to your oral questions is another way to elicit active participation. Imagine that you want to review the major aspects of communicable diseases. You could ask, "Who remembers something we learned about communicable diseases?" You probably would elicit some comments, but you might notice that they come from the same few individuals. Do those who remain silent not know or simply not care to participate? A review activity that gets every-one involved would be to have everyone take out a sheet of scrap paper and quickly write three things they remember about communicable diseases. Then you might randomly nominate students to share their thoughts.

Academic Challenge and Support

One of us (David Moore) has played racquetball regularly. David marks his great-est gain in racquetball enjoyment and skill during a two-year time span when he had a weekly game with Dean, a one-time state-level doubles champion in Iowa. Dean loved the game; he would play anyone just so he could be on the court. The first time they played, David scored only a few points, but Dean commented on his potential and suggested ways he could improve his backhand strategy. David re-members walking away from that game believing he could do better.

Sometimes, Dean would give David an advantage by hitting only straight drives to his backhand or serving only at half speed, and Dean continued demon-strating stroke and court positioning techniques. Over time, David's racquetball technique improved so much that Dean actually worked up a sweat when they played—and David even won a few of their matches just before moving from the state.

As with racquetball, literacy improves in situations with appropriate chal-lenges, ones that stretch students' abilities. Appropriate challenges call for special effort, but they are not defeating. They strengthen students' wills to succeed. They are at the cutting edge of students' abilities—neither too easy nor too demanding. Appropriate challenges are tasks that students are unable to accomplish at first but are able to accomplish with the help of others or with reasonable individual effort. Such levels of challenge allow students the pleasure of exerting themselves and ex-periencing success. Dean's racquetball challenge was such that David always be-lieved he was within sight of a higher level of play.

For challenging learning environments to be most effective, students require support. David's racquetball would have improved little if Dean had left him in a sink-or-swim situation. Fortunately, they entered into something like a master–apprentice relationship. Before, during, and after the games, Dean supported David's development by offering encouragement—along with an occasional criti-cism—and demonstrating and explaining pertinent techniques to get to the next level. Using terminology from the previous section of this chapter, Dean scaffolded then faded his instruction. Dean bridged the gap between David's existing racquet-ball abilities and more sophisticated abilities, then Dean removed his supports as David's performance improved.

Social Support

Social support calls attention to interpersonal relations and to identity formation. It focuses on the emotional and attitudinal climate of a class. Social supports are as

Students can actively participate in collaborative learning groups.

necessary as the preceding academic supports in promoting learning. Teachers provide social support and promote positive academic identities by shaping their classrooms so students see themselves belonging there.

Perhaps the key social support is *respect*. Among other things, respect is apparent when teachers and students treat each other like long-time members of a club. Each member is an insider; there is a sense of community. Social divisions such as achievement level, ethnicity, gender, and peer affiliation do not affect concerns for individuals' well-being. Rapport is evident during face-to-face interactions; efforts are made to enfranchise those who feel alienated.

Positive expectations are an important type of social support that indicates respect. Teachers' expectations for students are especially important because they often result in self-fulfilling prophecies: teachers who believe students will (or will not!) succeed with challenging activities communicate this to students, and students follow suit. Positive expectations assume that all students can and will learn. Additionally, learners do best when they and their teachers expect their efforts to result in high-quality accomplishments. To return to the racquetball account, Dean seemed convinced that David's racquetball game would improve to an A level, and David came to believe it, too.

Projecting enthusiasm is another way to support learners. You project enthusiasm when you convey an intense eagerness to explore class contents. Being theatrical or being low-key is not crucial as long as you are passionate and sincere about the value of the topic under consideration. As with respect and expectations, enthusiasm is contagious.

LISTEN, LOOK, AND LEARN Talk with a student about the classroom settings he or she prefers, asking this person to describe the best teacher he or she had. What did the teacher do that he or she liked? What was so good about that teacher's class? Compare your findings with the dimensions of effective settings presented in this section.

LOOKING BACK Instructional practices, cycles, and settings set the stage for developing readers and writers in the content areas. These staging devices provide good general structure for your instructional plans. Three key ideas were presented in this chapter: (1) Practices are a basic ingredient of literacy instruction; (2) literacy instruction occurs in cycles; and (3) settings influence literacy instruction.

ADD TO YOUR JOURNAL Think about the three key ideas of this chapter, and use the eight thinking processes from Chapter 1 to compose a response. You might organize the chapter by summarizing or outlining it. You might connect the chapter's information with past experiences and report events that are associated with what is presented. You also might evaluate the chapter and pass judgment on its contents. What is your opinion of the ideas so far? Why do you think this way? Finally, you could begin to apply what you have read. How do you plan to use what you have learned so far? What applications do you foresee between what has been presented in this chapter and your future teaching?

Additional Readings

Two good research-based summaries of principles and practices of effective literacy instruction are as follows:

Hoffman, J. V., & Duffy, G. G. (2001). Beginning reading instruction: Moving beyond the debate over methods into the study of principled teaching practices. In J. Brophy (Ed.), *Subject-specific instructional methods and activities. Advances in Research in Teaching* (vol. 8), (pp. 25–49). New York: Elsevier Science, Ltd.

Langer, J. A. (2002). *Effective literacy instruction: Building successful reading and writing programs.* Urbana, IL: National Council of Teachers of English.

The following describes specific reading and writing practices that are consistent with the general ones this chapter describes.

Buehl, D. (2001). *Classroom strategies for interactive learning* (2nd ed.). Newark, DE: International Reading Association.

Burke, J. (2000). *Reading reminders: Tools, tips, and techniques.* Portsmouth, NH: Boynton/Cook.

Tierney, R. J., & Readence, J. E. (2000). *Reading strategies and practices* (5th ed.). Boston: Allyn & Bacon.

3

Instructional Units

The first two chapters of this text provide background on the teaching of reading and writing in content areas. This chapter more specifically explains how to plan your teaching so that you promote students' literacy along with subject matter learning.

By moving from general to specific—by first planning the year, then units, then lessons—teachers produce a series of connected experiences. Yearly plans are at the long-term end of instructional decision making. Yearly planning is the time to think about grand outcomes. It calls for you to decide on the major goals you want students to accomplish. At this level of planning, you think about all the content to be covered (or uncovered!) and about helping students become critical thinkers, autonomous learners, productive individuals, and so on.

Establishing year-long outcomes before meeting students the first day of class is crucial because, as the old saying goes, "When you're up to your neck in alligators, it's hard to remember that you came to drain the swamp!" Having a vision for your class helps maintain your aim at what is important while managing immediate everyday details.

Lessons are at the short-term end of instructional decision making. Lessons specify day-to-day learning activities; they detail, sometimes down-to-the-minute, the actions teachers and students will perform. Beginning teachers often write lesson plans that are specific enough for a knowledgeable outsider—such as a substitute teacher—to step into a classroom, read the lesson plans, and lead a class.

Units, which are at the middle level of teachers' planning, offer a productive means for bringing together and teaching information, ideas, and skills (Erickson, 2002; Mitchell, Willis, and the Chicago Teachers Union Quest Center, 1995; Brown & Wiggins, 2004; Wiggins & McTighe, 2005). Units indicate how the year's curriculum will be divided among blocks of time, lasting from a few days to a few weeks. Space, weather, and plants name units of study commonly addressed in the early

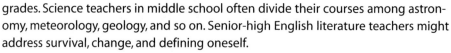

grades. Science teachers in middle school often divide their courses among astronomy, meteorology, geology, and so on. Senior-high English literature teachers might address survival, change, and defining oneself.

What follows are some major decisions to be made when planning units. This chapter presents four key ideas:

1. Selecting a topic begins unit planning.
2. Framing a topic structures unit planning.
3. Working within a frame focuses unit planning.
4. Interdisciplinary units are a special type.

Selecting a Topic Begins Unit Planning

Topics express in one or two words what units are about. They can be considered the titles, or organizing centers, of units. If you ask teachers or students what a class is studying, they generally will respond with something like "Fractions," "We're doing cell differentiation," or "We're reading *Ender's Game*."

When looking over what needs to be taught during the school year, teachers often begin with what their school districts, schools, academic departments, grade-level committees, or textbooks have listed. The contents of such lists readily serve as unit topics.

Dinosaurs, neighborhoods, and the weather are topics in countless primary-grade units. Pioneers, land formations, and adventure often appear in the middle grades. Radiation, constitutional government, and identity are found in the upper grades. These subject matter concepts readily divide into even more parts. For instance, land formations readily divide into mountains, plains, valleys, and plateaus, to name a few. These subtopics often are presented as individual lessons.

Teachers often choose topics that are deliberately open ended and invite exploration. They call these *themes* rather than *topics* because they underlie so much. For instance, patterns, flight, and bridges open the door to much creative thinking and exploring. Bridges, for instance, physically connect land and socially connect people. Complex topics, or themes, such as justice and relativity have proved effective because they offer rich possibilities for inquiry. The following table lists common secondary-school topics that form the basis of units:

Content Areas

Language Arts	Mathematics	Science	Social Studies
The Giver	Congruent triangles	Atomic theory	Civil rights
Heart of Darkness	Logic	Bonding	Legislative branch
Drama	Nonpolynomial equations	Digestive system	Macroeconomics
Shakespeare	Quadratic equations	Genetics	Mexico
Angelou	Statistics and probability	Plate tectonics	Westward expansion
Identity		Water cycle	World War II
Flight			
Conducting research			
Writing essays			

As the table shows, English/language arts teachers often employ distinctive topics. They might select ones that consist of

- a novel (*The Giver, Heart of Darkness*)
- a genre (drama, short story)
- an author (William Shakespeare, Maya Angelou)
- a theme (identity, flight)
- a skill (conducting research, writing essays)

Novels frequently serve as unit topics during English/language arts instruction and occasionally during social studies instruction. A middle-grade English/language arts teacher might select *A Wind in the Door*. In this story, Charles Wallace is seriously ill and others must miniaturize themselves and enter his body in order to combat his disorder. Students could examine plot and theme along with human anatomy, cell structure, and medical innovations. As students read *Roll of Thunder, Hear My Cry* during middle-grade social studies instruction, they could explore injustice, rural life, and post–Civil War social patterns.

Once you determine the topics for your units, you are ready to begin more detailed planning. Establishing frames for the topics is an important next step in this process.

LISTEN, LOOK, AND LEARN   Visit with a high-school department head, middle-school team leader, or elementary-school grade-level leader and ask for a list of units taught during the year. Then ask how these particular unit topics were chosen. How were they sequenced in their particular order of presentation? Compare your findings with those of others in your class.

Framing a Topic Structures Unit Planning

Frames provide structure. They enclose items and mark borders. A picture frame, for instance, holds a picture while setting it off from others. When producing units, teachers frame their unit topics by planning standards-based outcomes, central questions, and culminating activities.

Standards-Based Outcomes

Standards-based outcomes express what students are responsible for learning as a result of a particular instructional unit. They designate what students are expected to do and provide clear direction when planning units (Conley, 2005; Hurt, 2003; Zmuda & Tomaino, 2001). Standards-based outcomes became especially important after the 1994 *Goals 2000: Educate America Act* prompted practically every state to establish what educators and students are responsible for accomplishing.

Practically every school now is explicit about what they expect of students following each unit of instruction.

The terminology related to standards-based outcomes is confusing. Some educators use terms such as *standards* and *outcomes* interchangeably, and some differentiate these terms. Some use other terms, such as *goals, objectives,* and *benchmarks,* and some distinguish such things as *content standards* from *performance standards.*

We use the term *standards-based outcome* because it is relatively brief, descriptive, and common—but not universal. Many educators refer to expectations written at this level as *objectives.* To repeat, *standards-based outcomes,* or *objectives,* are academic expectations based on state or school district mandates.

Producing Standards-Based Outcomes   If you are in a situation in which standards-based outcomes are not established explicitly for each unit you teach, begin with the unit's topic—in migration, for instance. Working by yourself or with a team, consult applicable state or local standards-based outcomes—including those that address reading and writing—for ones that fit the unit.

Considering the mandated standards-based outcomes and your students' needs, you might decide that for this topic students require understandings of examples of noteworthy immigrations, personal experiences of immigrating, conditions that generate immigrations, and the consequences of immigrations. These decisions might be articulated into standards-based outcomes such as the following:

1. Students will be able to describe noteworthy immigrations.
2. Students will be able to portray personal experiences of immigrating.
3. Students will be able to explain conditions that produce immigrations.
4. Students will be able to evaluate the consequences of immigrations.

Features of Standards-Based Outcomes   A crucial feature of how these standards-based outcomes are stated is their plan for observable actions. Each outcome calls for students to do something that can be seen or heard. The terms *describe, portray, explain,* and *evaluate* emphasize overt, external responses. They are not entirely covert, internal processes such as *understand, appreciate,* and *learn.* To be sure, understanding, appreciating, and learning are critical, but they are not appropriate terminology for planning standards-based units of instruction because they can remain invisible too easily. Ask yourself, "What might learners do that demonstrates, or provides evidence of, understanding, appreciating, or learning?"

Another crucial feature of these outcomes is their overall plan for essential thinking processes. The majority of the outcomes call for students to go beyond the information given, to transform what they encounter. Expecting students to *describe, portray, explain,* and *evaluate* what they learn about immigration goes beyond recalling or reproducing ideas already stated. *Describing, portraying, explaining,* and *evaluating* engage students in higher-order thinking that generates ideas.

Some verbs useful for producing standards-based unit outcomes are as follows:

analyze	express
characterize	identify
classify	interpret
compare	invent
compose	judge
construct	justify
convince	map
create	paraphrase
critique	persuade
debate	portray
decide	produce
defend	rate
describe	recommend
design	recount
develop	sequence
distinguish	show
dramatize	solve
explain	summarize

Finally, for the reasons Chapter 1 presented, include a minimum of at least one reading or writing outcome with each unit topic. Many schools now have curriculum guides, or maps, that order reading and writing outcomes across content area curriculums. You might enter a teaching situation that expects you in September to present summarizing along with your subject, self-questioning in October, visualizing in November, and so on. If you do not inherit such guidance, then decide on literacy objectives on your own.

To decide on a literacy objective, determine how reading and writing connect with each of your content objectives, then determine which connection would require preliminary teaching in order for your students to accomplish it. To illustrate, with the immigration unit, ask yourself how literacy connects with students' descriptions of noteworthy immigrations, portrayals of personal experiences, explanations of causal conditions, and evaluations of consequences. If you decide that composing the explanations of conditions that produce immigrations will require extensive preliminary teaching, then you are en route to a literacy outcome. You might consult your state's standards, identify what best expresses your expectations, and produce a concise standards-based outcome that focuses on literacy like this:

Students will be able to write an explanatory, multi-paragraph essay.

Central Questions

Central questions are individual queries that provide students with an overarching purpose for examining unit topics and accomplishing unit outcomes. With regard to immigration, a productive central question could be, "Why do people immigrate?" If 1950 to 2000 were the topic of a middle-grade history unit, you might pose a central question such as, "In which decade of the late 1900s were people better off?"

Central questions position students as problem solvers in authentic situations. They serve as a stimulus, provoking and sustaining students' thinking and learning during day-to-day unit activities. They serve as a connector, too, gluing together what students encounter across several days of instruction. They allow all students to form an appropriate answer, although the sophistication of the answers might vary.

When addressing a unit's central question, you still help students grasp the numerous facts associated with the topic, but these facts become the building blocks of thinking. With central questions in mind, students treat potentially inert ideas and facts as ideas-in-action and facts-in-action. Students use facts and ideas to construct personal insights into the topic. Examples of central questions include the following:

History/Social Studies

- Is the United States today more like Athens or Sparta?
- What are appropriate limits to freedom of speech?
- Was the U.S. civil rights movement successful?

Literature

- What makes a short story outstanding?
- What does it take to be a hero?
- What is the heart of darkness?

Mathematics

- How economical is it to buy food from a convenience store compared to a full-service grocery store?
- How can statements such as "The lake has an average depth of 3 feet" and "The region has an average temperature of 70 degrees" mislead people?
- Is a straight line always the shortest possible distance?

Science

- What would happen if the Earth's gravity doubled?
- What factors most influence plant development?
- Why is the weather difficult to predict?

Interdisciplinary

- What new city in our state would be ideal?
- How can we stop violence?
- How can our community be better prepared for natural disasters that probably will occur?

Producing central questions is difficult. They need to be general enough to provoke thinking, yet specific enough to guide it. They need to allow multiple responses and have no single, obviously correct answer, yet they need to elicit answers that are supportable. They need to encompass substantial amounts of content, yet be limited to what can be explored deeply during the unit. They need to provoke students' thinking and hold their interest, yet cover content mandated by state standards and tests.

To produce central questions, begin by using "wh" words (*who, what, when, where, why*) and *how* to combine the unit's outcomes into a question. Search for commonalities underlying the outcomes. For instance, answers to "Why do people immigrate?" can touch on economic, political, social, and environmental issues, distinguishing them between approach factors and avoidance factors.

To maintain attention to central questions, post them on a bulletin board and on unit handouts for continual reference. At the end of each class, for instance, direct students to the central question with inquiries such as, "How does what you learned today help you answer the central question?" "Given what we've studied today, why do you think people immigrate?" and "Now that we know about the civil rights and youth movements, do you think people were better off in the 1960s or today?" Students use their minds fully to solve the problem, bringing together information and constructing significant ideas.

Culminating Activities

Culminating activities end units of instruction. They provide closure. Like central questions, they focus and connect what is being taught and learned. Culminating activities specify how students are to express their responses to units of instruction.

Culminating activities can consist of students' written, spoken, or artistic **exhibits** produced during the unit. To illustrate, students might respond to "Why do people immigrate?" or "In which decade of the late 1900s were people better off?" in one of the following ways:

Performance: a panel discussion, role play, persuasive speech, poster talk, or debate

Product: editorial, essay, magazine article, art display, newspaper report, multimedia production, videotape, powerpoint presentation, pamphlet, or children's book.

As these possibilities suggest, culminating exhibits can be somewhat open-ended (e.g., a debate) as well as closed (e.g., a newspaper report). Culminating exhibits can capitalize on creative outlets such as dramatic productions and visual displays as well as on traditional pencil-and-paper assignments.

Culminating exhibits often involve some public display of what students accomplish. Students share what they learned with their classmates, with younger or older students, and with adults such as parents, teachers, school administrators, political leaders, and community members. The public nature of such displays offers a chance to refine students' presentation abilities and recognize what they accomplished. The next chapter, "Reading Materials and Exhibiting Responses," details several types of exhibits appropriate for culminating units.

Some culminating activities can be part of **unit exams**. Students can focus their attention productively during unit activities when they know they eventually will encounter an essay-type test item consisting of an essential question such as "Why do people immigrate?" or "In which decade were people better off?" Having unit exams serve as culminating activities is a time-honored practice—one that certainly has a place in instruction, yet one that can be supplemented with the exhibition practices just noted.

Finally, culminating activities can be **enrichments**. Students might tour a museum, an historical site, a business or manufacturing center, an arboretum, or a zoo. They might attend guest speaker or video presentations. Such activities end the unit on a high note with or without an accompanying assignment and with or without being graded.

Framing Units Coherently

Standards-based unit outcomes, central questions, and culminating activities work best when they fit together as a coherent frame, when they correspond with each other. In effective units, one part of a frame leads to another; each is consistent with the other. For instance, a standards-based outcome calling for critical thinking corresponds with a central question asking about the decade in which people's lives were best. And this outcome and central question fit a culminating activity calling for a persuasive pamphlet. The parts are coherent; they fully correspond with one another.

DO IT TOGETHER   Discuss characteristics of standards-based outcomes, central questions, and culminating activities. Practice generating possibilities. First, select a topic you anticipate teaching. Then construct possible standards-based outcomes, central questions, and culminating activities for the topic. In class share these possibilities for framing instructional units and decide on the most effective sets.

Working Within a Frame Focuses Unit Planning

After establishing a unit's topic and frame, you are ready to plan the details. Working within a clear, coherent frame enables you to focus instruction effectively. You are better able to plan assessments, introductory grabbers, resources, general instruction, and a schedule.

Assessment

Assessment involves gathering information to monitor actions and inform decisions. We regularly gather information to help us determine how we are doing in the present and decide what we will do in the future. Assessing student performance contributes to teaching and learning largely by the following:

- *Maintaining attention*: Assessment clarifies outcomes and signals what is important in the unit.
- *Providing feedback*: Assessment alerts teachers to what needs to be retaught, and it alerts students to what needs additional attention.

Because assessment involves numerous complex decisions, the remainder of this text addresses it as it pertains to each chapter's topic. Moreover, you might consult resources relative to performance assessment (e.g., Stiggins, 2005) and grading (e.g., Arter & McTighe, 2001) if you have not already studied these issues during your professional development efforts. What follows are two assessment concerns that are especially pertinent during instructional units: scoring guides and student self-assessment.

Scoring Guides   Scoring guides, or rubrics, describe what is needed to achieve a level of performance. If a culminating activity is a panel discussion, the scoring guide would specify how the discussion is to be scored. If a culminating activity is a pamphlet, the scoring guide would specify how the pamphlet is to be scored. The following scoring guide has been used to assess personal stories middle-school students produced:

Personal Story Scoring Guide

Beginning action					
Story problem is clear.	4	3	2	1	Story problem is unclear.
Ending action					
Solution to the problem could really happen.	4	3	2	1	Solution to the problem probably would not happen.
Creativity					
Story events go beyond the examples presented during class.	7	5	3	1	Story events are identical to the examples presented during class.
Mechanics					
Spelling, grammar, and legibility promote understanding of the story.	4	3	2	1	Spelling, grammar, and legibility interfere with understanding of the story.
Cover Sheet					
Yes		2		0 No	

Scoring guides like this one consist of three components: criteria, scales, and performance indicators.

Criteria   Criteria are what assessors look for when scoring. They are the specific features, or traits, to be scored. The preceding personal story scoring guide contains five criteria: *beginning action, ending action, creativity, mechanics*, and *cover sheet*. Other criteria certainly contribute to personal stories, but the five listed here are the ones to be emphasized and directly taught this time. Other criteria that might have been scored earlier or later in the school year are *story content, voice, vivid language*, and so on. The mechanics criterion might have been divided among *spelling, grammar*, and *legibility*.

Scales   Scales are the series of points possible for each criterion. Most scoring guides consist of 2-, 4-, or 6-point scales. Having an even number of points requires scorers to stay off the middle, choosing either the high or the low side of the scale.

The points possible for each criterion depend on the emphasis placed on each. For instance, in the scoring guide shown here, *creativity* is worth 7 points, 3 points more than several other criteria and 5 points more than one other criterion. The highest point possible for *beginning action, ending action*, and *mechanics* are the same because the teachers decided these were of equal importance; the *cover sheet* criterion was considered to be worth fewer points. Additionally, two-point scales typically require either–or decisions; in the preceding example, personal essays either do or do not contain a cover sheet.

Performance Indicators   Performance indicators describe what each scale point represents. A 4 for *beginning action* means the story problem is clear; a 1 means the story problem is unclear. This scoring guide does not contain performance indicators for every scale point (i.e., 2 or 3 on this scale), although many guides do. Writing performance indicators for every scale point—not just the points at the extremes—is especially important for tests with high stakes, such as whether students graduate or enter special education.

Student Self-Assessments   Student self-assessments mean involving learners in estimating their own proficiencies. Bringing students into the assessment process promotes independence, removing them from reliance on others. It helps students internalize outcomes. Having students assess their own academic work promotes self-reflection, self-awareness, and self-direction. It engages learners with subject matter specifics, clarifying the standards educators use. It increases personal responsibility. There are numerous ways to promote student self-assessments:

1. Enlist students in completing scoring guides for their own work. After a scoring guide such as the one provided here is distributed, have students act as the scorer for their own and others' work before teachers or other authorities do so.
2. Enlist students in producing guides for their own work. Present an activity, then have students design their own criteria, scales, and performance indicators. Ask something like, "How should your pamphlets be assessed?"

3. Display standards-based unit outcomes, refer to them throughout the unit, and reflect on progress toward them. Teachers might display a unit outcome such as "You will be able to write an explanatory, multiparagraph essay," then regularly ask students about their proficiencies doing this.

4. Have learners gauge their ongoing reading and writing development by completing questionnaires and supporting their ratings. This might occur during small group discussions, individual conferences, or as journal entries. Students might answer open-ended questions—without a scoring guide—such as "I rate my summaries . . . because . . ." or "This paper deserves a . . . because . . . ."

5. In writing and during conferences and discussions, have learners explain how they accomplished strategies such as learning key vocabulary or following the author's organization. Learners also might estimate how well they performed the strategies.

6. During units' culminating activities, learners not only complete scoring guides, but also reflect orally or in writing on their work and growth as learners. For instance, they might answer questions such as, "What advice would you give someone who is doing this project next year?" and "What did you find out about your reading and writing while completing this activity?"

Features of effective self-assessments (Bruce, 2001) are evident in the ways to promote student self-assessments just listed. Note that the six ways all emphasize clear targets; they generate understandable goals and objectives. All six also provide opportunities for students to define quality work. They enable learners to specify in detail what counts, for instance, as *creative*, as *a clear story problem*, and as *events that go beyond the examples presented in class*. Each of the ways to promote student self-assessments also permits feedback, allowing students to obtain reactions to their work. Finally, there are opportunities for self correcting. Students can consider the feedback and decide on improvements.

TRY IT OUT Construct a scoring guide for a unit's culminating activity. Decide what criteria, scales, and performance indicators are appropriate for the activity. Obtain feedback from your classmates about your guide. Additionally, describe at least one way you would promote students' self assessment during your unit.

Introductory Grabber

Once you have framed a unit topic and determined your assessments, you know where you and your students are headed. Introductory grabbers then launch, or kick off, the journey. They set learning in motion. Introductory grabbers prime students for upcoming reading, writing, and subject matter (Readence, Moore, & Rickelman, 2000).

Teachers continually address students' literacy during instructional units.

For an introductory grabber in a unit on immigration, for example, you might display and talk about maps and census data depicting mass movements of people; visuals of poverty, warfare, and other conditions that trigger immigrations; and terms such as *melting pot, cultural pluralism*, and *brain drain* that address immigrations' effects. Such an introduction goes far in setting the stage for instruction that centers around why people immigrate.

Five practices that are especially appropriate as introductory grabbers are real-world observing/participating, reading aloud, previewing passages, brainstorming, and writing. These practices are flexible; they fit countless units and combine with each other in countless arrangements.

Real-World Observing/Participating   Connecting classroom talk with real-world objects, media, skits, and guest speakers puts students in touch with abstract ideas. For instance, the following content areas and unit topics might begin with the following real-world observations and participations:

Language Arts	*Mathematics: Statistical*
Shabanu, Daughter of the Wind • Photos, slides, and videos of rural Middle Eastern life • Guest speakers share firsthand experiences and momentos • Burn incense and play Middle Eastern music	Measures of central tendency • Survey of food or entertainment preferences • *USA Today* portrayal of data

Science	*Social Studies*
Oceans and marine life • Photos, slides, and videos of oceans and marine life • Sea shells, seaweed, driftwood • Maps and globes	Middle ages • Photos, slides, and videos of middle ages • Action figures/dolls representing people at different positions in society • Cardboard cutout of castle

Reading Aloud Reading aloud passages that introduce a topic and engage students with it is a good introductory grabber. Hearing vivid presentations of personal experiences and exciting or unusual events arouses interest. When hearing someone read aloud well, students can come into contact with ideas they might miss due to a passage's difficulty. Picture books—those in which pictures and print independently convey a message—launch units well for lower- as well as upper-grade students (Albright, 2002; Carr, Buchanan, Wentz, Weiss, & Brant, 2001). Picture books typically can be read aloud in one class sitting, so students experience the entire telling of something, and the books' artistic representations engage students in ways that words do not.

Previewing Passages Previewing passages is like touring reading materials before studying them. When students have been led through a number of passage previews by their teacher, they can do so with any material they choose.

- Display library and classroom materials related to unit contents. Teachers often set aside a table or display case to hold these materials and allow student access during the unit.
- Show the cover of some reading material related to the unit. Students describe what they see in the cover and predict upcoming unit contents.
- Students examine interior pages with an open discussion of what they encounter. Direct attention to pictorial displays such as illustrations, photographs, maps, diagrams, tables, and graphs as well as the text notes about these displays. Also examine the materials' titles, section headings, and boldface print. Insert target vocabulary into your comments about the material. Elicit from students the materials' commonalities.

Brainstorming Having students brainstorm what they know about a topic is a flexible and popular way to introduce units. Brainstorming occurs best in a free-wheeling atmosphere with just enough structure to maintain focus. First, stimulate students' brainstorms with real-world observations and participations, reading aloud, or previewing passages as previously suggested. Then use a device such as KWL or a web to record what students call up.

KWL is an abbreviation for the three steps of a well-known procedure: What we know, what we want to learn, and what we learned (Carr & Ogle, 1987). The following chart adds *focus questions* to KWL to promote deep examination of subject matter in a manageable way (Huffman, 2000). When launching a unit, stu-

KWL Chart for Washington, D.C.

	Where is it located?	Why is it a district and not a state?	What are its major landmarks?
What We Know			
What We Want to Learn			
What We Learned			

Web for Washington, D.C.

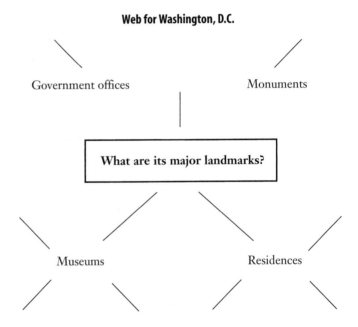

Government offices   Monuments

What are its major landmarks?

Museums   Residences

dents complete the first two rows of the chart. During the unit, they return to the chart and revise the second row, "What we want to learn" and complete the third row, "What we learned." Consider including other rows, such as, "How we will find out," "What we still need to learn," and "What we think about what we're learning."

Webs such as the one displayed for *Washington, D.C.*, also can be used to graphically depict relationships among the ideas and information students brainstorm. You might provide headings like the ones in the figure to direct students' thinking toward certain topics. Or you might simply list whatever students produce, then revisit the list and organize the items in web form.

Writing   Writing as an introductory grabber is especially appropriate because it helps clarify thinking. It goes far in focusing attention on a topic. Two writing practices useful as introductory grabbers are quick writes and extended personal writes.

Quick Write

- You now have had a brief introduction to desert habitats. Take sixty seconds and write down all that you think of when you think of a desert. The clock starts now!
- Starting with pennies, list all the different currencies we have in the United States. Then jot down any patterns you see.

These writing prompts are quick writes, the least formal kind of writing and, in some ways, the easiest one to fit into a crowded content curriculum. When using quick writes to launch units, emphasize the quickness of this practice. Students have a very brief time to blast down what they are thinking in "sloppy-copy," first-draft, rough fashion. Occasionally have students tell what they have written down as you list this on the board and point out that this is the starting point, the "What we know" phase of a KWL-type event. Occasionally collect the quick writes, using these to help guide the planning of later activities. And occasionally, use small index cards for recording the quick writes and have students hand them to you as their "tickets" for exiting class.

Extended Personal Write

- Pretend you are your current age in 1845, heading for the Oregon territory. Based on what you know of the westward movement, write a letter home to your best friend, describing your experiences and feelings.
- You are a saltwater fish who is able to keep a journal. Based on what you know of these animals, describe a day in your life.

Extended personal writes such as these take longer than quick writes, but they are intended to produce deeper, longer lasting knowledge. Extended personal writes encourage students to synthesize ideas and connect with subject matter at a somewhat emotional level. When using extended personal writes to launch units, have students maintain the writing in a journal. Redirect students to the compositions for revision as the unit progresses, and have students read their compositions in groups or to the class.

DO IT TOGETHER Get together in groups and examine the unit frames each individual produced. Then plan introductory grabbers that would launch the units effectively.

Collecting Resources

At this point, you should be clear about where the unit is going and how you intend to launch it. You have in mind the unit's ending and its beginning—the culminating days and the introductory day. You have a plan for assessing student performance. Now you are ready to begin devoting attention to the unit's middle—what happens throughout the unit that actually takes up most of the time.

The resources available to you go into your decision making as you plan your unit. Instructional resources define what you have to work with. Be sure to determine what instructional resources you have for the unit.

Effective, experienced teachers learn to collect resources over time. When a classroom magazine contains a good article about a topic, teachers save that issue. They might maintain picture files for what they teach. They locate and request library books and audiovisual materials each year when the appropriate unit of study comes up because they have kept a list with their unit materials, and they update that list to include new resources and eliminate ones that are less useful. They bookmark good web sites for teacher and student use on the Internet.

There are many ways to obtain print resources for your students without spending money. You can check materials out of the school or the public library to use in your classroom. Many public libraries will compile a "Book Box" for teachers, with fifty to one hundred books on a topic. Although searching is time consuming, the number of books and magazines available makes it worthwhile. You can also have students produce reading materials for their peers. In only a few years, you will have collected a veritable cornucopia of resources.

Planning General Instruction

To structure your general instructional planning, list your unit's standards-based outcomes and culminating activities, then begin deciding how you could best enable students to accomplish them. Ask yourself what support students require to meet these challenges. To illustrate, the immigration outcomes noted earlier are challenging:

1. Students will be able to describe noteworthy immigrations.
2. Students will be able to portray personal experiences of immigrating.
3. Students will be able to explain conditions that produce immigrations.
4. Students will be able to evaluate the consequences of immigrations.
5. Students will be able to write an explanatory, multiparagraph essay.

How would you enable students to accomplish these outcomes? How would you provide access to subject matter as well as to reading and writing strategies? Generate ideas about how you would help students accomplish these tasks.

During this planning stage, seek help from department heads, team leaders, media specialists, experienced teachers, friends, and acquaintances. Post notes in conspicuous places, and personally contact potential helpers. Notify your colleagues about units you are planning; you may be amazed at the amount of assistance you receive.

The remaining chapters in this book designate ways to help students accomplish the reading and writing aspects of your units. They suggest how to support students as they, for instance, evaluate printed matter. These later chapters on comprehension, vocabulary, writing, study, and inquiry detail practices that guide students toward course content through literacy.

Scheduling Unit Events

The final step is to design a timetable of events. You decide the sequence (the order) in which instruction will occur.

Figure 3.1 shows a three-week calendar for a unit on immigration. Seeing what is to be done each day helps you determine the feasibility of your plans. If your unit turns out to need three months, then you probably need to reduce it. Schedules also help determine how to overlap activities. For instance, you can plan to have students work in groups on one aspect of the unit while you confer with individuals about another aspect.

A schedule of unit events also helps organize your efforts, informing you about what lessons to plan and helping you monitor the pace of instruction. To be sure, your schedule might change once you begin a unit: a school assembly, fire drill, or power outage might disrupt a day's planned procedures; particular resources such as a video or a guest speaker might not arrive as scheduled; and students might accomplish tasks faster or slower than expected.

TRY IT OUT

Figures 3.2 through 3.6 present plans and schedules for units on space for the primary grades, Native Americans of the Southwest for the intermediate grades, and smoking for the upper grades. These figures show how unit plans can be portrayed as webs; they show finished products rather than what is produced at each step of the planning process. Evaluate the unit plan appropriate for the grade level you intend to teach. Determine what you would keep and what you would change for your classroom instruction.

Monday	Tuesday	Wednesday	Thursday	Friday
Introduce unit. Brainstorm understandings, beliefs, and questions.	Continue general introduction. Introduce objectives.	Present CD program on noteworthy immigrations and have students take notes. Present readings on immigration.	Engage students in cooperative groups with the task of describing noteworthy immigrations.	Have groups complete their descriptions then report to the class what they learned.
Have guest speaker share personal immigration experience.	Engage students individually with the task of portraying a personal immigration through poetry.	Conduct a brainstorming discussion of the human conditions that produce immigrations. Display resources on human conditions.	Demonstrate how to produce the explanatory, multiparagraph essay on human conditions that produce immigrations. Have students examine the resources.	Have students produce their essays; circulate through the class to support the writing.
Present the consequences of immigrations through a lecture and video clips.	Have students evaluate the consequences of immigrations.	Finalize essay on conditions triggering immigrations.	Culminate unit.	Culminate unit. Display exhibits.

Figure 3.1 A Three-Week Calendar for a Unit on Immigration.

Unit Introduction

Procedures

(wg) Announce topic and read several books to students.

(wg) Build bulletin board of solar system as reading.

(i or sg) Place books, filmstrips, and activity cards in center.

(wg) Chant poems and sing songs.

(sg) Select space body about which to learn and report.

(sg) Begin planning for planetary bazaar and museum.

Resources

Commander Toad series—J. Yolen
Space Case series—E. Marshall
The Magic School Bus: Lost in the Solar System—J. Cole
If You Were an Astronaut—D. L. Moche
Gravity and the Astronauts—M. Freeman
A Day in Space—S. Lord & J. Epstein
Our Solar System and Beyond—Q. L. Pearce
Amazing Space Facts—D. L. Moche
Songs and poems on space in Scholastic's *Banners: Space learning kit*
Space Songs—M. C. Livingston
Filmstrips, space songs record from media center

Students will be able to describe space exploration equipment.

Procedures

(wg) Guided viewing and discussion of films on space exploration

(i) Nighttime viewing of stars with telescopes

(wg) Presentation by head of astronomy club

Assessment

(sg) Each group selects a kind of tool, instrument, or machine used for exploration and examination of space bodies. Produce a picture and a description of what it does and what it has found.

Resources

The First Space Pioneers and *Lunar Landings* films from district office
Rockets and Satellites—F. M. Branley
How to Draw Spacecraft—E. Fischel & A. Ganeri
Telescopes borrowed from astronomy club
Guest speaker—Dr. Artis, president of local astronomy club
Pictures of space exploration equipment

Key:	i = individual
	sg = small group
	wg = whole group

Figure 3.2 Primary-Grade Unit on Space

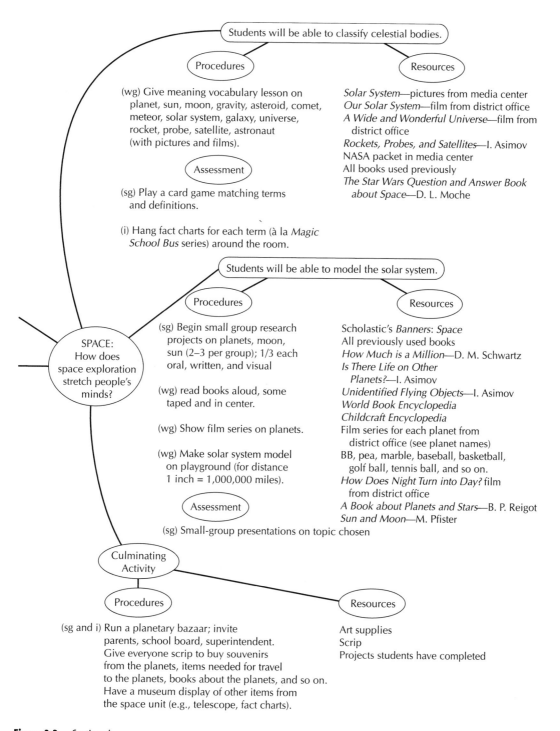

Students will be able to classify celestial bodies.

Procedures

(wg) Give meaning vocabulary lesson on planet, sun, moon, gravity, asteroid, comet, meteor, solar system, galaxy, universe, rocket, probe, satellite, astronaut (with pictures and films).

Assessment

(sg) Play a card game matching terms and definitions.

(i) Hang fact charts for each term (à la *Magic School Bus* series) around the room.

Resources

Solar System—pictures from media center
Our Solar System—film from district office
A Wide and Wonderful Universe—film from district office
Rockets, Probes, and Satellites—I. Asimov
NASA packet in media center
All books used previously
The Star Wars Question and Answer Book about Space—D. L. Moche

Students will be able to model the solar system.

Procedures

(sg) Begin small group research projects on planets, moon, sun (2–3 per group); 1/3 each oral, written, and visual

(wg) read books aloud, some taped and in center.

(wg) Show film series on planets.

(wg) Make solar system model on playground (for distance 1 inch = 1,000,000 miles).

Assessment

(sg) Small-group presentations on topic chosen

Resources

Scholastic's *Banners: Space*
All previously used books
How Much is a Million—D. M. Schwartz
Is There Life on Other Planets?—I. Asimov
Unidentified Flying Objects—I. Asimov
World Book Encyclopedia
Childcraft Encyclopedia
Film series for each planet from district office (see planet names)
BB, pea, marble, baseball, basketball, golf ball, tennis ball, and so on.
How Does Night Turn into Day? film from district office
A Book about Planets and Stars—B. P. Reigot
Sun and Moon—M. Pfister

SPACE: How does space exploration stretch people's minds?

Culminating Activity

Procedures

(sg and i) Run a planetary bazaar; invite parents, school board, superintendent. Give everyone scrip to buy souvenirs from the planets, items needed for travel to the planets, books about the planets, and so on. Have a museum display of other items from the space unit (e.g., telescope, fact charts).

Resources

Art supplies
Scrip
Projects students have completed

Figure 3.2   *Continued*

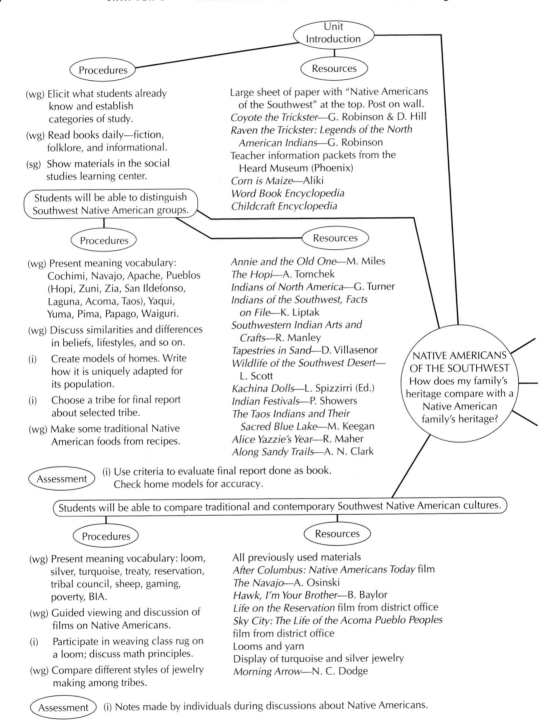

Unit Introduction

Procedures

(wg) Elicit what students already know and establish categories of study.

(wg) Read books daily—fiction, folklore, and informational.

(sg) Show materials in the social studies learning center.

Resources

Large sheet of paper with "Native Americans of the Southwest" at the top. Post on wall.
Coyote the Trickster—G. Robinson & D. Hill
Raven the Trickster: Legends of the North American Indians—G. Robinson
Teacher information packets from the Heard Museum (Phoenix)
Corn is Maize—Aliki
Word Book Encyclopedia
Childcraft Encyclopedia

Students will be able to distinguish Southwest Native American groups.

Procedures

(wg) Present meaning vocabulary: Cochimi, Navajo, Apache, Pueblos (Hopi, Zuni, Zia, San Ildefonso, Laguna, Acoma, Taos), Yaqui, Yuma, Pima, Papago, Waiguri.

(wg) Discuss similarities and differences in beliefs, lifestyles, and so on.

(i) Create models of homes. Write how it is uniquely adapted for its population.

(i) Choose a tribe for final report about selected tribe.

(wg) Make some traditional Native American foods from recipes.

Resources

Annie and the Old One—M. Miles
The Hopi—A. Tomchek
Indians of North America—G. Turner
Indians of the Southwest, Facts on File—K. Liptak
Southwestern Indian Arts and Crafts—R. Manley
Tapestries in Sand—D. Villasenor
Wildlife of the Southwest Desert—L. Scott
Kachina Dolls—L. Spizzirri (Ed.)
Indian Festivals—P. Showers
The Taos Indians and Their Sacred Blue Lake—M. Keegan
Alice Yazzie's Year—R. Maher
Along Sandy Trails—A. N. Clark

NATIVE AMERICANS OF THE SOUTHWEST
How does my family's heritage compare with a Native American family's heritage?

Assessment (i) Use criteria to evaluate final report done as book. Check home models for accuracy.

Students will be able to compare traditional and contemporary Southwest Native American cultures.

Procedures

(wg) Present meaning vocabulary: loom, silver, turquoise, treaty, reservation, tribal council, sheep, gaming, poverty, BIA.

(wg) Guided viewing and discussion of films on Native Americans.

(i) Participate in weaving class rug on a loom; discuss math principles.

(wg) Compare different styles of jewelry making among tribes.

Resources

All previously used materials
After Columbus: Native Americans Today film
The Navajo—A. Osinski
Hawk, I'm Your Brother—B. Baylor
Life on the Reservation film from district office
Sky City: The Life of the Acoma Pueblo Peoples film from district office
Looms and yarn
Display of turquoise and silver jewelry
Morning Arrow—N. C. Dodge

Assessment (i) Notes made by individuals during discussions about Native Americans.

Figure 3.3 Intermediate-Grade Unit on Native Americans of the Southwest

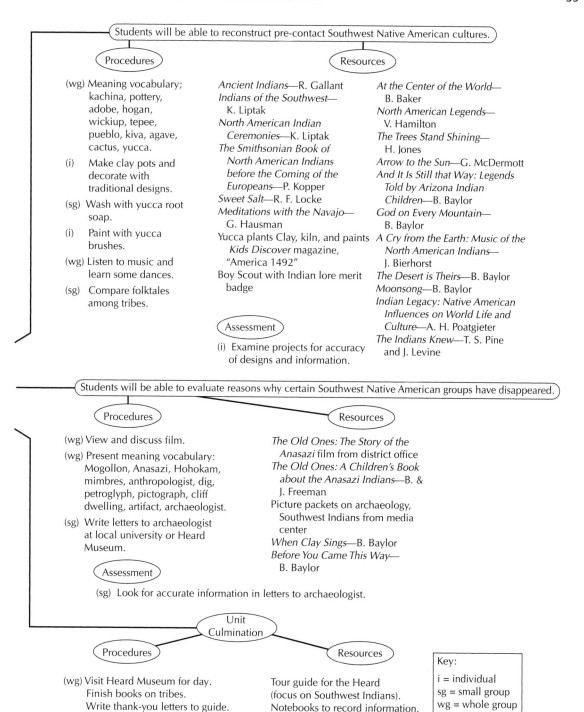

Students will be able to reconstruct pre-contact Southwest Native American cultures.

Procedures

(wg) Meaning vocabulary;
kachina, pottery,
adobe, hogan,
wickiup, tepee,
pueblo, kiva, agave,
cactus, yucca.

(i)   Make clay pots and
decorate with
traditional designs.

(sg) Wash with yucca root
soap.

(i)   Paint with yucca
brushes.

(wg) Listen to music and
learn some dances.

(sg) Compare folktales
among tribes.

Resources

Ancient Indians—R. Gallant
Indians of the Southwest—
K. Liptak
*North American Indian
Ceremonies*—K. Liptak
*The Smithsonian Book of
North American Indians
before the Coming of the
Europeans*—P. Kopper
Sweet Salt—R. F. Locke
Meditations with the Navajo—
G. Hausman
Yucca plants Clay, kiln, and paints
Kids Discover magazine,
"America 1492"
Boy Scout with Indian lore merit
badge

At the Center of the World—
B. Baker
North American Legends—
V. Hamilton
The Trees Stand Shining—
H. Jones
Arrow to the Sun—G. McDermott
*And It Is Still that Way: Legends
Told by Arizona Indian
Children*—B. Baylor
God on Every Mountain—
B. Baylor
*A Cry from the Earth: Music of the
North American Indians*—
J. Bierhorst
The Desert is Theirs—B. Baylor
Moonsong—B. Baylor
*Indian Legacy: Native American
Influences on World Life and
Culture*—A. H. Poatgieter
The Indians Knew—T. S. Pine
and J. Levine

Assessment

(i) Examine projects for accuracy
of designs and information.

Students will be able to evaluate reasons why certain Southwest Native American groups have disappeared.

Procedures

(wg) View and discuss film.

(wg) Present meaning vocabulary:
Mogollon, Anasazi, Hohokam,
mimbres, anthropologist, dig,
petroglyph, pictograph, cliff
dwelling, artifact, archaeologist.

(sg) Write letters to archaeologist
at local university or Heard
Museum.

Resources

*The Old Ones: The Story of the
Anasazi* film from district office
*The Old Ones: A Children's Book
about the Anasazi Indians*—B. &
J. Freeman
Picture packets on archaeology,
Southwest Indians from media
center
When Clay Sings—B. Baylor
Before You Came This Way—
B. Baylor

Assessment

(sg) Look for accurate information in letters to archaeologist.

**Unit
Culmination**

Procedures

(wg) Visit Heard Museum for day.
Finish books on tribes.
Write thank-you letters to guide.

Resources

Tour guide for the Heard
(focus on Southwest Indians).
Notebooks to record information.

Key:
i = individual
sg = small group
wg = whole group

Figure 3.3   *Continued*

Monday	Tuesday	Wednesday	Thursday	Friday
Introduce Space unit. Read books throughout day. Sing songs. Read poems. Introduce science center. Explain planetary bazaar.	Introduce Space unit. Read throughout day. Sing songs. Read poems. Start bulletin board (add to as can).	Introduce Space unit. Read throughout day. Sing songs. Read poems. Choose space body for report.	Meaning vocabulary lesson. Show *Solar System* pictures. Show *Our Solar System* film. Continue reading.	Meaning vocabulary lesson. Show *Solar System* pictures. Show *Wide/ Wonderful Universe* film. Continue reading. Play card game to practice terms.
Meaning vocabulary lesson. Show *Solar System* pictures. Use pictures and information in NASA space packet. Continue reading. Construct and hang fact charts.	Show *Sun* film. Read books and parts of encyclopedias. Visual display by small group.	Continue to read. Oral report by small group.	Continue to read. Written report by small group.	Show *Earth* film. Visual display by small group. Make solar system model on playground with balls to show distances and proportional sizes.
Show *Moon* film. Oral report by small group. Show *How Does Night Turn into Day?* film.	Written report by small group. Plan for bazaar and museum.	Visual display by small group. Prepare materials for planetary bazaar and museum.	Oral report by small group. Prepare materials for planetary bazaar and museum.	Show *Jupiter* film. Written report by small group. Prepare materials for planetary bazaar and museum.
Visual display by small group. Prepare materials for bazaar and museum.	Oral report by small group. Prepare materials for bazaar and museum.	Show *1st Space Pioneers* film. Evening: View stars with telescopes.	Show *Lunar Landings* film. Select tool and so on for research. Make pictures and one-paragraph report of tool.	Culminate unit. Hold planetary bazaar and museum. Guest speaker. Display pictures, reports, and so on.

Figure 3.4   Schedule for Unit on Space

Monday	Tuesday	Wednesday	Thursday	Friday
Introduce unit. Show pictures. Show map. Read passage from informational packet.	Introduce unit. Brainstorm knowledge. Browse and free read.	Introduce unit. Brainstorm knowledge. Share learning objectives. Browse and free read.	Meaning vocabulary: Southwest tribes. Emphasize similarities and differences among groups as shown in movie.	Choose a tribe/ group to study and report in book form. Begin collecting information from classroom resources.
Meaning vocabulary: Precontact cultures and artifacts. Illustrate and plan construction of models of homes and cultural artifacts.	Read folktales aloud. Construct models of homes and cultural artifacts.	Monitor tribe/ group reports. Perform traditional dances.	Read folktales aloud. Construct models of homes and cultural artifacts.	Display models of homes. Cook traditional recipes.
Meaning vocabulary: Extinct groups. Read folktales aloud.	Compare folktales. Construct cultural artifacts.	Meaning vocabulary: modern and ancient lives. Monitor tribe-group reports.	Watch movie and orally compare differences in modern and ancient lives. Plan letter to archaeologist.	Display artifacts (pots, rugs). Cook traditional foods from recipes.
Submit letter to archaeologist.	Plan questions and observations for museum visit.	Monitor tribe-group reports.	Culminate unit. Visit museum.	Culminate unit. Write thank-you letters to museum guide. Share books on tribes.

Figure 3.5 Schedule for Unit on Native Americans of the Southwest

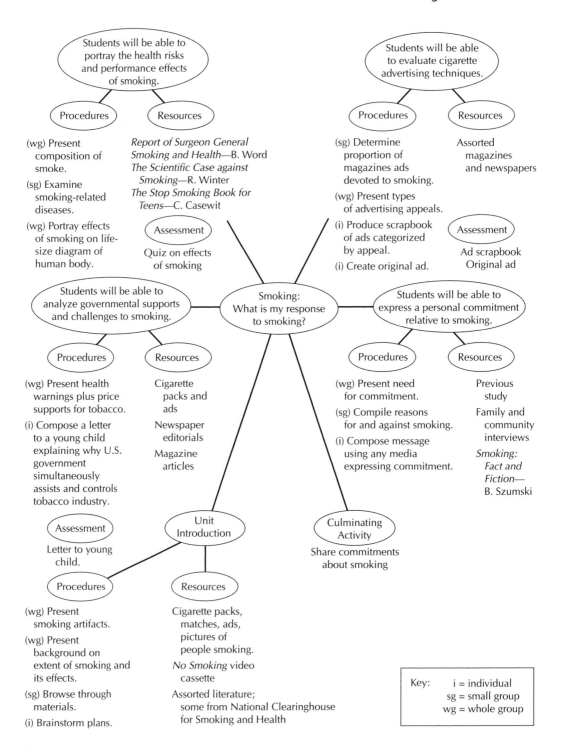

Figure 3.6 Upper-Grade Unit on Smoking

Interdisciplinary Units Are a Special Type

As the preceding sections demonstrate, units readily occur within the confines of a single discipline. Interdisciplinary units go beyond subject matter confines (Clark & Agne, 1997; Drake & Burns, 2004; Wood, 2001). Interdisciplinary units are a special type that link the various disciplines while exploring a particular topic. The base word of interdisciplinary is *discipline*, here referring to content area disciplines such as science, social studies, mathematics, language arts, and fine arts. For instance, the disciplines could be readily connected about the upper-grade topic of tobacco smoking according to the following:

> *Fine arts*: Dramatize tobacco's role in society.
> *Language arts*: Critique and produce advertisements for and against tobacco.
> *Mathematics*: Determine the spread of second-hand smoke.
> *Science*: Investigate the physical effects of tobacco.
> *Social studies*: Evaluate tobacco companies' product liabilities.

Planning Wheels

Planning wheels are useful graphic aids for designing interdisciplinary units. Teachers of self-contained classes can use them to ensure balanced treatment of all the disciplines they cover. Teachers who are part of interdisciplinary teams, such as those found in many middle schools and in some high schools, can use these wheels to initiate joint planning.

As Figure 3.7 shows, a unit's topic is written in the hub of the wheel, and unit standards-based outcomes are placed in the pie-shaped, discipline-designated sec-

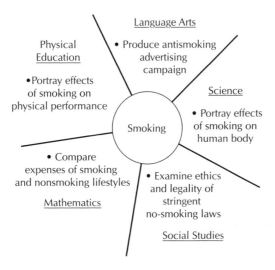

Figure 3.7 Planning Wheel for Interdisciplinary Unit on Smoking

tions connected to the hub. The number of sections about the hub can change as topics change. By providing a good overview of instructional experiences planned for a group of students, this planning tool allows you to identify appropriate connections. Planning wheels help organize discipline-specific outcomes for interdisciplinary units.

Getting Started

The decisions involved in planning interdisciplinary units might seem intimidating, but your concerns will lessen when you actually begin preparations. One way to reduce anxiety is to remember that planning is an ongoing, repetitive process. It does not occur overnight. Additionally, you often have access to plans produced by others. Previously designed units, district curriculum guides, commercial teaching materials, and plans available on the Internet are good beginnings for your own instruction. A good indication of interdisciplinary units' popularity is the presence of 774,000 links we found to date with a Google search of "interdisciplinary unit plans."

Don't forget your students as unit planners. Students can and should participate in the planning process. You might identify a topic and then enlist your class in producing central questions, culminating activities, assessments, resources, and general instructional procedures.

Additionally, teachers employ interdisciplinary units to various degrees. Elementary teachers sometimes offer traditional instruction in spelling while integrating language arts, social studies, science, and fine arts. Some units might include all the major disciplines; others might not. Secondary teachers often integrate their instruction in certain classes but not in others. A social studies teacher might collaborate with an English teacher to offer two American studies classes per day, yet teach drama in a more traditional manner. And some might combine instruction for one month and not another.

TRY IT OUT Produce an overview of an interdisciplinary unit using a planning wheel. Include at least three content areas in the plan.

LOOKING BACK In this chapter, we emphasized unit-level planning; information on more specific, lesson-level planning comes next. This chapter is meant to get you started with plans for meaningfully engaging students with reading and writing. It contains four key ideas: (1) Selecting a topic begins unit planning; (2) framing a topic structures unit planning; (3) working within a frame focuses unit planning; and (4) interdisciplinary units are a special type.

ADD TO YOUR JOURNAL Record in your class journal your reactions to this chapter. What units have you experienced? What were their strengths and limitations? What were their similarities and differences? What experiences have you had with interdisciplinary units? How do you plan on implementing units in your teaching and why?

Additional Readings

Descriptions of unit planning that include—but do not emphasize—reading and writing are found in the following:

CAMPBELL, D. M., & HARRIS, L. S. (2001). *Collaborative theme building: How teachers write integrated curriculum*. Boston: Allyn and Bacon.

GROSS, P. A. (1997). *Joint curriculum design*. Mahwah, NJ: Lawrence Erlbaum Associates.

JORGENSEN, C. M. (1998). *Restructuring high schools for all students*. Baltimore: Paul H. Brookes.

Concept-oriented reading instruction (CORI) is a promising research-based framework for integrating language arts and subject matter instruction that emphasizes academic engagement. These two books detail the theory, practice, and results of implementing CORI in elementary classrooms:

GUTHRIE, J. T., WIGFIELD, A., & PERENCEVICH, K. C. (Eds.) (2004). *Motivating reading comprehension: Concept-oriented reading instruction*. Mahwah, NJ: Lawrence Erlbaum Associates.

SWAN, E. A. (2003). *Concept-oriented reading instruction: Engaging classrooms, lifelong learners*. New York: Guilford Press.

4

Reading Materials
and Exhibiting Responses

LOOKING AHEAD   Think of traveling via different types of roads. Freeways hurry you through the landscape quickly and efficiently. Although freeways might speed your journey to a certain point, you probably would use them for only part of your trip if you want to take in the surroundings or get to a special area of interest—such as a small town, a lake, a state park, or an historical site.

Traditional content area textbooks are like freeways. They move you through a lot of territory, but they do it so quickly that you are unable to obtain close, personal insights into the area. In order to genuinely know where you are and have been, you need to exit the freeway and travel the connecting roads.

The connecting roads of subject matter study are materials such as library books, magazines, newspapers, the Internet, and computer software. These materials provide multiple avenues to thinking and learning.

Students deserve access to diverse print and nonprint materials in order to learn the subject matter and literacy proficiencies expected today. Students who regularly use brochures, encyclopedias, periodicals, telecommunications—and textbooks—have an advantage over those who rely on a single source of information. These materials can foster advanced thinking as well as positive values. Having access to various reading materials and opportunities to report on and respond to goes far in promoting subject matter and literacy learning. Students who produce collages, represent ideas with concrete displays, dramatize scenes, and write and talk about what they are reading have an advantage over those who react only one way. This chapter, which introduces content area reading materials and ways readers might react and respond to them, contains three key ideas:

1. Students deserve various reading materials during instructional units.
2. Various reading materials are available for instructional units.
3. Exhibits take many forms.

Students Deserve Various Reading Materials during Instructional Units

Students benefit from exiting the subject matter freeways of textbooks and traveling the connecting roads of various materials because such reading enriches the mind (Cunningham & Stanovich, 1998; Krashen, 2004). Students deserve a variety of content area reading materials for at least four reasons: (1) depth of information, (2) distinctive points of view, (3) materials that fit reading competencies, and (4) opportunities for a range of thinking.

Depth of Information

A major reason for providing students access to many reading materials during subject matter study is to deepen understandings. Reliance on a single source of information can lead to superficial knowledge. Think of how a typical middle-school social studies textbook presents the ancient Greeks. The textbook probably devotes ten to twenty pages to such topics as Greek mythology, government, social order, culture, art, architecture, warfare, and overall influence on modern life. The text most likely gives passing mention to landmarks such as Zeus, Aesop, Homer, Plato, and Alexander; to Athens, Sparta, and Macedonia; and to city-states, democracies, and republics. This is quite a lot of ground to cover in only ten pages, but the Roman Empire comes next, and it, too, has several noteworthy features that must be covered.

But now think of library books and magazine articles on ancient Greece. For instance, *Gods, Men, and Monsters from the Greek Myths* takes 156 pages to describe only one aspect of ancient Greek life: mythology. This book contains a full account of the exploits of the mythical characters, memorable graphics depicting scenes from the various myths, a chart depicting the relationships and roles of the gods, and an index. Prometheus, Apollo, Jason, Helios, and others come alive in this book. Such a carefully detailed, well-crafted treatment of a topic is not possible in a textbook because textbooks must cover too many topics.

To further appreciate the differences between the depth available in traditional textbooks and well-written library books, think back to what you learned in this text about the organize and connect thinking processes. Remember that good readers arrange information into categories and form associations between what they already know and what a passage contains. Likewise, good writers enable readers to readily apprehend the organization of a passage and make connections. Proficient authors are well aware of the pitfalls of typical textbook writing, so they make organizing and connecting seem effortless. They do not produce baskets of facts.

Distinctive Points of View

Students also deserve a variety of content area reading materials because such literature can present distinctive points of view on a topic, whereas textbooks tend to present no specific viewpoint or only a traditional perspective (Ravitch, 2003). For instance, *The Way Things Never Were: The Truth about the "Good Old Days"* (Finkelstein, 1999) presents an alternative history of the United States during the 1950s and 1960s that includes sections on health care, eating habits, family life, environmental issues, and the condition of the elderly. It demonstrates that looking at the past only through rose-colored glasses misrepresents actual conditions. *Lies My Teacher Told Me* (Loewen, 1996) takes this stance even further by revealing ways that American history textbooks slant and even distort the past.

Norma Klein's *No More Saturday Nights* helps students understand the implications of becoming an unwed parent and trying to continue an education. An interesting wrinkle in this one is that the parent is a teenage boy who has custody of his child. Readers will empathize as this boy makes the transition to adulthood. Content area materials also present alternative, interesting points of view on issues such as the environment, genetic engineering, UFOs, war and conflict, and those with mental or physical disabilities.

Materials That Fit Reading Competencies

If you took students out on a football field and had them run 100 yards, individuals would finish at different times, and some would enjoy the exercise more than others, no matter how they placed. In fact, the differences between students' running times and feelings about running probably would increase as they got older. The same holds true for literacy. When you give your class a reading and writing assignment, you can count on students finishing at different times, with different amounts of understanding and degrees of interest. Thus, a variety of materials is needed to match the variety of students you meet. Incorporating many library books, periodicals, encyclopedias, newspapers, brochures, and other reading materials into the study of subject matter allows students to work with what they can best handle.

Students learn best when reading and writing tasks are well within their limits. In addition, students' behavior on a task is related to the task's level of difficulty. Understandably, students tend to avoid frustrating assignments and search for something else to do. Making available a variety of reading materials allows more students to succeed. For instance, useful references for linking accessible materials with upper-grade English literature are *From Hinton to Hamlet: Building Bridges Between Young Adult Literature and the Classics* (Herz & Gallo, 1996) and *Adolescent Literature as a Complement to the Classics* (Kaywell, 1997).

Opportunities for a Range of Thinking

A final reason why students deserve a variety of content area materials involves opportunities to employ the various thinking processes. Teaching practices centered about a textbook tend to emphasize only information recall. This situation seems

Students enjoy opportunities to browse through a variety of reading materials.

due partly to the authoritative tone of textbooks. Textbook language has an all-knowing stance, dispensing information in domineering fashion. Multiple materials help demystify print by showing that some authors present a topic more clearly and completely than others.

Multiple materials are conducive to problem solving and decision making. For instance, teachers who use a variety of materials can have students compare different versions of the same Greek myth or, with *Realms of Gold: Myths and Legends from Around the World*, compare Greek myths with those from other cultures.

LISTEN, LOOK, AND LEARN Informally interview a teacher who uses multiple reading materials during subject matter study. Ask why he or she uses multiple materials rather than a single text. Compare the reasons you obtain from the interview with the ones listed in this section.

Various Reading Materials Are Available for Instructional Units

We hope that by now you plan to provide your students with a variety of reading materials during instructional units. You should realize the advantages of allowing students to interact with multiple sources of information. To repeat, multiple materials give students a chance at getting something meaningful from their reading;

they meet students halfway. Some of the time you might spend helping students understand their textbooks would be better spent getting other materials into their hands.

This section presents general types of materials for students to access. It describes six major categories of content area reading materials: reference materials, periodicals, computer technology, trade books, multicultural literature, and textbooks. We offer these six categories as a sample of what is available. You can engage your students with countless types of reading materials during instructional units throughout the year.

Reference Materials

Students consult reference materials for facts or general background information. These materials typically display information in a straightforward, concise manner. Two types of reference materials are common: compendiums and special-interest publications.

Compendiums   Compendiums are handy collections of information. They include encyclopedias, dictionaries, atlases, almanacs, and yearbooks. Students frequently are intimidated by compendiums because the information in them is presented differently than the information in other books. Compendiums usually have extremely dense text summarizing a great deal of information in very little space. Nonetheless, some materials are better than others. Some publications contain striking visuals, accurate information, and accessible writing. In one book's presentation of the layers of the atmosphere, an illustration shows the sea, the world's tallest building, an eagle flying, Mount Everest, and an airborne jumbo jet in order to provide concrete examples of height.

Computer-based compendiums have features that are lacking in traditional print. Multimedia sound and film clips enhance available information. Seeing and hearing portions of President Kennedy's inaugural address through multimedia differs from reading about it. Computerized encyclopedias also allow searches using combinations of terms (e.g., mammals + North American), and they offer immediate links from one topic to another. Finally, computer-based encyclopedias allow students to copy information from the reference and paste it into a word-processing application. Although this might raise concerns about plagiarism, it offers opportunities to explain how reports are to be constructed in the Information Age.

Technological innovations continue affecting the world of encyclopedias. CDs overwhelmed print-based materials, and the Web seems to be overwhelming CDs. To illustrate, the Encyclopaedia Britannica (www.britannica.com) affords searches through its more than 76,000 entries and provides fresh information daily, along with links to other web sites. At the free Microsoft Encarta site (http://encarta .msn.com), you can access 4,500 articles with links to related information. As of this writing, Encyclopaedia Britannica, Grolier, and World Book charge for access.

Special-Interest References   Brochures and pamphlets exemplify special-interest references. When studying cities or states, students often obtain colorful promotional literature from chambers of commerce. When investigating occupations, students examine brief publications produced by trade unions, professional organizations, and government agencies. Classrooms stocked with special-interest references have filing cabinets and shelves full of such real-life reading materials as maps, application forms, menus, food labels, legal documents, and telephone books. More and more they have web bookmarks, such as the following that lead to travel information, in place of print versions.

- www.webbrochures.com/
- www.travelinformation.com/

When searching for reference materials, keep student reading abilities in mind and examine the composition of the materials. Are they well organized? Are examples provided? If the material is too sparse, students will not be informed and may even go away from the material confused because information was missing.

Periodicals

A wide range of published material is available by subscription. Periodicals are excellent content area materials because they are timely and include short, lively, well-illustrated articles on interesting topics. Periodicals can provide students with an introduction to a new subject, pique student interest in a subject not considered interesting, and summarize information after students have done other research. Periodicals from *Ranger Rick's Nature Magazine* to *Popular Mechanics* to the community newspaper are available for class or individual subscriptions. Practically every subject area has at least one periodical appropriate for upper-grade students, and general periodicals that report the weekly news and special features exist for all grades. The Thomson Gale web site (www.gale.com/title_lists) maintains the *InfoTracKids*, *InfoTrac Junior Edition*, and *InfoTrac Student Edition* databases that provide extensive lists of magazines for young people.

Computer Technology

Fundamental shifts in education occurred when print replaced the oral tradition and again when printing presses resulted in affordable books. Learners depended less on others and more on themselves to become educated; learners also could access quantities of information and ideas that previously had been inaccessible. Computer technology is affecting education every bit as much as these past innovations. More and more educators now talk about *new literacies*, the reading and writing of digital, multimodal, multigenre representations displayed on screens, as opposed to traditional *print literacy* (Kist, 2005; O'Brien & Bauer, 2005). The International Reading Association recognized this impact on literacy with its 2001 position statement, *Integrating Literacy and Technology in the Curriculum*, which stated, "To become fully literate in today's world, students must become proficient in the new literacies of the Internet and communication technology" (International Reading Association, 2001).

Computers have incredible potential in making information accessible (Grabe & Grabe, 2004; Wiske, 2005). With appropriate resources and training, students can click and enter vast storehouses of information. Students can experience multimedia presentations that include print but go far beyond the capacity of books. They can participate in real-time video conferencing and long-distance collaborations. They can observe and produce vivid presentations with streaming technology.

Separating the hype from the reality about what technology actually offers classrooms can be difficult, but educational possibilities and occupational realities make computer technology an important part of content area materials. The computer applications most suitable as content reading materials include online resources, simulations, gamelike simulations, and multimedia.

Online Resources   Going online provides access to vast amounts of information. Students using web search engines such as *Yahoo* (www.yahoo.com), *AltaVista* (http://altavista.com), and Google (www.google.com) can access countless sources on countless topics. Many students' inquiries now are based largely on information obtained online. In fact, so much is available that the information superhighway remains at risk of becoming the information flea market. Students often need to negotiate their way through countless commercial offerings and individuals' home pages to find worthwhile information. Separating the wheat from the chaff is essential for effective use of telecommunications. But the incredible richness of contents ranging from primary sources such as slave narratives, weather data from around the world, and views from space as well as secondary sources such as that provided by online multimedia encyclopedias make the search worthwhile.

A good way for teachers to locate useful information is to rely on publications and home pages of individuals and school-based teams who serve as selection guides. Selection guides list only recommended sites, sometimes annotating web site contents and offering links that bypass introductory menus and go directly to the heart of the information. Teachers who use these guides have access to instructional tips, lesson plans, event updates, and subject matter information, which they, in turn, can make available to their students. A useful printed publication about the Internet is by Leu, Leu, and Coiro (2004).

A sample of reliable professional organizations' web sites that link to many informative sources are as follows:

- American Library Association (www.ala.org)
- Center on English Learning and Achievement (http://cela.albany.edu/)
- International Reading Association (www.ira.org)
- National Council of Teachers of English (www.ncte.org)
- National Reading Conference (www.nrconline.org)
- Regional Educational Laboratory Network (www.relnetwork.org)

- Wisconsin Literacy Education and Reading Network Services (http://wilearns.state.wi.us/)
- Young Adult Library Services Association (www.ala.org/yalsa)

Two first-rate sites associated with universities that direct you to countless web-based resources for youth are as follows:

The Literacy Web (www.literacy.uconn.edu/)
The home page of Dr. Alice Christie (www.west.asu.edu/achristie/)

Two search engines that review sites for youth are

Ask Jeeves for Kids (www.ajkids.com)
Yahooligans (www.yahooligans.com)

Finally, educational portals to vast amounts of information are

Big Chalk (www.bigchalk.com)
Blue Web'n (www.kn.pacbell.com/wired/bluewebn)
MarcoPolo (www.marcopolosearch.org/mpsearch/basic_search.asp)

Simulations Students who cannot participate in scientific or historical events firsthand can take part in them vicariously through computer simulations. Simulations allow students to investigate phenomena through virtual reality. *The*

Students access literacy through computer technology.

Human Body: The Ultimate Machine (www.aimsmultimedia.com) details the functioning of each of the human body's major systems: muscular, circulatory, respiratory, digestive, skeletal, urinary, endocrine, lymphatic, nervous, and reproductive. Through video and CD, it presents animation, microphotography, and actual surgical procedures to portray the systems. A more sophisticated application is found online amid the educational sites at the Lawrence Berkeley Laboratory home page (www.lbl.gov). In *Operation Frog*, students explore multiple biological aspects of this amphibian through virtual reality.

Gamelike Simulations   Many simulations have gamelike features, with points scored for desirable decisions, that only hint at actual firsthand experiences. For instance, the classic *Oregon Trail IV* (www.Learningcompany.com) has students reenact part of the westward expansion saga. Players decide what provisions they should set out with; what food rations and travel pace they should follow; and how they should acquire food, cross rivers, and handle adversity. Successful players reach Oregon's Willamette Valley; unsuccessful ones are said to die on the trail. On the *Europe Inspirer* (www.tomsnyder.com/) teams of students compete against each other as they participate in a scavenger hunt for resources across Europe. They interpret maps, recognize geographic patterns, and collaborate to be successful.

Multimedia   Like the electronic encyclopedias noted previously, multimedia contain incredible amounts of information in the form of print, still images, graphics, sound, animation, and video. Students can view multimedia individually on a monitor or as a group by having the visuals projected onto a screen. The presentation of multimedia can be controlled by moving from one link to another in a desired order. For instance, science teachers might talk through the human heart's system of blood circulation by presenting pictures one at a time, then showing a video of an actual heart beating, then displaying a diagram of the human body's arteries and veins. Deciding whether to show blood passing through the lungs can be made relative to how the class is responding.

The PBS award-winning documentaries *Eyes on the Prize* and *Eyes on the Prize II*, which are available on video (www.pbsvideodb.pbs.org), present America's Civil Rights movement from the mid-1950s to 1980s. They contain videotaped speeches by equal rights activists, texts from pertinent documents, anthems and theme songs, maps, and profiles of key people and organizations. In this case, students have access to the sights, sounds, and printed words of a social movement. National Geographic (www.nationalgeographic.com) offers multimedia kits with titles such as *Geokit: Cells & Microorganisms*, *Picture Atlas of the World*, and *PictureShow Library: Ancient Civilizations*. These collections include stunning pictures and drawings, narration accompanied by music and sound effects, and interactive picture buttons that invite exploration.

Multimedia projects are possible as students gather, organize, and report on information contained in multimedia courseware. For instance, in *Cultural Debates* (www.teachtsp.com/) a team of four upper-grade students watches a movie about an issue faced by an indigenous rainforest community. Each student uses a debate worksheet with a different point of view to present a position on the issue to the team. The team debates the issue, using examples from the movie, their worksheets, and their own community. The team reaches a consensus about the issue, then team members assess their work on a performance evaluation. *PrimeTime Math* (www.teachtsp.com/) engages intermediate-grade students class in real-world dramatic stories about professional people using math in compelling situations, such as wilderness search and rescues, medical emergencies, crimes, and fires. The situations portray how math applies to the world in which they live.

Trade Books

Trade books are intended for sale in general bookstores; they make up a bookseller's trade. Some educators use the terms *trade book* and *library book* as synonyms. Trade books differ from textbooks, technical manuals, reference materials, and the like.

Content area trade books come in a wide range for preschool children through adults. Trade books are available for all content areas, even those that typically limit wide reading. For instance, *Ultimate Sports* (Gallo, 1995) is an excellent collection of sports-related short stories. Marlette and Gordon (2004) present various texts physical education teachers can incorporate into their classes when addressing issues like body image, wellness, and teamwork. Hunsader (2004) presents trade books appropriate for mathematics topics. Along with books that focus on one topic like exponential growth or fractals, others deal with fundamental personal issues connected with mathematics. For instance, *The Curious Incident of the Dog in the Night-time* sensitively discloses an autistic boy's logical mathematical predisposition toward experiencing and coping with life.

Here we present only a few major genres appropriate for subject study in order to exemplify the possibilities. The following are some major genres likely to be found in elementary-, middle-, and secondary-school libraries: picture books, poetry, fiction, nonfiction narrative, nonfiction exposition, and biography.

Picture Books Picture books, which are appropriate for all ages, refer to texts whose artwork is crucial for their understanding and experience (Miller, 2000). For young children, these books introduce such concepts as size, shape, color, spatial relations, the alphabet, numeral recognition, and number sets. For instance, *Exactly the Opposite* depicts various opposites. This wordless book of photographs allows preschoolers and early readers to identify more than one correct response. In *Animalia*, each page contains dozens of lavish pictures of items that begin with that page's letter of the alphabet. *The Handmade Alphabet* uses sign language to illustrate each letter.

For older readers, *One Grain of Rice* vividly portrays the mathematical principle of exponential growth. Language arts teachers might introduce literacy devices through picture books and then transfer the lesson to more challenging material (Jurstedt & Koutras, 2000). They could present alliteration with *Some Smug Slug*, imagery with *Owl Moon*, and parody with *Prince Cinders*.

Poetry   Poetry develops mood, visceral connections, and frequently a sense of playfulness with subject matter. Poetry across the curriculum deserves your attention. For instance, poetically portray various endangered species with Heard's *Creatures of Earth, Sea, and Sky*. Enhance a unit on weather with haiku poetry from *Weather*. Engage playful attention on insects with *Flit, Flutter, Fly! Poems About Bugs and Other Crawly Creatures* and on dinosaurs with *Tyrannosaurus Was a Beast*.

Upper-grade students might find connections with the young Native Americans' poems collected in *When the Rain Sings*. When teaching a unit on the late nineteenth and early twentieth centuries, let students appreciate what life was like with Lewis's two books, *Long Ago in Oregon* and *Up in the Mountains and Other Poems of Long Ago*. *Hand in Hand: American History in Poetry* complements social studies instruction well.

Fiction   A great deal of your knowledge about the climate, language, flora, fauna, and ethnic groups in certain parts of the world probably came from reading fiction set in those locations. For instance, *Downriver* is an exciting story about troubled teens escaping their Colorado River guide, then battling themselves and the river. Readers access much information about the terrain and conditions of the U.S. southwest's Colorado Plateau while following this adventure. Other books that follow a story line while presenting extremely valuable and valid information include *Tchaikovsky Discovers America* and *Voices of the Wild*.

Two types of fiction especially suitable for content area classrooms include realistic fiction and historical fiction. *Realistic fiction* portrays events and people that seem to be involved in the recognizable trials and uncertainties of life. Books such as *I'll Get There, It Better Be Worth the Trip*, and *A Day No Pigs Would Die* are classic statements of young adults' changes from dependent children to independent adults. Many books are now available that deal with such issues as divorce, developing sexuality, mental and physical disabilities, and death and dying. For instance, *Johnny Got His Gun* is a compelling and classic piece of antiwar fiction that has a place in a high school English or a social studies class. Homelessness becomes more than a word to young children when they read engaging literature like *Fly Away Home, Monkey Island*, and *Sophie and the Sidewalk Man*.

Historical fiction attempts to re-create a believable past. Authors of such works often create fictional characters who interact with people who actually shaped events in history. Readers step into the past when they vicariously experience events through imagined and real characters. After reading *Across Five Aprils, Bull Run*, or *Behind the Lines*, students begin to understand much better why the Civil War was so devastating on a personal as well as a national scale. Historical fiction portrays countless eras and events, from prehistoric Ice Ages to the present.

Nonfiction Narrative   A content area trade book genre that deserves attention is accounts of actual happenings, called *nonfiction narratives*. This genre presents events and dialogue as they are remembered or recorded by the participants. Authors typically maintain a journal of the events if they were participants, or they interview those who actually participated and present a story that documents the events. Classic examples of nonfiction narratives appropriate for secondary students include *Black Like Me, The Double Helix, Into Thin Air, Never Cry Wolf,* and *The Right Stuff.*

You could accommodate readers' ranges of ability by offering a range of nonfiction narrative that addresses the same topic. When examining the end of World War II and the first use of an atomic bomb, you might offer *Hiroshima,* which is somewhat challenging, along with *Sadako,* which is quite accessible.

Nonfiction Exposition   Much nonfiction examines a single topic in expository fashion, with no story line for conveying ideas. This genre contains some exceptionally vivid writing and visual display. Nonfiction exposition is written for very young children through adults. *What Lives in a Shell?, Is a Blue Whale the Biggest Thing There Is?,* and *The Story of Money* are examples of nonfiction exposition books written for young readers. Books within this genre that address particular social groups and are appropriate for upper-grade readers include *Lest We Forget: The Passage from Africa to Slavery and Emancipation, World of our Fathers: A History of Jewish Life from Eastern Europe to America,* and *Crews: Gang Members Talk with Maria Hinojosa.*

Biography   Books about people who have made contributions to the content areas are numerous. Biographies are available about people prominent in reform movements, politics, sports, medicine, war, and entertainment, to name only a few fields. Abraham Lincoln, Jim Thorpe, Marie Curie, James Audubon, Anne Frank, Elizabeth Blackwell, and Bill Cosby are only a small sampling of those whose life histories have been written. Young readers often appreciate biographies as they search for heroes and heroines to emulate. Unfortunately, some biographers let their own infatuation with the subject interfere with the honest depiction of a multifaceted human being. Students need to be on the alert for folklore that passes for truth from one book to another. For instance, the story about George Washington and the cherry tree is not substantiated. Some myths are easily spotted; others pass into the general culture as truths. Though more biographies exist for people in the content areas of the arts, humanities, and social sciences, biographies have been written about important figures associated with all major curricular areas.

Multicultural Literature

Multicultural literature is a genre that differs from the others in this section because it refers to the content of materials rather than to their form. Multicultural literature is printed matter that reflects diversity; it recognizes features such as ethnicity, race, religion, age, gender, socioeconomic class, and exceptionality. Reference materials, periodicals, computer technology, trade books, and instructional materials and textbooks might or might not acknowledge our multicultural diversity.

Multicultural awareness during subject matter study is part of educators' responses to a pluralist vision of society. This vision prizes diversity, viewing group membership as an integral and a beneficial part of individuals' identities. The pluralist position holds that various groups in a society should honor their cultural heritages as long as all the groups coexist in peace. Pluralists often present a metaphor of the ideal society as a mosaic, something that contains identifiable elements contributing to a first-rate whole.

Culturally sensitive instruction honors and builds on styles of responding to print that students bring to classrooms from their communities (e.g., retelling passages as a group or individually; interpreting characters' actions playfully or seriously) (de la Luz Reyes & Halcon, 2001; Figueira, Hudelson, & Smith, 2002).

Including multicultural reading materials during subject matter study is an important aspect of this instruction. Students should have access to reading materials whose contents, illustrations, and language accurately and fairly represent diverse groups. This approach goes beyond merely displaying posters, having a one-day multicultural fair with ethnic foods for lunch, and adding a list of diverse heroes and holidays to be memorized. When studying the age of discovery, provide *The First Voyage of Christopher Columbus*, which maps out the voyage in exceptional detail, along with *The Encounter*, an account of the arrival of Columbus as seen through the eyes of the Tianos people who met him.

Myriad books with multicultural perspectives fit the myriad topics covered in school. Young children studying shelter will gain perspective on the children who live in different types of houses built throughout the United States in *The House I Live In: At Home in America*. *Rosa Parks: Mother to a Movement* offers older children a personal account of the events that led this courageous woman in 1955 to refuse to give her bus seat to a white man in Alabama, turning the civil rights movement into a national issue. *New Kids on the Block: Oral Histories of Immigrant Teens* presents adolescents' voices from various cultures.

The emphases you place on passage contents go far in determining what students make of diversity. For instance, *Shabanu, Daughter of the Wind*, a novel about a Pakistani girl commonly found in middle schools, can be approached different ways. You might help students enter the novel through multiple entry points, such as enacting key scenes from the book and bringing in Middle Eastern artifacts (Benedicty, 1995). Or you might approach the novel with a critical eye, using it as a resource for discussing and cultivating positive views toward women (Ruggieri, 2001). You might directly address two issues the book portrays—violence toward women and girls' attitudes toward their physical appearance—along with other more subtle issues, such as gender roles in the household and gendered customs relative to universal actions like weddings and childbearing. Or you might approach it from a multicultural stance (Boyd, 2003). Journal responses, PowerPoint presentations, and body biographies could all be pointed toward comparing Shabanu's traditions and customs with others.

Transforming your curriculum with multicultural literature allows you to help students understand diversity. It can sensitize members of one group to the heritages of others, resulting in the appreciation of their contributions. And it can affirm individuals' particular cultural identities.

Textbooks

Textbooks play a needed role in education: They systematically introduce readers to a body of knowledge; they save teachers time by outlining learning sequences for students; and they specify content beforehand so that teachers know how to plan. Textbooks provide the glue that holds together a wide assortment of facts and generalizations.

Although textbooks are found in practically every classroom, the way teachers use them varies substantially. At one extreme, some teachers slavishly cover their texts' contents from front to back, following suggestions from the teacher's manual and piloting students through as many of the activities as possible. Those who teach by the book daily might have students take turns reading orally and answering end-of-chapter questions. At the other extreme, some teachers leave textbooks on the classroom shelves or in the closet. These individuals might have students rely only on lectures, audiovisual presentations, and hands-on manipulatives.

Teachers in the middle of these extremes use textbooks selectively. They guide students through parts of the book that present content appropriately, point out textbook portions that reinforce what was introduced in class, and consult the text as a reference source. They selectively use accompanying textbook resources such as supplemental readings, workbooks, and tests; simulations and gamelike simulations; overhead transparencies, videotapes, and computer software; cassettes and CDs; bulletin board materials; and manipulatives such as flash cards, geometric shapes, and puzzles.

Assessing the match among textbooks, students, and the curriculum is an important aspect of teaching. Deciding if one book—or one section of a book—is more effective than another comes into play when adopting materials for course use and deciding what specifics to use when teaching. One way to make such an assessment involves textbook rating scales.

Textbook Rating Scales Rating scales focus on text aspects such as the clarity of introductions and the depth of explanations offered for a topic. Scales can go into these complex aspects of a text because they rely on individuals' judgments; they call for you to examine material and assign a subjective, but informed, rating. Rating scales pinpoint aspects of a text, and you judge their quality.

Figure 4.1 contains a textbook rating scale that we have found to be useful. As you rate each aspect of text this scale identifies, continually ask yourself how much support your students would probably require.

As you study this scale, ask yourself what you might add, modify, or delete. For instance, you might add to item 15. One way to ensure accurate and fair treatment of groups is to check materials for stereotyping, omissions, distortions, and language bias:

- Stereotyping occurs when all individuals in a particular group are depicted as having the same attribute: Are Native Americans characterized as warlike? Are women presented as dependent?

Title _____

Author(s) _____

Publisher _____ Copyright date _____

School district's intended audience _____

Directions: Rate the text according to each item below using a four-point scale, with 4 being high and 1 being low. Compare the text to an ideal instead of known materials.

After rating each item, decide how much you would need to guide students through the material in order to compensate for its shortcomings. Finally, form a holistic rating of the overall value of the text.

Very Desirable—"I would love to teach with this text!"

Desirable—"With a little support on my part, this text could be quite useful."

Undesirable—"I would have to spend a great deal of time and energy making up for the short-comings of this text."

Very Undesirable—"I would not even hand out this text to my students!"

Adjunct Aids

____1. The text contains a detailed table of contents, index, and glossary.

____2. Objectives, introductions, graphic overviews, and summaries occur at appropriate intervals and indicate major ideas.

____3. Headings, subheadings, and italic and boldfaced words occur at appropriate intervals and indicate major ideas.

____4. Graphic aids such as illustrations, maps, and tables occur on the same page as the discussion or at least the facing page. These graphics clarify major ideas presented in the text; they do not introduce new ideas or simply decorate the page.

____5. Review, extension, and application activities such as questions, suggested readings, and projects occur at appropriate intervals. They relate directly to the major ideas and elicit a wide range of thinking.

Conceptual Development

____6. The chapters emphasize fundamental concepts or principles; they are more than encyclo-pedic collections of related information. Facts are presented to develop the explicitly stated concepts or principles.

____7. Explanations of new ideas include memorable analogies, clear references to previously presented information, and concrete examples. The explanations consist of more than dull dictionary-type wording.

____8. The amount of technical vocabulary on each page is appropriate for the intended audience.

Motivation Arousal

____9. The text includes introductory comments, questions, and scenarios to arouse curiosity about the upcoming contents.

____10. The text explains how learners might use the information in real-life situations.

____11. The text cover, print size, graphics, and layout are appealing to the intended audience.

Organization

____12. The chapters could be outlined easily. The paragraphs and sections move forward in a logical manner.

____13. The text explicitly signals how information is arranged. Topic paragraphs and sentences include such statements as, "There are three reasons for this outcome" and "The following presents the key events."

Special Concerns

____14. The text fits the course objectives.

____15. Groups of people are presented authentically. There is no bias.

____16. A teacher's manual provides helpful suggestions for presenting the textual information.

Figure 4.1   Textbook Rating Scale

- Omissions occur when the contributions of particular groups are underrepresented: Are women's roles in westward expansion described? Are scientific discoveries by physically disabled individuals noted?
- Distortions systematically misrepresent certain groups. For instance, referring to Asian Americans rather than to Japanese or Chinese Americans gives a false impression of uniformity between these two groups. And depicting Native Americans in only historical or ceremonial settings ignores their contemporary status.
- Language bias happens when subtle, frequently subconscious choices about words affect the message about certain groups. Are revolutionaries working to overthrow an established government called terrorists or freedom fighters? Did Americans in the 1860s fight a Civil War or a War Between the States? Were African Americans given the right to vote, or did they win it?

The most effective textbook rating scales seem to be ones that school and school district staff produce on their own. Such scales can be based on the one shown in Figure 4.1 yet modified to fit local standards and particular student populations. Among other things, one group of social studies educators might consider primary sources to be essential in a textbook; a group of math teachers might emphasize vivid and feasible application activities; and a group of English instructors might be quite interested in authors from a particular region.

DO IT TOGETHER Form small groups of three or four students each according to academic specialization (e.g., social studies, mathematics, English). If you teach all subjects, select a particular one for this activity. Go on a scavenger hunt to locate and bring to class on a certain date published materials that fit your specialization in each of the following categories. On the day that everything is brought in, share the materials you found. Indicate what is special about their contents, writing styles, and potential classroom uses.

Reading Materials Scavenger Hunt List
Reference material
Periodical
Computer technology
   Simulations
   Gamelike simulations
   Multimedia
   Online resources
Trade books
   Picture book
   Poetry
   Fiction
   Nonfiction narrative

Nonfiction exposition
Biography
Multicultural literature
Textbooks

Exhibits Take Many Forms

The term *exhibit* refers to what students construct after they engage with instructional unit materials such as the ones just described. Exhibits typically are somewhat open ended and flexible. They can be in response to any single material or set of materials, and be assigned by the teacher or designed by the student. Effective exhibits include combinations of visual displays, concrete displays, dramatizations, writing, and discussing.

Visual Displays

If a culminating activity is "Portray why people smoke" or "Describe why the Grand Canyon is so grand," visual displays might be a key part of the exhibit. Visuals such as the following might be computer generated, produced freehand, or gathered from published resources.

Illustrations   Students often draw pictures, collect photographs, take their own photographs, and make posters or bulletin boards in order to depict what they encountered in a passage. Realistic or impressionistic sketches in response to literature stretch minds in ways that verbal reports cannot (Whitlin, 1996). Such visuals graphically depict what words can only suggest. For example, the Grand Canyon, cell division, parts of the body, and geometric figures are natural candidates for illustrated projects.

Time Lines and Murals   The key events of a phenomenon are frequently displayed on a time line. Any number of illustrations, or none at all, may be on a time line. The essential feature is that events are labeled and represented in sequence on a linear chart. Murals can be similar to time lines in that they represent a sequence of events; the difference, of course, is that murals consist solely of pictures.

Storyboards   The film industry originated storyboarding to represent scenes to be filmed, but educators now use the term to refer to any set of illustrations that depict a sequence of events. Readers can storyboard the key scenes from a narrative they have read or plan to write. They can storyboard scientific processes such as photosynthesis and the water cycle as well as social events depicting an era or political movement.

Maps   Representing an area graphically requires careful reading and composing. Students need to decide what locations to represent and then produce that representation. Illustrations can be added to maps for greater detail. Maps can depict locations on many scales. For instance, locations within a building, a neighborhood, a community, a state, a nation, the world, or the universe can be mapped.

Collages Collages are groups of pictures and various other materials glued to a surface. These artistic compositions generally symbolize a topic. Making a collage of an area of study such as ethnic and racial groups, geographic locations, inventions, or animal groups is a good project for students of all ages.

Tables, Graphs, and Charts Poster-size displays of data represented through tables, graphs, and charts and accompanied by written explanations are effective visuals. Students compare findings from public opinion polls as well as what they learn about various phenomena.

Concrete Displays

Students can buy, borrow, or make concrete displays as part of their projects. Such displays could be the centerpiece of what students then talk or write about. Science fairs and open-house displays, which are traditional parts of many schools' curricula, are excellent examples of projects centering around concrete displays.

Representations Concrete displays frequently represent, or model, real-world phenomena. Students who read about the formation of islands could fashion clay-and-water representations of geological actions. Large entities such as buildings and land formations, as well as invisible processes such as evaporation and covalent bonding, can be modeled.

Realia Actual phenomena being studied, called *realia*, might be collected and displayed as part of an effective project. Displaying pieces of sandstone, limestone, and shale concretely depicts types of sedimentary rock when examining land formations. Young students constructing a project on frontier living might collect objects that represent life on the western frontier in the 1800s. They can bring into class farm tools, kitchen implements, clothing, and assorted household items to depict aspects of a bygone way of life. A table of books and realia that students prepared for a unit of study in American history is shown in the photograph on page 80.

Dramatizations

Performing before others is a powerful device for promoting reading, writing, thinking, and learning (Smith & Herring, 2001; Worthman, 2002). Students dramatically reading selected portions of a passage to their classmates or to older or younger students is one form of dramatization. Dramatizations are ways for students to express ideas and understandings in a highly visible and active format. Four popular formats are described here.

Skits Many students like to stage short skits in reaction to what they have read, simulating certain phenomena through action and dialogue. For example, older students might read Elisabeth Kubler-Ross's *On Death and Dying* and then present different skits that portray the stages people exhibit when facing their own imminent deaths. Other students might take Studs Terkel's *Working* and present selected scenes wherein people talk about the emotional side of their jobs and how their jobs affect their whole lives. Young students who read about collecting rocks could go through a series of scenes that illustrate the recommendations for gathering a personal collection.

Another option is for students to break into pairs or small groups and simulate an interview with the author of or a character from the reading. Television talk shows provide a model for the interviewing format. Along this same line, students can form pairs to review what they have read, with one student emphasizing the positive features and the other stressing the negative. Finally, students dramatically reading selected portions of a text to their classmates or younger students is another form of dramatization.

Pantomimes Students use creative physical movement to nonverbally represent a procedure, event, or concept. Selections from fiction, nonfiction, drama, and poetry can be pantomimed. One person, often the teacher, might begin pantomime in the class by orally reading a passage while student-actors use gesture and movement to represent what is being said. As class members become adept with this

Assembling a display of objects and related reading materials is an effective book project.

technique, they can pantomime subject matter with no accompanying reading. After the performance, discuss the actors' accomplishments and the audience's thoughts. Some content area topics conducive to pantomime are as follows:

- *Mitosis* can be enacted with same-sex pairs of students wearing identically colored jerseys to represent chromosomes and students without jerseys encircling the pairs by joining hands in a large ring to represent a cell membrane. The group then depicts how it would produce another cell like itself (Wyn & Stegink, 2000).
- *Viral infections* can be presented with students acting as viruses entering, multiplying, and exiting cells.
- *The French Revolution* can be depicted with students acting as Louis XVI, members of the second estate, Robespierre, national assembly members, and Napoleon Bonaparte.
- *Paul Revere's ride and the battles of Lexington and Concord* can be portrayed with students acting as Paul Revere, colonists and the minutemen, and the British military.

Role-Play Interviews   Questioning figures in role-play interviews promotes inquiry. Investigative reporters interview important figures from science, social studies, literature, or mathematics. The questioning can occur during a fictional news conference, talk show, or on-the-scene report.

Demonstrate role-play interviews before students perform one. Generate questions that prompt long responses; follow up short yes/no responses with "Why?"; include various types of questions. Have students dress and talk (as much as possible) in the manner of the participants. After the interview, discuss the actors' accomplishments and the audience's thoughts.

- When studying the ancient world, famous individuals can be interviewed, such as

Alexander the Great	Confucius	Siddharta Gautama
Iceman of the Alps	Liu Bang	Menes
Paul	Socrates	Thutmose III

- Interviews can be conducted with unnamed individuals representing groups such as

archaeologists	artisans	barbarians
caravan riders	disciples	martyrs
patricians	plebeians	regents

As students become adept with role-play interviews, they can include multiple reporters and/or figures during one interview session (e.g., bring together and interview Confucius, Siddharta Gautama, and Paul).

Readers' Theater   Readers' theater is a productive way for students to dramatize what they have read (Campbell & Cleland, 2003; Moen, 2004). It is a method of oral interpretation that provides a relevant purpose for reading orally. You do not need to prepare special scripts for readers' theater; have students read directly from the passage. Most children who have basic reading proficiencies enjoy reading plays; readers' theater allows playlike reading with regular prose.

When you first introduce readers' theater, have a small group demonstrate the process. Show how each speaking part is indicated in the text with quotation marks and how the speaker is revealed by the flow of the conversation. The narrator's role of reading all the material outside the quotation marks should be made clear. When first presenting this activity, the narrator might read all the "he said" and "she said" phrases, but this practice should be stopped when the students become adept. Explain that only the key parts of a book and the parts that contain extensive dialogue should be selected for readers' theater.

When readers' theater groups are formed, have the students first react to the entire passage so they have a good understanding of what they are staging. Then have them identify and practice their parts before reading. Some groups tape-record themselves and submit the recording as their response project, and others perform for the class. Simple props and sound effects frequently are included. Readers' theater is quite popular among students, so you might consider setting aside a certain time of the week for these presentations.

TRY IT OUT   Produce a visual display, a concrete display, or a dramatization in response to this chapter. Share your project with your class or a small group of classmates.

Writing

Writing is part of most projects. Visuals and concrete object displays usually contain some written explanation; dramatizations involve notes, directions, and scripts. In addition, writing—with little or no accompanying props or performances—can be the basis of reading projects. You might have students regularly write very brief compositions, such as notes or reactions during a unit, and then collect all the writing as a culminating exhibit. Or you might have students work toward one large composition to submit at the end of a unit. Chapter 7, "Writing", and Chapter 9, "Student Inquiry," add to what we present here relative to writing.

To stimulate and structure students' projects, teachers often provide writing prompts. Prompts urge and inspire action; they cue people to move forward. Prompts can be questions ("What was the most important word in what you just studied?") or directives ("Describe the most important word in what you just studied.").

Generic prompts fit any material. They contain language that is appropriate for anything students read. Generic prompts apply to more than one piece of text. For instance, students can learn to ask, "What have I learned?" after each reading. To do so is a powerful strategy. In addition, teachers can regularly demonstrate how they answer a question such as, "What have I learned?" thereby providing a pattern for students to follow. Figure 4.2 contains numerous generic prompts. Two common writing projects that utilize prompts are response journals and reaction guides.

Response Journals Response journals allow students to explore ideas, ask questions, and express feelings about what they are learning. Teachers often introduce journals by presenting an entry or two and showing how they respond to particular prompts.

Numerous response journal prompts can be added to the questions presented in Figure 4.2. When reading a narrative, readers might respond in the form of a character journal, a written log readers keep as they assume the identity of a main character. Readers write in the first-person voice of the character, expressing feelings, thoughts, and reflections about the events unfolding in the story. Readers note the chapter they are responding to, then typically relive one episode. They might parenthetically (actually using parentheses) insert their own thoughts about the character or the author into their first-person accounts.

Another option is to provide writing stems that address various aspects of a passage. After first exemplifying appropriate responses, you might have students complete stems such as the following:

- The most important word in the chapter is . . .
- The most important thing about . . . is . . .
- The most incredible thing about . . . is . . .
- The worst thing about . . .
- An unbelievable thing about . . .
- The simple facts about . . .
- The truth about . . .

Students typically write in their journals several times a week. Replying to the students as an aunt or uncle instead of as teacher-as-examiner goes far in allowing you to express interest in students' insights and strategies and prevents the journals from becoming an exercise no different from assigned writing. Students who write on their own terms about what they are reading and who receive sincere reactions to their entries tend to respond more than they would to assigned factual prompts. At the same time, teachers are able to monitor students' progress in reading and writing when they read the journals. A special feature is that these journals allow teachers to stay in touch with each individual in class, not just the vocal ones; teachers can maintain a dialogue with the shyest student through journals.

Reaction Guides Teachers frequently distribute reaction guides to promote students' thinking. Reaction guides typically offer more structure than journals. Reaction guides for literary writing during English language arts instruction might contain items grouped according to traditional literary elements such as character, plot, setting, and theme. For instance, Figure 4.3 displays a sample guide for older

Universal Reading-Response Prompts

What will I/you remember about this material?

What ideas did I/you gain from my/your reading?

How did this material help me/you better understand the world?

What is the most important word, sentence, or section?

What materials have I/you read that are similar?

What does this material remind me/you of?

What was the author trying to share?

What is the most important message of this material?

How will I/you think differently after reading this material?

What questions did the material leave unanswered?

Information for a Best Friend

How could I convince my best friend to read this material?

What would my/your best friend like to know about this material?

Should I/you tell a friend to read this? Why?

Image

What pictures, sounds, and other sensory feelings did I/you experience while reading this material?

Evaluation

What did I/you like best about this material?

What was my/your favorite part of this material?

Should the material receive a literary award? Why?

Is anything missing that should be included? What?

If I/you rewrote this, what would I/you change?

Is the material unique? Why?

What part of the material was realistic or unrealistic?

Literary Structure

What event begins the story?

What situation in the story reminded me/you of a situation from my/your own life?

What did I/you think was going to happen when _____?

How would I/you have reacted to the situations in the story?

If I/you were _____, what would I/you have done when _____?

If I/you could become a part of the story, at what point would I/you like to enter? What would I/you do?

Characterization

Why did the main character behave as he or she did?

Which characters, if any, did I/you especially like or dislike? Why?

Did any characters change? If so, how?

What did the characters learn?

What advice would I/you give the characters?

Figure 4.2   Generic Prompts for Written and Oral Compositions

Emotions

How did _____ feel when _____ happened?
What parts made me/you feel the strongest?
Did any part of the material surprise me/you? Why?

Author's Craft

How did the author hold my/your attention?
How did the author signal important information?
How did the author reveal the meanings of difficult or unfamiliar terms?
How did the author organize the material?
How did the author balance illustrations and print?
How did the author develop his or her ideas?

Figure 4.2 *Continued*

readers that contains two items under each literary element; others certainly might be included. Figure 4.4 shows a sample literary response guide for young readers.

Reaction guides for expository writing differ from guides for literary materials because expository guides do not refer to story characters or the main problem and solution of the plot. Figure 4.5 shows an expository guide that fits younger as well as older readers.

Guides also can be produced that contain items fitting only the one book under consideration. For instance, if an adolescent chooses *Shipwreck at the Bottom of the*

Directions: Complete one task that is listed under each literary element.

Character

1. Write to a friend, a member of your family, or an actor or actress a letter that describes how he or she is like a character in your book.
2. Pretend that you are one of the characters in your book. Write a letter to Ann Landers to get her advice on coping with the main problem you faced. Write her response.

Plot

1. Produce a calendar of events that reflects the story line. (The calendar can be divided among hours, days, weeks, months, or years.)
2. Produce a diary that one of the characters might have kept in order to chronicle the events of his or her life.

Setting

1. Pretend that the book is being turned into a one-hour special or a miniseries for television. Describe at least five locations where five different scenes should be filmed.
2. You are responsible for obtaining the props for a stage production of your book. List five props that are essential for the production and justify their use.

Theme

1. Describe at least one insight that the main character gained by the end of the book.
2. Describe how another book that you know makes the same point as the one you read.

Figure 4.3 Sample Literary Response Guide for Older Readers

1. Tell how far you read before you knew for sure that you wanted to finish the book.
2. Describe your favorite part of a chapter or of the entire book.
3. Think of a book that is like the one you just read and explain how the two are alike.
4. Identify the main problem and its solution in the book.
5. Explain why you would or would not choose someone in the book for a friend.

Figure 4.4   Sample Literary Response Guide for Younger Readers

World, an award-winning account of the ill-fated 1914 Shackleton expedition to Antarctica, then the teacher or peers might help him or her decide which questions to address: Should the student portray and explain what caused Shackleton's ship, the *Endurance*, to be destroyed? Should he or she generate the most important reasons for no one dying during this ordeal? Should connections be made among this saga and contemporary ones? Should the quality and accuracy of Armstrong's presentation be evaluated?

Many teachers produce reaction guides that fit certain types of materials. For instance, the following prompts fit only their respective genres:

- *Biography*: Describe how the individual was influenced by others as well as how he or she exerted an influence on others.
- *Movie tie-in*: Describe at least three differences between the book and the movie.
- *Mystery*: List the clues that led to the solution.

To be sure, reaction guide writing prompts vary tremendously beyond the few displayed here. Teachers provide access to generic prompts such as the ones listed in Figure 4.2. They often have students choose the items they wish to complete or create ones for themselves. They might require one or two activities, provide options (e.g., "Select two of the following four choices"), and encourage students to create their own way to react. Figure 4.6 displays a reaction guide that calls for choices.

Discussion

Discussions are verbal explorations of ideas among teachers and students and among students themselves. Individuals purposefully exchange their views.

1. Tell what you learned from this book.
2. Explain why you would or would not choose to read other books by this author.
3. Describe what information in this book you would like to know more about.
4. Describe what made this book interesting.
5. Explain how you might use what you learned from this book.

Figure 4.5   Sample Expository Response Guide

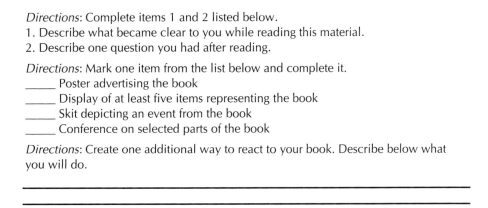

Directions: Complete items 1 and 2 listed below.
1. Describe what became clear to you while reading this material.
2. Describe one question you had after reading.

Directions: Mark one item from the list below and complete it.
_____ Poster advertising the book
_____ Display of at least five items representing the book
_____ Skit depicting an event from the book
_____ Conference on selected parts of the book

Directions: Create one additional way to react to your book. Describe below what you will do.

Figure 4.6   *Sample Reaction Guide Offering Choices*

Discussions provide opportunities for participants to think of things they otherwise might not have considered. They obtain new insights and perspectives (Applebee, Langer, Nystrand, & Gamoran, 2003). "I hadn't thought of that!" is a common response during effective discussions.

Discussants engage in a dialogue—not in a recitation in which an answer or a solution has been determined beforehand. Ideal patterns of group talk move from student to student rather than only from teacher to student in ping-pong fashion.

When using discussion as a unit's culminating activity, be sure to plan for it. Present a unit's essential question and highlight on the class calendar when the class will be able to publicly and thoroughly discuss responses to it. Prepare students for the culminating discussion by helping them gather and organize ideas for this event. You might have your class move their seating arrangement into a large circle in order to face one another during the discussion; sometimes you might have your classes move into several small circles.

To begin a discussion, you might use an open-ended item such as one of those listed in Figure 4.2. An important rule is to ask only those questions that you consider to have more than one possibly acceptable answer. If you are committed to a single correct answer, then the students' task becomes one of determining what is in your mind rather than of thinking on their own terms. Discussions are give-and-take dialogues in which teachers are not committed to single correct answers.

To keep talk going after a student has finished speaking, consider the classic four moves presented by J. T. Dillon (1988): statements, student questions, signals, and silence:

1. *Statements* are someone's selected thoughts to what has just been said. You might state your understanding ("As I understand it, you're saying. . ."), describe what you would like to have expanded ("I'm interested in hearing more about . . ."), indicate your state of mind ("I'm confused about . . . "), or relate what has just been said with what has been previously stated ("So you're saying . . . , while _____ is saying . . . "). Interestingly, students respond to statements.

2. *Student questions* often seem to invigorate discussions more than teachers' questions. Your role, then, is to encourage and facilitate such questions. You might state, "This seems to be a good time to know what else we should be asking about," then wait for someone to initiate a new direction in the exchange. Many teachers post questions for students to ask to keep a discussion moving. Questions such as the following move a discussion forward while addressing rigor and accountability: "Can you support that?" "Where did you find that information?" "Can you give us some examples?" "Why do you think that?" and "Can you explain that more fully?"

3. *Signals* are somewhat neutral gestures that indicate you heard what a student said and are ready for someone else to talk. Signals might consist of a comment such as, "All right," "Well said," or "Okay." You can nod your head in agreement or lift your hands and eyebrows in wonder.

4. *Silence* can go far in encouraging students to speak. Keeping silent for at least five seconds after a prompt by you or after a comment by a student might not seem like much, but it is a clear indication that someone should speak. This wait time can be powerful.

To keep discussions focused, you might record and display ideas. Using a Discussion Web (Alvermann, 1991), for instance, write a statement in the center and then have discussants generate ideas to be recorded about it. The following illustration shows a web for recording ideas affirming and negating the assertion that the printing press is the most important invention.

Affirmative	*Negative*
_____	_____
_____	_____
_____	_____
_____	_____
The printing press is the most important invention.	
_____	_____
_____	_____
_____	_____
_____	_____

Maintaining appropriate social support during discussions is especially important. Free-flowing talk about compelling issues risks inflaming passions and diminishing civility. It potentially enables powerful, outspoken individuals to marginalize others. Consequently, a classroom climate that promotes respect is essential. Respectful discussions are accomplished in part by articulating and demonstrating what respect looks like, sounds like, and feels like. Clarify expectations along these lines, have students enact them in small-group demonstrations, and hold individuals accountable for them. You might display expectations such as the following:

Respectful Discussions

Look Like	Sound Like	Feel Like
• People face each other.	• One person at a time talks.	• My ideas are being taken seriously.
• People concentrate on what each other is saying.	• Remain on task.	• I'm confident that I will learn from others and they will learn from me.
	• Give-and-take of ideas	
• Friendly faces		

A useful way to distinguish two types of discussions contrasts seminars with deliberations (Parker, 2001). Seminars are open-ended arenas for exploring meanings of passages. Seminar discussants generate multiple interpretations, digging deeply into what authors might have intended and what they might make of it. Seminar leaders and participants always are skeptical about what is said, stirring up ideas by challenging and questioning each other's reactions. When talking about the most important invention, readers would generate and examine multiple possibilities. Through vigorous talk, they would explore diverse reasons for diverse inventions being considered most important.

Seminars are crucibles for divergent thinking. After a seminar, when leaders do not emphasize convergence and closure, students might choose to reach closure individually by recording their final thoughts in a journal or notebook.

Deliberation is a form of discussion that expressly seeks closure. Discussants arrive at an answer to a question or a solution to a problem. The opening question generally is some version of "What should we decide?" Participants in a deliberation then hash out ideas en route to the decision. They weigh alternatives, evaluating as much relevant information as possible before reaching conclusions.

When talking about the most important invention, students in a deliberative discussion would talk about possibilities and then begin converging onto a choice. A debate might be held. Students might vote on the most important invention to reach a collective decision, or each person might decide individually. But the discussion is guided to inform participants' decisions.

LOOKING BACK When you use multiple reading materials in your classroom, you and your students will benefit greatly. Your teaching and your students' learning are energized. Reading materials vary from computer technology to trade books to periodicals. Students can respond to these materials in many ways, too. In this chapter, you encountered three key ideas: (1) Students deserve various content area reading materials during instructional units; (2) various content area reading materials are available for instructional units; and (3) exhibits take many forms.

ADD TO YOUR JOURNAL   Think about the role of multiple reading materials in the classes that you will be teaching. How far beyond the text do you intend to go? What types of materials will you use? How do you intend to have students react to what they read?

Additional Readings

This book is a comprehensive yet accessible guide to children's and young adult literature:

GILLESPIE, J. T. (2005). *The children's and young adult literature handbook: A research and reference guide*. Englewood, CO: Libraries Unlimited.

The following present literature across the curriculum for children:

CULINAN, B. E., & PERSON, D. G. (Eds.) (2003). *The Continuum encyclopedia of children's literature*. New York: Continuum, 2003.

LIMA, C. W., & LIMA, J. (2005). *A to zoo: Subject access to children's picture books* (7th ed.). Englewood, CO: Libraries Unlimited.

WOLF, S. A. (2004). *Interpreting literature with children*. Mahwah, NJ: Lawrence Erlbaum Associates.

ZARIAN, B. B. (2004). *Around the world with historical fiction and folktales: Highly recommended and award-winning books, grades K–8*. Lanham, MD: Scarecrow Press.

These references present literature across the curriculum for young adults:

BROWN, J. E., & STEPHENS, E. C. (2003). *Your reading: An annotated booklist for middle school and junior high* (11th ed.). Urbana, IL: National Council of Teachers of English.

CARTER, B., ESTES, S., & WADDLE, L. (2000). *Best books for young adults* (2nd ed.). Chicago: American Library Association.

GILLESPIE, J. T., & BARR, C. (2004). *Best books for high school readers: Grades 9–12*. Westport, CT: Libraries Unlimited.

LESESNE, T. S. (2003). *Making the match: The right book for the right reader at the right time, grades 4–12*. Portland, ME: Stenhouse Publishers.

NILSEN, A. P., & DONELSON, K. L. (2001). *Literature for today's young adults* (6th ed.). New York: Longman.

SCHALL, L. (2003). *Booktalks and more: Motivating teens to read*. Westport, CT: Libraries Unlimited.

Wise uses of information and communication technology for subject matter study are suggested in the following:

GRABE, M., & GRABE, C. (2004). *Integrating technology for meaningful learning* (4th ed.). New York: Houghton Mifflin.

KUIPER, E., VOLMAN, M., & TERWEL, J. (2005). The web as an information resource in K–12 education: Strategies for supporting students in searching and processing information. *Review of Educational Research, 75,* 285–328.

WISKE, M. S. (2005). *Teaching for understanding with technology.* San Francisco, Jossey-Bass.

Reading materials that expose students to new, possibly controversial ideas risk offending parents and community members. Prepare for this possibility by examining the following.

REICHMAN, H. (2001). *Censorship and selection: Issues and answers for schools* (3rd ed.). Chicago: American Library Association.

SIMMONS, J. S., & DRESANG, E. T. (2001). *School censorship in the 21st century.* Newark, DE: International Reading Association.

Leading discussions of what students have read is complex. The following books suggest ways to conduct productive discussions.

COPELAND, M. (2005). *Socratic circles: Fostering critical and creative thinking in middle and high school.* Portland, ME: Stenhouse.

HOLDEN, J., & SCHMIT, J. S. (Eds.) (2002). *Inquiry and the literary text: Constructing discussions in the English classroom.* Urbana, IL: National Council of Teachers of English.

Multicultural book selection guides such as the following suggest appropriate children's and young adults' titles:

HELBIG, A. K., & PERKINS, A. R. (2001). *Many peoples, one land: A guide to new multicultural literature for children and young adults.* Westport, CT: Greenwood Press.

HANSEN-KRENING, N., AOKI, E. M., & MIZOKAWA, D. T. (2003). *Kaleidoscope: A multicultural booklist for grades K–8* (4th ed.). Urbana, IL: National Council of Teachers of English.

HORNING, K. T., KRUSE, G. M., & SCHLIESMAN, M. (1997). *Multicultural literature for children and young adults* (vol. 2). Madison, WI: Cooperative Children's Book Center.

KUHARETS, O. R. (Ed.) (2001). *Venture into cultures: A resource book of multicultural materials and programs* (2nd ed.) Chicago: American Library Association.

The following summarize what researchers have learned about readers' interactions with literature.

GALDA, L., ASH, G. A., & CULLINAN, B. E. (2000). Children's literature. In M. J. Kamil, P. B. Mosenthal, P. D. Pearson, & R. Barr (Eds.), *Handbook of reading research* (vol. 3) (pp. 361–379). Mahwah, NJ: Lawrence Erlbaum Associates.

MARSHALL, J. (2000). Research on response to literature. In M. J. Kamil, P. B. Mosenthal, P. D. Pearson, & R. Barr (Eds.), *Handbook of reading research* (vol. 3) (pp. 381–402). Mahwah, NJ: Lawrence Erlbaum Associates.

MARTINEZ, M., & ROSER, N. L. (2003). Children's responses to literature. In J. Flood, D. Lapp, J. R. Squire, & J. M. Jensen (Eds.), *Handbook of research on teaching the English language arts* (2nd ed.; pp. 799–813). Mahwah, NJ: Lawrence Erlbaum Associates.

MORROW, L. M., & GAMBRELL, L. B. (2000). Literature-based reading instruction. In M. J. Kamil, P. B. Mosenthal, P. D. Pearson, & R. Barr (Eds.), *Handbook of reading research* (vol. 3) (pp. 563–586). Mahwah, NJ: Lawrence Erlbaum Associates.

Childrens' and Young Adults' Trade Books Noted in Chapter 4

ARMSTRONG, J. (1999). *Shipwreck at the bottom of the world.* New York: Crown.

ARMSTRONG, W. H. (1969). *Sounder.* New York: Harper & Row.

BASE, G. (1987). *Animalia.* New York: Abrams.

BODE, J. (1989). *New kids on the block: Oral histories of immigrant teens.* New York: Watts.

BUNTING, E. (1991). *Fly away home.* New York: Clarion.

COERR, E. (1993). *Sadako.* New York: Putnam.

COLE, B. (1988). *Prince Cinders.* New York: Putnam.

DEMI. (1997). *One grain of rice: A mathematical folktale.* New York: Scholastic.

DONOVAN, J. (1969). *I'll get there, it better be worth the trip.* New York: Harper & Row.

EDWARDS, P. D. (1996). *Some smug slug.* New York: HarperCollins.

FLEISCHMAN, P. (1993). *Bull Run.* New York: HarperCollins.

FOX, P. (1991). *Monkey island.* New York: Orchard.

GIBSON, M. (1982). *Gods, men, and monsters from the Greek myths.* New York: Schocken.

GRIFFIN, J. H. (1977). *Black like me.* Boston: Houghton Mifflin.

HADDON, M. (2003). *The curious incident of the dog in the night-time.* New York: Vintage.

HEARD, G. (1992). *Creatures of earth, sea, and sky.* Honesdale, PA: Wordsong/Boyds Mill Press.

HERSEY, J. (1946). *Hiroshima.* New York: Knopf.

HINOJOSA, M. (1995). *Crews: Gang members talk with Maria Hinojosa.* New York: Harcourt.

HOBAN, T. (1990). *Exactly the opposite.* Westport, CT: Greenwillow.

HOBBS, W. (1996). *Downriver.* New York: Dell.

HOLLAND, I. (1994). *Behind the lines.* New York: Scholastic.

HOPKINS, L. B. (1992). *Flit, flutter, fly! Poems about bugs and other crawly creatures.* New York: Doubleday.

HOPKINS, L. B. (1994). *Weather.* New York: HarperCollins.

HOPKINS, L. B. (1995). *Hand in hand: American history in poetry.* New York: Simon & Schuster.

HUNT, I. (1964). *Across five Aprils.* Chicago: Follett.

KALMAN, E. (1995). *Tchaikovsky discovers America.* New York: Orchard.

KLEIN, N. (1988). *No more Saturday nights.* New York: Knopf.

KRAKAUER, J. (1997). *Into thin air.* New York: Villard.

KUBLER-ROSS, E. (1974). *On death and dying.* New York: Macmillan.

LEWIS, C. (1987). *Long ago in Oregon.* New York: HarperCollins.

LEWIS, C. (1991). *Up in the mountains and other poems of long ago.* New York: HarperCollins.

LONDON, J. (1993). *Voices of the wild.* New York: Crown.

MAESTRO, B. (1993). *The story of money.* New York: Clarion.

MELTZER, M. (1996). *World of our fathers: A history of Jewish life from Eastern Europe to America.* Northvale, NJ: J. Aronson.

MOWAT, F. (1963). *Never cry wolf.* Boston: Little, Brown.

NATIONAL MUSEUM OF THE AMERICAN INDIAN, Smithsonian Institution. (1999). *When the rain sings: Poems by young Native Americans.* New York: Simon & Schuster.

PARKS, R. (1992). *Rosa Parks: Mother to a movement.* New York: Dial.

PECK, R. N. (1972). *A day no pigs would die.* New York: Dell.

PILLING, A. (1993). *Realms of gold: Myths and legends from around the world.* New York: Kingfisher.

PRELUTSKY, J. (1988). *Tyrannosaurus was a beast.* New York: Greenwillow.

RANKIN, L. (1991). *The handmade alphabet.* New York: Dial.

SELTZER, I. (1992). *The house I live in: At home in America.* New York: Macmillan.

SMITH, B. (1992). *The first voyage of Columbus.* New York: Viking.

STAPLES, S. F. (1989). *Shabanu, Daughter of the wind.* New York: Knopf.

TERKEL, S. (1981). *Working.* New York: Simon & Schuster.

THOMAS, V. M. (1997). *Lest we forget: The passage from Africa to slavery and emancipation.* New York: Crown.

TOLAN, S. S. (1992). *Sophie and the sidewalk man.* New York: Four Winds.

TRUMBO, D. (1939). *Johnny got his gun.* Philadelphia: Lippincott.

WATSON, J. D. (1968). *The double helix.* New York: Atheneum.

WELLS, R. E. (1993). *Is a blue whale the biggest thing there is?* Morton Grove, IL: Whitman.

WOLFE, T. (1979). *The right stuff.* New York: Farrar, Straus & Giroux.

YOLEN, J. (1987). *Owl moon.* New York: Philomel Books.

YOLEN, J. (1992). *The encounter.* San Diego: Harcourt Brace Jovanovich.

ZOEHFELD, K. W. (1994). *What lives in a shell?* New York: HarperCollins.

5

Comprehension

Most of the time, readers take comprehension for granted. They decode words and automatically understand the message. But comprehension does not always occur automatically. Excellent decoding skills sometimes are not enough. The following passage from a classic statistics book (Kirk, 1972) shows that comprehension is more than a matter of merely pronouncing each word:

> Fractional factorial designs have much in common with confounded factorial designs. The latter designs, through the technique of confounding, achieve a reduction in the number of treatment combinations that must be included within a block. A fractional factorial design uses confounding to reduce the number of treatment combinations in the experiment. As is always the case when confounding is used, the reduction is obtained at a price. There is considerable ambiguity in interpreting the outcome of a fractional factorial experiment, since treatments are confounded with interactions. For example, a significant mean square might be attributed to the effects of treatment A or to a BCDE interaction. (p. 256)

Did you understand this passage? Could you retell it to someone in your own words without looking back at the text?

Comprehension is automatic when reading about topics for which you have adequate background, know most of the appropriate vocabulary, and understand enough to sort out important from trivial information. People who are knowledgeable about statistics fully comprehend the sample paragraph; typically, it makes little sense to nonstatisticians. Students often are in this position when reading in the content areas, so they require support. This chapter on supporting comprehension contains four keys:

1. Vary levels of comprehension support.
2. Guide readers through challenging passages.

3. Teach reading comprehension strategies.
4. Promote collaborative comprehension practices.

Vary Levels of Comprehension Support

Not all content reading is—or should be—like what you probably just experienced with the fractional factorial design passage. As Chapter 4 showed, countless well-written, richly presented books, pamphlets, online sites, and so on, are available. Extensive reading of high-quality informational literature increases students' subject matter knowledge and reading competence. Engaging your class with accessible materials as Chapter 4 described goes far in promoting comprehension. However, students sometimes require support with even the best reading materials.

Determining appropriate levels of support is a good way to begin planning how to give students what they need to comprehend satisfactorily. Sometimes substantial support is needed because students are far from ready for the challenge certain materials present. Sometimes, practically nothing is needed. In order to begin planning comprehension supports appropriately, consider reader–text matches.

Reader–Text Matches

Assessing the match between readers and the texts they have to read informs your instructional decisions. It involves determining how challenging particular passages are relative to particular readers. Educators traditionally have discerned three levels of reader–text match: frustration, instructional, and independent.

Frustration   When passages are as challenging as the one on fractional factorial designs presented earlier, frustration readily sets in and students often skip it, have others explain it, or—if there is a test—try to memorize its contents. Students might eventually gain partial knowledge of the passage, but it would take too much time. The fractional factorial designs passage presents nonstatisticians an academic challenge that requires undue amounts of help and individual effort to be a worthwhile classroom teaching tool. For ease of reference, reading educators refer to this reader–text match simply as *frustration*.

Instructional   Reader–text matches conducive to effective instruction are called *instructional*. A good word for matches at this level is *teachable*. Like the racquetball situation between David and Dean described in Chapter 2, instructional level is at the cutting edge of learners' abilities—neither too difficult nor too easy. After receiving some support, learners can accomplish a task independently, and they can learn to accomplish similar future tasks independently, too.

Instructional, teachable text is one that students will best understand and remember if someone supports their efforts. It also is the level at which students develop their strategies best. Teachable text is just challenging enough that a teacher is needed to help the majority of students understand and remember it. It is not so easy that most students can read and learn from it on their own. In brief, instructional-level, teachable texts are those in which the support of an instructor, or teacher, is appropriate.

Independent   When you read about something that is so familiar and well known to you that comprehension seems effortless and automatic, you probably are reading text with a challenge educators describe as *independent*. The write-up in the sports page of last night's basketball game, which your favorite team won, is probably independent for you. Even if you did not see the game, you know all the players, their positions, and the likely moves they would make. You could independently use the essential thinking processes described in Chapter 1, seeing scenes from the game in your mind's eye, connecting new information with what you already knew, organizing the ideas, and so on. The novel you read last summer probably was independent for you, too. You did not know exactly what would happen to the characters, but your experience with novels having similar characters and plots enabled you to follow the action and enjoy the book independently.

To be sure, readers match up with texts according to more than three isolated points. Frustration, instructional, and independent reader–text matches are best seen as points on a support continuum, such as the following:

Frustration	Instructional	Independent
Maximum Support		Minimum Support

When readers are fully independent with materials, they require minimum support. When readers are on the frustration end of the continuum, they benefit from maximum support. Most of the time, however, readers are somewhere between these points.

Another way of considering reader-text matches and appropriate levels of support involves Vygotsky's (1978) zone of proximal development (ZPD). This zone designates what learners can accomplish only with assistance. For instance, many young students could comprehend Eve Bunting's *Fly Away Home* as long as someone assisted them by orienting them to the contents and explaining some key words. These same students could not comprehend Watson's *The Double Helix* no matter how much assistance they received because the concepts and words simply are too complex for them. *Fly Away Home* would be in the students' ZPD, and working there would afford students maximum learning opportunities. As you present units to your students, be sure to provide a range of reading materials so that some are within your students' instructional reading levels—their zones of proximal development—where the most effective instruction occurs.

DO IT TOGETHER Choose a four- or five-page section from a book used in a course in your major or area of expertise and interest. Read it once, close the book, and quickly write everything you remember from your reading. Have a friend who has a different major or area of expertise and interest do the same thing with a book section he or she selects.

Once you have separately read and recalled as much as possible from the books you chose, swap books, read the same sections the other read, close the book, and write everything you recall.

Compare the results. Did you recall more from the book you chose than from the one your friend chose? Can you see from the amount recalled that your chosen book was probably easy for you and your friend's book was probably teachable text for you?

Study Guides

When readers encounter instructional-level passages, they require more support than what is needed with independent-level passages. They do best with guidance during the reading act. A common support along these lines is a study guide. Study guides consist of questions and statements that direct students' reading. Study guides have been used for years and, while well intentioned, can easily become monotonous busywork that many students do not find helpful. On the other hand, study guides can help teachers clarify reading when the materials that students read are teachable. We examine study guides early in this chapter because they are so widely used in content area classrooms.

The most useful and appealing study guides we have come across are the point-of-view reading guide and the interactive reading guide (Wood, Lapp, & Flood, 1992). The point-of-view reading guide (Figure 5.1) engages the reader by making that reader and his or her reactions the central focus of the questions. The guide

Roman Empire

1. You are Julius Caesar preparing to march your troops across the Rubicon. Record your thoughts and feelings about this bold action.
2. As a plebeian, explain to a group of patricians why you wish to form the Concilium Plebis and elect tribunes.
3. As a farmer who lived before and during the beginning of the Pax Romana, tell how it affected your life.
4. As a gladiator talking with your peers, tell why you are appearing in the Colosseum.
5. As Marcus Aurelius, portray your concerns about the decline of the Roman Empire to your son, Commodus.

Figure 5.1 Point-of-View Guide

invites students to become one of the participants in what is being described and asks for readers' thoughts about and reactions to the events. Notice the use of the words *you* and *your*. No doubt, you can see that many of the questions on a point-of-view study guide require students to evaluate.

The distinctive feature of the interactive reading guide (Figure 5.2) is the interaction it ensures among students. Activities are to be done by individuals, pairs, small groups, and the whole class. As you look through the guide, notice that students have clear purposes for reading and that the actual reading is often done alone or with partners. Small groups often provide the during-reading task completion and feedback. The whole class gets together at certain points to brainstorm and discuss what is being learned.

While giving students a lot of questions to answer individually in writing while they read is ineffective with students who really need extensive support, high-quality study guides of the two types discussed can help students comprehend moderately challenging texts better.

Types of Rocks

Task: Acting as a geologist, produce a brief picture book appropriate for primary-grade children that explains the three main kinds of rocks.

1. As a class, brainstorm what we know about the three main kinds of rocks:

   Igneous   Sedimentary   Metamorphic

2. Read the section in your text on igneous rocks (pages 204–205), then work with your partner to revise what was brainstormed about this topic.
3. Read the section in your text on sedimentary rocks (pages 205–207), then work again with your partner to revise what was brainstormed about this topic.
4. Read the section in your text on metamorphic rocks (pages 207–208), working one last time with your partner to revise what was brainstormed.
5. As a class, generate what we now know about the three main kinds of rocks:

   Igneous   Sedimentary   Metamorphic

6. In groups of three, each person select one of the three types of rock to explain. Each person then talk through what you plan to produce for your section of the picture book.
7. Each person produce a section of a picture book explaining one kind of rock.
8. Combine the three explanations into one finished product appropriate for donating to a primary-grade class.

Figure 5.2   Interactive Reading Guide

LISTEN, LOOK, AND LEARN Interview two teachers who use study guides and two students who have used study guides. If possible, look at the study guides and compare them with the two samples here. How do the teachers feel about the study guides? Is this different from how the students feel? What kinds of activities are included in the study guides? Do the questions require a variety of thinking processes? Do the study guides provide some activities that can be done with a partner or small group? Summarize what you learned, including the benefits and pitfalls of using study guides. Then apply this to your own teaching: What will be the place of study guides in your instruction? What kinds of study guides will you use?

Guide Readers Through Challenging Passages

Imagine now that it is the first week of school. You have a list of state reading standards. You have met your students and have a general idea of their varied abilities. You also have one or more books and other resources that provide you with some teachable text for most of your students. You have a unit plan, but you now are thinking about specific lessons. You are looking through the available reading, listening, and viewing materials and have several critical decisions to make about planning comprehension guidance and implementing it.

Planning Comprehension Guidance

Choosing What Material to Use Time is a teacher's most precious commodity. Using your time well is one of the keys to successful teaching. Books, curriculum guides, and other resources are filled with information, some of which is critical to understanding in your subject area, some of which your students already know, and some of which is trivial, highly technical, or boring. Good teachers are more interested in "uncovering the mysteries and joys of their subject" than in "covering the text." Good teachers know that you cannot teach it all and that if you try, many students will retain very little.

As we discussed in Chapter 4, one of the advantages of having a variety of materials is that the best treatment of a subject for your students can be chosen from several possibilities. Alternative sources of content information can often add clarity and depth to lackluster or even erroneous textbook sections.

As you look through your available resources, rate the various sections, chapters, parts, and so forth, on a three-star scale. The selections to which you give one star are parts or resources that may not be used at all or be used by individual students as they pursue their own interests. Selections that you decide are "interesting, important, but not critical" should be given two stars, and you should have students work with these selections individually or in small groups as time and student needs permit. Those resources and selections that you determine to contain critical content in instructional, teachable text should be given three stars. Whatever class time you can devote to helping your students learn as they read should be devoted to guiding readers through these three-star selections.

Determining What Everyone Is to Learn   Once you have determined which part of your books and other resources get the three-star rating and deserve attention, you are ready to decide what critical concepts you want students to learn from these selections. Try to read or view various selections from the naive learner's standpoint. Imagine yourself once again as a novice in your subject area.

Because you are an expert in this topic, it may all seem simple and important, but some concepts, generalizations, and ideas are surely more critical than others. Many teachers find it helpful to read the selection first and then (with the book closed) list the most important ideas and information that are aligned with your unit's standards-based outcomes, essential questions, and culminating activities. Listing what is critical does not limit students to learning or thinking about only these critical ideas, but it does mean that your students' attention will be focused on the critical concepts, thus greatly increasing the chances that most students will learn them. You now have the beginnings of objectives for your lesson.

Comprehension lesson planning involves many decisions.

Deciding How to Engage Students with Reading   Once you know what objectives you want students to accomplish from their reading, you must think about why they would want to accomplish them. The most common problems cited by content area teachers are the inability of students to read well and the "who cares?" attitude many students bring to reading. You can take care of the first problem by not asking students to read text that is clearly too challenging and by providing guidance so they can focus their efforts on a doable task rather than the frustrating one of "reading to remember everything and to be able to answer any question the teacher might think to ask you." You also must consider what to do about the second problem.

Many factors affect engagement (Guthrie & Wigfield, 2000). Students must feel that they can successfully do what is being asked of them or they won't even try. Many students have experienced failure with reading to learn so they identify themselves as nonreaders. When reading is assigned with little support, students do not know what they are "supposed to get out of it," so they just read and hope they will know whatever it is the teacher asks or they give up because their past experience tells them they won't know it. Guidance in which you provide maximum support will convince students that they can successfully read in your subject area and, over time, change their expectation of failure.

The interest factor, however, must still be considered. How do you engage students' interest?

- A social studies teacher might create an analogy between parliamentary and congressional forms of government when the class is studying England, Canada, or Israel. A science teacher might create an analogy between airplane and bird wings when the class is studying birds. An algebra teacher might compare solving an equation with two or more unknowns to how Sherlock Holmes solves mysteries.
- A math teacher might relate a personal anecdote about his or her experience learning how to solve quadratic equations in high school during that unit of Algebra I. While teaching about famous painters, an art teacher might relate a personal anecdote about his or her first visit to an art museum as a child.
- A health teacher might arouse readers' curiosity by explaining that the "no cholesterol" printed on packages of cookies or potato chips will not protect them from increasing their cholesterol level as a result of eating those foods. A French teacher might arouse readers' curiosity by stating that they will be reading a conversation in French between an advocate and an opponent of nuclear power plants.

Designing a Group Task   Once you know what students are to learn and how you will engage them with reading, you decide on a group task that students will complete during and after reading. This task must meet two criteria: Completing the task must result in the students learning what is important; and the task must be clear to the students before they read.

Imagine, for example, that your objectives are that students should be able to list the nine planets, know their relative positions and sizes, and explain their orbits. How would you communicate this clearly? What joint task could the class complete so that everyone learns the important information?

There are many possibilities for this. The most traditional is to make up questions. For our example, these are some logical questions:

What are the nine planets?
Which planet is the largest?
Which planet is about the same size as Earth?
Which planet is closest to the sun?

Of course, there would have to be at least twenty questions to cover all the important information. What else could you do to communicate your objectives clearly? Imagine that you drew the chart in Figure 5.3 on the whiteboard. Notice that you partially fill in the chart for students, talking as you write about what is needed in each column: "Earth is the sixth-largest planet. Its mean distance from the sun is 92,960,000 miles. The year is the number of days it takes a planet to orbit the sun, and the Earth year is 365 days." Now, you point to the second row and have students explain what they will try to figure out about Mars to put in each column. For the third row, you help them to notice that, since you put a "1" in the size column, this has to be the biggest planet. The fourth row must be completed for the planet that is 3,660,000,000 miles from the sun. The planet that takes 60,188 Earth days to orbit the sun goes in the fifth row. The last four rows are filled in with the remaining four planets.

This partially filled in chart is one example of a group task that makes the objectives clear and gets at the important information. Depending on what you want students to learn, there is an endless variety of group tasks that will clearly communicate a purpose for reading. You will see many more examples of group tasks in the section about the different forms content comprehension lessons can take.

Planet Name	Size (1 = biggest)	Distance from Sun (miles)	Earth Days in Year
Earth	6	92,960,000	365
Mars			
	1		
		3,660,000,000	
			60,188

Figure 5.3 Planets in Our Solar System

Building Background Knowledge Students vary in the background knowledge they are able to call up about a particular topic. Students who live in Florida or California may know about oceans and oranges; midwestern students may be more familiar with wheat and blizzards. The author of a textbook may have assumed that students can call up certain information that you know your students lack. For instance, a passage on volcanoes may assume that students are aware of the "bubbling" action of heated liquids. Thus, the passage may deal primarily with a volcano's effect on the earth's crust, while failing to explain what forces magma up through it. If students are confused about the initial thrust of the magma, they may not be able to follow the rest of the description of volcanic action. We suspect that you had difficulty understanding the paragraph on statistics at the beginning of this chapter because of your own limited background in fractional factorial designs. If certain information seems prerequisite to students learning from a text, then you should present it before having the students read or listen to the text.

Implementing Comprehension Guidance

Comprehension guidance has discernible beginnings, middles, and endings. While it is impossible to set firm guidelines about how much time to spend in each phase, many teachers find that dividing the time available roughly into thirds is a reasonable guideline. With this distribution of time, the before-, during-, and after-reading phases are seen as more or less equally important in determining what students will learn from their scaffolded reading. Younger and less-able readers usually do the during-reading phase in class and require more time for all three phases; older and more able readers usually do the during-reading phase outside of class and require less time for all three phases.

Before Reading In the preceding example about the planets, the teacher was building background knowledge while presenting the chart. The background concepts included these:

> There are nine planets.
> They are all different sizes.
> They are various distances away from the sun.
> They all orbit the sun, and it takes different numbers of Earth days for them to orbit. This orbit is called a year.

Partially completing the chart for students makes the task clear, so their success-driven motivation should be high. Some interest is also piqued by the students' guesses before they read.

Because most students have some prior knowledge and considerable interest in the solar system, the talk engaged in as the teacher sets up the partially completed chart might be sufficient for developing both background knowledge and motivation.

How much background building and motivation are required? Generally, the less familiar a topic is to students, the more time and effort you have to expend to build background and motivation.

Teachers support students' comprehension.

Perhaps the most important part of the introductory phase of a content comprehension lesson is making clear the students' purpose for reading. What is clear to you as the teacher is often a mystery to your students. Has an English teacher ever told you to read so that you can discuss how the setting of a story or novel affects the plot development? In order to accomplish this purpose you must understand clearly what setting and plot entail, then clearly perceive the setting, follow the plot, and finally get to the task of thinking about how setting and plot interact. This complex task is further complicated by the jargon—setting and plot. Many students are confused by such terminology as *setting, plot, main idea,* and *summary.* When alerting students to the purposes for which you would like them to read, try to avoid unnecessary jargon or make the jargon clear by including examples.

In a situation in which the interaction between setting and plot was important, students would be more apt to understand what you wanted them to read for if you drew on the board a diagram such as Figure 5.4.

After displaying the diagram, you could explain to students that the setting changes three times during the story and that certain things happen in the differ-

	Setting (Time and Place)	Plot (What Happened)
Beginning of story		
Middle of story		
End of story		

How did the setting at different points in the story affect what happened?

Figure 5.4 Plot/Setting Diagram

ent settings. Students should read so they can fill in the three settings and the major events that happened in each setting. They should also think about how the different times and places affected what did and did not happen.

In this example, you have clarified the purpose by making a little chart on the board and explained what is meant by the jargon *setting* and *plot*. You have also written the chart and the question on the board so that as students read, they can look up and think about what they can contribute to the group task of filling in the chart and discussing the question. When students have the necessary motivation and prior knowledge and know their purpose for reading, they are ready to move into the next phase.

During Reading Now as the students go to work and read to fulfill their purposes, provide guidance. Often students read silently, but the reading can take other forms. Students can be paired and read the passage together, with each one taking a page or a paragraph. They might highlight important ideas by recording notes or pasting sticky notes at appropriate spots in a passage. As they read, you may notice their eyes going up to the board as they come upon some piece of information they want to include. You may need to interrupt the reading after a few minutes and point to the purpose on the board to remind students of it.

After Reading If you have set a clear purpose, clarifying the objectives and task, and have guided students during their reading, what happens after comprehending is done readily: students complete the task, then review it.

Talk about what they did and how they did it. For the setting-plot purpose discussed above, you might say something like this:

> Today you charted the time and place and the major events. You could then see the relationship between the setting and the plot. Often in books and movies, the setting affects the plot as the charts show. If we think about the time and place in which things happen, we can see how this occurs.

In the planet example, your purpose is for students to learn some basic facts about the planets. Once you establish that the planet chart the group completed is as accurate and complete as possible, you might point out how much more they knew and how efficiently they had recorded it on the chart. If this information is what you want everyone to learn, you might have them copy the chart into a science notebook so that they have clear, concise notes to study.

Closing Words about Guiding Comprehension

Guiding readers through challenging—but not defeating—text as presented here goes far in developing comprehension of future passages as well as the particular one at hand. This practice promotes knowledge of the world, which is crucial background for making sense of print (Hirsch, 2003; National Reading Panel, 2000). As students develop their understandings of concepts such as the solar system and plot-setting relationships, they bring this new knowledge to future readings. They learn about the world incrementally, across multiple exposures, constantly connecting new ideas and information with what they already know.

The after-reading, culminating phase is critical to both the development of students' content knowledge and their reading strategies. As the students complete the task, they are guided to revisit parts of the texts to resolve disagreements or fill in gaps, so they learn not only how to self-monitor their comprehension but also how to use some fix-up strategies when comprehension fails.

Countless activities are possible when implementing the three phases of comprehension guidance. Indeed, the KWL practice (Carr & Ogle, 1987; Ogle, 1986), consisting of *Know-Want-Learn* phases as presented in Chapter 3, is a widespread version of comprehension guidance. Additionally, you might guide learners' actions during each phase as follows:

Before Reading
- asking and answering questions
- brainstorming
- examining pictures and graphic aids
- graphically organizing related information
- listening to selected portions being read aloud
- observing media presentations
- predicting
- previewing key vocabulary
- previewing the passage
- receiving directions and recommendations
- writing

During Reading
- answering interspersed questions
- completing a study guide
- posting sticky notes on the passage
- reading along with a passage recording or another individual reading
- recording notes while reading
- silently reading individually

- taking turns reading and talking about the passage with a partner, group, or class

After Reading
- applying contents to a related situation
- asking and answering questions
- completing assessments
- discussing with a partner, small group, or class
- following directions
- graphically organizing information
- paraphrasing or summarizing the passage
- producing concrete displays
- producing dramatic responses
- producing visual, artistic responses
- writing

Teach Reading Comprehension Strategies

Reading comprehension strategies are procedures that active readers use to enhance their understandings of text (Dole, 2002). Active readers do more than internally listen to themselves pronounce words; they direct their attention to various aspects of print and build meaning for themselves. In one of the first empirical investigations of reading comprehension, Thorndike (1917) put it this way:

> Reading is a very elaborate procedure, involving the weighing of many elements in a sentence, their organization in the proper relations one to another, the selection of certain of their connotations and the rejection of others, and the cooperation of many forces to determine final response. (p. 323)

Teaching students comprehension strategies fosters their independence for the present as well as for the future; it promotes lifelong learning. Some reading comprehension strategies that have been shown to reliably enhance understandings of text include graphically organizing ideas and information, predicting what comes next in a passage, summarizing passages, forming images, generating and answering questions, and monitoring comprehension (National Reading Panel, 2000). The following describes these strategies.

Graphic Organizing

Both the planet chart and the setting/plot chart in the preceding section are graphic organizers. *Graphic organizers* are visual diagrams that depict the relationships among concepts. There are many kinds, and you can create your own variations. Figures 5.5 to 5.10 contained in Chapter 5 Appendix, *Graphic Organizers*, show popular graphic organizers in various stages of completion by students.

On the semantic feature matrix (Figure 5.5), students indicate with a plus or minus which qualities are possessed by various Americans depicted in poetry. On the Venn diagram (Figure 5.6), students compare and contrast how animals and humans communicate. These graphic organizers are helpful in comparing and contrasting members of a particular group.

The time line (Figure 5.7) is an excellent device to use when sequence is important. Here, students fill in the important event that occurred on each date. A variation is to give students a time line of events and have them fill in the dates. If you want more details, draw two lines under each event line and have students fill in two details about each event.

Both the whale web (Figure 5.8) and the Yukon outline (Figure 5.9) help students organize information when they are to learn a variety of information about one big topic. Most students find it easier to web ideas than to outline them, because when they outline, they often get lost in the trivia of upper- and lowercase letters and indentation. The partially completed outline allows students to concentrate on the information and the relationships because the skeleton and a few pieces of information are included.

Notice in the cause-and-effect chain (Figure 5.10) that some causes have multiple effects, some effects have multiple causes, and an effect often becomes a cause of another effect. These diagrams help students sort through the complex relationships that comprise much of the information they need to understand in the real world.

These figures are a sampling of graphic organizers to spur your thinking about how to help students see important relationships by considering how you would depict those relationships graphically. When you determine that students need to learn compare-contrast relationships, time/order relationships, topic/subtopic relationships, or causal relationships, a graphic organizer is often your most efficient strategy.

It is obvious that teaching practices in which students complete a graphic organizer involve organizing, and teaching practices that use prediction involve predicting. What may not be so obvious is that higher-order thinking processes—generalizing, evaluating, imaging, and applying—are often included.

- After completing the Venn diagram on human and animal communication in Figure 5.6, the teacher may lead the students to conclude that "there are many similarities between humans and animals," a generalization based on the data students have put into the graphic organizer.
- After students complete the World War II time line (Figure 5.7), teachers may lead them to talk about the events and imagine what it would have been like fighting those battles on either side. This discussion would involve the students in forming images of the events they had just organized.
- Students who learned about whales and organized the information into a web (Figure 5.8) might take a stand on whether whales should be hunted. This discussion would involve the thinking process of evaluating.
- Applying what you have learned to your current and future life can also

Students construct time lines in order to display information they have gathered.

occur. After learning about the Yukon or Washington, D.C., students could be asked if they would like to live there.

TRY IT OUT   Select a five- to ten-page section of text. Consider the important facts and relationships. Construct a graphic organizer. Include enough of the pieces so that students would clearly understand what information goes where.

Predicting

We are predicting whether a particular book will interest us when we peruse the title, author name(s), and cover illustration. We are predicting when we thumb through a magazine, looking at the pictures before we start to read. We are predicting when we read a heading such as "Are We Once Again Headed into Recession?" and assume that the author will give us reasons to believe we are or are not. Across the years of reading instruction, various ways of teaching students how to make predictions have been devised. The introductory grabbers presented for units in Chapter 3 can work well for prediction. We will discuss two practices with some unique practical features for teaching prediction: an anticipation guide and DRTA.

Anticipation Guide   An *anticipation guide* is a list of statements or key words, some of which are true and some of which are false. The students are presented with the statements or key words, and they predict which are true and which are false. They then read to check their predictions. Below is an anticipation guide used before students read about the life of Babe Ruth. What are your predictions?

Babe Ruth
1. Orphan
2. Good kid
3. Only child
4. Irish
5. German
6. Over six feet tall
7. Right-handed
8. Pitcher
9. Catcher
10. New York Yankee
11. Still living

Do you have some predictions about which you are quite sure and others for which you do not have a clue? Do you want to know the answers? Of course you do, and you therefore see the power of prediction as a motivating device. Students who have made some predictions want to read to "see if they were right." Students who predict before reading are nearly always motivated to read and be clear about their purposes for reading.

DRTA   A Directed Reading Thinking Activity—DRTA (Stauffer, 1969)—is a way of teaching students to predict what they will learn. In a DRTA, the teacher usually leads the students to make predictions, read portions of the text, stop and make more predictions, read some more, and so on until the text is finished. Predictions are written on the board, checked when confirmed, and erased when not confirmed. How many times the students stop and make predictions depends on the length of what they are reading and their maturity. Here is an imaginary script for a modified DRTA on a science section about sound:

Teacher: Today we are going to begin learning about sound. What do you think we might learn?

The teacher waits for students to respond, then writes these responses on the board:

What sound is.
How you hear.

What different kinds of sounds there are.
Where sounds come from.

Teacher: Let's open our books now and see if we can predict anything else we might learn just by looking at the visuals.

The teacher directs students' attention to several pictures, a chart, and a diagram. Students add predictions, which the teacher writes on the board:

Sound travels in waves.
You make sounds with guitars.
Your ears let you hear sounds.
Sounds are measured in decibels.
Bats can hear sounds.

The teacher reads all the predictions aloud and ask students to read the first three pages to see which predictions are supported by the text. Students do so. They read a part of the text to prove each prediction, then the teacher puts a checkmark next to that prediction. The teacher asks if there are more predictions students would like to add before finishing the sections. After students make suggestions, the teacher writes this:

Soft sounds have decibels.
Loud sounds have really big decibels.
Pitch is how high or low the sound is.

Students finish reading the section on sound, then tell which predictions should be checked because they are supported and which should be erased because they either are not supported or not mentioned.

This section has presented two practices in which students make predictions about what they will read. Anticipation guides and DRTAs differ in how much input the teacher and students have into the predictions. Both, however, motivate students to think about what they know and might find out and then to read with clear purposes.

Summarizing

Summarizing is producing a shortened version of what one reads or hears. Readers form generalizations about the text message, integrating information and stating its main ideas in a few words. *GIST* is one productive practice that promotes students' summarizing.

In *GIST*, the group task is to write a summary in twenty words or less. The teacher explains that the *gist* of something is the main idea and that sometimes we do not need to remember all the details but read just to get the gist of the material. The teacher draws twenty word-size blanks on the chalkboard or on a transparency and explains to the students that, after reading, they will try to write a sentence or two of no more than twenty words that captures the gist of what they have read.

The students read a short section—no more than three paragraphs—then work with the teacher to record the gist of what they have read. Students take turns telling the teacher part of what to write. In no case will the teacher write a twenty-first word. Students must revise what they want the teacher to write so that it will fit into the twenty blanks. The discussion challenges students to distill what is really important. This is an example of a GIST statement a class might produce:

Tropical	rain	forests	are	lush
forests	near	the	equator	that
are	hot	and	get	a
lot	of	rain.		

Next, the teacher tells them to read the following section and says that they must now incorporate the information from both the first section and the second in just twenty words. Students groan but usually rise to the challenge of trying to compact twice the amount of information into the same limited set of words. This is an example of the revised GIST statement, including information from both sections:

Tropical	rain	forests	are	hot,
rainy,	and	important	because	of
the	many	species	of	plants
and	animals	that	live	there.

It is possible that the teacher might then have the students read a third short section and attempt to incorporate its information into the GIST statement. (No more than three sections should be used with this challenging task.) This is an example:

Tropical	rain	forests	lower	the
carbon	dioxide	in	the	air
and	provide	new	medicines	and
products.	They	must	be	protected.

During this process, students learn how to ignore the details and only get down to the core of what they are reading. Most students will be able to make a contribution at some point during the GIST process.

Imaging

Imaging is using the senses to learn. It involves imagining something, seeing it, and putting yourself there. When we want students to image, we must move away from the two-dimensional world of the chalkboard into the real world. Here are some suitable tasks:

- Draw, paint, or sculpt a pioneer.
- Create a diorama of a scene from pioneer days.

- Pick or create a piece of music that evokes Switzerland.
- Create a skit or play in which you act out a confrontation between the president and Congress.
- Imagine that two pioneers were transported to the twentieth century. Decide what kind of food each would most prefer. What kind of car would each drive? Which baseball team would each root for?

Asking and Answering Questions

Learners who ask and answer their own questions about what they are reading have a powerful comprehension strategy. Learners best acquire and develop this strategy when they begin with question signal words and stems such as the following (Kiewra, 2002).

Question Signal Words
- Who _____?
- What _____?
- When _____?
- Where _____?
- How _____?
- Why _____?

Question Stems
- What have I learned about _____? What should I remember about _____?
- What does _____ mean?
- What are the components of _____?
- How are _____ and _____ alike? How are _____ and _____ different?
- What are the strengths of _____? What are the limitations of _____?
- What caused _____ to happen?
- How does _____ affect _____?
- How does _____ relate to what I already know? How does _____ relate to _____ in the passage?
- What does _____ look (and sound) like?
- What is the significance of _____?

Monitoring Understanding Monitoring understanding means that readers determine how their comprehension is progressing. They assess the status of their reading, and they repair breakdowns as needed. Writing brief responses to questions that focus on monitoring understanding is an especially powerful strategy (Bangert-Down, Hurley, & Wilkinson, 2004). Providing students with prompts such as the following that question the author (Beck, McKeown, Hamilton, & Kucan, 1997) and point to areas needing clarification (Palincsar, 2002) are especially productive:

- How did the author put the ideas in order? How can I duplicate this arrangement of ideas on my own?
- What did the author do to help me understand the passage? How can I use this help?
- What are the key vocabulary words? How can I understand and remember them?
- What did the author not explain clearly? What concepts, words, or phrases are unclear? What can I do to improve my understanding?

Closing Words about Teaching Comprehension Strategies

A classroom program of comprehension strategy instruction calls for several actions on your part. First, select the strategies you plan to teach, then decide when to introduce them. In this current era of standards-based education, such decisions frequently will have been made for you, so mark your plan book accordingly. If no school-level decisions have been made, you might begin with one or two comprehension strategies at the beginning of the year that you intend students to use all year long, then you might introduce others during the units that naturally call for them.

Strategy Instruction   Once you decide when to introduce comprehension strategies, expect positive effects by presenting them directly and systematically (Alvermann, Fitzgerald, & Simpson, in press; Dole, 2002). First, model and explain the strategy for students. If you are introducing students to forming images, for instance, you might read aloud a brief portion of text accessible to everyone, then stop and think-aloud the images you are forming and the mental moves you are making to form them. You would continue with this start-and-stop process through a passage, continually sharing your images and explicitly explaining what you are thinking. You might explain the internal movie, the series of still scenes, or the senses of touch and smell you are constructing. You could record on a chart prompts such as, "First I see . . . ," "Then I see . . ." to publicize your mental processing. Such thinking aloud and recording reveals proficient readers' mental processes that otherwise remain concealed (Lloyd, 2004). Once you have modeled and explained the strategy and students are catching on, you can begin fading.

Let's say that you have introduced and used many webs in class. Your students have gotten good at reading to find information for the various spokes of the web. You should realize that partially completed webs will not mysteriously appear when students need them; if students leave your classroom forever dependent on you to start the web, they will not be able to use this valuable strategy independently. Consequently, it is now time to fade your scaffolding. In fact, the next time you think a web will make a good group task, have the students create it.

Have students read and write details on the spokes of their own webs. After their reading, put students in groups of four or five to compare webs. Encourage them to accept diverse webs but also to add to their own webs information that the group sharing convinces them they need.

When you have your students independently webbing, your task is nearly complete. One more piece of teacher fading is needed. Your students will not always have you there to decide how to organize the text information graphically, so let them decide. Have them preview the text and decide how best to organize the information. Let different students or groups organize the data as they think best, then share their work with the class. When students can preview something they are about to read, decide what kind of graphic organizer would most efficiently and clearly depict the important relationships, and create the graphic organizer, they are becoming independent learners.

This same kind of fading can be applied to the other comprehension strategies. Students who have been engaged in DRTAs can learn that, before they read, they call up what they already know and try to predict what questions the text might answer or what they might learn. They can preview the text and use the headings and visuals to make these predictions. After reading, they should ask, "What do I know now that I didn't know before I read?" and "Have I learned what I wanted to learn?" Students who have been involved in creating GIST statements and summary paragraphs learn to do this for themselves.

Fading is not difficult to do, but it is sometimes difficult to remember to do. Just when your lessons are going well and your students are succeeding with your support, you must remember that some day they will have to do these tasks on their own.

Strategy Self-Assessment

During fading, the emphasis is on teachers gradually providing less scaffolding while holding students to the same standards with respect to their comprehension. However, if students are to become truly independent comprehenders, they must also learn to assess their own comprehension beyond the *Monitoring Understanding* questions.

The first kind of self-assessment to help your students with comprehension is integrated with your fading process. This kind of self-assessment mirrors the thinking you do as a teacher when you attempt to determine the level of comprehension scaffolding a class needs to comprehend a particular piece of material. Ask your students to preview the material and help you decide which level of scaffolding to provide with that material. The class should gradually improve in their ability to predict how much help they need from you.

The second kind of self-assessment occurs within the task. After students are very familiar with the kinds of response activities you use to follow up their independent comprehension of material, they can be asked to help you construct the follow-up they will engage in for something they have just read. As they work with you to create these culmination activities, many students improve in their ability to assess what is important for them to understand and remember from the material.

The third kind of self-assessment involves scoring guides as described in Chapter 3. Students rate their performance while completing literacy tasks and afterward they set aside time to monitor what they have accomplished and what they might do to improve. They develop self-assessment as both a habit and an ability when regularly completing and talking about scoring guides for their own work.

Promote Collaborative Comprehension Practices

Collaborative comprehension practices bring people together to improve their understandings of texts. Chapter 4 of this text describes collaboration mainly as talk about texts through discussion webs, respectful discussions, seminars, and deliberations. It focuses on promoting free yet rigorous exchanges among students so they explore passages from multiple perspectives and generate rich understandings of them. Here, we focus on collaboration as a tool for developing comprehension strategies.

Discussion is essential during the fading process (Keene & Zimmerman, 1997). Talking with others about reading-related graphic organizers, predictions, images, and so on, goes far in developing independence (Block & Pressley, 2003; Vaughn, Klingner, & Bryant, 2001). Discussion exposes learners to diverse options. It provides opportunities to reflect on one's effectiveness. It refines one's thinking about possible strategies with text.

As you release responsibility for reading and learning to your students, structure opportunities for them to talk about their strategies. Such talk should be in the form of a dialogue, with speakers responding to what each other said. It should make public what readers and learners do internally.

After presenting a strategy like webbing or forming images, have students divide into small groups or pairs and discuss how they implemented the strategy. Of course, teach the social roles of interacting in groups (e.g., listen attentively, contribute often) so the interactions are productive.

Learners require common shared approaches to academic work in order to collaborate effectively (Palincsar & Herrenkohl, 2002). To develop commonalities, record and post the mental processes involved in comprehension strategies. Displaying such processes publicizes what to do and serves as a reminder to do so. Learners also require opportunities to lead the conversations about reading strategies. Keeping track of group roles and distributing them evenly accomplishes this. Further, group members share approaches best after teachers have modeled the expectations several times and had groups demonstrate them before the class. Finally, learners need to construct a common culture of support, one where they are willing to expose their confusions and misunderstandings about comprehension strategies. They need to build a community of learners. Adhering to a rubric such as the following goes far in specifying what collaboration requires and designating areas for improvement.

Collaboration Rubric

Productivity

We stayed on task and accomplished much. <u>Comments:</u>	4	3	2	1	We often got off task, accomplishing little.

Participation

Everyone acted like an insider, contributing ideas. <u>Comments:</u>	4	3	2	1	Some acted like outsiders, contributing little.

Communication

We listened attentively and responded to ideas in a give-and-take conversation. <u>Comments:</u>	4	3	2	1	We often ignored others' ideas and had a one-sided conversation.

Climate

We disagreed agreeably; the atmosphere was friendly and relaxed. <u>Comments:</u>	4	3	2	1	We often disagreed disagreeably; the atmosphere was tense and quarrelsome.

Roles

Each member played preferred (or assigned) roles to help the group move along. <u>Comments:</u>	4	3	2	1	Only a few played preferred (or assigned) roles to help the group move along.

Specific Content Area Applications

Comprehension in English/Language Arts Classrooms

Attention to reading comprehension in English and language arts generally centers about novels, short stories, plays, and poetry. English teachers have countless options for promoting students' understanding of these literary forms. Given this situation, the following focuses on one specific piece of children's literature. What you gain from examining this example in depth can be used to guide decisions about other materials and other situations.

Shabanu, Daughter of the Wind is a novel about a 12-year-old nomadic Islamic girl in Pakistan. This 240-page narrative tends to hold the interest of middle-school students. There are numerous ways to scaffold understanding of it (Benedicty, 1995).

Introducing the Novel/Before Reading   A good way to begin supporting students would be to enrich their understandings of the book's setting, desert life in Pakistan. You could accomplish this by displaying photographs and slides of rural Middle Eastern life and showing videos. You might elicit students' images and the information they have about this topic. If you are fortunate, you might have someone from your class or community share firsthand experiences they had in this region of the world. List housing, transportation, and clothing features mentioned in the book, and portray them as vividly as possible. Students might benefit from imagining themselves living in tents, riding camels, and wearing turbans. You could burn incense and play Middle Eastern music, having students close their eyes and visualize life in this setting.

While helping students experience the setting of a novel or short story before reading serves to develop background knowledge, it often arouses curiosity, too. After viewing scenes from a Middle Eastern desert, students might begin to wonder what life there would be like. You might pique their interest by asking what differences they would expect if they moved to rural living in Pakistan. By focusing on one feature—transportation, for instance—you could have students imagine all the ways life with camels would differ from life with cars.

Supporting readers' comprehension also can be accomplished by focusing attention on a central question. There are many possibilities for *Shabanu*; your choices depend on how this novel fits the unit you are presenting and the school curriculum guide you are following. One productive central question might be "What is the same and what is different about my life and Shabanu's?" This question is promising because the novel touches on universal coming-of-age themes such as clashing with parental expectations and meeting a first love. It portrays events common to all cultures, such as wedding rituals and religious worship, yet it offers insights into distinctive customs such as arranged marriages and informal schooling. Other questions might be "How does Shabanu change during the course of the novel?" "What is different about the qualities and concerns of the men and women in this novel?" and "How do the characters' attitudes toward obedience affect their actions in this novel?" Of course, students might produce their own central question(s) once they get into the novel, or they might choose from several offerings.

Reading aloud the first few chapters is a good way to support students' initial efforts with the novel. If you intend to read orally to the class, practice your presentation so you can effectively convey the information and tone of the story while enjoying it with your class. Demonstrate your interest in *Shabanu* by commenting on what you find fascinating and what you hope to learn in the future. To help students with self-monitoring, focus their attention on a central question: "So far, what similarities and differences have you found between your lives and Shabanu's?"

Guiding the Reading   Once students are under way with *Shabanu*, provide enough guidance to support their comprehension while you fade in and out of center stage. Many teachers use response journals for this purpose. Having students maintain a folder, perhaps a spiral-bound notebook or a stapled collection of papers, helps in recording thoughts about what they are reading. Be sure to produce a schedule so everyone knows when certain chapters—and the whole book—are to be completed. Also include a set of prompts to accompany the central question(s) and elicit thinking about what has been read. The prompts can be generic (e.g., "What will I remember about this section?") or content specific (e.g., "Should Shabanu marry her cousin?"). They can address essential thinking processes such as organization (e.g., "Summarize the events of this chapter"), prediction (e.g., "What do you think will happen in the next chapter?"), and generalization (e.g., "What have you learned about Muslim life?").

Along with prompts that focus attention on the contents of the novel, you can list prompts that encourage student responsibility, reflection, and self-assessment. Students might respond to questions such as "What part of this chapter was the most difficult to understand?" and "What did I do when I encountered the difficult parts of this chapter?" Questions such as these enhance students' thinking about and control of their reading processes.

Arranging a weekly schedule for moving through *Shabanu* allows you to structure your plans. You might establish outside-of-class expectations for students to read silently and record responses in their journals, realizing that time for these activities can be offered during class, too. Designate inside-of-class time for whole-class or small-group discussions and for conferring with individuals.

Setting aside time during the week for addressing key incidents in the novel is a good way to provide needed guidance. For instance, powerful events occur when Shabanu's father sells their prize camel and when her grandfather dies in a storm. Sharing these passages orally through a teacher or student read-aloud session or through readers' theater could be time well spent. When talking about these episodes, you can refer to the central question(s), and you can explain how you employed essential thinking processes such as image, connect, and evaluate while making sense of these parts of the novel.

Culminating the Novel/After Reading   Culminating students' experiences with *Shabanu* can be accomplished many ways. If a central question is followed throughout the novel, then students' answers to it are shared. Using ideas recorded in their journals, students express differences between their lives and Shabanu's through visuals such as illustrated and captioned time lines, collections of concrete objects, skits, or essays. These forms of expression can be combined. Writing about Shabanu as a multiday project or as a one-day in-class exam are options. Displaying individuals' reactions to *Shabanu* through a class book, bulletin board, or presentations to an audience also build on the activities conducted while reading the novel.

Comprehension in Second-Language Classrooms

Comprehension processes are quite similar when students read in their first and second languages because in both instances readers tap essential thinking processes, such as call up, connect, image, and organize. The main difference between comprehending passages written in one's primary and one's secondary language centers on the support that is required. Second-language learners require comprehensible input, exposure to language that they can and are motivated to make sense of.

Reading Materials   To ensure that reading materials provide comprehensible input—that they are challenging but not defeating—effective teachers provide a range of commercial and student-produced materials for students to read. They offer abridged, simplified versions of core reading materials so all students can access basic story lines or expository structures. They provide access to print written at various levels of difficulty so students can learn from and experience materials within their range of competence. For instance, they encourage students to read novels written for children, young adults, and adults, allowing students to select what they can handle.

Effective teachers also provide high-quality culturally relevant literature for students to read. They incorporate novels into their instructional units that center on settings and events their students recognize and characters with which their students identify. For instance, authors such as Rodolfo Anaya, Nicholasa Mohr, Gary Soto, and Gloria Velasquez have produced many young-adult novels with Hispanic characters. Providing access to such literature honors the cultural backgrounds of many Hispanic students while linking home and school endeavors. It goes far in helping Spanish-speaking adolescents gain proficiency and comfort in English.

Read-Aloud Sessions   Reading aloud to students who are somewhat proficient in their second language provides many opportunities to develop comprehension strategies. When reading aloud, take special care to select passages that are within students' capabilities. In fact, you might read vivid and interesting passages more than once so students are able to grasp them at different levels. As students listen, they should concentrate on understanding the passage's ideas and experiencing the characters' worlds. Teachers and students then might share what images they formed while listening, what connections they made between the passage and their lives, how they organized the information, and so on.

Response Sketches   Second-language students often benefit from responding to literature verbally and through sketches rather than through writing. After reading, have students sketch an illustration that represents their understanding of the passage. They might react to prompts such as "What did the passage mean to you?" "What is the author's message?" or "What do you see after reading the passage?" You might display some sketches you or your students drew for previously read texts to demonstrate the possibilities. (In our case, we rely on minimal stick figures and geometry as art forms!) After displaying a sketch to the class or small group, the illustrator remains silent and the audience interprets its message about the passage. The sketcher then explains what he or she meant the drawing to express. Following these sharings, you might explore the variety of alternative interpretations the sketches represent.

Fluency   Teachers also support second-language comprehension by enhancing readers' fluency or their ability to decode a passage's words automatically so they can attend to the passage's ideas. To promote fluency, teachers often have students first read silently and then orally. They occasionally have students prepare to read orally just as they would for an oral interpretation event. They encourage groups of students to read selected portions of passages chorally.

Having students read a passage repeatedly until fluency is achieved is a powerful teaching practice. Students might tape-record themselves, repeating a passage several times until they are satisfied with their performance. Teachers often provide audiotaped recordings of passages with which students repeatedly follow along while looking at the text. Students also carry books home so they can have daily access to repeated reading in their home environment. These fluency practices always are conducted with meaningful passages connected to units of study, and students always respond to the meanings of what they have read fluently.

Social Support   Another way effective teachers support second-language comprehension involves social support during classroom interactions. Effective teachers recognize cultural sources of students' behaviors and adjust their instruction accordingly. For instance, students' culturally patterned ways of taking turns and gaining the conversational floor during text-based discussions might differ from their teacher's. If students are used to interrupting others and the teacher is not, then the situation should be addressed. Get the issue out in the open and talk about it. The case could be that students view interruption as a way for group members to express community and solidarity and jointly produce a message, whereas teachers view an interruption as a takeover attempt by an outspoken individual. If this is the case, teachers might promote discussions that follow students' expectations, or they might promote students' self-monitoring so they can behave differently in different situations.

Effective teachers also accommodate the uncertainties and pressures second-language learners typically experience. Realizing how vulnerable language users can feel when practicing a non-native language, teachers promote risk-free, non-threatening learning climates. They make it clear to students that linguistic miscues are expected and are considered learning opportunities rather than mistakes. They allow second-language learners ample time to reply to questions, and they repeat and rephrase questions that appear unclear. They encourage students to initiate questions about what has been read. They elicit comments from all students in whole-class and small-group settings so that more than just a few vocal individuals participate.

Comprehension in Mathematics Classrooms

Because math teachers generally received no comprehension scaffolding when they were K–12 math students and did not observe other math teachers providing it when they were in teacher education, they often feel that it has no place in the mathematics classroom. Yet, math word problems are perennially difficult for most students. Math is among the most homework-intensive subjects; students need to be able to understand the explanations and directions in their math textbooks when they have trouble figuring out their homework problems. As in the example from a statistics book presented early in this chapter, one must not assume that students can comprehend math word problems or text explanations and directions simply because they can read them aloud, pronouncing most of the words correctly. Fortunately, the current standards for teaching mathematics recognize the failure of traditional mathematics instruction to address the literacy demands of mathematics. Here are some specific ways math teachers use the ideas in this chapter to help students learn how to comprehend the written language of mathematics.

Comprehending Word Problems   Students for whom word problems are highly challenging benefit from being taught short content comprehension lessons with a single word problem as the text. Before they read the problem, they are given the task they will complete after reading the problem or part of it. For example, when students have difficulty interpreting word problems, they can be given a set of solutions for that problem, all computed correctly, which they examine before looking at the problem. Only one of that set of solutions performs the correct operations in the correct order. The task is to circle the correct solution. The students then read the problem and circle the solution. The beauty of this lesson is that students cannot become distracted by whatever computation difficulties they have. They must focus entirely on figuring out how to go about solving the problem. Discussion during the group task is essential. Fading from whole-class to small-group to individual tasks with this particular task gradually helps students learn how to interpret word problems significantly better.

As another example, when students fail to read word problems slowly and carefully before trying to solve them, you can use GIST with them. In GIST, when the text is a word problem, the group task is to write a summary of the problem in twelve words or less. Draw twelve word-size blanks on the chalkboard or on a transparency and explain to the students that they will try to write a sentence of no more than twelve words that captures the gist of the word problem. The students read the first sentence in the problem and then work with you to record the gist of that sentence. Students take turns telling you part of what to write. In no case do you write a thirteenth word. Students must revise what they want you to write so that it will fit into the twelve blanks. Next, tell them to read the following sentence and say that they must now incorporate the information from both the first sentence and the second in just twelve words. Continue in the same way through all the sentences of the problem. During this process, students learn how to distill the essence of the word problem. At the end, the resulting GIST statement is solved and then compared with the solution to the full problem to see if the GIST statement is correct and complete.

Students who have some but not serious difficulty with word problems are often helped by having comprehension follow-up before they actually try to work the problem. For example, give them a copy of a word problem and ask them to read it. Then, have them mark through every word in the problem that will not actually be part of the computation they do to solve it. This follow-up is particularly helpful to students who are confused by extraneous numbers in a problem.

Comprehension of Text Explanations and Directions On occasion, students should be taught a content comprehension lesson in which the material to be read is the explanation in the math textbook of how to solve a certain kind of computational problem. A problem of the type being introduced that day, and different from any in the book, is written on the board. However, instead of working that problem while students watch and listen, students read the explanation in the textbook for how to solve that kind of problem and then take turns telling you how to solve the problem on the board. Over time, these content comprehension lessons can be faded from whole-class to small-group to individual tasks.

Students who cannot use the written explanations in their math textbooks to help them when they have trouble doing their homework are totally dependent on the math abilities of their parents. When the parents are unable to help, students experience frustration and failure.

Comprehension in Science Classrooms

Science is a subject in which there is always a great deal of new information to be learned. Students (and teachers!) are often overwhelmed by the sheer volume of what needs to be taught and learned. When there is so much to cover, helping children develop comprehension strategies is particularly critical. Here are some specific ways science teachers use the ideas in this chapter to help students understand critical science concepts.

Graphic Organizers Earlier in this chapter, you learned that graphic organizers help students see the relationships between various facts and pieces of information. Learning to create graphic organizers also helps students become aware of text structure. Text structure is the way ideas are tied together in written language. Some common text structures include sequence, compare and contrast, cause and effect, problem and solution, and description/listing of important characteristics. While all of these idea structures appear in science texts, two commonly used structures are description and compare and contrast. Students can learn to construct webs when the information they are reading describes one main topic, Venn diagrams when the information is organized to compare and contrast two or three topics, and data charts when the information includes many different members of the same category.

Most teachers begin with the web because it is the easiest graphic organizer to teach and the most valuable for helping students organize and remember descriptive information presented hierarchically (i.e., topic, subtopics, sub-subtopics, and so on). Working together you and the students write the main topic in the center of the web and then put the other information going out from the center, using subtopics as needed. Generally, you and the class work together to create the first several webs, and then students work together in small groups to create several more; finally, ask students to create individual webs. (Figure 5.8 shows the beginning of a science web on whales.)

Once students have become proficient at making their own webs, you can teach a second graphic organizer format. Direct students' attention to a part of the text that describes two things, telling characteristics they share and differences between the two. Using the same class, small-group, individual progression, students can learn to create a Venn diagram like that shown in Figure 5.6. Some teachers call this Venn diagram a "double bubble."

When students are good at creating webs, double bubbles, and triple bubbles, direct their attention to a text passage in which many different members of a category are described/compared and contrasted. Interlocking circles would get cumbersome and indeed impossible to construct when there are more than three things being contrasted, and students can learn to make data charts such as that shown in Figure 5.3.

Once students have learned to create these separate graphic organizers, help them see that, depending on the structure of the text they are reading, one or the other of these would help them better organize the material. Deciding which one to use is the final step, which allows students to use this valuable comprehension strategy independently when reading on their own.

If the students already know how to create these graphic organizers or if the text you want them to read and understand has many passages in which sequence or cause–effect is the dominant structure, use the same procedures to teach them to create time lines (Figure 5.7) or cause–effect chains (Figure 5.10).

Anticipation Guides In science class, prior knowledge, which is generally helpful in comprehension, can sometimes actually impede comprehension. Based on observation and prior experience, some students have misconceptions about the way things work. Students may have seen objects falling and assumed that objects always fall in a straight line. Some students may have been told that warts are caused by frogs or that getting one's feet wet would cause a cold. To help students access their prior knowledge before reading, some teachers create anticipation guides in which some of the statements directly confront the possible misconceptions. Students indicate whether they agree or disagree with the statements before reading and then read to see which of the statements are actually true. Research on misconceptions has shown that students must have their misconception directly refuted either by the text, the teacher, or peers. Otherwise they may learn the new information but fail to discard the old misconception. Many students who learn that colds are caused by viruses still believe that they are also caused by getting your feet wet!

An anticipation guide, which directs students to think about and predict what they will learn, can directly confront common misconceptions. Going back to the statements after reading (or listening or viewing), students discuss what their misconceptions were and how they now understand the phenomenon under consideration.

Critical Thinking We always want our students to think critically, but it is crucial that they get in the habit of thinking that way in science classrooms. As they confront their misconceptions, we want them to realize that some of these misconceptions were based on the "best scientific evidence" that was available a generation ago. They also need to realize that some ideas that many think science has "proved" are really only our current best theory or one—but not the only—theory. When we say that we want students to think critically, we usually mean the thinking processes we have called image, generalize, evaluate, and apply. As we go through our activities and lessons and help students predict and organize information, we must never lose sight of the reason students are required to take science courses. We want students who can imagine how things were and how things might be different. We want students who can generalize and draw conclusions from the facts they have organized. We want students who evaluate and form well-founded opinions and students who apply what they learn in science to their own lives. As science teachers help students improve their comprehension, they must always strive to remember that comprehension is thinking and that thinking includes, by definition, the higher-order critical thinking processes.

Comprehension in Social Studies Classrooms

Graphic Organizers Earlier in this chapter, you learned that graphic organizers help students see the relationships between various facts and pieces of information. Learning to create graphic organizers can also help students become aware of text structure. Text structure is the way ideas are tied together in written language. Some common text structures include sequence, compare and contrast, cause and effect, problem–solution, and description/listing of important characteristics. While all of these idea structures appear in social studies texts, sequence, cause–effect, and problem–solution structures are omnipresent. Students can learn to construct time lines when sequence or dates are important, cause–effect chains when causal relationships are what matters and problem–solution maps when that is the dominant theme.

Time lines are fairly easy to construct and are often the first graphic organizer taught in history classes. Working together, you and the students draw the line and put in a starting date and an ending date. Next, go through the text and add other dates and important events. In the space under the event, add one or two key facts to each event. Generally, you and the class work together to create the first several time lines, and then students work together in small groups to create several more; finally, students are asked to create individual time lines.

Once students become proficient at making their own time lines, you can teach a second graphic organizer format. Direct students' attention to a part of the text in which a certain "chain of events" unfolds, with each event resulting in another event. Using the same class, small-group, individual progression, students learn to create a cause–effect chain like that shown in Figure 5.10.

Another common text structure seen in social studies texts is one in which there is a problem and various attempts at a solution. Sometimes, the solution creates an unforeseen new problem, which then needs some kind of solution. Students can learn to create a problem–solution map.

Once students have learned to create these separate graphic organizers, you can help them see that depending on the structure of the text they are reading, one or the other of these would help them better organize the material. Deciding which one to use is the final step, which allows students to use this valuable comprehension strategy independently when reading on their own.

KWLs   Social studies tends to be a subject in which the pooled prior knowledge and interest of the whole class about any topic is substantial. When most students already know a little and a few students know a lot, a KWL is a wonderful way to activate everyone's prior knowledge and interest. When you place a large sheet of roll paper across the board, label a column *K* for what we know and say, "We're going to be learning about the civil rights struggle in this country, but I know that you already know a lot about this so I want to list here everything that we jointly know." Student interest is piqued. As you list everything they brainstorm (even if it is not correct and will need to be edited or deleted later in the unit), students enlarge their prior knowledge stores by listening to their most important experts— their peers. Perhaps you spend most of one period creating a gigantic list. For homework, you assign them to discuss this issue with someone they know who lived through or participated in the struggle and see if they can come to class the following day with something to add. After adding what they learned from their "informed sources," you begin the second column, the *W*—what we want to know! Again, list all their questions, even if you know some of the answers can probably not be found or agreed on. As you begin your class study of this unit, return each day to the scroll and add to the *L* column—what we have learned. You may want to also let them add to the *W* column because as students learn more, they generate more questions.

Prediction is the major thinking process used to launch and sustain the KWL activity. Prediction is when that little voice inside all our minds whispers, "I wonder if . . ." "I think that . . ." or "I wish I knew . . . ." Prediction helps keep our brains, and sometimes our hearts, actively engaged in learning.

Critical Thinking   We always want our students to think critically, but it is crucial that they get in the habit of thinking that way in social studies classrooms. In spite of the fact that there are a lot of facts, dates, terms, and so forth, to learn, we all know that these are only means to the end of having students think about what they are learning. When we say that we want students to think, we usually mean the thinking processes we have called image, generalize, evaluate, and apply. As we go through our activities and lessons and help them predict and organize information, we must never lose sight of the reason students are required to take history, economics, politics, and other social studies courses. We want students who can imagine how things were and how things might be different. We want students who can generalize and draw conclusions from the facts they have organized. We want students who evaluate and form well-founded opinions and students who apply what they learn in social studies to their individual and community responsibilities. As social studies teachers help students improve their comprehension, they must always strive to remember that comprehension is thinking and that thinking includes, by definition, the higher-order critical thinking processes.

Comprehension in Activity Classrooms

Have you been to a large newsstand lately? Isn't it amazing how many different kinds of magazines there are? Think about classifying all those magazines into the different content areas in school. There are a few titles that would fit best under English, a few more that would fit best under social studies, and several more that would fit best under science. There are almost none that would fit best under foreign language or mathematics. A very large number, however, would fit best under our "activity" category. In other words, they are magazines for people who engage in a particular pursuit, say gardening, golf, or gun collecting. And many of the articles in these magazines actually outline procedures for doing some aspect of the pursuit to which the magazine is devoted. Likewise, time spent in a major bookstore reveals that this is an era of "self-help" books and manuals for doing, using, or repairing almost anything.

In your course, you are attempting to teach your students to do a number of varied procedures. Wouldn't it be helpful to them to learn how to *read to do* in your subject? Granted, nothing beats the coaching or apprenticeship model for learning how to do something. Reading is a useful and practical substitute or source for review, however, for those who need to or prefer to learn independently.

You may well have a textbook for your course. If not, you may have access to brochures, manuals, or even trade books and magazines that exist to help people perform better in your field. That is the material, diagrams and all, that you can teach your students how to comprehend as a part of your course. If so, your students will be more able to take advantage of the books, magazines, and other reading materials available to them after they no longer have you for their teacher.

Comprehension follow-up is automatic in your course when you have students read to do something. Also, the materials you have are often study guides of a sort in that they lead students through the procedure, step by step. Content comprehension lessons can readily be planned and taught by previewing and describing the procedure students are to be able to perform during or after reading.

What is crucial is that students have opportunities to read what to do under your guidance and supervision. Most people are unable to follow directions to program their VCR or learn how to use their personal computer because no one ever taught them how to comprehend such material. Certainly, such materials are never included in reading or English courses.

Most students are totally dependent on their teachers in activity courses because they are unable to use reading to add to their skills. Reading should never become a major part of any activity course, but reading what to do is one aspect of what it means today to be educated in any field, from playing the guitar to playing the stock market, and from painting with watercolors to accomplishing weight loss.

LOOKING BACK   Most of what we choose to read is on topics for which we have a great deal of background knowledge; thus, motivation is usually quite high. When we read this easy (for us) material, comprehension seems to occur effortlessly and automatically as we process the words. In content area classrooms, however, students often read materials for which they have little prior knowledge and motivation. It is when students are reading teachable text that content comprehension lessons are needed. In this chapter, you learned the why and how of supporting students' comprehension and some strategies for weaning them off this support. These are the four keys:

1. Vary levels of comprehension support.
2. Guide readers through challenging passages.
3. Teach reading comprehension strategies.
4. Promote collaborative comprehension practices.

ADD TO YOUR JOURNAL   Reflect on this chapter's key ideas: Do you see why students need support as they read unfamiliar text? Does the procedure for planning comprehension guidance make sense? Can you imagine yourself guiding students through the before, during, and after phases of reading, listening, or viewing? Do you see that within the basic framework there are almost endless variations? Do some of these variations seem more applicable to your content area and your purposes for reading? Finally, what do you think about fading and self-assessment as ways to make students more independent learners? Describe your reactions to each of the four key ideas and generalize about the role of guidance and independence in your classroom. What do you believe will be most useful to you?

Additional Readings

The following present specific hands-on teaching practices that focus on particular aspects of reading comprehension:

BUEHL, D. (2001). *Classroom strategies for interactive learning* (2nd ed.). Newark, DE: International Reading Association.

BURKE, J. (2002). *Tools for thought: Graphic Organizers for Your Classroom*. Portsmouth, NH: Heinemann.

HARVEY, S., & Goudvis, A. (2000). *Strategies that work: Teaching comprehension to enhance understanding*. Portland, ME: Stenhouse.

MOORE, S. A. (2004). *Conversations in four-block classrooms: Encouraging literacy interactions with students*. Greensboro, NC: Carson-Dellosa Publishing.

READENCE, J. E., MOORE, D. W., & RICKELMAN, R. J. (2000). *Prereading activities for content area reading and learning* (3rd ed.). Newark, DE: International Reading Association.

SADLER, C. R. (2001). *Comprehension strategies for middle grade readers: A handbook for content area teachers.* Newark, DE: International Reading Association.

SCHERER, M. (Ed.) (2002). Reading and writing in the content areas [Special issue]. *Educational Leadership, 60*(3).

WILHELM, J. (2001). *Improving comprehension with think-aloud strategies.* New York: Scholastic.

WORMELI, R. (2005). *Summarization in any subject.* Alexandria, VA: Association for Supervision and Curriculum Development.

ZWIERS, J. (2004). *Building reading comprehension habits in grades 6–12: A toolkit of classroom activities.* Newark, DE: International Reading Association.

The following texts provide solid research-based insights into reading comprehension instruction:

BLACHOWICZ, C., & OGLE, D. (2001). *Reading comprehension: Strategies for independent learning.* New York: The Guilford Press.

BLOCK, C. C., GAMBRELL, L. B., & PRESSLEY, M. (Eds.) (2002). *Improving comprehension instruction: Rethinking research, theory, and classroom practice.* San Francisco: Jossey-Bass.

BLOCK, C. C., & PRESSLEY, M. (Eds.) (2001). *Comprehension instruction: Research-based best practices.* New York: The Guilford Press.

SWEET, A. P., & SNOW, C. E. (Eds.) (2003). *Rethinking reading comprehension.* New York: The Guilford Press.

The following six references report very reputable summaries of research on teaching reading comprehension:

ALVERMANN, D. E., FITZGERALD, J., & SIMPSON, M. (in press). Teaching and learning in reading. In P. Alexander & P. Winne (Eds.), *Handbook of Educational Psychology* (2nd ed.). New York: Simon & Schuster/Macmillan.

FARSTRUP, A. E., & SAMUELS, S. J. (2002). *What research has to say about reading instruction* (3rd ed.). Newark, DE: International Reading Association.

GERSTEN, R., FUCHS, L. S., WILLIAMS, J. P., & BAKER, S. (2001). Teaching reading comprehension strategies to students with learning disabilities: A review of research. *Review of Educational Research, 71,* 279–320.

NATIONAL READING PANEL. (2000). *Teaching children to read: An evidence-based assessment of the scientific research literature on reading and its implications for reading instruction: Reports of the subgroups.* Bethesda, MD: National Institute of Child Health and Human Development, National Institutes of Health.

PRESSLEY, M. (2000). What should comprehension instruction be the instruction of? In M. J. Kamil, P. B. Mosenthal, P. D. Pearson, & R. Barr (Eds.), *Handbook of reading research* (vol. 3) (pp. 545–561). Mahwah, NJ: Lawrence Erlbaum Associates.

RAND READING STUDY GROUP. (2002). *Reading for understanding: Toward an R&D program in reading comprehension.* Santa Monica, CA: Science and Technology Policy Institute, RAND Education.

Appendix: Graphic Organizers

Famous Americans in Four Poems

Qualities (+ / −)	Abraham Lincoln	Georgia O'Keeffe	Martin Luther King, Jr.	Betsy Ross
proud				
controversial				
artistic				
political				
———				
———				
———				
———				

Figure 5.5 A Semantic Feature Matrix is especially appropriate for comparing and contrasting as well as choosing among alternatives (e.g., Which famous American is least controversial?).

Human and Animal Communication

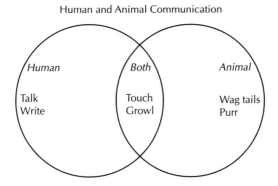

Figure 5.6 A Venn Diagram is especially appropriate for comparing and contrasting as well as describing (e.g., How does human communication differ from animal communication?).

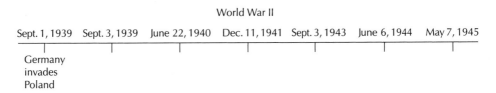

Figure 5.7 A Time Line is especially appropriate for describing sequences (e.g., Describe the major turning points of World War II.).

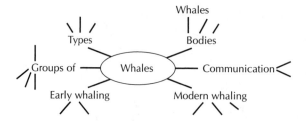

Figure 5.8 A web is especially appropriate for grouping items into categories and portraying relationships among the categories. Often used to begin and monitor the gathering of ideas and information during units and unit projects (e.g., What can we learn about whales?).

THE YUKON
A. Geography
   1.
   2.
   3.
   4.
B. Economy
   1. Fishing
      a.
      b.
   2. _____
      a. lynx
      b.
      c.
   3. Manufacturing
      a.
      b.
      c.

4. _____
   a. gold
   b.
   c.
   d.
   e.
C. Government
   1. Canadian
      a.
      b.
      c.
   2. Territorial
      a.
      b.

Figure 5.9 An outline is especially appropriate for grouping items into categories. Often used to introduce expository writing (e.g., List main points about the Yukon in the order that they are to be presented.).

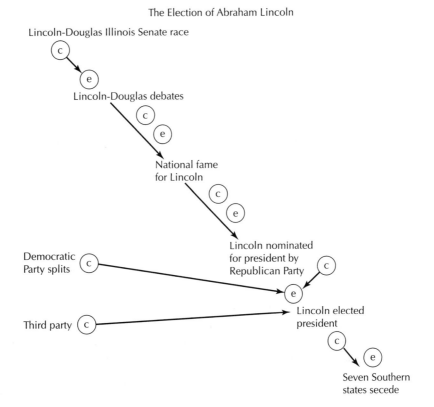

Figure 5.10 A Cause-and-Effect Chain is especially appropriate for explaining how events affect one another (e.g., How did events associated with Abraham Lincoln contribute to secession?).

6

Meaning Vocabulary

LOOKING AHEAD   Knowing the appropriate meanings for the words used to communicate ideas is essential for learning a subject. Because many students have not encountered the critical vocabulary for each content area through their general world experience or acquired it through previous schooling, content area teachers are responsible for teaching the meaning vocabulary essential to communicating their subject. Part of what it means to know biology, geometry, economics, and so forth is to be able to read, write, listen, and speak using their terminology. In order to provide students access to words, good understandings are needed of what it means to know a word, how learners grasp word meanings, and how teachers construct effective word-learning opportunities.

Words are used to communicate ideas. You are able to compose or comprehend ideas only when you can associate meanings with the corresponding words. Indeed, studies of what makes passages difficult to read consistently have shown word difficulty to predict passage difficulty. Correlations between students' vocabulary test scores and passage comprehension scores generally are among the highest of any school assessments. There is little doubt that those who do well with individual words also tend to do well reading and writing passages (National Reading Panel, 2000).

These are the keys in this chapter:

1. Vocabulary development is complex.
2. Promote wide reading.
3. Teach sets of words directly.
4. Promote word consciousness.
5. Teach word learning strategies.

Vocabulary Development Is Complex

Given the importance of vocabulary development to academic success, there are many aspects to vocabulary learning to consider. To illustrate, examine the following two sentences:

The avuncular man scratched his philtrum.
She painted all but her lunules.

These are simple sentences. You probably gained a general idea that a "certain" man scratched "something" that belonged to him, and that the woman painted all but some specific "things" that belonged to her. Because you probably lack meanings for some key words, however, your comprehension of these sentences is impaired. If you looked for dictionary definitions of these key words, starting with *avuncular*, you found that it meant "acting like an uncle." Depending on your experiences with uncles, you then conjured up a meaning for the previously unfamiliar word, *avuncular*. You also discovered that you have both a philtrum (groove in the middle of the upper lip, below the nose) and lunules (moon-shaped white areas at the base of the fingernails that at one time were fashionable for women to leave white while painting the rest of their nails).

Concepts and Labels for Concepts

Notice that you did not lack meanings for the three words in the preceding example. But you were unable to connect the meanings with the words. Psychologists would say that you had the concepts—how uncles behave, the groove in the middle of your upper lip, the moon-shaped white areas at the base of your fingernails. What you didn't have were these particular labels, or words, for the concepts. Having concepts and labels for concepts are two aspects of vocabulary knowledge.

Consider another example:

The pharmacist needed lupulin and lupulone.

Again, you know that the pharmacist needed two "things." But which two things? When you look up *lupulin*, you discover that it is the "glandular hairs of the hop." Lupulone is "a white or yellow crystalline solid." These meanings are not very informative because you probably do not know what the meanings mean. In this example, you probably lack the labels as well as the concepts. Dictionaries are very helpful when we have a concept but not the particular label by which it is being called. Dictionaries have limited usefulness when we lack both the labels and the concepts. Indeed, Beck, McKeown, and Kucan (2002) provide data-based support for their assertion that "the reality is that definitions are not an effective vehicle for learning word meanings" (p. 33).

As you consider how to teach word meanings, keep in mind the aspects of labels and concepts. If the word to be taught is one for which students already have the appropriate concept and lack only the label, the teaching task is relatively simple. If, as is more common during subject matter study, students lack both the concept and the label, the task is more difficult.

Depth of Word Knowledge

Knowing a word is like knowing a person. Asking "How many words do you know?" is like asking "How many people do you know?" If we ask the latter question, you will probably not respond, thinking that we could not be serious. If we persist, however, you might answer with a question of your own: "What do you mean by *know*?" There are many aspects to knowing word meanings.

There are many people whom you know only by name. There are also many words you know only by name, for which you have the label, but whose concept remains vague. *Truffles* is a word known to many people, but perhaps the whole extent of your meaning for *truffles* consists of "I think you eat them." Your meanings for the word *potatoes*, on the other hand, probably could fill pages. You might think of all the French fries you have eaten at fast-food restaurants, of the baked potatoes your mother served, and of the potato-head toy you had as a young child. You might call up your knowledge that potatoes are "vegetables," "underground tubers of a plant," "sometimes covered with eyes," "grown in great quantities in Idaho," "eaten in many forms: baked, mashed, french fried," "the crop that failed during the Irish famine of the 1840s," and so on.

Related Words

Just as most names stand for many different people, some of whom are related and some of whom are not, most words stand for many different meanings, some related, some not. Look up *root*, for example, and you will find many meanings. Plant roots, tooth roots, root words, and square roots all share a common concept, the idea of a basic part, often hidden, from which other parts, usually visible, emerge and grow. The related meanings of a word may be compared to related people who share the same name. Such people often share a family resemblance: physical (red hair, big bones) or behavioral (mannerisms, gestures, idiosyncrasies of speech). In some families, these resemblances are striking. In others, only the most astute observer would be able to detect family resemblances. So it is with words. The relationship among the many meanings for some words is apparent to everyone; other words reveal their kinship only to philologists. For instance, did you know that the words *sedimentary* and *presidential* are related? Their *sed/sid* bases all refer to *settle*. Sedimentary material is the sediment that settles at the bottom; presidents wield their presidential power when they preside over groups, settling them down. Thus, most students need a teacher's help to perceive the family aspect of words.

Symbols

We must be concerned with some terms not usually considered *words*. A few examples should illustrate this point:

The FBI and CIA directors met last week.
AB = CD.
N.Z. is ESE of Australia.
The president of ASCAP was a member of CORE.

Phrases, symbols, abbreviations, initials, and acronyms all occur in the material students read in content areas. While these terms are not technically "words," they are entities for which meaning must be built, and teachers should remember to teach meanings for any symbols that students will need to understand in order to read and write effectively in a particular content area.

Direct Experience

Think of a person whom you know very well. Most of the people whose names you know are people with whom you have interacted over a period of time. You have had firsthand, direct experience with them. Many of the words for which you have meanings are also words with which you have had direct experience. If you have actually seen a tiger in the wild or at a zoo, your meaning for the word *tiger* is based partly on direct experience. If you have run a *marathon* or played *tennis* or *basketball*, your meanings for these words are rooted in this direct experience. When you experienced *fear, love,* or *sorrow,* your meanings for these words are based on that experience.

Media and Technology

You have not directly interacted with all the people whose names you know, nor with all the meanings whose words you know. You know a lot about Ronald Reagan, Elizabeth Taylor, and George Washington, with whom you have probably not had firsthand experience. But you probably have seen them in pictures or films or on television. You "know" these persons through visual media. The meanings for some of the words you know are based on the media rather than direct experience. You know what pole-vaulting is because you have watched it on television, even though you may never have actually done it or been there watching someone do it. There are places you have never visited but have seen pictures of; thus, you have meanings for words such as *Jerusalem* and *Andes*. You have viewed representations of countless phenomena online, visiting web sites that portray automobiles, beauty products, consumer electronics, and so on.

Connection

You know some people whom you have neither met nor seen in the media and technology. These real or fictional people are ones you have read about in novels or historical literature. While you have never met these people, you use the knowledge gained from all the people you have met to understand the unknown people about whom you are reading. So it is with words. Imagine that you are reading this passage about the game of cricket:

The batsmen were merciless against the bowlers. The bowlers placed their men in slips and covers. But to no avail. The batsmen hit one four after another along with an occasional six. Not once did a ball look like it would hit their stumps or be caught. (Tierney & Pearson, 1992, p. 93)

Now, imagine that you have never played cricket nor seen it played, but you call up what you do know to help you build meanings for the word *cricket* and other words in the passage. "Baseball is a lot like cricket," you might think. "The bowlers must be like pitchers. The batsmen are obviously the batters. Maybe the stumps are bases." You use what you know to predict meanings for words. In situations in which you build meanings for words without any direct or visual experience with what the words represent, you still draw on your direct and visual experience, but you do so through comparisons: "It is like this known thing in these ways—but different in these ways." We refer to this way of learning as learning by connection.

TRY IT OUT

Words and meanings, like names and people, are learned through direct experience, media and technology, and connection. List three people and three word meanings you have learned through direct experience—people and concepts with which you have actually interacted. Then list three people and three word meanings you have acquired through the media and technology—people and concepts you have not actually met or experienced but that you feel you know through the power of the visual media and technology.

Finally, list three people and three words that you have learned by connection. These people and words were learned by calling up your direct and visual experience in similar situations and connecting those experiences to the new names or words to build meaning.

Authentic Settings

About 88,700 word forms (e.g., *history, historian, historical*) occur in print from the first through the twelfth grade (Nagy & Anderson, 1984). If children are to learn enough of these word forms to become literate adults, they need to know about 45,000 by the end of high school. Perhaps the best way to enable students to develop such a vocabulary is to focus on words in authentic settings.

In authentic settings, students use the rich natural language that is provided by books, guest speakers, role plays, informative media, and classmates as they explore ideas. Settings are authentic when they relate to students' worlds, when they tap individuals' interests and concerns. Students in authentic settings want to acquire new words for genuine reasons; they intend to apply what they learn. They develop vocabulary while engaging their minds fully in worthwhile ideas.

Authentic settings are found in units of study as described in Chapter 3, "Instructional Units." Units present the big picture before focusing on details, so students have something to help organize all the new words they encounter. This whole-to-part approach enhances vocabulary development. Such settings are the opposite of antiseptic ones filled with worksheet lists of unrelated words to define, synonyms to match, and rote drills to perform.

Authentic unit-based settings are especially appropriate for the complexities of teaching and learning vocabulary. In fact, the words that naturally emerge during units are the ones many teachers use as the core of their vocabulary instruction. To arrange this instruction, many adapt a four-part program described by Graves (2000) that consists of promoting wide reading, teaching sets of words, promoting word consciousness, and teaching word-learning strategies.

Promoting Wide Reading

Wide reading is a premier setting for learning vocabulary (Krashen, 2004). Reading self-selected materials provides a rich source of new words. Research is clear that students engaged with interesting and important books, periodicals, online sites, and so on, grasp the meanings of unfamiliar words, and they review and refine the meanings of familiar ones. When reading on their own, students tend to independently understand and remember the meanings of about fifteen of every one hundred unknown words they encounter (Swanborn & de Glopper, 1999). Reading only ten minutes per day can result in students learning about one thousand new words each year (Cunningham & Stanovich, 1998). In brief, if you want to increase students' vocabularies, you should do everything possible to increase the amount of students' wide reading.

Secondary students find a range of reading materials engaging.

Fictional and nonfictional printed accounts add to students' funds of knowledge about the world and about words. Reading about the Donner party, the Shackelton expedition, the way animals adapt, and how *Star Wars* was produced—to name a few topics—can be compelling experiences in their own right as well as valuable contributions to one's knowledge base. Chapter 4 of this text, "Reading Materials and Projects," describes materials appropriate for wide reading and explains how to set up and manage opportunities for reading and responding.

Teaching Sets of Words

Making new words available and accessible through wide reading is essential for vocabulary development, but more needs to be done. Learners also benefit from studying sets of words that correspond to units of instruction. Teaching sets of unit-based words presents students conceptually related items that are linked in meaningful networks. The best instruction involves rich, active practices that reveal words' meanings in multiple ways. This instruction focuses on deep and thorough understandings of the words, so that youth will have them for a lifetime.

Introduce your units' words as each one comes up during the normal course of instruction. To ensure that you are doing more than merely introducing and mentioning the terms as they arise, consider the following practices.

Selecting Sets of Words

Selecting sets of words that correspond to your units of instruction involves several considerations:

1. *Consider the unit you are presenting and list all the key words.* As Chapter 3 indicated, much instructional decision making occurs when planning units of instruction. When planning units, be selective about the vocabulary you intend to teach. Begin by identifying key words. Key words are words that unlock the meaning of a topic. Be sure to include multi-meaning words, such as *root*, for which the students might know a meaning that is not appropriate.

2. *Pare down this initial list by setting priorities.* Determining how many words to teach is a difficult task, but research indicates that ten new words per week per class is what we can expect students to learn (Beck, McKeown, & Kucan, 2002). Ten words per week may not sound like much, but consider that it means 360 new words per year! Furthermore, if a student is studying five subjects and each subject includes ten new words each week, that would add up to 1,800 new words per year—a considerable increase in vocabulary.

   To pare your list, first select the words that are important not only to the unit of study but also to the whole understanding of the content area. The word *cell* in a science unit on plants should be kept because it is crucial not only to understanding plants, but also to the whole study of biology. Likewise, the word *angle* is crucial to the whole study of geometry. In addition to words crucial to the whole discipline, keep on your list words that occur repeatedly in the unit of study and that are crucial to understanding it. A word appearing only once is probably less important than a word that occurs frequently throughout the unit.

3. *Include words that will be of particular interest to your students.* Sometimes, there is a word or two that are not critical to your discipline but that are interesting words. Including these words will increase the engagement of your students and help convince them that words are wonderful!

4. *Display the words for intensive study.* Many teachers reserve one of the bulletin boards in the room to display the important words associated with a unit. Sometimes these words are part of a graphic organizer such as a web or a chart. Other times, the words are displayed with pictures that help to clarify their meanings. Still other times, they are simply written on index cards and attached to the board. Some teachers put all the important unit words up at the beginning of the unit and refer to these words throughout the unit, periodically asking students what else they have learned about these important words. Other teachers prefer to add words gradually as the words occur and do some culminating activities at the end of the unit to help students tie all the words together.

TRY IT OUT   Select a unit of study you might teach to a group of students. Consider what you want them to learn. Preview CDs, DVDs, videos, and other teaching aids you might use. Read the text chapters and other sources students might read. As you think, preview, and read, list all the key words. Be on the lookout for multimeaning words. These are hard to spot because when we know the appropriate meaning, we often forget that students may only know the more common meanings.

Once you have listed your key words, cut the list to a reasonable number (no more than ten per week) following the guidelines given. Assume your unit will last three weeks, and cut your list of words to teach down to thirty.

Representing Word Meanings Productively

As you move through units of study, you can use numerous productive strategies for presenting the key words you have selected. How we teach something should parallel how something is learned. Because we remember best the things that we do, direct experience with the concept represented by the word is the most powerful and lasting way to teach. Providing this real experience, however, is not always possible, and thus we often look to the next best thing, media representations. We also can teach new words by helping students see the relationships between new concepts and already known concepts.

Remember that effective settings for learning include authentic situations in which learners are actively involved and well supported. And cycles of instruction occur during which teachers plan, introduce, guide, and culminate learning activities. Such settings and cycles apply to learning words. This section presents a variety of productive teaching strategies for developing students' vocabulary.

Real World Interactions   Real world interactions are exactly what they sound like. You want students to develop a meaning for a word, so you put them in direct contact with the thing that the word represents. Field trips are often good ways to show students the real thing. If you have ever taken a field trip to a state capitol to watch the legislative process, your teacher was providing you with real experience for a number of words: *capitol, legislature, gavel, quorum, debate, adjourn.* Field trips are some of the best ways of providing students with direct experience on which to base meaning for new words, but they are expensive and time consuming, and often the things you need to show students are not available at a reasonable distance from the school.

When you cannot take the students to the real thing, the next best option is to bring something to the students. Learners at all levels learn something best when they have actually seen it, touched it, smelled it, listened to it, or even tasted it.

Sometimes the actual subject of study could never be available for students to interact with, but a model could. Models of the human heart, a pyramid, or a DNA molecule, while differing in size and other features from the real thing, are still three-dimensional representations that can be explored by the senses.

You can provide students real experience with verbs like *cringe, catapult,* and *pontificate* by demonstrating these actions, then letting students act them out. You provide students with experience with such concepts as *assembly line* and *electoral process* by simulations in which each student takes part as the class manufactures something assembly-line style or participates in a mock election. Because of time and other constraints, not all meanings can be developed through this method. But the time and effort involved in providing the real thing must be weighed against the depth and the permanence of the learning and excitement that this method generates.

Scavenger Hunts   Have you ever had firsthand experience with a scavenger hunt? Have you actually gone to gather assorted items, competing to be the team that found the most in a limited time? If you have not, perhaps you have had visual experience of watching others go on one. Scavenger hunts are fun because they develop both competition and a sense of team spirit. For a scavenger hunt that helps your students build word meanings by collecting real things and pictures, follow these steps:

1. *Make a list of the items for which you want students to scavenge.* Include anything for which students might be able to find a real object, model, or picture, but make sure to include items represented by those words for which you need to build meaning. Be sure to add some well-known,

Students link concrete objects with vocabulary learning during instructional units.

easy-to-collect items so that some of the finds will be easy and immediately satisfying. Here is a list used for a scavenger hunt before beginning a unit on the desert:

sand	woodpecker	cactus	vulture
skunk	dune	fox	kangaroo rat
mesquite	dates	oasis	nomads
roadrunner	coyote	yucca	

2. *Divide your class into teams of three or four.* Explain how scavenger hunts work. Be sure students understand that they must bring in objects and pictures by a certain date.

3. *Allow the teams to meet briefly once or twice more.* Teams should check things off their lists and see what is still needed. If students protest that "No one could find a . . . ," assure them that "No one could possibly get objects or pictures for everything. The goal is to collect as much as you can." This will generally result in some students making sure that they have a picture, if not an object, for everything, just to prove you wrong.

4. *On the appointed day, have teams bring their finds.* Cards on which each word is printed might be attached to bulletin boards and all the pictures representing that object can be arranged in collage fashion around the word. Objects that are not alive, dangerous, or valuable can be labeled and placed on tables near the bulletin boards.

Pictures help develop meanings for words.

Media and Technology   Media provides us with the next best thing to being there. All of us have numerous concepts that we have not experienced directly but have developed through movies, television, still photographs, paintings, diagrams, or maps. Computer software and web sites now offer simulations that allow students to observe science phenomena like the body systems and mathematical phenomena like tessellations that were difficult to portray before. Imagine trying to explain the Grand Canyon to someone who has never seen it, or trying to describe with words the color teal, what fencing looks like, or life at the bottom of the ocean. Your words are meaningful only to those who have seen what the words represent.

Fortunately, we are surrounded by visual stimuli. Television programs offer great possibilities for content teachers. Most school system media centers contain videos, CDs, slides, and other visual aids. As you consider how to build meaning for words, ask yourself, "Where could I find a picture of this?" Often, the answer is as close as your textbook.

When you have your list of words for which you must build meaning, look at the textbooks and other books you have available. Note page numbers where various concepts are portrayed visually. You can introduce these concepts by writing the word on the board, pronouncing it and having students pronounce it with you, and directing their attention to the appropriate text visual.

Active participation engages learners with language.

In the case of visuals, if one is good, two are twice as good. Remember that developing a concept is not a matter of "one time—now you've got it." Your meaning for *ancient Greece* is not based on having seen just one picture. If your students see several visuals, the depth of their meaning for the word will be much greater than if they see only one. In addition to broadening their concepts, each visual provides review of the meaning represented by the word.

Organizing Words   Organization is a powerful avenue to understanding and remembering words and their meanings. If you provide category names before students organize words, correct answers would be expected. If students are allowed to invent their own category names, correctness is based on the students' explanations of their organizational schemes. Students typically like recording each word on a separate slip of paper in order to physically manipulate and group them. For instance, if young children were reading about food, they might organize the following items into categories:

apple	fried chicken	ice cream
hamburger	cake	peach
orange	hot dog	pie

You might produce one or more category topics, then have students supply subordinate terms in a format such as the following:

Fruit	Dessert	Meat Dish

Older students exploring land formations caused by glaciers might depict the relationships of the following words:

drumlin	rocking stone	moraine
erratic boulder	valley	continental
esker	kame	

You and your class might display the categories in a Venn Diagram or web according to the words' relationships with each other (see pages 131 and 132 of this text). Displaying terms in main idea–detail or sequential arrangements promotes deep understandings of the connections among vocabulary. It is like producing a map of a group of words.

Creating Analogies   To create an analogy, think of something your students are apt to know that is like the thing they do not know. It is very important that students be familiar with the concept being used to teach the unknown concept. Telling you that cricket is a lot like rounders is not helpful if you do not know rounders either. Once you have decided which analogy to make, consider the similarities and differences between the familiar and unfamiliar concepts.

Imagine that you want to teach the students about taxation without representation and its relationship to the Revolutionary War. You decide to compare this concept with the idea of belonging to a club to which you have to pay dues. You do not mind paying the dues, even though the club founders meet each year and decide how the dues are to be spent. After a while, it occurs to some club members who are not founders that because the dues are partly theirs, they should have some say in how the dues are spent. The founding members will have no part of this and insist that the power to spend dues is theirs, as is written in the club's bylaws. Once you have gotten from students what they know about clubs and dues, you may have to interject the notion that founding members could have control of the dues because this may not be in the experience of most students. Then, explain that taxation is like dues and that representation, in this case, means the power to decide how something is spent. A difference that should be pointed out is that you as a club member always have the right to quit the club and stop paying dues. When the colonists quit and stopped paying taxes, a war ensued.

Passage Impressions   In Passage Impressions, students compose a brief passage by fitting together words in a given order, reading a passage that contains the words, then refitting their original impressions. Here are the four steps of Passage Impressions:

1. Students write paragraphs using displayed words in order. Show students a list of key vocabulary on a chalkboard, overhead, handout, or chart. Say: *Here are some words contained in what we are going to be reading. First, write your own paragraph using all these words in the order they are presented.*

Grand Canyon Geology
Colorado Plateau
uplift
erosion
strata
sedimentary
limestone
sandstone
shale

2. After writing, have a few students read their paragraphs aloud to the class.
3. Then have students read the story or passage and see how their ideas compare with the author's.
4. After reading, have students compare the similarities and differences between the contents of their paragraphs and the author's actual composition. This comparison can be done through discussion, writing, or both.

Word Splash While Passage Impressions has students order words from first to last in entire paragraphs, Word Splash has students relate words in any order through graphic organizers and sentences.

To begin Word Splash, identify key terms from the reading passage that are adequately defined by their context. Display the words, like the Grand Canyon ones above, on cards so they can be manipulated. Then follow six steps:

1. Explore word relationships. Students might come to the front of the class and graphically organize the words to portray how they fit with each other.
2. Have students write sentences that each contain at least two of the key words, underlining them in each sentence. Words may be used in more than one sentence, but every word must be used at least once.
3. After writing, have a few students read their sentences aloud to the class.
4. Students then read the text to see how it supports their sentences.
5. Revise the sentences. Using the passage as a reference, students evaluate the information in each of their original sentences to determine which ones are supported and which ones need revision. Unsupported sentences should be made accurate.
6. Share the revised sentences. Ask for new sentences from the word list that conform with the passage information.

Promoting Word Consciousness

Word consciousness is an awareness of and interest in words as units of language (Graves, 2002; Scott & Nagy, 2004). Youth who are conscious of words willingly note their presence in different settings, analyze their distinctive spellings and meanings, judge whether certain ones are more appropriate than others in particular situations, and generally appreciate the power and wonder of language. Developing youths' word consciousness goes far to produce life-long readers and writers who value print. The following describes practices used to promote word consciousness.

Model Word Wonder

If you are fascinated by words, you need to realize that you probably developed that sense of wonder by interacting with someone—a parent, teacher, friend—who communicated his or her love of words. That gift is now one that you can pass on to your students, regardless of what subject you teach. If you have not yet developed an appreciation for words, it is never too late! Put *The New Shorter Oxford English Dictionary* on your holiday wish list. Read a few books, such as Isaac Asimov's *Words of Science and the History Behind Them*, John Ciardi's *A Browser's Dictionary*, Willard Espy's *Have a Word on Me*, or William Safire's *What's the Good Word?* that describe words' histories, or etymologies. These and other sources will help you overcome any lingering logophobia and help you and your future students become logophiles!

A student sorts cards by looking for the words with the same root.

Have Students Select the Words to Be Learned

Ruddell and Shearer (2002) suggest a vocabulary self-collection strategy in which students list words they consider important and relatively unknown. Help them consider whether the word is unknown not by their ability or inability to pronounce it but by their "I wonder what that word means" reaction. The list of words that students suggest can be modified by the teacher to fit the criteria for choosing which words to teach offered earlier in this chapter. Of course, you can add words not suggested by students if these words are crucial to the discipline or the unit.

Help Students Develop Self-Assessment Strategies

Helping students self-assess is one of the major ways of helping them develop responsibility for their own learning. Letting students select the words to be learned is one type of self-assessment, because, in selecting, they are deciding that these are relatively unknown words to them and that these words are likely to be important to the unit under study. You might also help students self-assess by presenting them with a knowledge-rating scale and have them put various unit words on that scale at the beginning and end of the unit (Blachowicz & Ogle, 2001). Students could then add up the number of points they have moved and have tangible proof of their vocabulary growth in your content-area.

Vocabulary Self-Assessment Scale
0 = I never heard of that word in my whole life.
1 = I have heard it, but I have no idea what it means.
2 = I couldn't tell you what it means, but I might be able to pick the right meaning from four choices.
3 = I can tell you a little about that word.
4 = I could put that word in a good sentence that would show its meaning.
5 = I could use that word correctly in discussion and writing.

Another way to support students' vocabulary self-assessment is to post questions that invite thinking about what to do upon encountering unfamiliar words. Harmon (2000, p. 525) suggests the following:

Do I know this word?
Do I need to know this word to understand what I am reading?
If I think this word is important, what do I already know about it?
What does the word have to do with what I am reading? What is it referring to?
How is it used in the sentence? Does it describe or show action?
Do I see any word parts that make sense?
Do I know enough about this word?
Do I need to know more information?
How can I find out more about this word?
Should I ask someone or use the dictionary?

Word Books

Many teachers have students make word books—vocabulary notebooks in which to record the words they are learning. Students may use a notebook or sheets of paper stapled together and decorated with an interesting cover. Words are then usually entered according to their first letter, but in the sequence in which they are introduced, alphabetical by first letter only. Depending on the age of the students and the type of word being studied, different information can be included with each word. Many teachers like students to write a personal example for each word ("*Frigid* is a February day when the thermometer hits 20°F.") as well as a definitional sentence ("*Frigid* means very, very cold."). Although students may consult the dictionary for help, it is best not to let them copy dictionary definitions because this requires little thought or understanding. In addition to the example and definitional sentence, other information may be included when it is helpful. A phonetic respelling may help students remember how to pronounce words. Sometimes, a common opposite is helpful in remembering the word. If the word has a common prefix, root, or suffix that will jog students' memory of its meaning, this can be noted. For some words, students can draw pictures, diagrams, or cartoons. The following table lists productive dimensions to use.

Dimensions of Words

Dimension	Example
1. Original Sentence (Copy the sentence containing the word.)	Pat was not used to the frigid weather conditions he now faced.
2. Dictionary Definition (What does the dictionary say the word means?)	extremely cold
3. New Sentence (Use the word in a sentence that shows what it means.)	A winter day at the north pole would be frigid.
4. Closest Experience (When have you seen it?)	My aunt has a big freezer, and the inside of it is frigid.
5. Explanation of Meaning (In your own words, what does it mean?)	Frigid means very, very cold.
6. Main Idea (What is it?)	a way to describe temperature
7. Details (What are some parts of it?)	you can see your breath, ice and snow
8. Synonym/Comparison (What words have nearly the same meaning?)	cold, freezing, polar

Dimension	*Example*
9. Antonym/Contrast (What words have nearly the opposite meaning?)	warm, hot, burning
10. Word Family Members (What words share the same root, or base?)	Frigidaire, refrigerator, fridge
11. Origin (What does the word come from?)	*Frigid* comes from the Latin word *frigus*, which means frosty or cold.
12. Translation (What is the Spanish [or other home language] word for it?)	frígida
13. Visual (Illustrate the meaning of the word.)	❄
14. Learning Key (How will you remember this word?)	The *fr* beginning makes me think of the first two letters in frosty, freezing and frozen, and the *rigid* part reminds me of something frozen solid. So frigid is something that is so cold that things barely move.

In the next chapter, on writing, we discuss having students keep content journals. Many teachers who have students create journals reserve special pages in those journals as a word book section. Students add new words and their own personal definitions as each unit is studied.

Word Play

As Blachowicz and Fisher (2004) put it, word play puts the *fun* back into *fundamental*. Word play is a motivating way to position youth as active manipulators of words, as being conscious of words. It focuses on different dimensions of word structures and meanings. The following word plays join time-honored activities such as classroom baseball, charades, password, and pictionary for promoting word consciousness.

Stump the Expert   Students play either individually, in pairs, or in small groups.

1. Designate the expert.
2. A stumper then offers an academic challenge in an attempt to confound the expert. With vocabulary, stumpers typically present a definitional statement (e.g., "This word is used a lot in the winter to describe extremely cold weather.") and the expert has a set time (e.g., ten seconds) to produce the term (e.g., *frigid*).

3. If the expert responds accurately, the next stumper offers a challenge. This continues until the expert is stumped—or until the expert answers a certain number of challenges (e.g., seven) and earns recognition (e.g., applause), a prize (e.g., food treat), or both.
4. Whoever successfully stumps the expert becomes the new expert, and the procedure begins anew.

Around the World   A student designated as the traveler moves from his or her seat and stands by a student in the next seat. Orally, present the traveler and the challenger a definitional statement; whoever says the matching word first is the traveler and stands by the student in the next seat. A traveler who continues responding first and returns to his or her seat has successfully gone Around the World.

Concentration   Patterned after the popular card game, vocabulary concentration relies on card pairs containing a term on one and a definitional statement on another.

1. Tape the cards containing the terms to one section of the board; randomly tape the cards containing the definitional statements on another section.
2. Students playing either individually, in pairs, or in small groups then direct the teacher or an assistant to uncover one card from each section. If a matching pair is uncovered, the students keep it and try to match another pair. If they do not make a match, the next set of students tries.
3. When all the pairs are matched, students determine who uncovered the most pairs.

Twenty Questions   One student silently holds in mind a word from the unit's vocabulary list. Other students then take turns asking yes–no questions—no more than twenty—to determine the word that was selected. One particular questioner might continue until he or she receives a "no," or questioners might be allowed to ask only one question at a time to allow greater participation. Questions should progress from general to specific.

Jeopardy   Patterned after the popular television show, Jeopardy contains columns with about five terms in each column, arranged from simple to difficult. The columns might be headed by unit categories (e.g., sedimentary rocks, metamorphic rocks, methods of erosion) or simply by letters.

A	B	C	D
5	5	5	5
10	10	10	10
15	15	15	15
20	20	20	20
25	25	25	25

Students then select a cell (e.g., "C for 15"), listen to the definitional statement, and attempt to produce the appropriate term.

Whatta' Ya' Know Put two words together in a way that students can answer only with "yes" or "no." You or your students can be the ones to make up the sentences. The responses can be written or stated orally, and hands can be raised for yes and then for no. For instance, the following questions might be asked about words associated with *volcanoes*:

1. Do *igneous* rocks come from *magma*?
2. Are *volcanoes* made from *lava*?
3. Would you find *igneous* rocks around *volcanoes*?
4. *Magma* is what *lava* is called when it's under the ground.

Be sure to talk about students' reasons for deciding whether two things can go together as stated in the sentences. Points can be kept for appropriate responses if desired.

Teach Word Learning Strategies

So far, this chapter mostly has stressed teacher-directed vocabulary development. The teacher selects words to study intensively. The teacher designates whether to conduct a scavenger hunt or form analogies. The teacher reviews words with Word Books or Around the World. To help students become truly independent word learners, especially when reading widely on their own, teachers must encourage independent strategies (Edwards, Font, Baumann, & Boland, 2004). Here are some ways to accomplish this goal.

Context Power

Do you know what a jingo is? Imagine that you are reading and come across the unknown word *jingo* in this context:

> All he ever talked about was war. His country was the best country, and anyone who disagreed should be ready to fight in battle. He was really quite a jingo!

You could now infer that a jingo must be a militaristic person ready to defend his or her country (or have someone else defend it) at the drop of a hat. The word *jingo* may have been unfamiliar, but if you have had experience with nationalistic, militaristic people, the concept was not. The context helped you associate your old meaning with a new label. Context is a valuable tool for associating meaning with words, because once you learn how to use context, you can do so independently without a teacher's help. Many students, however, do not make proficient use of context. They do not know how surrounding words often give clues to an unfamiliar word.

There are a variety of context clues, and you should try to use all the common types so that students become familiar with them. Common types of context clues include explanatory sentences, as in the jingo example; synonyms ("mean, cruel, and truculent"); antonyms ("Some things are easy, others are arduous"); similes and metaphors ("as fervid as a stove"); and appositives ("the pandowdy, a pudding made with apples"). Once you have chosen words, the steps of Context Power are as follows:

1. *Display the words without the context clues and have students work out the meaning.* Pronounce each word and have students pronounce it with you. Have students produce a meaning for each word.

2. *Display the word in its context and have students interpret the meaning a second time.* Emphasize that context only gives us clues to words, and sometimes these clues can lead us astray. Our ideas about what a word means when we see it in context should be considered tentative. Our context-based guesses, however, are more likely to be right than the guesses we make without any context.

3. *As students determine what words mean based on context, have them explain how the context clues helped.* Do not settle for "It said so." Students who do not understand how context clues are contained in language do not see what is obvious to those of us who do know how our language system gives clues. Through your questions, get students to explain the obvious: "*Mean* and *cruel* mean almost the same, so *truculent* probably does, too." "Stoves are hot; if something is as fervid as a stove, it must be hot, too." "The commas around 'a pudding made with apples' tell you that it is the same as pandowdy."

4. *As each word is defined from context and the reasoning behind the definition is explained, have a volunteer look up the word in the dictionary and read the appropriate definition to the class.* This reinforces the notion that minimal context gives only clues, not certain answers, and it models for students using the dictionary to check hunches and gain more precise information.

5. *Have students apply the context strategy by finding some unfamiliar words in their books and deriving meanings from the book context.*

In addition to these lessons, content teachers have the opportunity on a daily basis to explore with students how context helps figure out meaning for words (Harmon, 2002). When you and your class encounter a word whose meaning even you—the teacher—are not absolutely sure of, that is a perfect opportunity to model authentically how you use context as your first line of attack on a new word. In the next section of this chapter, we discuss the role that morphemes play in figuring out meaning for big words. Context and morphemic sophistication are a powerful combination for learning new word meanings.

Morpheme Power

Here is the first sentence from a *USA Today* article in which all the words of three or more syllables have been replaced with X's.

French XXXXXXXXX are XXXXXXXXX ways to XXXXXXXXX should the United States enforce laws XXXXXXXXXXX XXXXXXXXXXXXX trade with Cuba, Iran, and Libya.

You can easily see that without some ability to pronounce and access meanings for these words, comprehension would be impossible. Now, read the sentence again and put these words where the X's were: *officials, exploring, retaliate, restricting, international*.

Imagine that you are teaching a unit in economics class on international trade, and you want your students to write a letter to the editor expressing their opinions related to this topic. Writing a sensible letter would be impossible unless they could use some of these big, specific words in their writing. Even if you allow them to spell the words as best they can on a first draft and then fix them on a final draft, they must be able to remember the words and make some attempt at spelling them, or their writing will not reflect the kind of thinking you want them to do.

The simple truth is that learning about any content area topic requires students to learn to speak, understand, read, and write a new vocabulary. Throughout this chapter, we have emphasized strategies you can use to teach new vocabulary, but your students are going to meet many more words than you can possibly teach, and if they have a "skip it" or "quit reading" reaction to text with lots of big, not-immediately-familiar words, they are not going to be able to read much independently. This sets off a vicious downward cycle because vocabulary is developed primarily through wide reading, and students who avoid reading are cut off from this most important source of vocabulary development.

Let's look again at those five words your students might not have immediately recognized:

officials, exploring, retaliate, restricting, international

Two of these words, *exploring* and *restricting*, are what linguists call "morphologically transparent," that is, they are related to smaller words and would be almost instantly identified by a reader who knew the words *explore* and *restrict*. Two other words, *officials* and *international*, also have related words, but it requires a level of "morphological sophistication" to recognize the similarities. The word *officials* is related to the words *office* and *officers* and also to words such as *nationals* and *professionals*. *International* is related to the word *nation* and also to *interstate* and *intersection*. The only word for which many readers would not have some related words to help them figure out its pronunciation and meaning is *retaliate*.

The English language contains innumerable word families based on common morphemes (Venezky, 1999). (*Morphemes* are meaning-bearing parts of words, including suffixes, prefixes, and roots.) Linguists estimate that for every word you learn, you can transfer some part of its pronunciation, spelling, and meaning to seven other words! That is the good news. The bad news is that in order to do this transferring, you have to notice the letters, sounds, and meanings that words share! Even many high-school students have not noticed common word parts!

Of the ten thousand new words students from fifth grade and up encounter in school each year, only one thousand are probably truly new words, not related to other more familiar words. If we can help our students become more morphologically sophisticated, they will be able to take advantage of these morphological relationships when reading and writing on their own (Henry, 1997; Templeton, 2004). Word Bench is an activity designed to help students notice these relationships.

Word Bench   To help students become aware of the helpful links words share, there are two questions you should get them in the habit of asking themselves:

1. "Do I know any other words that look like this word?"
2. "Are any of these look-alike words related to each other?"

The answer to the first question helps students with spelling the word. The answer to the second question helps students discover what, if any, meaning relationships exist between this new word and others in their meaning vocabulary stores. These two simple questions can be used by every teacher in every subject area. Imagine that students in a mathematics class encounter the new word/phrase:

improper fraction

The teacher demonstrates and gives examples of these fractions and helps build meaning for the concept. Finally, make use of an instructional routine that focuses attention on the inner parts of words. Display a unit's word on an overhead projector, saying that this is the *wordbench*, something like a *workbench* where carpenters and mechanics assemble and reassemble objects. In this case, the objects are words. The teacher asks the students to pronounce and look at both words and see if they know any other words that look like these words: For *improper*, students might think of

impossible, important, impatient, imported
property, properly, proper
super, paper, kidnapper

For *fraction*, they might think of

fracture, motion, vacation, multiplication, addition, subtraction

The teacher lists the words, underlining the parts that are the same. The teacher then points out to the students that thinking of a word that looks the same as a new word will help them quickly remember how to spell the new word.

Next the teacher explains that words, like people, sometimes look alike but are not related. If this is the first time this analogy is used, the teacher will want to spend some time talking with the students about people with red hair, green eyes, and so on, who have some parts that look alike but are not related and others who are.

"Not all people who look alike are related but some are. This is how words work, too. Words are related if there is something about their meaning that is the same. After we find look-alike words that will help us spell new words, we try to think of any ways these words might be in the same meaning family."

With help from the teacher, the students may discover that *impossible* is the opposite of *possible*, *impatient* is the opposite of *patient*, and *improper* is the opposite of *proper*. *Proper* and *improper* are clearly relatives! *Impossible*, *impatient*, and *improper* are probably "distant cousins" because they all have *im* making it the opposite. Depending on their word sophistication, someone might be able to point out that a *fracture* is a break into two or more parts and that *fraction* also involves parts.

Imagine that the students who were introduced to improper fractions on Monday by their math teacher using Word Bench and were asked to think of look-alike words and consider if any of these words might be "kinfolks," had a science teacher on Tuesday who is beginning a unit on weather and does some experiments with the students using *thermometers* and *barometers*. At the close of the lesson, the teacher uses Word Bench with these words and helps them notice that the *meters* chunk is pronounced and spelled the same and asks the students if they think these words are just look-alikes or are related to one another. The students conclude that you use them both to measure things and the *meters* chunk must be related to measuring, as in *kilometers*. When asked to think of look-alike words for the first chunk, students think of *baron* for *barometers* but decide these two words are probably not related. For *thermometer*, they think of *thermal* and *thermostat* and decide that all these words have to do with heat or temperature.

Now imagine that this lucky class of students has a social studies teacher on Wednesday who uses Word Bench to point out the new word *international* and asks the two critical questions, an art teacher on Thursday who has them do the same with *sculpture*, and an English teacher on Friday with whom they encounter the new word *personify*. Such instruction benefits all students, and it is especially appropriate for Spanish-speaking English Language Learners when they capitalize on Spanish-English cognates (e.g., violencia/violence, farmacia/pharmacy) (Carlo et al., 2004).

Throughout their school day, our students from the intermediate grades up encounter many new words. Because English is such a morphologically related language, most new words can be connected to other words by their spelling, and many new words have meaning-related words already known to the student. Some clever, word-sensitive students become word detectives on their own. They notice the patterns and use these to learn and retrieve words. Others, however, try to learn to pronounce, spell, and associate meaning with each of these words as separate, distinct entities. This is a difficult task which becomes almost impossible as students move through the grades and the number of new words increases each year. Asking the two critical questions for key vocabulary introduced in any content area adds only a few minutes to the introduction of key content vocabulary and pays students back manyfold for that time.

DO IT TOGETHER In a small group or pair preparing to teach the same content subject, discuss the meaning vocabulary teaching and practice strategies described in the last two sections. Choose three of the strategies that your group or pair would be most

likely to use with students during content instruction and write a one-sentence rationale for choosing each. Compare your list and rationales with other groups or pairs who have engaged in the same activity. Did different groups or pairs pick different strategies for different reasons? Is a variety of meaning vocabulary strategies called for?

Dictionary Power

As you began this chapter on vocabulary, did you expect to find a chapter full of dictionary activities? That expectation is reasonable when you consider the experience you have probably had with vocabulary activities throughout your schooling. The most common vocabulary activity in classrooms at all levels is to assign students to look up words and write their definitions. This frustrating practice is like expecting that you could get to know some new people by looking them up in *Who's Who* and writing down their distinguishing characteristics. Such an activity is helpful only if you already know something about the people and want to find out more. In the same way, dictionaries are wonderful resources for adding to or clarifying a word's meaning.

Students need to see how real people use the dictionary. Real people do not look up lists of words and write definitions that they memorize for a test. Real people consult a dictionary when they cannot figure out the meaning of a word they encounter in their reading. They look up a word they know a little about when they meet it in a new context and need some clarification or elaboration on its meaning. Sometimes a dictionary is used in the real world to check the spelling of a word needed in writing.

All teachers should keep a dictionary handy and model its real use. When students meet a new word and ask what it means, you may respond with a little information and then say, "I don't really know exactly what that means. Let's look it up and find out." As described in the context power lesson, you can have students use the dictionary to check or flesh out a meaning derived from context. When you are at the board recording a brainstormed list or some other student-generated responses, they can model how to check the spelling of a word of which you are unsure. Showing students that you, the teacher, see the dictionary as the natural tool to discover and clarify meanings and check spelling will go a long way toward making them independent vocabulary learners.

LISTEN, LOOK, AND LEARN   Interview three of your friends about their vocabulary remembrances: Are they logophiles or do they suffer from logophobia? Do they remember teachers who were word wizards? Do they remember looking words up and writing the definitions? How did this affect how they felt about the dictionary? Do they use a dictionary now, and how do they use it? Ask them also if they remember teachers that let the class choose the important words and let students

plan lessons to teach the words. What did they think of these activities? If they never experienced this, ask them to decide if they thought these types of experiences would have made them more independent word acquirers.

Specific Content Area Applications

Vocabulary in English/Language Arts Classrooms

Two primary goals of reading novels, short stories, plays, and poetry is to gain insights into the human condition and to participate vicariously in the text worlds authors create. To accomplish these goals, readers must understand the words they encounter. Understanding vocabulary, then, is the means to the end of literary insights and experiences. Understanding vocabulary is not the end.

Effective English teachers perform a balancing act when addressing vocabulary: they work at developing word understandings while keeping those understandings subservient to the larger purposes for which students read. They achieve balance before students read by teaching the specific word meanings needed to grasp overall passage meanings. Effective English teachers achieve balance after reading by focusing attention on the key words that elicited the messages and experiences students gained. This balancing act fits situations involving single passages as well as multiple passages.

Single Passages   To consider effective ways to promote vocabulary when students are reading a single passage, think of *Shabanu, Daughter of the Wind*, the novel addressed in Chapter 5 (pages 117–119). Vocabulary learning readily can be folded into the study of this piece of literature.

Before students read *Shabanu*, introducing unfamiliar words that are crucial to understanding a section but are not fully explained is a good way to balance vocabulary and passage understandings. To illustrate, desert *oases* play a large role in *Shabanu*. Readers who lack clear and extensive understandings of this term risk substantial difficulties with the novel because it assumes readers already know about oases. Presenting the word in depth to students before they read the book is appropriate. As part of the introduction to the novel, you display *oasis* before the class and call attention to its pronunciation, then develop in-depth knowledge of its meaning. You ask students to call up what they already know about oases, present pictures and videos of them, and create analogies. You connect this individual term to the overall novel by explaining how it is a central part of the setting.

Folding vocabulary instruction into the study of *Shabanu* also can be done in the during- and after-reading phases. Asking students, "What is the most important word in this section?" and discussing their choices goes far in promoting active comprehension and in-depth vocabulary learning. A student who selects *storm* for the scene in which Shabanu's grandfather dies might focus on the denotations and connotations of this word. What exactly is a storm? Does *storm* refer to a physical weather disturbance or to characters' turmoil? How can personal relationships or the course of one's life be stormy?

If students are maintaining response journals for *Shabanu*, some of the writing prompts can highlight vocabulary. Offering a menu of prompts allows readers to select a vocabulary response format they find most productive. For instance, students illustrate the meanings of three words from a chapter (e.g., show people wearing *chadors* and *turbans* or having their bodies painted with *henna*). They present word families (pilgrim, pilgrimage; nomad, nomadic). They maintain a list of "words I should learn more about" for weekly follow-ups, or they complete vocabulary self-assessment scales of words that peers select. Students maintain a "language gems" section in their journals for recording vivid comparisons, strong verbs, and other phrases they find compelling.

Multiple Passages   A standard recommended practice for increasing vocabularies is for students to read widely in materials that are within their capabilities. This recommendation is based in part on realizations of the inefficiency of teaching isolated terms in a word-by-word fashion. A large volume of reading provides students opportunities to encounter the thousands of new terms they need to develop their vocabularies.

English teachers who stimulate their students to read widely for pleasure and for academics certainly assist vocabulary development, but additional actions are needed to enhance the impact of this practice. Because it is impossible to introduce unfamiliar words that are crucial to understanding a section when each student selects his or her own materials, focusing on vocabulary in the during and after phases of self-selected reading is appropriate.

A good way to incorporate word study while students are reading on their own is to have them maintain journals with a section devoted to vocabulary. Students select their own materials for silent reading, and they enter into their journals sections of text that contain words or phrases find appealing, that they want to remember, and that they believe deserve sharing with classmates. They might cite author, title, and page number for each section they record. About once a week students share what they have recorded, and they engage their peers in a discussion of the passage context and meaningful word parts (if any) that determine the word's meaning. Students might first meet in groups to nominate one they consider most important for class consideration. When group representatives present their words to the class, they explain why they believe others should know them by articulating their contribution to the unit of study being conducted. Favorite sections might be gathered, posted on a bulletin board, and published every few weeks in a class anthology.

Vocabulary in Second-Language Classrooms

Understanding the words of a second language is only part of understanding the second language, but it is a crucial part. Here are some ways to build on the suggestions presented in this chapter when teaching word meanings to learners of a second language.

Scavenger Hunts   Realia and visual aids are used in many second language classrooms to teach vocabulary meaningfully. One way to add to these concrete teaching tools is by enlisting students' help through scavenger hunts. Present a list of terms for each instructional unit, and have students individually or in groups bring in concrete objects, models, pictures, and illustrations that represent the terms. Afterwards, you have an almost instant bulletin board or display table for introducing and practicing vocabulary.

Looking beyond obvious sources and representations is a good way to extend what you gather during scavenger hunts. For instance, children's action figures, dolls, and other toy people often come with physical settings such as dollhouses, forts, and farms. Leading your class to describe the locations and actions of scenes ("The man is hiding behind the large house hoping to surprise the enemy.") can result in active participation and meaningful applications of terms. You also might provide well-illustrated magazines for students to scavenge during class time. Calendars, catalogues, and newspapers are other frequently untapped teaching aids that provide useful tools for promoting second-language vocabularies.

Capsule Vocabulary   The capsule vocabulary teaching strategy provides students good practice using the vocabulary of a second language. In this strategy, you first present the pronunciations and meanings of topically related words (e.g., fruits), then students use these words (e.g., apples, oranges, bananas) while conversing with each other. This strategy is most productive when the terms refer to common concepts that require little explanation, because the emphasis here is on students practicing and applying new terms in a supportive setting. Capsule Vocabulary stresses attaching labels to concepts already understood more than developing conceptual knowledge.

Several options are available for practicing the Capsule Vocabularies that are introduced. Using the words in oral conversations certainly is appropriate. In written conversations, or buddy journals, students take turns composing notes to each other in a manner similar to the surreptitious note passing that sometimes occurs during class. Written conversations are like pen pal situations; however, the pals are in the same classroom and they are using certain terms associated with units of study.

Another Capsule Vocabulary practice option is for students to write one term each on a card and categorize the cards in whatever groupings come to mind. Additionally, students might write sentences with each one containing two or three target terms. The class could play Twenty Questions in the second language, a game in which one word is selected and players try to determine what it is by asking yes–no questions ("Is it an animal?" "Is it four-legged?" "Is it domestic?"). Charades and Password are two other games appropriate for practicing Capsule Vocabulary Terms.

Using Cognates   Successful readers of second languages often apply their knowledge of word cognates when they encounter unfamiliar vocabulary. Cognates are words derived from a common earlier form. Spanish and English have especially large numbers of cognates due to their historical bases in Latin. Here are some Spanish–English cognates:

naturalmente	naturally	novelas	novels
clima	climate	decidir	decide
curioso	curious	farmacia	pharmacy

Using cognates to help understand and remember unfamiliar words involves several mental operations. Learners identify unfamiliar words that justify the time and energy to be figured out, they examine target words' spellings and pronunciations to determine if they might be cognates of known words, and they test possible meanings for the unfamiliar words in the contexts of the passages to decide upon specific meanings.

Teaching students to transfer their knowledge of word meanings in one language to help in another can be done according to the recommendations in this chapter for teaching morphological sophistication. Indeed, a shared morpheme is what makes up a cognate pair. In essence, students act as detectives when figuring out word meanings, and cognate relationships are powerful clues to solving the mystery of what many words mean. When attention is directed to long unfamiliar words, remind students to ask themselves,

"Do I know any other words that look like this word?"
"Are any of these look-alike words related to each other?"

And when meanings are suggested through possible cognates, have students ask themselves,

"Does my understanding of this word make sense in this passage?"

Consider the following description by a Mexican American woman of one of the healing plants in her garden:

Estas hojas tienas se hiervan para hacer un te. Este te es para los diabeticos. Ellos lo toman para su enfermedad. (These tender leaves are boiled to make a tea. This tea is for diabetics. They drink it for their illness.) (Brozo, Valerio, & Salazar, 1996, p. 164)

Te–tea and *diabeticos–diabetics* are two word pairs with obvious cognate relationships. Students could be expected to capitalize on these relationships when assigning meaning to what they read. Somewhat more obscure relationships are apparent in *un–a* and *enfermedad–illness*. Explaining that the *un* in *unit*, *unite*, and *union* refers to *one* or *single* and that *infirmity* is a synonym for *illness* would offer students powerful clues for understanding and remembering the meanings of *un* and *enfermedad*.

Vocabulary in Mathematics Classrooms

When most people think of mathematics they think of numbers, but math is a subject with its own very particular vocabulary, and if you don't know precisely what its words and symbols mean, you just can't do mathematics! Here are some activities teachers use which help students master the language of math.

A Symbol Board   Cover a bulletin board or attach a banner to your wall and add symbols to it as they are introduced. Put the symbol and a "class-created, user-friendly" definition. Add pictures and opposites as appropriate. Use different colored markers and make it as appealing as possible

Math Morphemes   The Word Bench activity in which you ask your students if they know any other words that look and sound like a new mathematics term and if they think any of these words might be related will help your students become more morphologically sophisticated. In addition, you have the unique opportunity to teach your students the meaning for some morphemes that occur most commonly in mathematics words. Seize this opportunity when introducing one of these words because your students might not meet these morphemes in any of their other classes:

Morpheme	Math Usage	General Usage
bi (two)	bisect, binomial, bimodal	bicycle, bifocals, bilingual
cent (hundred)	centimeter, percent	century, centipede
circu (around)	circle, circumference	circumvent, circumstances
co, con (with)	coefficient, cosine, collinear	cocaptains, coordinate, concurrent
dec (ten)	decimal, decagon	decade, decibel
dia (through)	diagonal, diameter	dialogue, diagram
equi (equal)	equilateral, equiangular	equator, equinox, equitable
inter (between)	intersect, interpolate	interception, international
kilo (thousand)	kilometer, kilogram	kilowatt
milli (thousand)	millimeter, milligram	millennium, million
peri (around)	perimeter	periphery, periscope, periodontal
poly (many)	polygon, polynomial	polygamy, polyunsaturated
quadr (four)	quadrant, quadruple	quadrangle, quadruped
tri (three)	triangle, triple	tricycle, tripod, trilogy

Multimeaning Luck   Math has more than its share of words such as *base*, *product*, *power*, *point*, and *ray* for which students have one meaning but for which they need to develop a math-related concept. Multimeaning Luck is a fun activity to review the mathematical meaning for these words. Prepare for the lesson by writing down each word, with one math-related and one non-math-related definition. (Overhead transparencies work best for this lesson, but you can also write the words on the board.) On the bottom of the transparency or on a part of the board you can cover temporarily, write one sentence for each word. Be sure to include in these sentences both math-related and unrelated meanings, as students will have to guess which definition your sentence uses. If you use only math-related meanings, they will easily figure out the system. The following is a sample lesson.

Begin the lesson by displaying the words and their two definitions:

times   1. multiplied by
         2. periods of life
gross   1. disgusting
         2. 12 dozen
line   1. a piece of rope, cord, wire, or string
         2. the shortest distance between two points
mean   1. unkind
         2. average
face   1. front part of the head
         2. any surface of a solid figure

As you read each word and its two definitions, have each student write the word and a 1 or 2 to indicate a guess of which meaning you have used in the covered sentences. Be sure to tell students that doing well on this part of the lesson is simply a matter of luck. You may want to tell students this is a way to find out how their luck is running today.

When all students have made their guesses, display the sentences one at a time. Have students give themselves five points for every lucky guess and deduct five points for every unlucky guess. The person with the most points is the lucky person for the day. Once lucky and unlucky persons have been applauded and commiserated with, respectively, review the math definitions and remind your students that they will often find words in math for which they have other meanings, and that they must not let those words lead them astray but must try to figure out and remember the mathematical meaning.

Are you curious as to how you did with your guesses? If so, you will see one of the advantages of Multimeaning Luck. Once you have made a guess, you want to know how you did. You care about and pay attention to which meanings the multimeaning words had. Here are your sentences.

We had some good times together.
She ordered a gross of pencils.
I've got a huge fish out here on my line.
The mean temperature for Hawaii in July is 84 degrees.
My aunt is in the hospital having a face-lift.

Give yourself five points for every lucky guess and subtract five for every unlucky guess. Are you having a lucky day? Did you pick only the math-related meanings even though we told you to include others?

Vocabulary in Science Classrooms

Could You Say That in English?   Each content area has unique vocabulary, but the technical vocabulary load in science is probably greater than in any other subject. Look at the "key vocabulary" listed for each chapter and you will often find thirty to fifty words. If you are going to follow the ten-words-a-week guideline, you would need about a month to teach each chapter, and the typical textbook contains thirty or more chapters! It can't be done! Another problem is that much of the vocabulary used in science falls into the lupulin/lupulone category—students know neither the word nor the concept—rather than the lunules/philtrum/avuncular category in which students have the concept but simply lack the label. One advantage that science teachers have is that much of their class time is spent with hands-on activities and experiments that are intended to provide the direct experience essential for building meanings for these completely new concepts. Generally, the hands-on experience should occur first and then students should be led to attach the associated vocabulary with the phenomena experienced.

Science teachers must be ruthless about limiting the number of words, following guidelines listed earlier. Textbook and curriculum guide writers often list all words not apt to be known by students without consideration for the fact that some listed words only occur once and are not essential for understanding the unit, much less the whole discipline. Once you have identified the key vocabulary, it is a good idea to let students know exactly which words it is critical to master. One way to do that is to post critical vocabulary on a board along with a "plain English" translation and/or picture or diagram whenever possible. It is also helpful to show the phonetic pronunciation next to each word because many students have difficulty pronouncing these strange, big words. Psychologists believe that while we can put concepts in our long-term associative memory stores without pronouncing them, retrieval from that memory store often follows an auditory route. Students who cannot pronounce the critical vocabulary may understand what they are reading and what you are telling and demonstrating for them, but they may lack the auditory route to retrieve that information if they have not said the critical words.

Science Morphemes   The Word Bench activity, in which you ask your students if they know any other words that look and sound like a new science term and if they think any of these words might be related, will help your students become more morphologically sophisticated. In addition, you have the unique opportunity to teach your students the meaning for some morphemes that occur most commonly in science words. Seize this opportunity when introducing one of these words, because your students might not notice the morphemes on page 166 in any of their other classes.

Morpheme	Science Usage	General Usage
astro (star)	astronomy, astronaut	astronomical, asterisk
bio (life)	biology, biome, biosphere	biography, antibiotic
chlor (greenish)	chlorophyll, chloroplast	chlorine
eco (habitat)	ecology, ecosystem	economy
hydro (water)	hydrogen, hydroelectric	hydrant, hydroplane
hypo (under)	hypothermia, hypodermis	hypodermic
hyper (too much)	hyperglycemia	hyperactive, hypertension
meta (change)	metamorphosis, metabolism	metaphor
micro (small)	microscope, microorganism	microphone
logy (science)	biology, geology, physiology	psychology

Morpheme	Science Usage	General Usage
photo (light)	photosynthesis, phosphorescent	photograph
sym, syn (together)	symbiosis, symmetry	symphony, synchronize
therm (heat)	thermometer, thermal	thermos, thermostat
vor (eat)	omnivore, herbivore, carnivore	devour, voracious

Vocabulary in Social Studies Classrooms

Fighting Words   In social studies, more than any other subject area, students have to become attuned to the connotations as well as the denotations of words. In describing various events, the point of view of the writer colors the reporting and interpretation of these events, and this point of view is usually evidenced by the words used. To help students become sensitive to word choice and to review important vocabulary, give students lists of words/terms and have them indicate with a plus, check, or minus sign whether they think the word generally has positive, neutral, or negative connotations, respectively. After students complete this activity separately, have them get together with peers and discuss their decisions. This is an activity in which you want them to use the evaluate thinking process. Don't expect everyone to agree, because their point of view will affect their decisions. But, considering the different connotations of common social studies terms will help them be more critical readers and better understand and retain the word meanings. Here are some starter words/terms. Pick similar words from your units.

liberal	conservative	Stars and Stripes
hawk	dove	AFL-CIO
corporation	pro-choice	pro-life
John Bircher	revolutionary	capitalist
reactionary	hillbilly	feminist
media	minority candidate	third world

Social Studies Morphemes   The Word Bench activity in which you ask your students if they know any other words that look and sound like a new social studies term and if they think any of these words might be related will help your students become more morphologically sophisticated. In addition, you have the unique opportunity to teach your students the meaning for some morphemes that occur most commonly in social studies words. Seize this opportunity when introducing one of these words, because your students might not notice these morphemes in any of their other classes:

Morpheme	Social Studies Usage	General Usage
anti (against)	antitrust, antislavery	antibody, antisocial
com, con (with, together)	community, congress, conspiracy	compile, committee, company, conform
counter, contra (against)	counterintelligence, counteroffensive	counterfeit, contradict
ex (out)	exports, explorers	expedition, exit

Morpheme	Social Studies Usage	General Usage
form (shape)	conform, reformers	deformity, formula
geo (earth)	geography, geopolitical	geometry, geology
im, in (in)	imports, immigration, invasion, inauguration	implant, impoverish, indent, intruder
im, in (opposite)	immoral, independence	impatient, inefficient
inter (between)	international, intervention	interrupt, interfere
ism (state of)	communism, capitalism	patriotism
ist (person)	communist, nationalist	pianist, scientist
mono (one, same)	monarchy, monopoly	monorail, monastery
non (opposite)	nonviolence, nonpartisan, nonproliferation	nonprofit, nonstop
sub (under)	subcontinent	subway, substitute
trans (across)	transAtlantic, transcontinental	transport, transfer
uni (one, same)	unilateral, unified, universal	uniform, united

Acronym Board Cover a bulletin board or attach a banner to your wall and add acronyms to it as they occur in your study. List the acronym and the word for which it stands. Have your artistically talented students draw something to symbolize each acronym. Here are some examples of common social studies acronyms:

> AID—Agency for International Development
> CARE—Corporation for American Relief Everywhere
> CORE—Congress of Racial Equality
> SADD—Students Against Drunk Driving
> HUD—Housing and Urban Development
> MIA—Missing In Action
> SNCC—Student Nonviolent Coordinating Committee
> VISTA—Volunteers In Service To America
> WHO—World Health Organization

Vocabulary in Activity Classrooms

In many subjects, the emphasis is on doing rather than on reading and writing. In order to do anything successfully, however, you have to develop the vocabulary—the lingo—of that area. Whether you teach physical education, music, art, a vocational subject, or some other activity-oriented course, your students will learn more and like it more if you expend a small amount of time and effort identifying the key vocabulary in your area and making sure your students attach the appropriate meanings to the words and symbols. Here are some specific activities teachers in nontextbook courses have used to develop meanings for critical words.

Multimeaning Luck In every field there are words with a subject-specific meaning for which students have a more commonly used meaning. Music class can be pretty confusing when the teacher is talking about *keys*, *scales*, and *notes*, and the students are picturing car keys, bathroom scales, and messages to their friends!

Common words such as *rack* and *tolerance* have very specific meanings when used in a mechanics class. Students who are becoming computer experts must realize that you can't fish with this *net*, bet with this *chip*, and shouldn't scream at this *mouse!*

Multimeaning Luck is a fun activity to review the content-specific meaning for words. Prepare for the lesson by writing down each word, with one math-related and one non-computer-related definition. (Overhead transparencies work best for this lesson, but you can also write the words on the board.) On the bottom of the transparency or on a part of the board you can cover temporarily, write one sentence for each word. Be sure to include in these sentences both subject-related and unrelated meanings, as students will have to guess which definition your sentence uses. If you use only subject-related meanings, they will easily figure out the system. Here is a sample lesson from a computer class. Begin the lesson by displaying the words and their two definitions:

menu	1. list of available foods
	2. options in a computer program
boot	1. footwear often used in rain or snow
	2. load an operating system into a computer
ram/RAM	1. Random Access Memory
	2. crash into
virus	1. an infection from a submicroscopic organism
	2. a computer program that can attack other programs
bug	1. error in a program
	2. small insect

As you read each word and its two definitions, have each student write the word and a 1 or 2 to indicate a guess of which meaning you have used in the covered sentences. Be sure to tell students that doing well on this part of the lesson is simply a matter of luck. You may want to tell students this is a way to find out how their luck is running today.

When all students have made their guesses, display the sentences one at a time. Have students give themselves five points for every lucky guess and deduct five points for every unlucky guess. The person with the most points is the lucky person for the day. Once lucky and unlucky persons have been applauded and commiserated with, respectively, review the subject-related definitions. Remind your students that they will often find words in your subject for which they have other meanings, and that they must not let those words lead them astray but must try to figure out and remember the appropriate meaning.

Are you curious as to how you did with your guesses? If so, you will see one of the advantages of Multimeaning Luck. Once you have made a guess, you want to know how you did. You care about and pay attention to which meanings the multimeaning words had. Here are your sentences:

You can check your spelling by pulling down the edit menu.
The only clue at the scene was a size 11 boot print.
I was just sitting there and I saw this car ram right into the house!

I found a virus on my computer.
There must be some kind of bug in this program.

Give yourself five points for every lucky guess and subtract five for every unlucky guess. Are you having a lucky day? Did you pick only the computer-related meanings even though we told you to include others?

Word/Symbol/Picture Board   Fortunately, many of the new meanings that students must learn in activity courses are words that represent concrete, real things. Learning the names of the parts of the lathe becomes a much simpler task when a picture or diagram is displayed with these parts labeled. Coaches have long made use of diagrams for various plays and positions. A music board might display the symbols for *sharp, flat, note, repeat*, and so forth, along with the words for which they stand. A display of art labeled for its style and media catches the eye while simultaneously giving reality to confusing terms such as *impressionist, neoclassical*, and *acrylic*.

Word Detectives   Just as in all areas, many of the new words your students will encounter are big words for which your students have other words that will help them figure out and remember pronunciations, spellings, and meanings. Students in an art class who are dealing with the concepts of *foreground* and *background* and whose attention is drawn to words such as *forehand, forehead, backhand*, and *backpack* should have no trouble understanding and using the new art terms. The strange new words *micrometer, variometer*, and *magnetometer* are not so strange when connected with *speedometer, thermometer, microscope, variations*, and *magnetic*. With a little help, students can even be led to see the "strong" relationship in such words as *fortress, fortitude, fortify*, and *fortissimo*.

   When you are on the lookout for these morphemic relationships between words and point them out to your students, your students benefit in two ways. The obvious benefit is that they can more easily learn your new vocabulary and retain it fairly effortlessly. Less obvious—but actually more important in the "scheme of things"—you help your students become "word detectives" who, whenever they encounter a new word, are apt to look for clues in already-known words and thus can grow independently in vocabulary knowledge from all the reading they do. Not a bad return on a small investment of time and energy!

LOOKING BACK   Having a thorough knowledge of the key words is essential to learning in any content area. The vocabulary of each content area is specific to that area and not apt to occur in normal conversation, recreational reading, or television viewing. All content area teachers must teach the vocabulary essential to communicating about their subject. These are the keys you explored in this chapter: (1) Vocabulary development is complex; (2) promote wide reading, (3) teach sets of words directly, (4) promote word consciousness, and (5) teach word learning strategies.

ADD TO YOUR JOURNAL   Reflect upon the five key ideas in this chapter and decide what you think: Do you remember learning words through direct and visual experience? Can you think of words for which you have had no experience and that you learned by connecting them to known words? Do you remember teachers who worked hard to provide you with direct experiences? Do you remember taking field trips? Engaging in simulations? Building models? Do you remember teachers who used films and videos effectively? Can you think of ways in which teachers tried to develop abstract concepts by creating analogies to real situations? Did any teacher help you learn to use context or become morphologically sophisticated? Think about the teaching strategies described. Which ones could you most profitably use in your content area? Finally, think about independence. Students will not always have you there to ferret out the critical words and devise nifty ways to learn them. What will you do to make your students independent word learners?

Additional Readings

Some notable books devoted specifically to vocabulary instruction are as follows:

ALLEN, J. (1999). *Words, words, words*. York, ME: Stenhouse Publishers.

BAUMANN, J., & KAME'ENUI, E. J. (Eds.) (2004). *Vocabulary instruction: Research to practice*. New York: The Guilford Press.

BEAR, D., INVERNIZZI, M., TEMPLETON, S., & JOHNSTON, F. (2003). *Words their way: Word study for phonics, vocabulary, and spelling instruction* (3rd ed.). Englewood Cliffs, NJ: Prentice-Hall.

BECK, I. L., MCKEOWN, M. G., & KUCAN, L. (2002). *Bringing words to life: Robust vocabulary instruction*. New York: The Guilford Press.

BLACHOWICZ, C., & FISHER, P. (2002). *Teaching vocabulary in all classrooms* (2nd ed.). Upper Saddle River, NJ: Merrill Prentice Hall.

GANSKE, K. (2000). *Word journeys: Assessment-guided phonics, spelling, and vocabulary instruction*. New York: The Guilford Press.

Books like the following that present the origins of peculiar English words and phrases help develop your and your students' word consciousness:

ASIMOV, I. (1969). *Words of science and the history behind them*. New York: New American Library. (Asimov has written many insightful books on English; all are recommended.)

BARNHART, R. K. (Ed.). (1995). *The Barnhart concise dictionary of etymology*. New York: HarperCollins.

CIARDI, J. (2001). *A third browser's dictionary*. New York: Akadine Press. (Ciardi's first two browsers' dictionaries also provide insight into curious English formations.)

LEDERER, R. (1991). *The play of words*. New York: Pocket Books. (Lederer has produced many joyful books on English; all are recommended.)

SAFIRE, W. (2004). *The right word in the right place at the right time*. New York: Simon & Schuster. (This book is one of several Safire has published that consist of collections of his weekly *New York Times* magazine column, *On Language*. These are rather sophisticated entries.)

7

Writing

Writing is thinking you do with a pen, pencil, or word processor. Because writing is primarily thinking, you use some or all of the thinking processes as you write. Students who write about what they are learning are engaged in thinking. In order to write, students call up what they know and even seek out more information or clarifications. They show the connections they have made. Writing is an application of new knowledge. As people write, they monitor what they know, what they think, and how well they are communicating. Teachers support students' thinking by planning and carrying out instruction in which the writing tasks are made clear and the fulfillment of these purposes is ensured by group sharing and feedback.

Writing is thinking made external. When we write, we record our thoughts and discover new thoughts. Writing, like reading, has before, during, and after phases. Thinking pervades all these writing phases. If you come upon someone who is sitting with a pen in hand or fingertips poised over the keyboard and staring at the blank page or screen, you might ask, "What are you doing?" The person will often respond, "I'm thinking."

Continuing to observe, you will see the person eventually move into the writing phase, but the writing is not nonstop. If you are rude enough to interrupt during one of these pauses and ask, "What are you doing?" the writer will probably again respond, "I'm thinking." Eventually, the writer will finish the writing, or more accurately, finish the first draft. The writer may put the writing away for a while or ask someone to "take a look at this and tell me what you think." Later the writer will return to the writing to revise and edit. Words will be changed and paragraphs added, moved, or deleted. Again, the writer will pause from time to time during this after-writing phase; if you ask the writer what he or she is doing, you will likely get the familiar response, "I'm thinking!"

We offer this common scenario to show that writing is, at its essence, thinking. Because writing is thinking and learning requires thinking, students who write as they are learning think more and thus learn more (Bangert-Downs, Hurley, & Wilkinson, 2004; Newell, 2005). The following three keys head the contents of this chapter:

1. Vary informal writing.
2. Guide writers through challenging tasks.
3. Teach writing strategies.

Vary Informal Writing

Informal writing can take just a few minutes but can help students focus on what they know, what they don't know, and what they think. In some classrooms, students regularly record short bursts of thoughts about a topic and keep daily journals which record their ideas, questions, and feelings throughout a unit. In this section we describe two types of informal writing—quick writes and content journals—that can occur on a daily basis in almost any class and that serve a multitude of purposes.

Quick Writes

1. We are about to begin learning about machines. Take thirty seconds and write down all the words you think of when you think of machines. The clock starts now!
2. Before we begin our exploration of matter, write down everything you know about matter. You have one minute.
3. We have been talking about communities today. Write one sentence in which you come up with your own definition for community. Try to include the big ideas we have talked about.
4. We have been learning about habitats. List as many habitats as you can in thirty seconds.
5. Today's math lesson had some difficult concepts. We will work more on this tomorrow. List at least one thing you don't fully understand.
6. I didn't hear from many of you today and I am wondering what you are thinking. Tell me in a sentence or two what you thought of today's activity.
7. The topics of race and prejudice are emotional ones. Tell me in a few sentences how you are feeling about the difficult issues we have talked about today.

These are all examples of quick writes used in content area classrooms. Quick writes are the least formal kind of writing and in some ways the easiest ones to fit into a crowded content curriculum. Quick writes are used for a variety of purposes.

- Examples 1 and 2 are previewing quick writes, intended to help both students and teacher assess the entry-level knowledge of the class about a new topic.
- Examples 3 and 4 are quick writes that help students synthesize the day's learning and let teachers know how well the concepts were understood.
- Examples 5, 6, and 7 are self-assessment quick writes. Students have to assess their understanding, their involvement, their attitudes, and their emotions.

By reading these quick writes, teachers could determine common confusions, evaluate the success of the activity, and determine if an emotional topic under consideration was at or beyond students' comfort level.

What you do with quick writes depends on why you did them and how much time you have. If the quick writes are like examples 1 and 2 and intended to get students accessing prior knowledge and thinking about a topic, use them for a unit's introductory grabber as Chapter 3 suggested. You may want to have students tell what they have written down as you list this on the board and point out that this is the starting point, the "what we know" from Chapter 5. You may also ask volunteers to share what they have written in response to examples 3 and 4 in order to let students see how others defined *community* or how many habitats they have listed. This helps students cement their learning and monitor their level of understanding.

Sometimes teachers collect the quick writes, telling students that these will help guide the planning of tomorrow's activity. In this case, you may want to ask students not to put their names on quick writes to make sure students know you are evaluating the lesson, class learning, mood, and so forth, and not individual students. Many teachers hand students small index cards for these assessment quick writes. Because of their size and their "real world" uses, index cards are unintimidating and help students to view this writing as different from some of the other more formal class assignments. Collecting the cards as an informal exit slip is a good way to manage this practice and bring closure to the day's lesson (Andrews, 1997).

Cubing *Cubing* is a quick-write practice that emphasizes different purposes for writing about the same topic (Readence, Bean, & Baldwin, 2000). The name, *cubing*, comes from the practice of designating a purpose for each side of a cube (totaling six), then rolling it to see which one emerges. Cubing is a good way to practice writing; many teachers use it to prepare students for state-level writing assessments. The way we have seen it practiced most commonly differs from process-writing approaches that emphasize continual shuttling among planning, drafting, and revising to produce finished products. Cubing seems to have become a fast-paced approach that emphasizes short bursts of output. Students have relatively brief amounts of time to produce final products.

You might designate writing purposes that correspond with your state tests along with ones considered important in their own right. For instance, given any topic, students might set out to perform the following:

- *Narrate*: Tell a story connected with it.
- *Persuade*: Convince someone of an assertion about it.
- *Explain*: Specify its parts and compare it with others.
- *Apply*: Describe how it can be—or might be—used.
- *Image*: Portray it through an art or craft and describe the portrayal.
- *Synthesize*: Present conclusions, or generalizations, about it.

First, teach students how to perform each of the tasks with simple topics. Then randomly select one for students to accomplish in a brief amount of time. If the Grand Canyon were the lesson topic, students might have the following purposes:

- Narrate a story with the Grand Canyon as the physical setting.
- Persuade potential tourists that the canyon truly is grand.
- Explain how natural forces carved the canyon.
- Apply understandings of the Grand Canyon's formation to future land formations.
- Create an image of the Grand Canyon, depicting its strata, and describe each layer.
- Present generalizations about land formation based on what the Grand Canyon and other formations reveal.

Like most teaching practices, cubing can be modified multiple ways. You might gradually decrease the amount of time students have to complete the tasks, generating excitement while inducing concentration on writing. You might randomly or selectively assign one or several tasks. You might have students complete all six tasks, with you or them designating the order of completion. You might include one purpose (e.g., persuade) more than once and delete another (e.g., image) according to curricular emphases. Cubing can be performed readily with topics as diverse as the Grand Canyon, cell division, fractions, and personal identity.

Timed Writing   Timed Writing reflects the on-demand time-sensitive writing people frequently do for reports, proposals, and correspondence such as e-mail (Gere, Christenbury, & Sassi, 2005). It is designed to promote written fluency, to accelerate the flow of written words. Timed Writing is meant to promote a habit of focusing and producing text quickly. In content area classrooms, it directs students to concentrate on aspects of the current topic of study.

The inclusion of Timed Writing in many state tests, as well as in the SAT and ACT college entrance exams, has encouraged its practice in many classrooms. During Timed Writing, students compose in response to a prompt or choice of prompts for a specified amount of time, from thirty seconds to an entire class period. Note that the first two quick writes listed earlier contain a time deadline:

- We are about to begin learning about machines. Take **thirty seconds**, and write down all the words you think of when you think of machines. The clock starts now!
- Before we begin our exploration of matter, write down everything you know about matter. You have **one minute**.

These quick write/timed writes allow very brief amounts of time because they are meant only to help students call up prior knowledge. Others might allow more time for composing better-developed thoughts, although a deadline still is vigorously enforced.

When students produce timed writings, you might select particular groups for editing and assessing (Fisher & Fry, 2003). They might edit first at home, then at school, before submitting the preliminary and final drafts to you for assessment. This practice helps you manage the paper load by dealing only with selected groups, and it focuses students' attention on their writing when they realize you could randomly select them.

Content Journals

We hope that you have been keeping the journal suggested at the end of each chapter. This is just one example of a content journal. A content journal is a place for students to record their personal insights, questions, confusions, disagreements, and frustrations about what is being learned (Abrams, 2000; Bromley, 1999). (Some teachers call these journals *learning logs*.) Journal writing is primarily writing students do for themselves; it helps them sort out what they think about what they are learning.

Content journals may have a great deal of structure or very little. When there is little structure, students choose what to write about. One student might write a diary-style account of what was learned, while another might write a letter to the teacher, complete with visuals, explaining his or her reaction to what is being studied. When students have control over the specific content they are writing about, the journals are said to have *low structure*.

With *high-structure* content journals, the teacher requires students to react to specific ideas they are exploring in class. Students may be asked to explore some controversial issue associated with the content. For instance, if westward expansion were the unit of study in American history, students might be asked to record their impressions of the similarities between nineteenth-century movement by U.S. citizens into Texas and twentieth-century movement by Mexican citizens into Texas. Students could be asked to call up impressions they had before beginning the class and compare them with their current impressions. They might be asked to summarize chapters or articles they are reading. The structure is high because the teacher assigns the writing task; students have little to say about what they are to write.

Typically, students are expected to write in their journals from five to ten minutes each day. Some teachers begin class each day with a five-minute journal-writing time. During the five minutes while students are completing their journal entries, teachers do the routine chores of attendance taking, talking to a student who was absent yesterday, and so on. On some days, a high-structure entry is required and prompted by a sentence or two written on the board. On other days, students write whatever they want related to the topic being studied. Teachers who establish this five-minute beginning-of-class journal-writing routine report that journal writing does not take away from their teaching time, because they must spend a few minutes at the beginning of each class with routine chores, and that students settle in and get back into the content of the class much more readily.

Journals are collected several times a term in order to make sure that students have been writing regularly, and in order to determine whether students are learning course content and reacting thoughtfully to the ideas they are encountering. While reading the journals, some teachers write comments to the students, creating a written dialogue, about how well students are learning the course material and how clearly they express what they have learned. Students' attitudes and efforts regarding journal writing seem to be directly related to the frequency and quality of a teacher's comments in the journals. Weekly reactions are ideal, although bi-weekly or monthly input is generally more feasible. Most teachers don't grade each journal entry, but they do give students points for keeping their journal up to date and for demonstrating good thinking.

TRY IT OUT

Think about a unit you will be teaching. Come up with three quick writes, one each for previewing, synthesizing, and self-assessment. Write down each including how much time you would give students or how many words, sentences, and so forth, you want them to write. Next come up with three prompts for high-structure journal entries that your students could complete in five to ten minutes.

Students explore their feelings and reactions to classroom experiences by writing in journals.

Guide Writers Through Challenging Tasks

Imagine that you have a frame for a particular instructional unit as described in Chapter 3, and you are satisfied with your standards-based outcomes, essential question, culminating activities, and so forth. If you have decided that students will do more than write informally during this unit of study—perhaps they will produce an exhibit that features writing—then planning how to guide students through this task is your next step.

Planning Writing Guidance

With regard to planning, as we said about comprehension in Chapter 5, you must decide on clear learning purposes and decide what background knowledge and motivation students would need to achieve these purposes. When planning writing guidance, you follow similar steps.

Deciding What Students Are to Think About   Once you become convinced that the main purpose for writing in a content area classroom is to get students thinking about content topics, then you must decide what you want them to think about. For every unit of study, there is a host of possibilities. Imagine that you are teaching about twins and the incredible similarities that exist between identical twins separated at birth. Here are some issues that you might consider important and that deserve your students' attention:

1. What genetic traits do twins share?
2. What are the advantages and disadvantages of having a twin?
3. How does research on twins help us understand the heredity versus environment issue?

There are many different issues and questions about which you might want students to think. They could be formed into a unit's objective, central question, as well as culminating activity. In doing so, they will use different thinking processes. Almost all writing tasks require students to call up what they know and connect new information. Likewise, students must monitor what they know and are communicating as they write. Students' use of the other thinking processes will depend on what you want them to focus on and the writing task you set for them.

Designing a Writing Task   In Chapter 5, we noted that once you decide what you want students to learn, you should design a task that will focus their attention. When writing, once you know what you want students to think about, you design a writing task that focuses their attention. A writing task has four major components: topic, form, audience, and role.

Topic   The topic is both the "what?" and the "what for?" of writing: the content and the intent. The topic chosen can include what the students will write about and the purpose the writer should attempt to accomplish during writing. In a content class, the writing topic is related to the unit of study and selected so that students focus their thinking.

The best writing topics are narrowed so that the writer knows how to focus attention. Teachers narrow the topic by specifying the intent, or aim, of the writing. Here are some possible intents for writing:

1. Describing
2. Explaining
3. Expressing feelings
4. Narrating
5. Persuading

Form   Form is the medium of writing. How are students going to write about the topic? Are they going to write a poem, a story, an essay, or a newspaper article? Writers use a variety of forms, and their choice of form is related to their topic. For example, your writing on a unit topic might take the form of a play, a letter, a short story, or even a comic strip.

Specifying the form of a passage usually includes specifying its length. Knowing the expected length of their writing helps students understand how much information to include. Imagine that you are assigning a paper describing the metric system. Do you expect the paper to be one page or five pages long? A one-page paper would leave space for few examples, but a five-page paper would need many examples. Assigning approximate lengths for writing helps clarify the depth of discussion you expect to find in the writing. Often, the teacher will have more success by setting a maximum length than a minimum one. For students to have to meet the demands of the topic within a constraining length, they will have to plan carefully before writing.

Much school writing is limited to a few forms—paragraphs, stories, letters, poems, and reports. Actual writing, however, contains countless forms. In the real world, people write lists, journal entries, and directions. The following list gives just a sampling to get you thinking about the possibilities for writing forms:

A Sampling of Writing Forms

ads	
allegories	interviews
announcements	journals
autobiographies	lab reports
biographies	letters
book jackets	lists
book reviews	magazine articles
brochures	memoirs
campaign speeches	memos
character sketches	mysteries
children's books	myths
comic strips	newspaper articles

commercials	newspaper columns
contracts	obituaries
debates	observational notes
diaries	plays
dialogues	poems
directions	position papers
editorials	posters
encyclopedia entries	PowerPoint presentations
epitaphs	questionnaires
essays	recipes
fables	reports
scenarios	reviews
scripts	stories
song lyrics	summaries
	thumbnail sketches

Audience   Imagine this vignette:

> It was a dark and foggy night, and you were driving home from class. You did not stop at a STOP sign that had only recently been installed at a familiar intersection. Fortunately, there were no other cars in the intersection, so you got through safely. Unfortunately, a police officer was parked along the curb ahead. You were given a ticket for running the STOP sign.

Now imagine that you are going to write a letter about this sad incident to a seven-year-old cousin, your best friend, your father (in whose name the car is registered), and the judge who will decide on your fine. The topic and form will be the same for all the letters, but the audience for each is quite different. Think about how the four letters would be different.

Audience refers to the person or persons who might read your writing. An authentic audience is preferable. For example, students write pieces to be read by their classmates, students in other classes, younger children, pen pals, parents, school personnel, newspaper readers, and public officials. Sometimes the audience cannot really read the piece, but the writer writes as if the audience could. For example, letters are written to George Washington, or descriptions of life as it is today are put into time capsules for some possible readers, years or even decades into the future.

Often writers write for themselves. People keep diaries and journals; make lists, schedules, and notes; and write to clarify their own thinking rather than to communicate that thinking to others.

In schools, a common audience is the teacher, probably the hardest audience for whom to write. Students who know that their teacher will be the only reader often leave important data unstated because they know that the teacher already knows the information.

Having an authentic audience other than the teacher has been shown to improve greatly the quality of student writing (Dyson & Freedman, 1991). Students write more clearly and use more examples when they know that someone who really needs the information is going to read it. Whenever possible, students should write for a variety of audiences, including themselves, their classmates, and other people in the real world. Before students begin to write, they should be clear about who will be the audience for that piece of writing.

Role   Role is the identity, or the perspective, you take. Often we write from our own perspective so that we do not think about our role; sometimes we write from different perspectives. Assuming different roles helps students produce clear, interesting writing.

Students could write to Abraham Lincoln, and thus Lincoln would be the audience; or they could write what they think Abraham Lincoln would say in a speech today, and thus they would assume the role of Lincoln. For actors, getting into the part, believing they are who they are portraying, is crucial for believable acting. For writers, assuming different roles helps them write more vividly.

A writing task thus has four components: RAFT (Holston & Santa, 1985) is a mnemonic device for remembering the four components:

Role—Who is doing the writing?
Audience—For whom are you writing?
Form—In what format will you write about the topic? How long will your writing be?
Topic—What are you writing about and for what intention?

When teachers design a writing task for a content area class, they think about the topic first and then the forms, audiences, and roles that would help students think about the topic. Writing tasks have these four components, but you do not have to specify all four. Sometimes you may want to decide on the topic and form but let students choose their audience and role; other times you may want to specify the topic and let students decide on the rest.

Here are some examples of central questions and culminating writing tasks that could frame a unit on twins:

1. *Central question*: What genetic traits do twins share?
   Task: Write a two- to three-page scenario to be shared with your classmates describing the following scene: Imagine that you had an identical twin who was separated from you at birth. You meet twenty years later at a restaurant. Describe your similarities and differences.
2. *Central question*: What are the advantages and disadvantages of having a twin?
   Task: Locate a twin to interview about the advantages and disadvantages of being a twin. Write a one-page magazine article summarizing your interview, which will be compiled with others into a special class magazine on twins.
3. *Central question*: How does research on twins help us understand the heredity versus environment issue?
   Task: Imagine that you are a scientist who is thinking about how you

might use twins in research to shed light on the heredity versus environment issue. You are talking on the phone to a scientist from another country and seeking advice on how to proceed. Write what each of you might say in this conversation.

TRY IT OUT

Analyze the three writing tasks just presented and decide what the topic, form, audience, and role is for each. For example, for the first writing task, the topic was a restaurant meeting with an identical twin who had been separated at birth, the form was a scenario, the audience was classmates, and the role was yourself. (Remember that not all of these must be specified in every writing task.) Choose two of the tasks and change one or more of the components (form, audience, or role) to create a new writing task. Be sure, however, that your new writing task is still getting students to think about what you want them to think about.

Designing a Scoring Guide   Although teachers frequently look over quick writes and content journals just to determine whether or not they represent students' reasonable efforts, more formal writing typically is assessed. As Chapter 3, "Instructional Units," indicated, students as well as teachers have legitimate rights and needs for assessments. Assessments help teachers and learners focus attention on what is important; they are sources of feedback regarding ongoing efforts. Assessment instruments indicate expectations for students' writing. Scoring guides, or rubrics, as presented in Chapter 3 are useful when you deem writing assessment to be appropriate.

The 6+1 Traits of Analytic Writing Assessment Scoring Guide, produced by the Northwest Regional Educational Laboratory (www.nwrel.org/assessment), is found in practically every state. In fact, several educational governing boards have adopted this scoring guide for their state- and district-level assessments. This instrument contains the following seven traits:

1. Ideas and content
2. Organization
3. Voice
4. Word choice
5. Sentence fluency
6. Conventions
7. Presentation

Note that the term *trait* is a synonym for the term *criterion* as used in Chapter 3 of this text. The following is a skeleton version of this popular scoring guide, showing maximum and minimum performance indicators for each of the traits:

Ideas and Content

5	1
This paper is clear and focused. It holds the readers' attention. Relevant anecdotes and details enrich the central theme.	As yet, the paper has no clear sense of purpose or central theme. To extract meaning from the text, the reader must make inferences based on sketchy or missing details.

Organization

5	1
The organization enhances and showcases the central idea or theme. The order, structure, or presentation of information is compelling and moves the reader through the text.	The writing lacks a clear sense of direction. Ideas, details, or events seem strung together in a loose or random fashion; there is no identifiable internal structure.

Voice

5	1
The writer speaks directly to the reader in a way that is individual, compelling, and engaging. The writer crafts the writing with an awareness and respect for the audience and the purpose for writing.	The writer seems indifferent, uninvolved, or distanced from the topic and/or the audience.

Word Choice

5	1
Words convey the intended message in a precise, interesting, and natural way. The words are powerful and engaging.	The writer demonstrates limited vocabulary or has not searched for words to convey specific meaning.

Sentence Fluency

5	1
The writing has an easy flow, rhythm, and cadence. Sentences are well built, with strong and varied structure that invites expressive oral reading.	The reader needs to practice quite a bit in order to give this paper a fair interpretive reading.

Conventions

5	1
The writer demonstrates a good grasp of standard conventions (e.g., spelling, punctuation, capitalization, grammar, usage, paragraphing) and uses conventions effectively to enhance readability. Errors tend to be so few that just minor touch-ups would get this piece ready to publish.	Errors in spelling, punctuation, capitalization, usage, and grammar and/or paragraphing repeatedly distract the reader and make the text difficult to read.

Presentation

5	1
The form and presentation of the text enhances the ability of the reader to understand and connect with the message. It is pleasing to the eye.	The reader receives a garbled message due to problems relating to the presentation of the text.

Appropriate criteria for writing tasks balance issues pertaining to your prior instruction, students' competencies, school or school district curriculum guides, state standards, and the task at hand. Create a set of about five criteria that are feasible and build incrementally from the past; including more or less than five depends on the sophistication of your scoring guide and your students.

Appropriate criteria also connect directly with the task's subject matter. For instance, students might be writing an essay that compares twins' portrayal in literature with what science has uncovered about twins. You might include only three criteria from the list: organization, word choice, and conventions. Then you might create two that are specific to this task, such as the following ones addressing the validity of what students say about scientific discoveries and literary portrayals:

Scientific Discoveries

5	1
Statements about what scientists have discovered about twins' shared physical appearance and personality traits are valid.	Statements about what scientists have discovered about twins' shared physical appearance and personality traits are invalid.

Literary Portrayal

5	1
Summary of how specific authors have portrayed twins is valid.	Summary of how specific authors have portrayed twins is invalid.

Building Background Knowledge   Once you know what you want students to think about and how to assess the writing task they will perform, you can decide what knowledge you need to build to enable them to carry out the task. Building knowledge for writing is no different from building background knowledge for reading. Ask yourself what students need to know to complete the task; then think about how most efficiently to build that knowledge.

Background knowledge for writing usually includes content related to the topic but may also include how to write the form. Students cannot successfully write a letter, an essay, or a TV commercial if they do not know the way in

Knowledge of the world is essential for writing.

which this particular form is written. Modeling of the form and/or examples may be required.

Helping Students Plan   Once you have built background knowledge for the task, presented the task and score guide, and helped students do any required research, are they ready to write? Not quite. Their writing will be better if they plan what they are going to say. This is the point at which students prepare outlines or webs, jot down words or reasons or names of people or places they may include, discuss with others what they want to say, develop a working title, or compose a final sentence.

You should help students plan before they begin writing. Have them engage in some class activity that will involve them in the planning. If research is involved, help them organize their findings into a writing plan before they begin their paper.

One caution: Because writing is a discovery process, do not insist that students follow their plan too closely, even though there will be some relationship between the plan and the paper.

Implementing Writing Guidance

In a manner similar to comprehension guidance, implementation of the writing plan elements just described occurs in phases. Discernible beginnings, middles, and endings are apparent in writing guidance just as in comprehension. The following is an example of writing guidance based on the following central question and task:

> *Central question*: What personality traits seem to be most and least accounted for by heredity?
>
> *Task*: Explain which of your major personality characteristics you believe to be most attributable to heredity. You will present your conclusions on a poster to share with classmates.

Before Writing   Assume that this writing task is being done during a unit on twins. Students have already learned how research with identical twins who were separated at birth is providing insight into the heredity versus environment issue. They know that scientists at the University of Minnesota Center for Twin and Adoption Research have found amazing similarities between identical twins who were separated at birth. Present them with data from the Minnesota Twin Studies, which indicate that leadership, cheerfulness, optimism, imaginativeness, stress vulnerability, and risk avoidance are strongly influenced by heredity. Other traits, such as ability to establish emotional intimacy and the propensity to be sensible and rational, appear to be less influenced by heredity.

Write these traits on the board in two columns under these headings: *Personality Traits Most Influenced by Heredity* and *Personality Traits Less Influenced by Heredity*. Next, have the class brainstorm other personality traits, such as these: hot-tempered, impatient, cooperative, laid back, high-strung, nervous, and cautious.

Write these traits on the board also but not under either heading, then explain that some personality traits seem to be more influenced by heredity than others, but we do not know which. Students then write a self-description in which they compare their personality traits with those of their family members and try to conclude, based on their own family experiences, which traits they seem to share with other family members. Remind them that because they have shared the same environment with many of these family members, the traits they share are probably attributable to both heredity and environment.

Then suggest that the self-description should be about two pages long and that they can first describe themselves and then compare themselves with other family members or that they can concentrate on one personality trait, then another, and so on, as they go along. Finally, tell them that after writing, they will read their self-descriptions to others in a small group and the group will see if any conclusions can be drawn about shared personality traits based on that group's findings. Each group's information will then be compiled, and the class will decide if they can draw any generalizations from the separate experiences of all the class members. After this introduction and guidance, move to the writing phase of the lesson.

During Writing   Now the students write. The first two parts of their task, to describe their own personalities and compare them to those of other family members, should be clear for most students. Circulate about the class, conferring with students as needed. Make sure that students have enough time to write but not so much time that they will not stay on the task.

After Writing   Assemble the students in groups of three or four and give them about twenty minutes to share their writing. When all students in the group have had a chance to read what they wrote, the group lists all the different personality traits discussed in all the papers and tries to classify them as more or less attributable to heredity. The whole class then reconvenes to culminate the activity. You record the small-group decisions on the board, and you lead the class to see if there is any agreement across the groups.

LISTEN, LOOK, AND LEARN   Visit a classroom to observe writing instruction or watch a videotape. Summarize what you saw during each phase of writing. Evaluate based on what you have learned so far in this chapter. What worked? What might the teacher have done differently?

Teach Writing Strategies

Teaching students strategies for writing and learning fosters their independence for the present as well as for the future; it promotes lifelong learning. Some writing strategies that have been shown to promote learning include ones that occur in the before, during, and after stages of writing production as well as ones associated with self assessment.

Before Writing

The before-writing phase is sometimes called *prewriting*. In the South, some people call it "fixing to write," and others call it "getting it together." There are various ways that teachers teach students how to get ready to write. Background knowledge is often built through such strategies as these:

brainstorming	charting
webbing	outlining
researching	discussing

Sometimes these strategies for building background knowledge are taught with the teacher directing the whole class, but small groups learning these activities allow for much more participation of each student.

Once students have sufficient background knowledge and motivation to write, you must make sure that they understand how to produce the form. If students do not understand how to write a particular form, you will have to teach it. Students cannot write a lab report, TV commercial, or brochure if they do not know the form.

The most efficient way to teach students the form is usually demonstration. Using the overhead projector, a science teacher can write up the lab report while thinking aloud. As students watch and listen, the teacher talks about what is important to include, what the scoring guide calls for, and produces actual writing. This teacher demonstration is *modeling* and has been shown to be an effective and straightforward way of teaching (Graham, 2005). Teacher modeling is more effective than just presenting students with an already completed paper, because when students watch teachers write and listen as teachers think aloud, they learn how the product is produced.

Already completed models are quicker than teacher modeling and are best used when students need just a quick review or a reminder of a form with which they are familiar. Showing students a letter or brochure and pointing out the salient features that all letters or brochures share may enable them to produce the desired form. Whenever possible, these already completed models should be student-produced, and you should provide several. Multiple models help students find their own writing style and make it clear that there is never just one right way to write. Students are more motivated if they see something similar done by last year's class. Some students are even challenged to excel as they respond to last year's models with a "We can do it better!" attitude.

During Writing

If prewriting is "getting it together," during writing is "getting it down." Three during-writing strategies include communal efforts, technology, and conventions.

Communal Efforts Writing is usually conceived of as an individual activity, but in the real world many excellent pieces of writing (this textbook, for example) are group-written. Students often achieve much and enjoy learning when it is arranged in some kind of cooperative learning format. This is especially true of writing. When you want students to write communally, you have available a variety of classroom grouping patterns.

Students might work in a group of three or four, with one person recording the ideas of the entire group. This communal writing seems to work best if everyone contributes ideas and one student acts as scribe and produces a first draft and reads it to the group. All group members can suggest ways to make the writing better and clearer. This communal strategy of *plan collaboratively-draft individually-revise collaboratively* blends group effort with individual accountability. Individuals have access to group support, but they submit their writing individually and no classroom grades are awarded to the group. This promotes group interaction while eliminating the free-rider problem of students being rewarded for efforts they didn't exert.

For a lengthy piece, students might divide up the sections (as we did with the first draft of this book). They would first plan which part each would write and set some guidelines about content to be covered and writing style to be used. Each person would then write his or her part to which everyone in the group would respond. The group would work together producing sections that make up one item to which they all had contributed.

Technology   In classrooms today, students write using computers. Those who have regular access to computers for word processing are more willing to write, write more, revise more, and feel more confident in their writing. In addition to basic word-processing programs that allow students to write, edit, check spelling, and so forth, other software supports writing in much more sophisticated ways (Bruce & Levin, 2003). Programs like *Inspiration* (www.Inspiration.com) and *Expression* (www.Sunburst.com) are available that provide computer-assisted brainstorming, idea mapping, and outlining. Other software, like *Author's Toolkit* (www.Sunburst.com), extends prewriting planning to drafting and editing. And still

Students record their thoughts in the writing phase.

others, like *Kidspiration* (www.Inspiration.com), take it one step further by enabling young writers to hear their work read aloud by the computer or by their own recorded voices.

Desktop publishing software such as *Print Shop Deluxe* (www.Learningco.com) allows writers to customize their own professional-looking books, reports, announcements, and so on, by formatting text with student-made illustrations, clip art, and other visuals. Popular presentation software, like *PowerPoint* (www.Microsoft.com), enhances written notes students might display during multimedia presentations. And web sites such as *Homestead* (www.Homestead.com) readily enable older students to embed writing with music, video, pictures, and other media on their own web sites. Your role is to provide students the strategies for using this information and communication technology efficiently and wisely.

Conventions   Spelling, of course, is a concern for writers and teachers, but it seems best to underemphasize it during first-draft writing. Students should be encouraged to brainstorm lists of words, use a dictionary (if they know how and want to), and write words as best they can. Some teachers encourage students to leave blanks for letters about which they are uncertain or put an asterisk in the margin where they think their spelling is probably wrong.

The procedure just described sounds easier than it is. Because students are afraid of misspelling words, teachers feel a natural tendency to want to help. But, students will write longer drafts and use more sophisticated words if they are freed from real or perceived "perfect spelling" demands on their first-draft writing. Students should learn that perfect spelling is not required for them to share their work with a small group and that when their writing is to be publicly displayed or graded, they will be given time and help to fix the spelling.

Fixing spelling, and many more conventions such as grammar and punctuation is what some teachers do while students produce their first drafts. In some classrooms, teachers work with individuals or small groups who are revising an already completed first draft while the rest of the students are writing their first drafts. These writing conferences are usually conducted quietly in a corner of the room so that the writers are not disturbed.

After Writing

During the culminating, after-writing phase, possibilities range from doing nothing to sharing the writing by reading it aloud to revising, editing, and publishing it. Let's consider the doing-nothing option first. If your major purpose for having students write is to promote their thinking about content, you may have accomplished that goal with the thinking engaged in by the students before and during writing. In this case, you would simply check to see that the writing was indeed done and that a sufficient effort was made.

The problem with the doing-nothing response is that students do not get any feedback on how well they performed. This feedback can be provided by you, by

A writer getting editing help from a friend.

the person who wrote the piece, or by classmates. Using the scoring guide, you can assess how well each student has done and make some notes on the writing about what the student might have misunderstood or might need to clarify. You can have a short conference with each student and give feedback in this setting. Some teachers use a scoring guide to structure the feedback they give about how well writers have completed the task.

When the writing is a culmination to a consequential project that will be displayed or publicly shared in some way, the after-writing phase becomes more extended and more complex. (If you have used the terms "getting it together" and "getting it down" to help students conceptualize the before- and during-writing phases, you might want to tell them that now they are engaged in "getting it right.") Here again, students could work with a partner, a small group, or the teacher to do the revising and editing process. This help needs to address both the message contained in the writing and the conventions. The message should be dealt with first, then attention should focus on conventions. PQS (praise, question, suggest) is a nifty mnemonic for a strategy to help students remember how to help one another.

Each writer should share his or her paper with a willing partner or partners (teacher, buddy, or small group). The writer elicits **praise** by asking something like this: "What did you like about it?" The partner or partners then provide some positive comments:

"You really learned a lot by interviewing two sets of twins."

"Your reasons for why twins might not become famous really made sense to me."

"Your conversation with the other scientist sounded like a real phone conversation, and you had some good ideas for using twins in research."

Next, the writer elicits **questions** by asking, "Do you have any questions?" or "Was there anything you didn't understand?" These are sample responses:

"I didn't understand if the twins finally thought it was better or not to have been born twins."

"You lost me in the middle part."

"How would you find the twins for your research?"

Finally, the writer asks the partners to **suggest** how to improve the paper. The writer might ask, "Can you think of words to make the writing more interesting, informative, or compelling?" Using the comments, the writer has some concrete things to do in order to revise the piece.

The next step is editing for mechanics, with which students and teachers can help. The goal of editing for mechanics is to produce a finished product of which the writer can be proud. How perfect that needs to be depends on the age and ability of the students and the expectations of the audience who will read the final copy.

Once the writer has had help revising the message and editing for mechanics, the piece should be recopied, retyped, or reprinted. This finished product should then be displayed or published, because the reason for revising and editing first drafts is to make them more readable for a new reader.

TRY IT OUT Plan a writing activity. Make a sheet like the one in Figure 7.1 (on page 192) and fill in what you will do during each phase.

Self-assessment

To produce independent lifelong writers, teachers need to encourage responsibility and reflection and help students develop self-assessment strategies. Once students understand that a writing task has four components—topic, form, audience, and role—they should be given some responsibility for deciding on appropriate writing tasks. Returning to our twins example, you may decide that students should think about the advantages and disadvantages of being a twin. This topic might be given to the students, then the students might decide what would be an appropriate form, audience, and role.

Once students have a writing task in mind, they need to reflect upon their own background knowledge and what additional knowledge they might need. Again teachers help by making suggestions:

Before writing:
   Decide what students are to think about
   Design a writing task
     • Topic
     • Form
     • Audience
     • Role
   Design a scoring guide
   Build background knowledge
   Help students plan
During writing:
   Write alone or communally
   Technology
   Teacher input
After writing:
   Teacher or peer conference
     • Praise
     • Question
     • Suggest
   Display or publish
   Celebrate

Figure 7.1   Planning Writing Instruction

- What do you need to know?
- How could you find out more about twins?

Finally, if students are to become independent writers, they must learn to reflect upon their own writing and assess their own writing products. Some teachers provide students with a reflection sheet they can use to evaluate any piece of writing they do. The reflection sheet might include questions such as these:

- What do I like best about what I wrote?
- What is not clear? How can I make it clearer?
- Will the reader be interested in reading it?

Many teachers use scoring guides to help students learn the strategy of assessing their own writing. Scoring guides fit specific writing projects or tasks and may take the form of checklists in which questions are answered with a "yes" or a "no."

- Does the paper give a clear and accurate definition of anxiety?
- Does the paper make at least two different and accurate distinctions between anxiety and fear?

Writers get editing help from a teacher.

Scoring guides are usually explained to students before they write. After writing, students work with a peer to evaluate their paper according to the criteria set up in the guide. Some teachers send the guides home and ask parents to help the writer read the piece to determine if the criteria are being met. The essential factor with guides is that students are taught how to use them to improve their own writing.

While scoring guides help students learn what is expected in their writing and how to assess their own writing, there is a danger that students will become too dependent on these devices and "write to the formula." The most successful teachers use these devices but gradually help students determine what the criteria on particular assessment devices should be and eventually help students reflect upon and assess their own writing based on their own criteria.

Additionally, writing prompts that focus students' attention on their current knowledge, confusions, and learning processes have been found to be especially effective at promoting subject matter learning (Bangert-Drowns, Hurley, & Wilkinson, 2004). For instance, students might ask themselves questions like the following:

- What is becoming clear to me about _____?
- How did the author/teacher put the ideas in order? How can I use this order to understand and remember _____?

- What are the key vocabulary words? How can I understand and remember _____?

DO IT TOGETHER   In this chapter, we offer suggestions for what students might write; for how you can guide, support, and encourage that writing; and for how you can help students become more independent in their writing and learning. Discuss these suggestions with two or three colleagues. Decide how you plan to implement particular suggestions in your classroom.

Specific Content Area Applications

Writing in English/Language Arts Classrooms

Countless opportunities exist for writing in English/language arts classes. Indeed, if you review the English/language arts classroom suggestions for comprehension and vocabulary in the preceding chapters, you will see writing activities already incorporated (e.g., maintain a response journal, compose a resolution to the central question, record passage sections containing words worth remembering). The following suggestions go beyond the ones already presented, building on ideas introduced in this chapter specifically related to quick writes, journals, and lesson tasks. The following would be appropriate for students engaged with the novel *Shabanu, Daughter of the Wind*.

Quick Writes   Quick writes help when calling up prior knowledge on a topic. Students might produce quick writes in response to the following:

What three things should nomadic people do when desert sandstorms occur?
What wedding customs have you seen or heard of?

To have students predict what comes next in *Shabanu*, you might offer these prompts:

What will happen to Shabanu's betrothal to Rahim-Sahib?
What will happen in the next chapter?

Synthesizing ideas about the novel can be elicited by having students write in response to these items:

What Islamic customs differ from the ones you are used to?
List the similarities and differences you can think of so far between Shabanu and her sister, Phulan.

To help students reflect on their processing of *Shabanu*, they might write briefly on the following:

What part of *Shabanu* has been confusing?
Why is *Shabanu* maintaining—or losing—my interest?

Journals   Journals contain writings that take numerous forms. Indeed, students might maintain reactions to these quick-write prompts listed above in their journals. To facilitate writing, students might have available a menu of generic prompts from which to react. Here are some generic prompts we have found to be productive that would fit *Shabanu*:

What have I learned from reading this passage?
What images did I experience while reading this passage?
What do I not really understand so far?
What did this passage remind me of?
What would I like to see changed?
How did I feel when reading this passage?

Designing Tasks for Lessons   Thinking of RAFTs (roles, audiences, forms, and topics) when designing tasks for writing lessons helps produce meaningful and connected learning opportunities. Students tend to find writing tasks explicitly based on RAFTs more engaging than traditional ones. If the topic you are addressing is the wedding of Shabanu's sister, Phulan, here are some ways RAFTing could be done to transform conventional writing tasks.

Modifying Forms   Students benefit from modifying forms of expression while maintaining essentially the same role and audience. We call this practice *translation writing*. After students read the passage describing Phulan's wedding, they might rewrite the description of it in a form selected from the following:

play	song lyrics
interview script	newspaper article
illustrated strip	diary
poem	contract
personal letter	

Modifying Roles   Considering different roles that writers might assume also contributes to the design of writing tasks. For instance, if students decide to produce a poem or a set of diary entries centering on Phulan's wedding, they might consider the multiple perspectives that are available. They might write a wedding poem while acting in the role of Phulan, Shabanu, the girls' mother, or the girls' father. They might write poems from the points of view of all four story characters.

Modifying Audiences   When thinking about possible wedding poem audiences, students again have several options. They might write for those in attendance, for Phulan's husband, for other members of the family, for younger children, or for readers of a literary journal. Associating different roles and forms with different audiences as we have done here produces writing task possibilities with space for most students' interests and abilities.

Supporting Writing   The tasks listed provide good momentum for students writing about *Shabanu* in English classrooms, but there certainly is more to writing instruction than this. Students require support, or scaffolding, to accomplish goals along with opportunities to reflect on and assess their writing performance. This section concentrated on tasks for writing because teaching and learning are greatly facilitated when there are clearly stated engaging tasks guiding the attention and action of teachers and students.

Writing in Second-Language Classrooms

Writing in second-language classrooms is much the same as writing in first-language classrooms. Students plan what they will write, produce written drafts, and sometimes revise what they have written. The main difference between writing in one's first language and in one's second language involves the support that is required. Effective teachers support second-language writing in several ways.

Connections   Writers who easily sustain a line of thinking are able to concentrate on overcoming the word choice, grammar, spelling, and other such challenges a second language presents. One way effective teachers support second-language writers and help sustain their lines of thought is by offering them access to life experience topics that have personal connections.

Topics from life experiences enable writers to focus on expressing themselves. Life experience topics that promote ready connections include student favorites with regard to the following:

foods	books/comics/magazines
clothes	weekend activities
sports	adventures
games	pets/animals
hobbies/collections	television shows/movies
friends	songs/musical groups

Teachers often suggest topics such as one's preferences for food, entertainment, and clothing, and students go into depth on particular ones. Producing a personal crest that heralds one's identity and explaining the crest is another common practice that capitalizes on personal connections. Of course, when describing one's personal background or family history, students should realize they are free to decide how much they will reveal about themselves.

Oral history projects with family or community members are good ways for second-language learners to capitalize on life experiences and personal connections. When students interview parents and grandparents, aunts and uncles, and neighbors and business people in their communities, they are connecting the stories of others' lives with their lives. They can see how past actions might have affected their lives and how conflicts and circumstances from the past might be similar to those of the present. Writing comes into play during oral history projects when students research the times in which people lived, prepare questions, record interviewees' responses, and write up reports.

Finally, writers who address topics associated with their cultures also have ready access to personal connections. Practically everyone has personal experiences and understandings of distinctive holidays, foods, ways of dress, and pastimes. Addressing such topics allows writers to concentrate on expressing themselves, and it provides opportunities to honor and celebrate differences in culturally diverse classrooms. Teachers who share their interest and respect for others' cultures model ways that students can do the same.

Collaboration Promoting collaboration is another good way to support students who are writing in a second language. Collaborative writing projects call for students to work together in whole-class, small-group, or paired situations. Students with high proficiency and those with low proficiency in the second language might collaborate sometimes, and those with similar levels of proficiency might collaborate other times.

One key to the success of collaborative writing is the instruction students receive about how to act. Teachers typically demonstrate positive face-to-face interactions (e.g., praising others, encouraging participation, finding common ground) so students will do the same when they interact. Teachers often specify particular interactions, then they and the students reflect on the behaviors during and after collaborative work.

Collaboration during the planning, before-writing phase occurs many ways. If students are writing in their second language about particular life experiences, they first might jointly brainstorm possibilities. They could list key words that are related to what each plans to write. They could help each other decide on terms that would most appropriately articulate what they want to say. They could talk about the order in which they would use the words, stating orally what they plan to express in print. They could figuratively step back and talk with each other about what they want to write.

When students are getting their writing down, they still can benefit from collaboration. They might request a partner's help with a particular term or a grammatical form (How do you say, "May I help you?"), or they might consult about the spelling of a word. Writers who cannot produce a particular word or phrase in their second language might insert a few words from their first language to get past the difficulty, later getting help to replace the native language terms.

Collaboration also is appropriate in the after-writing phase. Students can read their writing orally to a single partner or to a small group, and all concerned individuals can listen for points to praise and to question. Rather than listening, partners and small-group members can read what one has written, looking for points to praise and to question. Teachers typically model before a whole class the dynamics of small-group revisions. They demonstrate how to attend to specific features of writing as well as how to comment appropriately when they spot difficulties.

Writing in Mathematics Classrooms

For many of us, writing was not a part of how we learned in a mathematics class. Recently, however, all content areas have become concerned with students' ability to think and communicate, and writing is one of the major ways of promoting both of these. Here are some specific ways that math teachers use quick writes, journals, and word problems to help students think and communicate mathematically.

Quick Writes   As previewing activities, math teachers ask students to

> List as many kinds of different triangles as you can in thirty seconds.
> Draw and label three shapes that have different names.
> List ways you use decimals in real-life activities.

To synthesize what was learned at the end of a class, ask students to

> Define in your own words what parallel lines are.
> Write in words what this formula means.
> Use the symbols =, <, and > to write three true sentences.

To help students self-assess understanding, attitudes, and so on, you could use these prompts:

> What did you not understand about today's lesson?
> List one or more terms you cannot clearly define.
> I have the feeling many of you are not "with me" on this topic. Write what you are feeling about what we are doing and if there is anything I could change to help you feel more involved and successful.

Journals   Journals call for more extended entries than quick writes and are most successful if used on a daily basis. Both high-structure and low-structure journals can be used in math class. Here are some examples of high-structure journal prompts math teachers use:

> Draw and label pictures that will help you remember each of the shapes we have studied so far.
> Write a paragraph using as many of the following words as possible. (List math terms you are studying.)
> Analyze the mistakes made on your homework (or in-class work). What have you learned that will help you avoid making these same mistakes again?

Write an explanation of why we need to study _____, which would make sense to a younger friend who hasn't yet taken this course.

Word Problems   Solving word problems is an essential math skill but one that presents problems for many students. To understand word problems from the inside out, students are often helped by trying to write some. Most teachers find that because this is a difficult task, it is one at which students are more successful and are willing to tackle if they write cooperatively as a team of two or three members. Team members are asked to write word problems similar to the ones they have been trying to solve, and then two teams are paired to try to solve each other's problems. The solving team points out any missing information or unclear language and the writing team rewrites. Finally, the combined team picks its "best" and most challenging problem for the whole class to solve.

Guidelines for changing word problems into easier ones include the following:

Using fewer words
Using shorter sentences
Using smaller numbers
Using simpler figures
Having fewer steps or operations
Putting the information in the order it will be used
Including a chart or diagram
Suggesting the use of manipulatives

Writing in Science Classrooms

Many students (and teachers!) don't see many connections between science and writing. But scientists are inveterate writers. They write down hunches and sketch possible arrangements of whatever they are studying. They observe carefully and write down their observations. They conduct experiments and write down what they think will happen as well as what they actually observe. Writing and sketching are important tools real scientists use to help themselves think. Here are some specific ways that science teachers use quick writes, journals, and lab reports to help students think and communicate.

Quick Writes   As previewing activities, science teachers ask students to

List as many different animals with backbones as you can in thirty seconds.
Draw and label the parts of a tomato plant.
List ways that chemistry is important to us in real-life activities.

To synthesize what was learned at the end of a class, you might offer students these prompts:

Define in you own words what an ecosystem is.
Your book says, _____. Write what that really means in English.
Use the words _____ and _____ and _____ to write a true sentence.

To help students self-assess understanding, attitudes, and so forth, you could offer these prompts:

> What did you not understand about today's lesson?
> List one or more terms you cannot clearly define.
> I have the feeling many of you are not "with me" on this topic. Write what you are feeling about what we are doing and if there is anything I could change to help you feel more involved and successful.

Journals   Journals call for more extended entries than quick writes and are most successful if used on a daily basis. Both high-structure and low-structure journals can be used in a science class. Here are some examples of high-structure journal prompts science teachers use:

> Draw and label the parts of the digestive system.
> Arrange the following words into a web that shows their relationships.
> Analyze how you did with today's experiment. Were you able to follow the directions? Did the experiment turn out as you had predicted?
> Explain to a younger person (brother, sister, cousin) why it is important for everyone to understand about toxins in our environment.

In addition to content-oriented journal entries such as these, science teachers may want to use "personal history" journal entries early in the year to help students come to terms with their science "attitudes." Many students have not had good experiences with science and in spite of all the recent efforts to have science classes be "hands-on" active learning environments, many students associate science with hard-to-read textbooks and big unpronounceable words to memorize. If students see themselves as inadequate and uninterested learners in science, their attitudes will affect their motivation, learning, and thinking. Science teachers can engage students and begin to alter self-concepts in a number of different ways, including having students reflect on their own personal science histories.

To use journal entries in this way, tell students that we all have personal experiences in all areas of our lives that affect how we feel about things. Use a few examples to which your students can relate, perhaps telling about some of your life experiences which helped you to feel positively about something and negatively about something else.

> "My mom made me take piano lessons for four years and I hated it. I generalized that hate to all music and only in recent years have I learned to enjoy jazz and some other types of music."
> "When I was your age, I had a friend who was a great baseball player. All he ever talked about was baseball. Eventually, I got interested in baseball too, even though I didn't play well. I still love baseball."

Let students share some of their earlier experiences with real life—not science—topics and then tell them that since your job is to teach them science and their past experiences with science will affect their attitudes, you would like to know about those experiences. Explain that each day for a week or two you will ask them to write about specific science experiences. After students write, you can let them tell about what they have written, either to the whole class or in small groups, or you can collect their journals and read them so that you get to know their science stories. Be sure that if you read them, the students know that the entries won't be graded (although doing them may add some points to their grade) and that you want to know both the high points and the low points of their experiences. Here are some possible prompts that could be used across several days of journal writing time:

- Of all the school subjects you study, is science one of your best or one of your worst? Rank it on a 1 (worst) to 10 (best) scale and explain why you chose the number you did.
- Regardless of how much you like science, some of your science teachers/ classes were probably better or worse than others. Write what you remember about your worst science teacher/class. What grade were you in? What made it so awful? How did things work in the class? Change the name of the teacher of that class to X to protect the guilty.
- Today reflect on your best science teacher/class. What grade were you in? What made it good? How did things work in this class? No need to change the name of this teacher!
- How do you feel about science experiments? Can you usually do them? Do you like to do them? Do they help you learn?
- Have you ever done projects for the science fair? What did you do? Did anyone help you? Did you like doing this? (If you never did, talk about why not and tell about your feelings about science fairs in general.)
- Do you do anything out of school that is science related? Do you like sci-fi TV shows, movies, books? Do you like to read *National Geographic* and similar magazines? Do you like any science/nature shows on TV? Have you ever belonged to the scouts, 4H, or another group through which you had any wilderness experiences? Do you have a microscope, telescope, or other science paraphernalia?

While recognizing, expressing, and taking ownership of attitudes will not alter these attitudes, it is a first step. Students who don't like science will enjoy telling you why, "ranting and raving" about their awful experiences. They will get it out of their system and be amazed that you, a science teacher, know and accept the fact that some of them don't like science. If you let them share their responses, they will discover that others have had different experiences with science and begin to realize that with different experiences, they might have developed different attitudes. Science teachers are always concerned with helping students recognize their misconceptions. If your students have misconceptions about science, spending some of your journal time exploring personal science history issues will help you and them begin to change those misconceptions.

Lab Reports   Many students feel about lab reports the same way they feel about book reports. They don't mind the lab (book) and even enjoy it sometimes, but they detest writing it up. Successful science teachers find ways to make the writing of the lab report less tedious and more successful. They usually begin by modeling at the overhead or chalkboard the writing of the report. This is not the same as giving the students an already completed model because as the teacher writes, he or she "thinks aloud," allowing students to see how the teacher decided what to include and how to word it. Most teachers do the modeling and thinking aloud themselves several times and then continue modeling but asking students to give them ideas of what to write next and how to write it. Once students are participating in the writing being modeled by the teacher, many teachers move to a small-group writing format. One person in each group is appointed as writer, but all group members share in deciding what to write and how to write it.

Once students have had lots of experience watching and helping the teacher model the writing of a lab report and participating in group writing, many teachers like to have the class create a frame for a lab report which can then be displayed in the room (and/or duplicated for their science notebooks) and will serve as a reminder of the form and essential elements of a lab report. This frame is most useful if it is constructed by the class after teacher modeling and group work. A generic frame is given here but should only be considered as an example and not as *the* frame for lab reports. Frames more specific to the particular area of science being studied, the age, and scientific sophistication of your students will support student writing of lab reports.

> **Laboratory Report**
> Problem
>   Why does . . . ?
> Hypotheses
>   I think that . . .
> Materials
>   (List materials used)
> Procedures
>   (List in order what you did)
> Data
>   (List what you observed, including numbers, pictures, etc., as appropriate)
> Conclusions
>   My problem was . . .
>   The results showed that . . .
>   These results supported (did not support) my hypotheses because . . .

Writing in Social Studies Classrooms

Writing in social studies is more common than in many other content areas. Because you are studying about people and events, there are endless opportunities for students to "think things through" while writing.

Quick Writes   As previewing activities, social studies teachers ask students to

> List as many names of people important in the Civil War as you can in thirty seconds.
> Write down one question you have about our federal budget.
> List three major inventions of the twentieth century.

To synthesize what was learned at the end of a class, ask students to

> Define in your own words what a democracy is.
> List two things that changed after the *Brown v. The Board of Education* ruling.
> Use the words *interest rates*, *inflation*, and *stock market* to write a true sentence.

To help students self-assess understanding, attitudes, and so forth, offer these prompts:

> What did you not understand about today's lesson?
> List one or more terms you cannot clearly define.
> I have the feeling many of you are not "with me" on this topic. Write what you are feeling about what we are doing and if there is anything I could change to help you feel more involved and successful.

Journals   Journals call for more extended entries than quick writes and are most successful if used on a daily basis. Both high-structure and low-structure journals can be used in a social studies class. Here are some examples of high-structure journal prompts social studies teachers use:

> We have been studying the controversial topic of our welfare system and the law which limits welfare benefits. Are you for or against this law? On balance, is it going to make us a better or worse society? If you could have voted on this issue, how would you have voted? List three reasons to justify your vote.

> Arrange the following words into a web that shows their relationships.
> Explain to a younger person (brother, sister, cousin) why it is important for everyone to understand the concept of global interdependence.

In addition to content-oriented journal entries such as these, many social studies teachers use "historical figure diaries" to help students relate to events often far away in time and space. While studying about the Vietnam War, students may become major players such as John F. Kennedy, Lyndon Johnson, Henry Kissinger, Ho Chi Mihn, Ngo Dinh Diem, or "common people" such as a marine sent to Vietnam, a college student with a draft deferment, a soldier in the Viet Cong, a civilian living in North Vietnam, and the child of an American soldier left in Vietnam. Teachers may let students choose their character or have them pick a character "from a hat" so that all points of view are represented. As the unit continues, characters write each day "diary style" what they are doing and thinking. If two people have the same character, they can write separately or can collaborate on a joint entry. To make this more effective, have the "common people" characters name themselves and decide on their personal characteristics (age, occupation, family status, etc.) before beginning. From time to time, let characters share their diary entries with the whole class or in small groups.

Getting students involved in events that occurred long before their birth is not easy. Having students assume the role of a person in an historical setting promotes their use of the imaging and evaluating thinking processes. Keeping a diary is a real-world writing task. Anne Frank kept one, as did Richard Nixon! Incorporating historical figure diaries into your social studies routine increases student motivation and engagement and gives students a real purpose for writing.

Oral History Projects   Oral history projects use interviews with real people who have experienced an event as the primary source of information. They can be used anytime the event or phenomenon being studied is one that friends and relatives of the students have experienced. Many teachers use oral history projects when studying about immigration or societal changes. Often the oral history project begins in the middle of the unit when the students have enough background information to construct good questions. The first time this project is used, it is probably best to lead the class as a whole to construct the questions. As this format is incorporated into other units, students can work in small groups to construct questions and finally construct their own questions. Students may conduct the interviews individually or with a partner. After conducting the interview, students can report to the whole class about what they learned. In many classes, students write a book in which each interview is summarized and printed, perhaps with a picture of the person being interviewed.

Oral history projects make history come alive for students. Learning about the flood of immigrants that arrived after a particular war and the personal and societal upheaval that accompanies immigration takes on a whole different dimension when someone you actually know was one of these immigrants. Students develop new respect (and sometimes even awe!) for neighbors and relatives often previously ignored. Teachers of two-language children and newcomers find that incorporating oral history projects into their social studies classrooms is a way of involving and validating the experience of students struggling with English and with a new culture. Of course, personal involvement increases motivation and engagement, and writing becomes a tool for thinking as students write down the questions, write down the answers, and construct the written summary of what was learned. The name *oral history* refers to how the student gathers the information but, for the student, oral history projects involve a lot of purposeful, focused writing.

Writing Your School's History   Beverly Fazio (1992) describes a wonderful social studies writing project in which U.S. history students began their study of history with their own school. Using old school yearbooks, newspapers, minutes of school board meetings, and interviews with community members, students studied the history of the 84-year-old school. One of the respondents to their advertisement in the local newspaper soliciting information from bygone days was a 1918 graduate who told the students that their high school in her day had three grades and three teachers—one for each grade. The building that housed the high school had neither electricity nor plumbing. Men who had left school in the 1940s to fight the war came forward to decry the fact that they couldn't graduate and to explain the lack of a football team during the war years—not enough male students left in school! (The article describing this school history project gives many details about how to proceed, along with other fascinating tidbits.)

Doing the school's history involved oral history along with lots of other research using primary sources. Writing was involved in all stages of this project, which culminated in the printing of a real book, eagerly bought by students past and present. History and how historians "do" history was directly experienced by these lucky students of American history.

Writing in Activity Classrooms

Many students (and teachers!) don't see connections between art, music, physical education, vocational subjects, and writing. But all teachers are constantly seeking ways to get students to think more deeply about their subjects, and writing is one way to focus and organize thinking. In addition, almost all jobs require an astonishing amount and variety of writing. Here are some specific ways that teachers of activity courses use writing to help students learn and think.

Quick Writes   As previewing activities, ask students to

List as many different materials sculptors might use as you can in thirty seconds.
Sketch what you think a miter box looks like.
List ways that knowing first aid is important to us in real-life activities.

To synthesize what was learned at the end of a class, ask students to

Define in your own words what syncopated rhythm is.
Draw a stick figure to show what the backhand position looks like.
Use the words _____ and _____ and _____ to write a true sentence.

To help students self-assess understanding, attitudes, and so forth, you could offer these prompts:

What did you not understand about today's lesson?
List one or more terms you cannot clearly define.
I have the feeling many of you are not "with me" on this topic. Write what you are feeling about what we are doing and if there is anything I could change to help you feel more involved and successful.

Journals   Journals call for more extended entries than quick writes and are most successful if used on a daily basis. Both high-structure and low-structure journals can be used in activity classes. Here are some examples of high-structure journal prompts:

> Draw and label a _____.
> Arrange the following words into a web that shows their relationships.
> Analyze how you did with today's activity? Were you able to follow the directions? What problems did you experience? What did you do to help yourself understand?
> Explain to a younger person (brother, sister, cousin) why it is important for everyone to know how to do CPR.

Interviewing Real People about On-the-Job Writing   Many students have the idea that once they are done with school, they won't need to write anymore! In today's advanced society, this is hardly ever true. Mechanics, technicians, computer specialists, and store managers expend a huge amount of time and effort writing everything from letters to orders to e-mail messages to reports. Every student needs to see writing as an important part of any job to which they aspire. Of course, preaching this to them is rarely effective. Some teachers of activity-oriented courses send the students out to find out for themselves. Students select some people in a variety of nonacademic jobs and then interview them to find out specifically what they write. When all the information obtained from these interviews is compiled and shared with the whole class, students may develop some real-world motivation for learning to write clearly and well.

Writing Directions in Plain English   Everyone knows that directions are hard to read. Students who experience frustration reading directions feel better if teachers demonstrate an "It's not your fault; they should write them more clearly" attitude. Students are more willing to work through a set of directions and try to make sense of them when they realize that not being able to follow the directions easily says more about the writer of the directions than it does about their own reading ability. One effective writing activity to use when you and your students are faced with complex written directions is to rewrite them "in plain English." When you come across poorly written directions, have the students work together in small groups to first try to follow the directions. Once they have assembled the object or carried out the procedure, have them rewrite the directions so that they are easier to follow. Here are some guidelines for making directions easier to follow:

1. Use shorter sentences.
2. Use "plain" English words instead of technical terms.
3. Include only one thing in each step.
4. Make sure the steps are in logical order.
5. Include a drawing for each step when possible.
6. Include a list of materials/parts with each one clearly labeled.
7. List important "don'ts" at the beginning. (Sometimes, knowing what not to do is more important than knowing what to do!)

Once students have rewritten a particularly difficult set of directions, have another group of students carry out the directions to see how they work. You may want to compile their simplified directions in a resource book for other classes to use. Tell them that they are providing a service to all the students who will follow them in this course and who will not have to wrestle with that particular set of poorly written directions. Students who rewrite directions to make them simpler and clearer become better at reading all kinds of directions—including the poorly written ones they will encounter in the future!

LOOKING BACK Writing can be more than a way to assess what was learned; it can be a tool for learning. Learners who record thoughts in print crystallize and refine them and cement them in memory. In this chapter, you encountered ways to promote the power of writing. The ideas are divided among three headings: (1) Vary informal writing, (2) guide writers through challenging tasks, and (3) teach writing strategies.

ADD TO YOUR JOURNAL Reflect upon the three key ideas presented in this chapter and decide what you think. Do you see ways that writing can help your students think and learn in your content area? Does the procedure for planning writing guidance make sense to you? Do you agree that some writing tasks are more motivating than others and that helping students think about role and audience as well as topic and form can help them focus their writing? Can you imagine yourself guiding students through the before, during, and after phases of writing? Finally, what do you think about encouraging student responsibility, reflection, and self-assessment as ways for students to become more independent learners? Describe your reactions to the three key ideas and generalize about the role of writing in your classroom. What and how large a role do you see for writing in your classroom?

Additional Readings

A persuasive case for attention to writing is provided by the following:

NATIONAL COMMISSION ON WRITING. (2003). *The neglected R: The need for a writing revolution*. Retrieved August 14, 2005, from the National Commission on Writing website: www.writingcommission.org.

This article provides a compelling sketch of a young person's writing and writing instruction from elementary to high school:

CASEY, M., & HEMENWAY, S. I. (2001). Structure and freedom: Achieving a balanced writing curriculum. *English Journal, 91*, 68–75.

Comprehensive views of writing instruction in elementary and middle schools are found in the following:

BROMLEY, K. (2003). Building a sound writing program. In L. M. Morrow, L. B. Gambrell, & M. Pressley (Eds.), *Best practices in literacy instruction* (2nd ed.; pp. 143–166). New York: The Guilford Press.

FEARN, L., & FARNAN, N. (2001). *Interactions: Teaching writing and the language arts.* Boston: Allyn and Bacon.

The following describes grade 3–6 practices that integrate reading and writing to teach the distinctive elements of literary and nonfiction genres:

BUSS, K., & KARNOWSKI, L. (2000). *Reading and writing literary genres.* Newark, DE: International Reading Association.

BUSS, K., & KARNOWSKI, L. (2002). *Reading and writing nonfiction genres.* Newark, DE: International Reading Association.

These books address writing to learn at middle- and secondary-school levels:

OLSON, C. B. (2003). *The reading/writing connection: Strategies for teaching and learning in the secondary classroom.* Boston: Allyn and Bacon.

SCARBOROUGH, H. A. (Ed.). (2001). *Writing across the curriculum in secondary schools: Teaching from a diverse perspective.* Upper Saddle River, NJ: Merrill/Prentice-Hall.

Two solid reviews of research on writing are presented here:

DYSON, A. H., & FREEDMAN, S. W. (2003). Writing. In J. Flood, D. Lapp, J. R. Squire, & J. M. Jensen (Eds.), *Handbook of research on teaching the language arts* (2nd ed.; pp. 967–992). New York: Macmillan.

GRAHAM, S. (2005). Strategy instruction and the teaching of writing: A meta-analysis. In C. A. MacArthur, S. Graham, & J. Fitzgerald (Eds.), *Handbook of writing research.* New York: The Guilford Press.

8

Studying

Have you ever heard a joke, laughed out loud at the punch line, then found yourself unable to recall and retell it to friends a few days later? If so, then you experienced the difference between comprehending and studying. You understood the joke well, but you did not study it well. Chapter 5 of this text presents comprehension; this chapter presents study.

Studying is understanding and remembering. Students in K–12 schooling seldom develop effective and efficient study abilities from merely being required to study. Explicit instruction in how to study is necessary if most students are going to acquire those abilities. Study strategy instruction involves, among other things, teaching students how to take notes, question themselves, and organize what they read. A team approach, in which each teacher helps students learn how to study that subject that year is an effective way for schools to teach studying.

Thinking processes are the building blocks of studying; they are its fundamental elements. The essential thinking processes described in Chapter 1—connect, preview and predict, organize, generalize, image, self-monitor, evaluate, and apply—are also the processes of studying. Students learn more and remember it longer when they actively think about a subject. The thinking processes are the antidote to the passive rote learning achieved by reading something over and over until it is memorized. With a few important exceptions like multiplication tables, that which is memorized by rote is usually forgotten soon after a test.

This chapter presents four key ideas:

1. Studying is complex.
2. Studying includes several major components.
3. Important principles of instruction apply to studying.
4. Teaching all students how to study requires a team approach across content areas and grades.

Studying Is Complex

The term *study* denotes any conscious effort to learn independently. Students study when they deliberate over subject matter, working to understand and, especially, to remember it (Devine & Kania, 2003). Studying is something students do for themselves, orchestrating and monitoring their own learning. Because reading and writing are major tools for learning, most studying involves reading or writing or both.

Providing learners with regular, explicit instruction in how to study faces three major challenges. In the first place, because studying is something students do for themselves, studying is personal. Students vary tremendously in their strengths, weaknesses, preferences, and peeves. They have different academic histories, including differing opportunities to have experienced successful independent learning. As a result, there is probably no area of strategic functioning with more room for individuality to display itself than studying. It is probably true that no two successful students study exactly alike.

In the second place, studying is particular to the content area being learned. As we discussed in Chapter 1, content teachers can teach content area reading and writing best because different subjects' different perspectives on the world require different literacies, because students are most receptive to receiving help in literacy when they need it to accomplish specific content assignments, and because content teachers know how best to read and write in their subjects. For these same reasons, it is difficult to teach students how to study in a generic way. When students try to transfer generic approaches to a particular content area, they often find that they are unable to get them to work, given the specific demands of that subject. For example, being taught how to take notes outside of math class often fails to help students take notes in math because the summarizing one usually uses when taking notes in other subjects ignores the sequential, step-by-step nature of much mathematics instruction.

In the third place, because studying is something you do rather than something you talk or write about, it can only be learned by doing. Learning to study is more like learning to play the piano or basketball than it is like learning American history or English literature. We don't expect students to learn how to be soldiers or poets by studying World War II or William Wordsworth. Likewise, we should not expect students to learn how to study from just reading or hearing about approaches to studying that one could take. The only way most students learn how to perform any complex action is through receiving explicit directions in how to perform the action, watching others correctly model the action, participating in successful guided practice, and engaging in successful independent application. Studying can best be taught to most students through those same means.

Studying would certainly be easier to teach if these three challenges were not in the way. If there were only one way to study effectively, if that one way worked equally for all content areas, and if students could learn that one way by just reading or hearing about it, studying would be a breeze to teach. Because of these three challenges, however, students benefit most from experiencing a variety of ways to study each content area as they move up through the grades.

Studying Includes Several Major Components

Knowing where to begin studying instruction is difficult because the domain of studying is huge. Philosophers have commented on studying throughout recorded history, and U.S. educators have published voluminous research-based and professional reports about it starting in the 1920s (Moore, Readence, & Rickelman, 1983). This section describes four central components of learning that fall under the name of studying: strategies, systems, resource management, and self-regulation.

Study Strategies

Proficient learners merge individual thinking processes into study strategies. Strategies are plans for accomplishing specific actions. They are how-to forms of knowledge (Kiewra, 2002). When summarizing material, for instance, learners might apply strategies such as identifying topic sentences, disregarding redundant information, and collapsing ideas into single statements. Practically all meaningful learning with print elicits some evidence of strategies. The following study strategies are used and recommended often:

Defining Learning Expectations
Previewing
Setting a purpose

Creating Mnemonic Devices
Analogies
Images
Abbreviations
Acronyms
Acrostics
Rhymes
Phrases

Questioning
Answering prepared questions
Self-questioning

Creating Special Word Associations
Meaningful word parts
Idiosyncratic associations
Mnemonic keyword method

Organizing Information Graphically
Outline
Time line
Flow chart
Venn diagram
Web
Cause-and-effect chain

Mental Learning
Retelling
Discussing

Writing
Study card
Note taking
Summarizing
Learning log/Journal
Essay

Test-taking Strategies

Defining Learning Expectations   Proficient learners define expectations by clarifying what they intend to learn. They create multistep plans for bringing thought into the learning act. One way of defining learning expectations is *previewing*, when proficient learners look over what they are to learn before examining it closely. They preview printed materials by surveying many sources of information: titles, headings, italic and boldface print, and other typographical aids; illustrations, maps, graphs, and other pictorial aids; introductions, first sentences of paragraphs, summaries, and conclusions; guiding questions, stated objectives, end-of-chapter exercises, and other adjunct aids. Previewing helps learners define learning expectations by establishing a general idea of what a passage has to offer.

Another aspect of defining learning expectations involves *setting a purpose*. Learners set purposes when they discern what they should acquire from a passage, lecture, video, CD, DVD, or other teaching device. Learners incorporate what they gathered from a preview with their understanding of the learning task to decide what deserves special attention. They attend to their instructors' stated and unstated cues about what they should learn. The age-old tradition of "psyching out" vague instructors to anticipate what should be in a paper or might be on a test exemplifies part of this strategy. When learners set a purpose, they decide what they want to or need to learn and go after it.

Questioning   Students who read and then answer questions tend to learn more than students who only read (Peverly & Wood, 2001). *Answering prepared questions* often seems like busywork to students, but it can be a potent study strategy.

Self-questioning taps learners' creativity. To learn how to self-question, students might be encouraged to pattern their questions after the teacher's, using certain stems like the following:

- What have I learned about _____?
- What should I remember about _____?
- What does _____ mean?
- What are the components of _____?
- How are _____ and _____ alike? How are _____ and _____ different?
- What are the strengths of _____? What are the limitations of _____?
- What caused _____ to happen?
- How does _____ affect _____?
- How does _____ relate to what I already know? How does _____ relate to _____ in the passage?
- What does _____ look (and sound) like?
- What is the significance of _____?

More open-ended self-questions include the following:

- What might be other examples of _____?
- What conclusion can I draw about _____?
- Why is it important that _____?
- What would happen if _____?
- What do I have to say about _____?

Organizing Information Graphically   Graphic representations arrange key terms in order to depict their relationships. *Outlines, time lines, Venn diagrams,* and *webs* (which are discussed in Chapter 5, pages 107 to 109) are different formats for graphically organizing concepts. They all show how selected concepts are organized. A graphic representation of the desert, for example, could consist of terms arranged about such topics as climate, location, plant life, and animal life; it would not be an illustrated scene of coyotes and cactuses.

Writing   Although such strategies as defining learning expectations and questioning might involve writing, study strategies grouped under this heading typically refer to other techniques. Writing strategies that promote learning progress from simply recording facts to assimilating and reflecting on bodies of knowledge. These strategies activate thinking when learners compose the message; they also provide a record for review or revision.

Study cards are one kind of writing strategy. Each study card usually contains a question or vocabulary term on one side with a corresponding answer or definition on the other. These cards are especially useful for factual learning. Many students would not have been successful in fact-filled courses without resorting to study cards.

Note taking is another writing strategy that promotes learning. Note taking assumes many forms. Learners sometimes copy definitions and key ideas verbatim from a passage, comment in the margins of texts, paraphrase information, or add personal examples. They benefit from rewriting their notes, clarifying and consolidating information from class presentations and readings.

Summarizing uses writing to involve learners in selecting and condensing important information. When summarizing, students may abstract important contents.

Learning logs/journals are a variation of class notebooks that require summarization. Students summarize when they record information from class presentations, readings, or outside experiences. Later, students sometimes develop their summaries into more lengthy compositions. In addition, they sometimes use learning logs or journals to pose questions or state confusions about what they are learning. Many mathematics teachers have students write—rather than orally ask—questions about their homework in order to clarify the questions. This practice often leads the students to reach independent solutions.

Essays that call for integration of subject matter or persuasive writing from a particular point of view are forms of writing that powerfully promote content learning, even though they are also time consuming for teachers to read. Most of us still remember papers we wrote in high school and college classes even though we have forgotten much of the rest we learned in those courses.

Creating Mnemonic Devices   Mnemonic devices—memory aids named after the Greek goddess of memory, Mnemosyne—include several disparate techniques (Glynn, Koballa, & Coleman, 2003). *Analogies* stress the similarities between phenomena. For instance, the cell structure of a plant might be compared with the factory structure of an industry. Effective speakers, writers, and teachers frequently use analogies to help students use what they already know to help them understand and remember new knowledge.

Images become mnemonic devices when they are used to represent abstract concepts. For example, a visual image of mist coming from a block of dry ice might be used to represent the physical process of sublimation, the change of a solid directly into a gas. Most of us associate personal or public events of the past with certain images that make those events come alive for us even now.

Mnemonic devices also take such forms as *abbreviations* (FBI, NAACP, NCAA), *acronyms* (HOMES for the first letters of the Great Lakes), *acrostics* ("My very educated mother just served us nine pizzas" for the first letters of the planets in order from the Sun), and *rhymes* ("In 1492 Columbus sailed the ocean blue"). They also can be *phrases* that help with meaning ("Hang on tight" for remembering that stalactites are on cave ceilings rather than floors) as well as pronunciation ("It's hot again" indicates the accent to Betatakin, a cliff dwelling in Arizona's Navajo National Monument).

Creating Special Word Associations   A set of mnemonic devices that is large enough and important enough to warrant separate treatment involves individual words. Because understanding and remembering subject matter vocabulary consumes a great deal of students' attention, we present word-study techniques both here and, at greater length, in Chapter 6.

Meaningful word parts, or morphemes, are found in derived words with their prefixes, roots, and suffixes. Contractions and compound words also contain these parts. Students often benefit from attending to the meaningful parts of such words as *underground, triangular*, and *immortalize*. Identifying the meaningful parts of words provides control of them and a tool for identifying new words.

Idiosyncratic associations are similar to meaningful word parts, although the word parts are not from our linguistic heritage. Knowing that the principal should be your friend and that latitude runs the same way as the equator represent idiosyncratic associations.

The *mnemonic keyword method* requires first an acoustic link, then a visual one. For instance, to remember that a credenza is a piece of furniture like a buffet or sideboard, the students might recode the word to an acoustic link, such as dents. A visual image of someone bumping into and denting the furniture could then be constructed.

Mental Learning   This somewhat amorphous category of study strategies produces no written or visual products. It stresses learning activities to be done either with others as part of a study/discussion group or inside one's own head.

Retelling is one way to initiate mental learning. After reading, students individually or in groups recount what has been learned. They focus on specific information, sometimes repeatedly verbalizing or paraphrasing it and sometimes reading it aloud. When uncertainties occur, proficient learners return to the source to clarify it or make a note to ask the instructor for clarification.

Discussing is an open-ended arrangement for students to come together and refine their learning. They might retell particular portions of subject matter, teach it to one another, or ask and answer questions about it.

Test-taking Strategies As standards-based accountability systems increasingly control education, students take more and more tests. And test performance substantially influences the futures of students and their schools. Consequently, preparing students for tests is a study strategy that now is an educational priority.

Test preparation is not the same as test practice (Kraemer, 2005; Santman, 2002). As one student who felt authentically ready for testing put it, "You prepare us for the test without teaching to the test." Teachers who prepare students for tests authentically connect test demands with coursework, integrating what is tested into the ongoing curriculum rather than only allocating separate time to isolated activities. These teachers do not focus on raising schools' test scores; they focus on improving youths' reading proficiencies. They first teach students how to improve their reading, then they teach how to succeed with tests.

When the focus is on succeeding with tests, teachers approach the task like any other genre. They explain the special forms and functions of tests, calling attention to how tests are similar to and different from other types of reading. They engage students in the genre, talking through the process of understanding it. They have students read test items carefully, deliberate with others over appropriate answers, and generate guidelines for succeeding with this genre. Figure 8.1 contains a list of test-taking strategies that are appropriate for middle-grade and older students. Note the three types: (1) general, (2) objective (i.e., response select), and (3) essay (i.e., response construct).

Systems

Study systems are multistep plans for bringing thought into the learning act. They combine several strategies.

SQ3R The classic study system recommended in the literature is SQ3R. Many years ago one of us examined the learning-from-text professional literature and found the book presenting SQ3R (Robinson, 1941) to be the most frequently cited reference; since 1941 it has been presented in many study skills courses (Readence & Moore, 1984). SQ3R consists of the following strategies, performed in order:

> *Survey*—Preview the material to obtain a general overview of what is to come.
> *Question*—Generate questions from the titles, headings, and subheadings to be answered while reading.
> *Read*—Process the print in order to answer the questions just asked.
> *Recite*—Deliberate over the passage contents, questions, and answers.
> *Review*—Look back over the passage to confirm answers and clarify uncertainties.

Reciprocal Teaching Reciprocal teaching (Palincsar, 2002; Slater & Horstman, 2002) is a highly acclaimed study system. In reciprocal teaching, students in small

General Strategies

1. Survey the test. Estimate its difficulty and plan your time for each section.
2. Read each direction or question carefully. Underline the important words in each direction or question. Be especially alert for closed terms such as *always, never,* and *most.*
3. Answer every required question (unless there is a penalty for guessing).
4. Do not spend too much time on any one question.
5. Drink water and eat a nutritious snack as needed.
6. Take a deep breath if you are becoming anxious.
7. Think like a test maker.

Strategies for Objective Tests

1. Answer the easy questions first. Mark the ones you skip and go back to them when you are ready. Remember that information contained in later items can help you answer previous items.
2. Look for the most correct answer when two items seem to be similar.
3. Narrow multiple-choice items to two, then make your choice when you are not sure of an answer.
4. Rephrase questions and answer questions in your head before inspecting the choices.
5. Change your answers only if you misunderstood the question the first time or if you are absolutely sure that your first response was wrong.
6. Shuttle among the passage, the question, and the choices.

Strategies for Essay Tests

1. Briefly outline all answers before writing. Jot down key terms and then add to those terms while working on your answers.
2. Include only information that you believe is correct.
3. Plan your time for each question and stick to that schedule.
4. Include topic sentences and supporting details in each paragraph.
5. Proofread your writing.

Figure 8.1   Test-taking Strategies

groups take turns leading discussions about sections of a piece of reading material they have all read and have open in front of them. RT consists of the following four strategies:

Summarize—Identify and integrate the most important information in the passage.
Question—Pose information in question form to test self and ascertain understanding.
Clarify—Identify specific impediments to understanding (e.g., unfamiliar terms, unclear ideas) and take necessary measures to restore meaning.
Predict—Preview upcoming text and hypothesize what it contains.

The student leader begins the group's discussion of the section by asking questions of the other students about the section's content. After the questioning period, the student discussion leader summarizes the section aloud for the others. The rest of the students in the group respond to this summary and, if there are disagreements, everyone returns to the text until a consensus is reached. After consensus on an oral summary is achieved, attention turns to clarifying. A student specifies troublesome aspects of the text, such as unclear referents, unfamiliar vocabulary, disorganized structure, incomplete information, and unusual expressions. Older readers often respond best to this strategy by pointing out what younger readers might need to have clarified. Next, the student discussion leader elicits predictions from the others about the content of following sections. The leader may also add predictions of his or her own. That ends the group's discussion of that section. If another section is to be taught reciprocally that day, another student in the group becomes the discussion leader for the new text section.

Initially during reciprocal teaching, the classroom teacher moves around, keeping students and groups on task. At opportune moments, the teacher models questions, summaries, clarifications, or predictions for students. The teacher also provides suggestions and feedback. As the students improve in their ability to teach text segments reciprocally, the teacher fades his or her guidance until each group is functioning independently.

Reciprocal teaching has been investigated in many research studies that, together, provide strong support for its effectiveness as a study system (Rosenshine & Meister, 1994). Its combination of the study strategies questioning/self-questioning, summarizing, clarifying, and predicting, mixed with mental learning, probably explains why it has been found to be so effective.

Study systems like SQ3R and RT share an important characteristic with teachers' unit and lesson plans: They have a beginning, a middle, and an end. Learners' study systems and teachers' instructional frameworks call for the learner to think deliberately about a passage before, during, and after reading. Preparation is done in the prereading, beginning stage; actual reading is done in the middle stage; and follow-up occurs in the postreading stage. Proficient learners realize this progression when studying with a system.

Resource Management

One of the authors wanted to attend a resource management seminar offered during the writing of this book but couldn't find the time. Resource management clearly is easier to talk about than actually to control. You probably will find this to be the case with your students, but we encourage you to continue emphasizing it because of its importance. Principles of resource management related to studying outside of school include the following:

1. *Maintaining a routine.* Establish a consistent time and place to study.

2. *Creating a productive environment.* Establish appropriate levels of noise, light, and temperature. Make sure school supplies are nearby. Have access to food and beverage. Take short breaks.

3. *Completing tasks in an efficient order.* Sequence tasks in an order such as easy to difficult, short to long, interesting to boring, or most favorite to least favorite (or vice versa). Then complete them in the way that is most efficient for you.

4. *Completing tasks on schedule.* Keep up with readings and assignments; do not procrastinate.

5. *Reviewing information at regular intervals.* Conduct frequent short reviews rather than infrequent long ones.

6. *Seeking help when needed.* Contact friends, classmates, or teachers to clarify information. Use tutors or study centers. Initiate study groups or pairs.

7. *Goal setting.* Chart a course to the future that includes career pathways and personal fulfillment.

8. *Getting along with others.* Collaborate as a team member more than a lone wolf. Develop teamwork skills, societal and workplace etiquette, and assertive communication. Channel emotions; manage stress and anger.

Resource management may be the component of studying that is most dependent on home support to develop. While home support may be crucial, teachers can help students improve their resource management by providing occasional opportunities during class for students to share how they manage resources. Schools can support students' development of good resource management by sending home a one-page description of resource management, focusing on the eight principles, and explaining how important home support is in helping students do well in school.

Self-Regulation

Proficient learners do what it takes to learn, employing the study strategies and systems they can use and have found helpful, and managing resources to enhance their learning. They also are self-regulated (Zimmerman, 2002), which encompasses control and motivation.

Control   Self-regulated learners control their learning actions. If deep understanding of a passage is needed, these students may preview it, take notes, and question themselves about it. If mastery of specific facts is the learning goal, these learners may decide to create mnemonic devices. Furthermore, they know whether an abbreviation, acronym, or acrostic is the best type of mnemonic device for the particular set of facts they intend to learn.

When self-regulated learners control what they read, they sometimes move forward at a medium rate, they sometimes skim, and they sometimes slow down considerably. They change their reading rate according to the demands of the material and their purpose for reading. If the passage is easy and learners want an overview of it, they read rapidly. If the passage is difficult and learners want to master the contents, they read more slowly, maintaining their focus. Proficient learners control themselves as they move through print, centering on ideas that they know to be important. At times, they regress to an earlier point in the passage and reread it to fix it in their minds or to compare it with a later one. These learners also focus on confusing ideas. If they are unclear about something, they return and attempt to clarify it or seek a third source to resolve an apparent conflict. This control of strategies and reading rate is essential for learning.

Think of a person skilled in a craft such as plumbing. Good plumbers have many tools and control them selectively to accomplish specific purposes. A plumber might size up a situation, then begin working with a socket wrench. If that tool is not getting the job done, she might employ a crescent wrench. When a plumber is at a delicate part of a job, she will slow down to be sure to get it right. Students with control use learning strategies like skilled craftspeople use tools. They plan to use strategies appropriate to specific learning tasks, check on how well they are progressing, and make adjustments as needed. They have well-developed and flexible repertoires.

Motivation   Along with having control, self-regulated learners are motivated. Students might be full of study strategy knowledge, but it will help only if they are motivated to apply it. Habit and will are as important as content and skill. Self-regulated learners have the predisposition to accomplish academic goals and persist with tasks even when they become difficult. They engage learning tasks with their full attention, blocking out distractions.

Students with little control of their efforts often attempt to escape learning. They may try to distract teachers or make excuses for their performance. They often create highly charged emotional scenes, acting out verbally and physically or withdrawing sullenly. Feelings of frustration and embarrassment rather than confidence and pride influence their actions.

A productive way to directly address the motivational aspects of self-regulation is to focus on students' academic identities as noted in Chapter 1. Acknowledging the influence of students' identities as readers, writers, and learners leads to many actions. Teachers recognize learners' difficulties but emphasize what students do well and begin instruction with these capabilities in mind. Such teachers maintain high standards and positive expectations for success. They promote learners' awareness of how academic success fits with personal fulfillment and career goals. They invite to the classroom role models from the community who attest to the value of reading, writing, and studying. Taking academic identity seriously means showing children and youth that studying in school counts for something, and individuals have the power to control it.

The affective motivational aspects of self-regulation deserve as much instructional attention as controlled strategic aspects. The roles of identity, curiosity, persistence, and confidence in learning should not be shortchanged.

A powerful method for motivation is described by Pearson and Santa (1995). Pearson is a high-school teacher who involves her students in an experiment for them to discover which of five study strategies are most helpful. This experiment is integrated with the content learning they are doing anyway. The students read five different text portions as part of their current unit of study. For each passage after the first one, the students are taught to use a different study strategy. After studying each of the five passages, the teacher gives the same kind of test. Each student graphs his or her performance on the test across the four study strategies and the control condition (passage 1). While prior familiarity with passage content makes some difference, students see that some study strategies seem to be more helpful to them than others. Pearson finds that this experiment motivates students to want to use the strategies they have found personally beneficial.

LISTEN, LOOK, AND LEARN   Interview a few high-achieving and a few low-achieving public school students of the same grade level. You may use the study questionnaire presented in Figure 8.2. Describe the similarities and differences between the students' reported approaches to studying. Explain how your beliefs about studying instruction were affected by interviewing the students.

Important Principles of Instruction Apply to Studying

At this point you probably realize the complexity of studying. Studying has many aspects, and many of these aspects rely on higher-order thinking. For instance,

---

Interviewer _____ Date _____

Student _____ Grade _____

School Subject _____

Note: If students are confused by a question, explain it until they understand. In addition, probe students' responses until they have no more to say about each item.

1. What do you do when you want to learn the information being presented in your (school subject) class? How do you go about understanding and remembering the information you need for this class?

2. How do you prepare for tests in (school subject)?

3. What do you do to understand and remember what you read?

4. How did you learn how to study?

5. When and where do you study?

6. How much reading do you do each week in (school subject)?

Figure 8.2   Study Questionnaire

such strategies as note taking, self-questioning, and representing information visually cannot be broken down into a fixed sequence of steps that always produce the same results. Long division can be reduced to such a series, but study strategies usually cannot. Because self-regulation is a major component of studying, the application of study strategies and systems requires countless decisions about the relative importance of information and the relationships among ideas. The individuality of knowing what some ways of studying are, understanding which ones to employ in particular situations, and being motivated to do so, add to the intricacies of studying.

You can and should be explicit when you teach students how to study, but you cannot expect an answer key to help you check students' notes, questions, or visual representations. Their approaches to studying should produce some common outcomes, but students' individual interpretations, preferences, and peeves will also cause these outcomes to vary.

TRY IT OUT   Compare the complexity of long division with that of study strategies. With a fellow student or teacher, compute an answer to an identical long-division problem; then both of you take notes on an identical passage. Compare both sets.

Given the complexity of studying, the best teachers can do is explicitly present general guidelines for strategy use, resource management, and self-regulation, then structure regularly occurring situations so students construct systems and habits that work for them. This section describes four principles of effective study instruction.

Combine Study Strategy Instruction with Content Teaching

An effective way to combine study strategy instruction with content teaching is by mixing isolated and integrated instruction (Langer, 2002). To illustrate, a school might focus on note taking as a study strategy all students will learn well. Effective teachers initially would demonstrate and have students practice note taking in isolation, with materials unrelated to unit topics. They would set aside brief portions of class time devoted only to this competency. They might use short, skill-building, commercial reading materials that are unrelated to the particular unit's topic. They would demonstrate and explain how to go about taking notes. Such an introduction is a way of separating a particular competency such as note taking from the ongoing flow of class life and highlighting it for students' undivided attention. It marks note taking for future use and signals its importance.

As students become proficient with note taking, effective teachers would ensure that it soon is integrated into instructional units with the actual tasks at hand. For instance, in science class, students initially might summarize materials unrelated to cell division, but, as their proficiencies increase, they would take notes when reading about the cardiovascular system and the nervous system. Students might record notes in journals or notebooks, then use them during inquiry projects or when preparing for a test.

Many upper-grade teachers introduce particular study strategies or systems during the first few weeks of school to help students study better throughout the semester or year. Teachers identify a few preferred ways to study or take ones from a school's curriculum guide, then present them to students immediately. For example, if they expect students to keep learning logs throughout a semester, they will demonstrate how to do so at the beginning. Or, if mnemonic devices make especially good sense to them and are applicable to a subject they are teaching, they will introduce the creation and use of mnemonic devices to students as early in the semester or year as possible.

Ways to study can also be presented after a semester or school year has gotten under way. Different ways to represent information visually might be presented throughout the year as opportunities and students' needs arise. In social studies, time lines might be appropriate during each unit of study, but outlining might be introduced only when students create the table of contents for a term paper. If students are having special difficulty with a portion of subject matter, then self-questioning might be introduced at that point to help them overcome that special challenge.

Follow an Apprenticeship Model

The best teachers of any subject are usually the teachers who are themselves successful students of that subject. It is difficult to teach science well, for example, unless one is interested in science. Learning how to learn any subject is most effectively done when it is conceived of as a classroom of apprentices learning from a master. Engage your students with meaningful units of study, then teach what is needed to succeed like a master craftperson instructing apprentices (Braunger, Donahue, Evans, & Galguera, 2005).

Fading and Self-Assessment

Fading is an effective approach for teaching students ways to study. As we explained in Chapter 2, fading occurs when teachers show students how to perform a reading or writing strategy, then gradually move back so students do it on their own. Teachers fade out, and students fade in.

Fading requires planning on your part to make sure it happens. Teachers often lead students through particular learning procedures, never fading out to relinquish control to students. But think about it: If you always ask the questions, when do students learn to question themselves? If you always present an outline of course topics, when do students learn to outline independently?

There is no question that teachers should fade out during instruction in how to study, but sometimes teachers can fade too quickly. Sometimes teachers simply tell students to "take notes on the upcoming material" or "get ready for a quiz on Friday," with little or no instruction on how to take notes or prepare for a quiz. Teachers sometimes assume students are proficient with these strategies when they are not. Guard against not fading out and fading out too soon. Plan studying instruction that balances demonstration, guided practice, and independent application.

Demonstration   During the demonstration stage, teachers begin as the dominant figure in the class. Teachers label and define the desired study strategy or system by naming it, presenting a general description of it, and making analogies to it whenever possible. Teachers explain the relevance of the strategy or system by indicating when and why it is useful. They model it by performing it publicly, explaining it as they go along. Finally, they list prompts for it.

When labeling and describing word study cards, you might tell students something like this:

> Today I will present word study cards to you. These cards are ways to focus on the technical vocabulary of this class. They are like snapshots of individuals rather than a total class picture. Word study cards contain a vocabulary term on one side and ways to understand the word on the other. Making these cards will help you understand the terms, and reviewing the cards will help you remember them.

To explain the relevance of the strategy, you might say something like this:

> Using these cards is one way to cope with the terrific amount of new terms you'll be encountering here. Knowing this strategy will help you in other situations, like getting a new job or being on a sports team when you suddenly have to learn a lot of specific new ideas.

As you model the strategy, you could say something like this:

> Watch how I produce word study cards. First, I acquire a stack of index cards. Then I decide which terms to transfer to the cards. I select words in boldface print, ones listed at the end of the passage, and ones that seem important to me. As you can see, I chose *monarch* as one of the words, so I print it on the front of the card. Then I turn the card over and produce learning aids that will help me understand and remember this word. I decide to write a definition, "Ruler. A king or queen"; a sentence containing the term, "Queen Elizabeth is the monarch of England"; and a note on word parts "mon = one (monorail)." I could have drawn a picture or produced other examples of monarch, but what I have here seems to be enough. Now I put this word card into my pile to review later. I might simply quiz myself on the meanings, separate known from unknown words, get with someone else and take turns quizzing each other, or group the words into different categories.

Finally, listing prompts consists of specifying as well as possible the procedure you followed. Prompts are general guidelines; they are not rules that always lead to the same outcome. You might tell your students something like this:

As you saw, I followed the three steps that I posted on the bulletin board:

1. Identify important terms.
2. Record one term on one side of a card and learning aids on the other.
3. Review the cards regularly.

Guided Practice   After demonstrating the study strategy or system, provide guided practice in doing it. Direct students to use it and provide feedback while they do. You might say, "Now it's your turn to produce your own study cards. Work with a partner or on your own. We'll get together as a whole class in fifteen minutes to check on progress." As you move around to work with students, you can probe their understanding of the strategy, praise and encourage their efforts, remind them of missing steps, and suggest improvements.

Independent Application   Showing students a strategy or system, and then having them practice it several times as you provide cues and feedback is a good beginning, but students need to apply the strategy independently and regularly to make it their own. During the independent application stage, teachers plan situations for students to use and refine the strategy; they determine students' grasp of it and reteach what is needed.

Plan your teaching so that your instructional routines incorporate study strategies and systems, and so that students succeed in class when they apply them. Open-notebook quizzes exemplify this type of planning. Regularly provide class time for students individually or in groups to take notes from their readings. Then allow students to use these notes, but not the readings themselves, during quizzes. Many teachers also collect students' learning logs or journals, comment on them, and record a plus or minus grade depending on the amount of writing students produced. Representing information visually becomes an instructional routine when every Monday you randomly select a student to share what he or she produced for an assigned reading. You ensure that self-questioning leads to success when student-produced questions appear on quizzes.

Self-Assessment   The necessary complement to your fading is for students to self-assess during studying instruction. For instance, as with any writing you could have your class complete score guides for their notes, learning logs, graphic organizers, or self-questions before you check them.

You could have your class complete open-ended questions such as the following:

- What did I find difficult to understand? What can I do to improve my understanding of _____?
- Does _____ make sense with what was presented before? If not, what can I do to make sense of _____?
- What did the author/teacher present to help me understand _____?

TRY IT OUT Select a study strategy or system, and plan an introductory lesson that contains the demonstration and guided practice steps. Conduct the studying lesson with a group of peers or public school students. Evaluate the lesson: Describe what you would keep and what you would change if you were to do it again. Also describe your next steps to follow up this introductory lesson with opportunities for independent application.

Scaffolding

Construction workers use scaffolding to prop up structures and gain access to them as they are being erected; scaffolds are used in various ways until the building can stand on its own. In education, scaffolds are the supports teachers and students use to construct new knowledge. Dialogue among students and their teacher is a central feature of scaffolded instruction. Students need a nonevaluative setting to verbalize their understandings and beliefs about study strategies and systems so teachers and other students can suggest the right actions at the right times. Scaffolds also can be teaching tools, such as cue cards, or teaching techniques, such as classroom grouping patterns (Rosenshine & Meister, 1992).

When you plan and present studying lessons through an approach based on fading, decide what scaffolding is needed. Working closely with your students will help you determine the supports to include, gradually decrease, and eventually remove. Thinking about the following types of scaffolding helps you plan what to fade: prompts, analogies, classroom grouping patterns, reading materials, strategy complexity, and process checks.

Prompts   Prompts stimulate thinking. They are questions or directions that cue learners to the critical features of the strategy. They induce learners to think a certain way.

Like the outcomes of a traditional task analysis, prompts indicate the actions to perform in multistep procedures. The three guidelines for producing study cards, presented earlier, exemplify prompts (identify important terms; record one term on one side of a card and learning aids on the other; review the cards regularly).

The five steps of SQ3R (survey, question, read, recite, review) cue readers to the actions they should take during this particular study system. Mathematics teachers usually present a multistep strategy for solving word problems with prompts such as the following:

1. Survey the problem.
2. Determine what is given and what is asked for.
3. Determine what operations to use and when to use them.
4. Estimate the answer.
5. Solve the problem.
6. Determine if the solution is reasonable.

The prompts should be recorded for students' reference. They might be placed on a bulletin board, distributed on cue cards, or copied into students' class notes. You should refer to the prompts frequently at first, then begin to fade them out.

Prompts do not specify invariant rules; they signal general actions. The survey part of SQ3R, for instance, involves examining many parts of a passage in no particular order. However, despite their generality, prompts are valuable supports that guide learners.

Analogies Another form of scaffolding to include in studying instruction is analogies that compare a study strategy or system to something vivid. Analogies can motivate students and make strategies concrete and sensible. They are good vehicles for discussions.

Many types of analogies are available. You can compare word study cards to snapshots, note taking to gold mining or eating digestible bites of food, and representing information visually to sketching a picture or framing a building. Teachers sometimes compare readers to detectives: Both search for clues, form hunches, and support their generalizations.

If you cannot think of an analogy for the strategy or system you are presenting, ask students for one. Their analogies frequently are more vivid and apt than the ones adults produce.

Classroom Grouping Patterns Adjusting classroom grouping patterns is a good way to scaffold instruction. Students can develop strategies when participating in whole-class, small-group, learning-pair, and individual configurations. Teachers change classroom grouping patterns to keep their instruction fresh, accommodate the type of lesson they are presenting, and promote dialogue.

Teachers often demonstrate ways of studying to a whole class, then begin fading by jointly performing the procedure with students still grouped as a class. After collaborating with students in a whole-class setting, have them perform the strategy or system in small groups or learning teams. Students who take turns teaching the strategy or system to one another go far in refining their knowledge of it. Small-group or learning-pair production of questions, visual representations, or mnemonic devices are clear tasks that fit group work nicely. Individuals can perform strategies on their own and then join a group or a partner to share what they produced and receive feedback. Finally, group support can be removed as students work to internalize the strategy on their own.

Reading Materials Ensuring that your instruction offers an appropriate challenge is an important feature of scaffolded instruction. The materials you use when introducing ways to study should present minimal difficulties to your students so they can concentrate on that strategy or system. We have seen many studying lessons torpedoed by lengthy, difficult reading materials; the students became confused about the material and, consequently, the strategy.

When you introduce a strategy or system, one way to ensure appropriate materials is to use ones already studied in class. Return to a passage that your class already read and show how the procedure applies to it. Another way is to locate very

Students can learn study strategies while working in groups.

easy topic-related materials. Secondary-school English teachers often introduce such literary elements as plot, setting, theme, and symbolism with children's literature. After introducing a strategy with short, easy materials, you can begin increasing the length and difficulty of the materials to meet your students' abilities. Once students have a strategy for identifying the plot of *The Three Little Pigs*, they can begin transferring it to *Charlotte's Web* and eventually *War and Peace*.

Complexity   Another way to control the difficulty of studying instruction involves the strategy or system being taught. Be sure that the prompts are appropriate for your students. If a step in summarizing is "Determine the main idea of the passage," you would need to ask yourself if your students can accomplish this step. Perhaps this main idea prompt should be modified to "Determine the topic of the passage."

You can regulate the difficulty of a multistep procedure by presenting each prompt gradually, giving manageable yet meaningful portions a step at a time. Ensure that students can perform the first step before beginning the second. If students are to ask themselves or one another generic questions, be sure that they understand each question and know how to go about answering it.

Strategy Checks   A final way to scaffold instruction involves strategy checks. These checks are good ways to keep students in pursuit of learning how to study, directing them to maintain what they are learning. Have students take stock of their use of study strategies or systems at various intervals. When they are preparing to read, ask them, "What are some things you might do to learn this information?" At other times simply remind students of strategies or systems they have learned: "Remember what you know about imaging when you read this passage."

Questions such as the following check on students' strategy:

Before Reading
How will you remember this? What can you do to learn this?

After Reading
What led you to that conclusion?
Why do you say that?
How did you figure that out?
How did you approach this?

Strategy questions focus students on how they studied rather than on what they learned. If a student claimed that the Spanish conquistadors were criminals rather than heroes, a product-oriented check would be: "What did they do that was criminal? Were the French settlers any more criminal or heroic?" Conversely, the following would be a strategy-oriented check: "Why do you say that? What led you to that conclusion?"

Teaching All Students How to Study Requires a Team Approach across Content Areas and Grades

Students benefit most from experiencing a variety of ways to study each content area as they move up through the grades. The ability to study develops over many years. What should or can be done to help students acquire the skills for lifelong learning in a dynamic society? As the numerous methods textbooks devoted to study indicate (see, for example, Fry, 2000; Greene, 2005), multiple approaches have been offered. We believe that the key to progress in teaching studying is for each content area at each grade level to have a few useful ways of studying that are seen by everyone as part of what is to be learned that year in that subject.

The concept of a *team* approach is crucial here. We are opposed to top-down mandates of study skills courses, modules, or units, because they cannot work given the nature of studying and studying instruction discussed so far in this chapter. Instead of mandates, we encourage the faculty of each school to work together as a team to decide what ways to study they will attempt to teach their students by the time they move on to the next level of schooling. For example, each K–5 elementary school faculty should engage in a process by which they decide what they will teach in each subject at each grade in the area of studying that will prepare all of their students to be able to study successfully in sixth grade.

In effective teams, knowledge is shared in an open, collegial manner. Teachers and administrators critically examine their beliefs and actions relative to a classroom concern, like study instruction. They review standards and the professional literature, consult with and observe the programs of knowledgeable others, and converse among themselves.

Team members plan instructional initiatives, then evaluate and report what happened. Study strategy initiatives might range from graphic organizing, to note taking, to the components of Reciprocal Teaching. Team members support each other, implementing initiatives by sharing resources, coaching each other, visiting one another's classes, videotaping class actions, evaluating what students produce, and providing feedback.

The outcomes of a team approach to teaching students how to study potentially cause changes so profound that schoolwide reform results (Langer, 2000). For instance, teachers and administrators might collaborate to learn about Reciprocal Teaching, identify program goals, gather appropriate resources, involve all faculty, and adjust schedules to allow focused teaching. Every teacher might present a Reciprocal Teaching minicourse to a group of students. When all goes well, the vocabulary and repertoire of Reciprocal Teaching becomes part of the school culture.

If you are fortunate enough to teach in a school where the faculty engages in a team approach to teaching studying, we encourage you to participate actively as a member of that team in advocating for the kind of studying instruction outlined in this chapter. However, if you teach in a school where there is no systematic or organized attempt to teach studying schoolwide through the grades, then present those study strategies and systems you understand, believe in, and can integrate with your content teaching. You will have helped your students learn to study your subject better.

Specific Content Area Applications

Studying in English/Language Arts Classrooms

English/Language Arts curriculums, like those of most other content areas, include a broad array of outcomes. Among other things, students in English/Language Arts are expected to learn how to write essays, letters, memos, and poems; understand advertisements, plays, short stories, and novels; present themselves during interviews, public presentations, and work groups; and value, appreciate, and personally respond to literary accomplishments. Concentrating on generic study techniques that provide students access to these outcomes is one way English/Language Arts teachers manage such crowded curriculums.

Reciprocal Teaching (RT) is an approach to studying English/Language Arts that deserves consideration. RT denotes an instructional approach for teachers as well as a study system for students. It offers a set of specific learning conditions as well as a set of specific mental operations.

The RT instructional approach emphasizes teacher–student and student–student conversations, or dialogues, about understanding texts. It calls for cooperative effort and sharing. While reading short sections of a passage, for example, teachers and students think aloud. They talk about the mental processes they are using to make sense of what they are reading.

Teachers typically fade their instruction during RT. They initially take the lead in describing particular strategies they are applying, then they gradually relinquish this role as students describe their use of the strategies with other segments of text. When participating in small groups, students often write their responses on overhead transparency sheets for whole-class sharing. Teachers scaffold instruction during RT by commenting on students' efforts ("That's a good start. What do others of you think might be important to say?"), offering additional modeling ("I think the reason for selling the camel needs to be included here."), and hinting at next steps ("Now what should you do to make sense of this passage?"). Praising valid actions, providing passages at different levels of difficulty, and posting written prompts about RT strategies are additional possible scaffolds. Teachers explain why and when particular strategies are appropriate.

The original RT study system, or repertoire of mental operations, consists of four cognitive strategies: summarize, question, clarify, and predict. Teachers and students talk about how they are employing these mental actions relative to specific sections of reading materials. If the class or a small group was reading *Shabanu, Daughter of the Wind*, individuals would take turns describing their summaries, questions, clarifications, and predictions. For the episode when Shabanu's father sells Guluband, the family's prize camel, one student might briefly summarize what happened, produce a question such as "Why was Guluband sold?", clarify the way Shabanu's father went about selling the animal, and predict what will happen next. As the student talks about these things, others chime in with their thoughts. They might add to the summary, suggest additional questions, offer other items for clarification, and produce their own predictions.

The RT learning target is independence. After multiple focused conversations about passages conducted in groups, individuals are expected to conduct their own dialogues internally. Individuals are expected to become independent and think through their own summaries, questions and answers, clarifications, and anticipations. When emphasizing this individual action phase of RT, you might call it "talking to yourself" or "having an internal dialogue." This aspect obliges individuals to utilize inner speech—the voices within their minds—to determine text meanings. Students are expected to address possible interpretations and evaluations internally before settling on certain ones.

When using RT in English/Language Arts class with narrative passages, you might retain its approach to instruction but modify its cognitive strategies. Consider modifications such as reducing the number of strategies from four, having students select only the one or two they believe most appropriate for a particular section, or substituting strategies. You might replace the original RT strategies (summarize, clarify, question, predict) with some of the essential thinking processes described in Chapter 1, such as connect, generalize, or image, if these seem more appropriate for your students and the materials they are reading. For instance, students internally might orchestrate connections among text ideas and previous experiences, think through possibilities for a passage's overall message, and construct and reconstruct images of key scenes until they are satisfied. Indeed, RT's value seems to come from its collaborative, explicit, sense-making approach to instruction more than from its specific strategies being taught. Students benefit when they exert concentrated efforts to learn and make public what they are doing.

Studying in Second-Language Classrooms

Helping students become independent lifelong learners is a central goal of education. In second-language classrooms, this means developing students' desires and abilities to continue their language learning after graduation. Promoting effective instructional settings and word-learning strategies are two ways to approach this goal.

Second-Language Instructional Settings   As noted in Chapter 2, the overall setting of a classroom substantially affects learning. Second-language learning is no exception. Teachers play an especially crucial role in promoting meaningful settings that begin a lifetime of second-language learning.

Effective second-language teachers promote meaningfulness by stressing cultural studies along with linguistic studies. Effective teachers go beyond having students translate printed passages, memorizing word meanings, and completing grammar exercises. Instead, they emphasize second languages as a means of examining and expressing the cultures from which they come. Students are immersed in the modern customs and ancient traditions of a culture, and they examine history and geography associated with the language. They experience the second cultures firsthand through field trips and guest speakers, and they experience audio-visuals of the culture's sights and sounds. Language learning is embedded in cultural learning.

Word-Learning Strategies   Teachers who present only the meanings of words encountered during class shortchange students when they leave class. Second-language users with few word-learning strategies are limited when they encounter unfamiliar terms and their teacher is not available to explain them. To avoid this situation, effective second-language teachers emphasize word-learning strategies.

A frequently underestimated word-learning strategy is determining the depth of knowledge needed for particular terms. Knowing only that *truffles* are edible and that *taupe* is a color might be sufficient for some learners but not for others. Learners need to become adept at determining the words that warrant their attention and the degree of knowledge that they require. Second-language teachers promote this adeptness by involving students in selecting words for study and determining their meanings. Teachers regularly have students identify the important words in reading materials, presentations, and audiovisuals, and they have students talk about the meanings they produce for the words. To stimulate these practices, effective teachers regularly hold discussions in response to questions such as these two:

"Which terms should be learned?"
"What needs to be known about each term?"

Second-language teachers also emphasize word-learning strategies by helping students become "word detectives," sleuths who take advantage of word-meaning clues. Effective second-language teachers stress context as a powerful clue to word-meanings. After deciding on a passage's terms that should be emphasized, teachers help students figure out their meanings by examining the ways they are presented. They do this by regularly talking about students' reactions to a question such as this one:

"What does the passage reveal about the meaning of this term?"

Searching for cognate relationships (e.g., discerning the connections between the Spanish *naturalmente* and the English *naturally* as described in Chapter 6) is another good way to utilize word meaning clues. Teachers can accustom students to search habitually for shared meanings among words that look and sound alike by regularly asking students:

"Do you know any words that look and sound like this word?"
"Are any of these look-alike/sound-alike words related to each other?"

To see how contextual and morphemic clues combine, consider this sentence: *All rocks formed from fiery hot magma are called igneous rocks.* The context clearly implies that *igneous* means *formed from fiery hot magma.* And since the beginning of *igneous* looks and sounds something like the beginnings of *ignite* and *ignition*, a morphemic connection based on *ign* becomes apparent. Students can generalize the meaning of *igneous* to something like, "rocks formed by fire or volcanic action." To help students combine contextual and morphemic clues, you might ask something like:

"What are the connections between what the passage reveals about the word and its relation to look-alike words?"

If contextual and morphemic clues are insufficient, then independent learners consult references such as dictionaries, glossaries, encyclopedias, and other people. References are consulted only after determining that a term is important to understand and that the available clues do not fully reveal its meaning. Indeed, learners consult references to confirm and refine word meanings as much as to gain completely new understandings. In the preceding example, learners might seek confirmation to the meaning of *igneous*, and they might look up *magma* for initial ideas if they don't have any clue to its meaning. To help students consult references at appropriate times, you could ask:

"When understanding a word is crucial and the clues to its meaning are insufficient, what do you do?"

Finally, making and reviewing word study cards is a time-honored word-learning strategy. Recording new terms on the front of study cards and supplying clarifying information on the back is a powerful tool for continually upgrading one's second-language learning. Writing the clarifying information in one's native language enlarges the possibilities of what can be included. Learners might record definitions, explanations, sentence contexts, mnemonic devices, related words, and illustrations to clarify the unfamiliar word meanings. Reviewing the study cards, separating the words that are understood immediately from the ones that are not, and resolving difficulties are additional steps that promote word learning over time.

Studying in Mathematics Classrooms

Mathematics may be the subject that most people feel inadequate about how to study. When students are doing math homework or preparing for a math test, their lack of effective study procedures can lead to frustration and poor performance. Here are some ways math teachers help students become more successful and independent in their learning of mathematics.

Study Cards Requiring students to make a set of study cards during a math unit and then teaching them how to use that set of cards to study for a test helps students develop an important study strategy that only a few above-average students would probably figure out on their own.

After each type of problem covered in the unit has been taught and practiced, require the students to pick one problem of that type from their math book. Choosing one of moderate, rather than low or high difficulty, is generally best. Each student should write that problem on one side of a four-by-six index card. It should be written in every different way the book or you, the teacher, would write it. (See Figure 8.3 for an example of a math study card from a middle-school math class.)

On the other side of that same four-by-six index card, each student should write the page number(s) in the book where the explanation of how to work that kind of problem is to be found, followed by the steps the teacher recommends for solving that kind of problem, followed by the problem worked correctly. (See Figure 8.4.)

After each student has completed this study card, it can be handed in or checked by a partner. Once it has been checked, it is added to the student's growing deck of math study cards.

$$\begin{array}{r} 23.2 \\ \times 14.1 \\ \hline \end{array}$$

23.2 x 14.1

23.2 14.1

(23.2) (14.1)

Figure 8.3 Math Study Card Front

pages 187–189

1. Copy the problem in vertical form.
2. Check to see if the decimals line up.
3. Check to see if the numerals line up.
4. Multiply the top number by the first numeral on the right of the lower number.
5. Put a zero on the right, then multiply by the second numeral of the lower number.
6. Put two zeros on the right, then multiply the third numeral of the lower number.
7. Add the part answers together, starting on the right and keeping numerals straight.
8. The answer has the number of decimal places that the two numbers have together.

$$
\begin{array}{r}
23.2 \\
\times 14.1 \\
\hline
232 \\
9280 \\
23200 \\
\hline
327.12
\end{array}
$$

Figure 8.4   Math Study Card Back

Before a test, you should demonstrate how to use the deck of math study cards for study. Shuffle your deck and then pick the top card. Work the problem on the front without looking at the back of the card. Then turn the card over to check both your answer and how you worked it. It is helpful to students if you get one or two problems right and then "miss" one. On the one you miss, show them how to use the card to check, step by step, what you did. Show them how to use the pages from the book that explain how to do that kind of problem when you can't remember exactly what one of your steps means or what your teacher said about it. Provide time during class for students to study some for the next test using their deck of math study cards. Encourage them to use their study cards outside of class as they prepare for the test. Students who use their deck of cards for study and feel that it helps them are more likely to begin developing their own decks of math study cards after you stop requiring all students to do so.

Self-Regulation   No component of studying is more important for mathematics than self-regulation. Consider the kinds of students who usually do well in math. They know when they "have it" and expend little effort and exhibit little anxiety afterward on that concept. On the other hand, they also know when they are having difficulty and seem able to formulate the right questions to ask to elicit the help they need. Moreover, they seem to know when a parent, a fellow student, or a teacher is the most likely person to know the answer to a particular question. At times, they are able to keep working at one or more problems until they figure out what they need to know without help. The successful student of mathematics is almost always a self-regulated student.

The problem with some math instruction is that it seems based on the assumption that all the students are already self-regulated learners of mathematics.

The teacher shows students how to work a particular kind of problem and then assigns them practice exercises. It is their responsibility to know when and what they don't know and to seek the appropriate help from the appropriate person at the appropriate time. Unfortunately, such an assumption is often inappropriate!

Successful teachers of mathematics help students become more self-regulated by requiring them to predict and self-monitor during math lessons. Instead of starting out by working a problem for the class, the teacher presents a problem to the class and asks them to predict individually whether they can solve it correctly or not (he or she can even require them to write down a "yes" or "no" in the margin of their notes). If a number of students are certain that they can or uncertain about whether they can or not, the teacher has the class take a minute and try to solve the problem at their seats. The correct answer is shared and students discuss any difficulties. Then, the teacher tries to help them determine how they could have anticipated where they would have trouble. If most of the students seem certain that they cannot solve the problem, the teacher has different students explain what there is about the problem that has them stymied. In either case, the teacher still teaches everything she would have otherwise taught, but only when students have been made aware that they really need to know what is being taught.

A different problem is presented to the class and, again, they are asked to predict individually whether they can solve it or not. This process takes a little longer at first until the students become more self-regulated, but it pays off in reduced math anxiety and negative attitudes toward math on the part of many students. Once students are more self-regulated during math lessons in class, they can be encouraged to be more self-regulated when studying math outside of class.

Studying in Science Classrooms

Science is an extremely important subject that many students have difficulty learning. Here are some ways science teachers help students become more successful and independent in their learning of science.

Graphic Organizers Graphic organizers are an extremely important tool for helping science teachers give their students the big picture and to show them relationships between that big picture and science facts, terms, and concepts. Just as importantly, students can learn to create their own graphic organizers independently so that they can assist in their own mastery of both the parts and wholes of science.

For example, some chemistry teachers make the Periodic Table of the Elements on the wall of their classrooms an integral part of their course. In the beginning, the teacher explains what a chemical element is and contrasts it with a compound. As students are taught the concept of *atomic number*, the teacher refers to the Periodic Table to show them how the elements are arranged in increasing order of atomic number from left to right and top to bottom. As students are taught that the elements can be subdivided into groups that act somewhat alike when forming compounds, and share other properties as well, the teacher refers to the

Periodic Table to show them how sections of it cluster together into identifiable groups such as alkali metals or noble gases. Later, as students are taught the chemistry of these different groups of elements, they learn about the K, L, M, N, O, P, and Q electron shells. The teacher then regularly refers to the Periodic Table to show the students how the number of electron shells that an element has determines which of the seven rows or "periods" that element is in. As the teacher teaches the students that the number of electrons in the outer shell of an element determines how it forms compounds with other elements, the teacher also shows students that the number of electrons in the outer shell determines which column of the table that element is in. Once they understand how it works, students are encouraged to refer to the Periodic Table in their chemistry textbook as they study. Throughout, students are not allowed to forget that all the specific facts, terms, and concepts about chemical elements they are learning fit together into a grand scheme.

A *data chart* (labeled rows and columns with information in the cells) like the Periodic Table is only one kind of graphic organizer that a chemistry or other science teacher can use to show the relationships between the whole of a course, unit, or topic and its parts. With respect to studying, however, it is important to follow the effective use of graphic organizers by teachers with activities that have students work in small groups to represent graphically the relationships they understand among a set of facts, terms, or concepts. For example, at the end of a unit on electricity in a middle-school physical science course, the students could be put in mixed groups of four or five students each and given a list of key terms from the unit: current, conductor, induction, insulator, resistance, semiconductor, and voltage. The task would be for them to web "electricity" using those terms and others they find helpful. The groups can do these webs on transparencies or sheets of chart paper and some can be shared with the whole class. Of course, this task assumes that the teacher has previously used webs as graphic organizers while teaching the course.

As students improve in their ability to represent graphically the key terms, facts, or concepts of a science topic or unit, they can be shown how such an activity helps them prepare to answer test questions about the relationships among those terms, facts, or concepts. This will motivate some of the students to construct graphic organizers as a study strategy.

Mnemonic Devices   What are the colors of the rainbow in order? If you are like we are, you know the answer to this question because you remember the memorable nonsense word, *roygbiv*, or strange name, Roy G. Biv (red, orange, yellow, green, blue, indigo, violet). One of us still remembers eras in the order he learned decades ago in historical geology by constructing the sentence, "Come over soon; don't miss pepperoni pizza" (Cambrian, Ordovician, Silurian, Devonian, Mississippian, Pennsylvanian, Permian).

No other subject is so vocabulary intensive as science. The number of terms which must be learned in any science course is often daunting for students. Teaching them a few mnemonic devices that you have found helpful will increase their ability to remember sets of terms. With respect to them learning how to study science better, it is important to have the class construct a mnemonic occasionally to help them remember a particular set of important terms. The students who find these mnemonics helpful are more likely to produce ones on their own when studying science outside of class.

Studying in Social Studies Classrooms

Social studies courses are often marked by their breadth of content coverage and thoughtfulness of conceptual issues. If students are to take advantage of this breadth and thoughtfulness, they must learn how to study both social studies content and its conceptual implications. Here are some ways social studies teachers help students become more successful and independent in their learning of science.

Graphic Organizers To learn social studies, a student has to acquire a large number of facts, terms, and concepts. Unfortunately, teaching this basic level of social studies knowledge causes many students to become unable "to see the forest for the trees" and to conceive of social studies as "just one darn thing after another!" Graphic organizers help social studies teachers portray the big picture and relationships among facts, terms, and concepts.

For example, some American history teachers use data charts to help their students see the significance of the people, events, and dates they are learning. A *data chart* is a graphic organizer consisting of labeled rows and columns with information in the cells. Figure 8.5 is an example of a data chart that helps students see relationships among the specifics they are learning about the years leading up to the Civil War.

After having students fill the cells of this data chart with information from their textbook, class notes, and other sources, the students can easily be led to consider expansion, slavery, and the economy across the five administrations instead of only within each. Moreover, the chart facilitates students seeing relationships among expansion, slavery, and the economy during these years. The data chart increases the likelihood that the students will think about the possible relationships across administrations and factors without the teacher having to tell them directly what those relationships are.

A data chart is only one kind of graphic organizer that an American history or other social studies teacher can use to show the relationships between the whole of a course, unit, or topic and its parts. With respect to studying, however, it is important to follow the effective use of graphic organizers with activities that have students work in small groups to represent graphically the relationships they understand among a set of facts, terms, or concepts. For example, at the end of a unit on types of government in a middle-school social studies course, the students could be put in mixed groups of four or five students each and given a list of key terms from the unit: anarchy, aristocracy, authoritarianism, autocracy, capitalism, communism, democracy, fascism, monarchy, oligarchy, republic, socialism, totalitarianism. The task would be for them to web "government" using those terms and

	Expansion	Slavery	The Economy
James K. Polk (1845–1849)			
Zachary Taylor (1849–1850)			
Millard Fillmore (1850–1853)			
Franklin Pierce (1853–1857)			
James Buchanan (1857–1861)			

Figure 8.5   The Five Presidential Administrations Leading Up to the Civil War

others they find helpful. The groups can do these webs on transparencies or sheets of chart paper and some can be shared with the whole class. Of course, this task assumes that the teacher has previously used webs as graphic organizers while teaching the course.

As students improve in their ability to represent graphically the key terms, facts, or concepts of a social studies topic or unit, they can be shown how such an activity helps them prepare to answer test questions about the relationships among those terms, facts, or concepts. This will motivate some of the students to construct graphic organizers as a study strategy.

Discussing   In social studies, conceptual understanding is crucial. That is why successful social studies teachers use as many essay questions on tests and assign students to write as many short papers as they have time to grade. Unfortunately, many students have real difficulty showing what they know in a short paper or an answer to an essay question. Perhaps the best way to prepare students to do the kind of thinking that essay questions and short papers require is to have class discussions from time to time on the kinds of questions the teacher asks and paper topics the teacher assigns.

Two-Column Notes   Two column notes is a note-taking system that helps students organize information under specific topics and gives them a study system that they can use alone or with a partner. Students take notes on one side only of loose-leaf notebook paper. Before taking notes, they draw a line vertically down the paper, leaving a three-inch column on the left. They leave this left column blank, making their notes based on the lecture, video, or reading only in the wider right-hand column. When they finish taking their notes, they go back through them and label each with a word or phrase that tells the topic of each section of notes. To study from these notes, they work by themselves or with a partner, folding their paper so that they can only see the left column with the topics. Trying to anticipate questions that might be asked, they answer the questions, using information they remember from the folded-away right column of details. To check their recall of important facts, they fold back the paper and see if they have included all pertinent ideas. While studying, they deal with all notes that have a particular topic entry, even if these are separated by other topic entries. If students who have taken notes on the same lecture, video, or text section study together, they can compare notes and add details from each other's that they omitted to enter into their own notes and then "test" each other by constructing possible questions for each topic and trying to recall the pertinent details.

Teachers use a variety of strategies to teach students how to take and study from two-column notes. Some teachers divide a transparency into two columns and, with the overhead light off, make notes in the right column while reading or viewing something with the students. The students are also taking notes simultaneously, and after each section, the teacher turns the light on and helps students compare their notes with those he or she has written on the transparency. When all the notes are taken, the teacher and students work together to decide on a topical word or phrase to write in the left column. Finally, teachers demonstrate how to use the notes to study by folding the paper, coming up with possible questions related to each topic, constructing an answer, and unfolding the right-side notes to see if important details were included in the answer.

Another way of helping students learn two-column note taking is to give them a set of notes with the right column already filled in and have them decide what topical word or phrase to put in the left-hand column. They then use these notes to study as described. Here is one page of some two-column notes taken about modern day South Africa:

South Africa Since 1994

Government	400-seat national assembly
	80-seat senate
	President Nelson Mandela
	1993 first all-race election
People	43 million people
	32 million Africans (blacks)
	6 million Afrikaners (whites)
	4 million Colored (mixed ancestry)
	1 million Asians (India)
Land	Southern tip of Africa
	Bordered by Namibia, Botswana, Zimbabwe, Mozambique, Swaziland
	mostly plateau
	mild climate

Studying in Activity Classrooms

Think of the studying you have done as you have learned the field you teach. While reading and writing play a significantly smaller role in your field than they do in social studies, science, or English, they have helped you at times to learn what you now know and can do. Your students may not be aware that reading and writing have *any* part to play in your course. Here are some ways teachers of activity courses use literacy to help students become more successful and independent in their learning.

Study Cards   Requiring students to make a set of study cards while they are learning a procedure in your class and then teaching them how to use that set of cards to study for a test helps students develop an important study strategy that only a few above-average students would probably figure out on their own.

As you are teaching the procedure, select an important term, step, or rule that your students in the past had trouble remembering. Each student should write that term, step, or rule on one side of a four-by-six index card. On the same side of that card, each student should write the page number(s) in the book, if there is one, where the explanation of that term, step, or rule is to be found.

On the other side of that same index card, each student should write the question that the term, step, or rule on the other side is the answer to. If the term, step, or rule on the other side is the answer to more than one question, then more than one question should be written.

After each student has completed this study card, it can be handed in or checked by a partner. Once it has been checked, it is added to the student's growing deck of study cards for this procedure or the procedures being taught during this unit.

Before a test, you should demonstrate how to use the deck of study cards to study from. Shuffle your deck and then pick the top card. Ask the question(s) on the front aloud and then try to answer it (them) aloud without looking at the back of the card. Then turn the card over to check whether you answered with the right term, step, or rule. It is helpful to students if you get one or two terms, steps, or rules right and then "miss" one. On the one you miss, show them how to use the card to study that term, step, or rule (put it in a "missed" pile that you review after going through the deck one time). Show them how to use the pages from the book that explain that term, step, or rule when you can't remember exactly what your answer means or what was said about it. Provide time during class for students to study some for the next test, using their deck of study cards. Encourage them to use their study cards outside of class as they prepare for the test. Students who use their deck of cards to study with and feel that it helps them are more likely to begin developing their own decks of study cards for difficult terms, steps, or rules after you stop requiring all students to do so.

Writing Summaries of Procedures   After you explain or demonstrate how to do a particular procedure, have students write a quick summary of the steps and rules you have taught them. Then, pair the students and have them swap their summaries. Each student reads her partner's written summary to see if she understands and agrees with it. This process is faster and less threatening than if you watch each one of the students try to do the procedure, and yet it usually reveals many of the misunderstandings and gaps in what the students understand about how to do the procedure. Respond to the questions that arise.

Images and Rhymes Mnemonic devices help us remember difficult or tricky procedures. Many people still remember how to use a screwdriver or wrench properly by reciting the ditty: "Righty tighty, lefty loosey." Great basketball players often practice hitting crucial, last-second free throws over and over again in their minds so that, if the situation arises, they will have an image to help them remember how it feels to make those shots when the pressure to panic is intense.

Share with your students any images or rhymes you have used to help you remember procedures at difficult or stress-filled times. Encourage and give them

Literacy in an activity class.

time to construct their own images or rhymes to help them remember the procedures you are teaching them or to prepare for tests or performance situations when they might forget under pressure.

LOOKING BACK   Teachers can instruct students in how to study. More and better studying instruction would help all students be better prepared to learn from their current courses, future schooling, and lifelong learning opportunities. You encountered four key ideas in this chapter: (1) Studying is complex; (2) studying includes several major components; (3) important principles of instruction apply to studying; and (4) teaching all students how to study requires a team approach across content areas and grades.

ADD TO YOUR JOURNAL   Record in your class journal your reactions to this chapter. What lessons or units in how to study have you experienced? What were their strengths and limitations? What were their similarities and differences? Which study strategies will you emphasize with your students? What instructional routines do you foresee for highlighting study? How do you plan on implementing studying instruction in your teaching?

Additional Readings

A good source for teaching students how to study is found in the following:

FLIPPO, R. F. (2004). *Texts and tests: Teaching study skills across content areas.* Portsmouth, NH: Heinemann.

These three classics present scholarly description of study strategies:

NOVAK, J. D., & GOWIN, D. B. (1984). *Learning how to learn.* New York: Cambridge Press.

PRESSLEY, M., JOHNSON, C. J., SYMONS, S., MCGOLDRICK, J. A., & KURITA, J. (1989). Strategies that improve memory and comprehension of text. *Elementary School Journal, 90,* 3–32.

WEINSTEIN, C. E., & MAYER, R. E. (1986). The teaching of learning strategies. In M. C. Wittrock (Ed.), *Handbook of research on teaching* (3rd ed.; pp. 315–327). New York: Macmillan.

Although this scholarly reference addresses the study of older, college-age students, it offers implications for younger ones:

FLIPPO, R. F., & CAVERLY, D. C. (Eds.) (2000). *Handbook of college reading and study strategy research.* Mahwah, NJ: Lawrence Erlbaum Associates.

Self-regulated learning is described well in the following scholarly book:

ZIMMERMAN, G. J., & SCHUNK, D. H. (Eds.). (2001). *Self-regulated learning and academic achievement: Theoretical perspectives*. Mahwah, NJ: Lawrence Erlbaum Publishers.

Many how-to-study handbooks written for students are available such as the following:

CORMAN, M. C., & HEAVERS, K. L. (2001). *How to improve your study skills*. Glencoe/McGraw Hill.

JAMES, E., JAMES, C., & BARKIN, C. (1998). *How to be school smart: Super study skills*. New York: Beech Tree Books.

LUCKIE, W. (1997). *Study power: Study skills to improve your learning and your grades*. Cambridge, MA: Brookline Books.

TURNER, J. (2002). *How to study: A short introduction*. Thousand Oaks, CA: Sage.

9

Student Inquiry

LOOKING AHEAD   A group of primary-grade children inspect the chart they are producing. One claims, "We need to show the difference between those who eat sugar cereal for breakfast and those who don't." Group members talk about how this might portray classmates' eating habits, and they decide to make the comparison. A class of middle-school youth call out ways to reduce, reuse, and recycle as their teacher records ideas under a heading entitled "Conservation." In a high school media center young adults are online searching for possible solutions to selected U.S. foreign policy issues. These glimpses of school life show learners engaged in inquiry, investigating meaningful issues, and informing others about what was learned. This chapter describes how to facilitate such inquiries.

Recognizing the need for information, locating good sources, gathering what is needed, and applying ideas to situations are becoming critical competencies. Well-formed decisions about personal, social, and occupational issues depend on well-developed inquiry processes.

Many consider inquiry and research to be mysterious and specialized endeavors. However, these terms can be demystified by thinking of them as a state of mind. *Inquiry* and *research* refer to the process of producing convincing answers to interesting questions. People become curious about something, so they set out to learn more about it.

This chapter describes inquiries that engage students with a range of materials and methods for independently learning about the world. These are its keys:

1. A special feature of instruction.
2. Asking engaging researchable questions.

3. Locating sources and information within sources.
4. Organizing information.
5. Representing what was learned.
6. Teaching independent inquiry.

A Special Feature of Instruction

Many models of teaching involve student inquiry. General educators (Kain, 2003; Lambros, 2004; Martinello & Cook, 2000) long have promoted learner-centered investigations. Many secondary schools now have graduation requirements that call for students to exhibit the products of inquiries conducted over several months. Inquiry advocates believe that the most permanent and transferable learning occurs through personal involvement and self-controlled analyses. Inquiry-based educators believe that students who receive just teacher-directed instruction are at risk of learning to perform only on command.

The professional literature typically groups inquiry with educational concepts such as problem solving, project method, research projects, experiential learning, and inductive teaching. Inquiry often is linked with information literacy, "to recognize when information is needed and have the ability to locate, evaluate, and use effectively the needed information" (Association of College and Research Libraries, 1998). Unlike direct didactic teaching, inquiry-based approaches take a somewhat indirect, facilitative role in students' learning. Teachers provide support in whole-class, small-group, and individual settings as students assume primary responsibility for planning, conducting, and evaluating their investigations. During inquiry activities, teachers act as a guide on the side more than as a sage on the stage.

Student inquiry readily occurs during instructional units. If a unit focuses on heroes, alienation, inventions, weather, space, or careers, then students take the lead in exploring aspects of these topics in depth. They might concentrate solely on the central question of a unit (e.g., "What does it take to become a hero?") or they might address a particular favorite sport hero (e.g., "What can I learn about this hero?"). Like interdisciplinarity (see Chapter 3), inquiry is a special feature of units.

Once students begin conducting inquiries, they take the lead—or at least share it. But even as a partner in the inquiry process, you play a significant role developing learners' proficiencies. Students require support posing engaging and researchable questions, finding information, synthesizing ideas among multiple sources, and representing what has been learned (Roser, Strecker, & Ward, 1996; Rossi & Pace, 1998; Stahl et al., 1996). You support, or scaffold, students' efforts when they conduct inquiries. The next four sections present ways to help students ask questions, locate information, organize information, and represent what has been learned.

DO IT TOGETHER As a group or pair, think back to the independent research projects you completed in elementary and secondary school. Which projects were your favorites? Why? Which were your least favorite? Why? Each group or pair should briefly summarize their discussion for the rest of the class.

Asking Engaging Researchable Questions

Asking engaging and researchable questions leads to effective inquiries. Engaging questions elicit a sense of connectedness. They involve students by linking academic contents with personal concerns. Students address issues and ideas that they choose and that they perceive to be useful and interesting in the present rather than in some unforeseen future.

Inquiring into what it takes to be considered a hero tends to be engaging and researchable for middle-grade students. Neither naming one hero from Greek mythology nor describing every recognized hero in the world would be engaging or researchable. Indeed, problem *finding* might be an inquiry activity that is as important as problem *solving*.

Teachers introduce inquiry by engaging students' attention and arousing their curiosity. They kick off units with concrete objects that stimulate thinking and questioning. When launching upper-grade inquiries into advertising practices, you

Research entails multiple aspects of literacy.

might spend time displaying and talking about selected magazine advertisements, reading aloud some ads, and having students recall memorable ones. You might read aloud an article on how advertisers position their products, then browse through ad-saturated periodicals. A guest speaker or video could present information and ideas. Some teachers call this stage of inquiry "presearch," the time when learners acquire sufficient knowledge and interest for a productive inquiry. Immersing learners in a topic before inquiring into it goes far in setting the stage for rich research (Guthrie, Wigfield, & Perencevich, 2004).

Brainstorming is appropriate for helping students form engaging researchable questions. KWL, as presented in Chapter 3 of this text, is a popular way to generate questions. Other powerful practices include WH Poster Questions and Question Stems, which can be performed with the whole class, small groups, or individuals.

WH Poster Questions

For WH Poster Questions, a topic is presented on a sheet of chart paper or the whiteboard, or projected with a computer presentation program or an overhead transparency, so students can brainstorm questions with the teacher. The *wh* words, who, what, when, where, why, and how, are the entry points for inquiries. Teachers initiate the topic to be studied—*danger*, for example—then help students frame inquiries by attaching *wh* words to the organizing center. A central question for the whole class, one for each small group, or one for each individual could be produced this way. Students ask questions such as, "*Who* are the most dangerous people we meet?" "*What* dangers occur inside and outside school?" "*When* do we encounter danger?" "*Where* are the most dangers encountered?" "*Why* do dangers exist?" and "*How* can we overcome dangerous situations?" Many more questions could be posed for each *wh* word.

The questions are posted for inspection. Those that are too narrow for engaging inquiry (e.g., "*Who* set the Chicago fire?") might be moved aside. Those that are too broad (e.g., "*What* dangers occur outside school?") might be reduced (e.g., "*What* common dangers exist in a kitchen?"). Commenting on questions at this point enables you to make public the question generation process. You and your class might think through the production of good questions, explaining the decisions you make. Refining questions this way so they are engaging and researchable has been called the "funneling process" (Kellett, 2005, p. 39), with classmates responding to ideas and you supporting the efforts.

Question Stems

Question Stems adds several words to the WH ones, guiding students somewhat directly (Rankin, 1999). Question Stems takes WH Poster Questions a step further by pointing students in particular directions. The following illustrate some possible stems that might be displayed in class to guide inquiries:

Children discuss WH Poster Questions in order to evaluate what has been learned and generate additional areas of investigation.

- What problems . . .
- What happens/happened when . . .
- What causes/caused . . .
- What are/were the effects/results of . . .
- What are the connections among . . .
- What is/was the role of . . . in . . .
- What is/was the difference between . . . and . . .
- What is the value of . . .

When exploring space, question stems might be expanded to "*What problems* face those wishing to travel to Mars?" "*What causes* meteorite crashes?" "*What is the role of* gravity in landing spacecraft on the moon?" and "*What is the value of* space exploration?"

Self-assessing Questions

Posting a set of criteria such as the following helps you and your upper-grade students self-assess questions:

- Neither too broad nor too narrow
- Interesting to the researcher

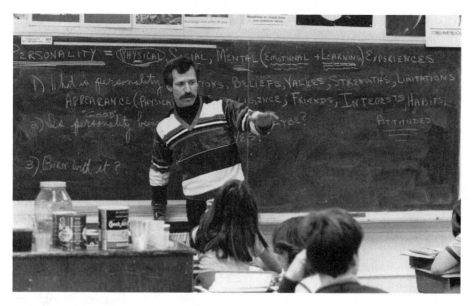

Students brainstorm researchable questions during inquiry units.

- Connected with the unit
- Resources available

Criteria such as these guide the self-assessments. Sometimes teachers configure students into small groups and have them act as critical friends, commenting on each others' questions.

Locating Sources and Information Within Sources

Along with engaging researchable questions, students need access to information. Efficiently locating sources and their appropriate information is essential to inquiry. A productive way to help students in this endeavor is to emphasize key words, online resources, and interviews.

Key Words

Key words open storehouses of printed information such as libraries, the Internet, textbooks, and encyclopedias (Callison, 2003). Key words encompass many concepts. "If you are going to the store for milk, orange juice, root beer, and diet cola," you might say to your class, "what word could you use to refer to all those items?" Discuss students' responses, such as *beverages* and *drinks*, in order to demonstrate that a few key words lead to many, many specifics. Point out how a few different key words can be combined with *and* and *or* to uncover the items. Adding *soft* to *drinks* specifies the list for the store.

Key Word Scavenger Hunt is a teaching strategy that allows students to practice locating information. It addresses information location strategies for multiple topics rather than for a student's particular inquiry. Students first are led as a whole class through introductory exercises to see how to locate information that answers various questions. Then they work in pairs or as individuals to locate information for a Key Word Scavenger Hunt list. The following are some practice items used with intermediate-grade students using textbooks, library books, and encyclopedias:

1. A word used in New England for factory is *mill*. How many kinds of mills does your textbook tell about?
2. What is adobe?
3. What is a nuclear reactor? What key words could you use to find information?

Online Resources

The Internet continues to offer dramatic opportunities for researchers individually and collectively to access, organize, and represent information (Leu, Leu, & Coiro, 2004; Stepien, Senn, & Stepien, 2000). When opening the Internet to students' searches, many schools focus on approved outlets. They provide access to youth-appropriate search engines such as Ask Jeeves for Kids (www.ajkids.com/) and KidsClick (http://sunsite.berkeley.edu/KidsClick!/). They link with services such as Marco Polo (http://marcopolo.worldcom.com) that provide panel-reviewed links to web sites, a search engine limited to those sites, and professional development resources. They visit portals (see, for example, www.west.asu.edu/achristie/sengines.html) that recommend Internet subject directories. Subject directories are arranged hierarchically with general topics divided into subtopics. For instance, Kids Web from Syracuse University (www.npac.syr.edu/textbook/kidsweb/) allows youth to progress from *science* to *biology and life sciences* to the *human body* to the *human heart*. The online exploration of the heart offers amazing print and visual information presented through static as well as streaming sources. They install filtering software to screen out objectionable material.

WebQuest names a particularly sensible type of inquiry activity conducted online. Short-term WebQuests last one to three class periods; long-term ones last between one week and one month. In a WebQuest, teachers or media specialists bookmark some or all of the information from online sites for students to access. Student researchers are not left to wander through cyberspace, hoping their search engines point them toward pay dirt. WebQuest designers include direct links to documents, searchable databases, experts' e-mail addresses, and nonprint media. This practice is especially sensible with younger students because the web is so unwieldy at present. Two excellent introductions to WebQuests are available at the following sites:

- http://webquest.sdsu.edu
- www.west.asu.edu/achristie/webquest.html

To illustrate, you might search a matrix of webquests from one of the sites listed above and find a topic you teach. If you use a webquest for young students on the Cinco de Mayo celebration of Mexican independence, you might introduce this topic and then present a task such as creating a book that describes this event's history and portrays its traditional dances, music, costumes, and food. You might have students click on a launch page's links to access preselected web pages that provide age-appropriate information. And you might present a rubric to guide students' inquiries.

Interviews

Conducting oral interviews seamlessly blends reading, writing, listening, and speaking as student researchers gain access to information (Kellett, 2005). Interviews can range from highly structured question–answer sessions between an expert and a novice, conversations among several people with varying degrees of expertise on a topic, and informal questions posed during guest presentations, field trips, and other outside-of-school explorations. We recommend interviews as standard features of inquiry projects.

When involved in somewhat structured question–answer interviews, young students should begin with familiar, friendly sources. Family members, school personnel, and peers are appropriate candidates for interviews in the early grades. Secondary students can begin interviewing unfamiliar people who are expert in students' inquiry topics. Once a person has agreed to be interviewed, many teachers send the person a brief letter outlining the nature of the students' projects and a description of how the information will be used. Such a letter is especially helpful if the interview is to be tape-recorded.

Question–answer interviews work most efficiently when the researcher has specific inquiries written in a set order. If students investigate schools of the past, asking the interviewee to "Tell me about your school days" may not be very productive. Instead, the students should be prepared to ask questions about teachers, other students, lessons, tests, discipline, and so on. These key words should be jotted down at first and then developed into complete questions before interviewing a subject. Interview questions, like the ones guiding an overall inquiry, should be specific, but not so narrow that they can be answered with a "yes" or "no." Asking source people follow-up questions such as, "Can you tell me more about that?" or "What else do you remember?" is a useful way of getting more complete information.

Tape-recording the interview is a good way to maintain a record of what was said; taking notes during the interview is also recommended. After leaving the interviewee, students should write down what they learned. This summary might be shared with the interviewee in order to check for accuracy and elicit additional pertinent information.

Before sending students out to conduct interviews, teachers frequently demonstrate the procedure by interviewing a guest in the classroom. Students also may want to practice interviewing one another before going outside the classroom.

TRY IT OUT   Form groups of about three. Conduct interviews with each other. Then talk about how you think these sessions would play out in a K–12 classroom. What would you need to do to ensure their success?

Organizing Information

Organizing information is an ongoing task facing student researchers (Burke, 2002). Young researchers who are seeking answers to "What do bears eat?" soon discover that information is available about the eating habits of different types of bears, at different times of the year, and at different ages and locations. Older students looking into how people measure time soon discover the great complexity with which scientists have addressed this issue. Students frequently report all the information they find because they consider everything to be of equal importance ("If it's not important, then why was it written there?"). Helping students be selective is essential to inquiry.

Computer software such as *Inspiration* and *Kidspiration* (www.Inspiration.com) helps students selectively organize their data collection by providing basic report structures or writing frames. Such software enhances students' abilities to produce notes, categorize information, and, in some instances, cite information. It helps students visualize patterns and relationships among ideas. Whether or not computer tools are available, students benefit from support in organizing information while conducting inquiries.

Interviewing guests contributes to research.

Producing Notes

A good way to introduce notes is to produce them on overhead transparencies or a Smart Board about a passage encountered during a unit. Think aloud your decision-making process while recording the notes you think most appropriate. After demonstrating and explaining your process several times, have students volunteer their ways of producing notes. Offer feedback, remembering that there are many avenues to good study strategies. Have students meet in small groups to produce notes jointly or to react to what each member produced individually. Again, display the notes so everyone can see the products.

Categorizing Information

As notes accumulate during an inquiry, students need to categorize what they find. It is not efficient to write bits of information on separate file cards, computer documents, or sheets of paper and organize them at the end of a project. It is far better to establish categories and group facts into categories as the research progresses. In this way, students can see which categories are lacking information and whether new information corroborates or contradicts earlier findings. When categorizing information, students might see the need for establishing new categories or revising old ones. The graphic organizers presented in Chapter 5 of this text and in other publications (see, for example, Burke, 2002) effectively group ideas into meaningful categories. Venn diagrams, time lines, outlines, and cause–effect chains visually portray the relationships among ideas. Two especially appropriate ways to categorize notes during inquiry projects are data charts and webs.

Data Charts Data charts are a tool to help students categorize information. Make a grid on paper, with the research questions listed across the top and the resources to be used listed along the side. Each box of the grid then contains the source's information related to the question. Sparsely worded notes are used in order to conserve space and encourage students to use their own words when writing the report. If a particular source provides no information about one of the questions, an *X* is placed in that square. Figure 9.1 shows a data chart for investigating the career of Ernest Hemingway. Show students how to record information in the proper location of the chart. Students should also be sent out to locate other sources to add to the left column.

Another type of data chart lists questions across the top of a chart and aspects of the questions down the side. For example, if the topic is wild animals, the questions across the top might be "What does the animal eat?" "Where does the animal live?" and "What dangers does the animal face?" Down the side, rather than listing sources, several different wild animals such as tiger, leopard, and lion are listed. Figure 9.2 is an example of this type of data chart.

Data charts are useful for arranging information, and they help students evaluate what they have gathered. For example, students might be directed to the wild animals chart and asked to decide which animal ate the widest variety of food, lived in the most unusual habitat, or faced the greatest dangers.

Sources	What was his life like?	What themes did he pursue?	What was his influence?
Smith & Jones			
Brown			
Linn			

Figure 9.1   Data Chart for Ernest Hemingway Report

Webs   Webs are flexible outlines that graphically depict the relationships of the parts to the whole and to one another. Figure 9.3 is a web of the history of Connecticut produced by a middle-school student. In the middle of a web is the topic being researched, and radiating out from the center are the subtopics stated either as questions or as words and phrases. Pieces of information about the subtopics are listed around the subtopics, though not necessarily in any specific order.

A web is a good way to depict information that students produce during brainstorming sessions and that students eventually gather. When you introduce webs to students, use the organizing center of the unit pursued and list questions around it. Next, have students tell what they know or think they know about the topic and list that information next to the questions. Students then find more information from their sources, return to the web, and revise it in light of the new information. The initial web is a good way to introduce an inquiry, and the final web is a good basis for a culmination.

Citing Information

An important point to convey to students is the need to record their sources accurately. Accurate records are necessary both for others to check the information and for the students themselves to return to, if necessary. The simplest way to record

Animals	What does the animal eat?	Where does the animal live?	What dangers does the animal face?
Tiger			
Leopard			
Lion			

Figure 9.2   Data Chart for Wild Animals Report

sources is to make a numbered list of all sources by title and date, including all visual, oral, and written sources. As shown in Figure 9.3, when students find something they want to use they can jot down the information, placing the appropriate identification number after the information, and including a page number if using a written source.

Maintaining and Clarifying the Focus of Research

A word of caution: Students who are seeking information frequently lose their focus. They often become so involved with tangential information that they are led far astray of their original question. One way to help students remain focused is to have them confer during the week and talk about how their projects are progressing (Rogovin, 2001). These conversations help students crystallize their learning and their next steps. When students meet with peers to talk about the status of their inquiries, they put into words what otherwise might be unclear. They stimulate each other to articulate what is being learned, what gaps exist in their knowledge, and how everything is fitting together. They think through what they intend to say in their final reports.

Teacher–student conferences also help young researchers maintain and clarify the focus of their inquiries. As you circulate among the class, you might serve the same function as peers by stimulating students to think deeply about their topics

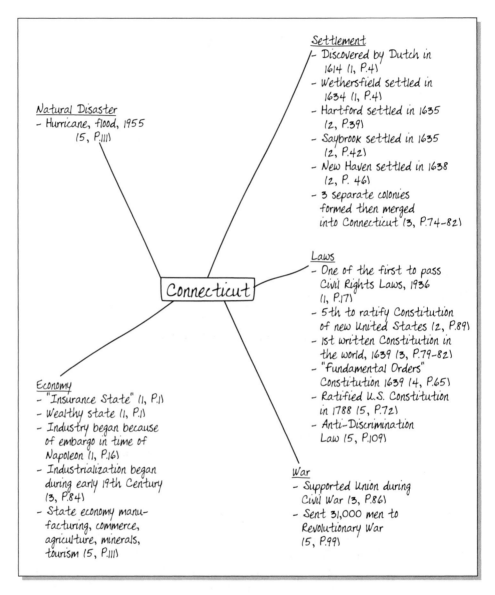

Figure 9.3
Web for Connecticut Report

and articulate their research status and plans. You might support their research efforts by answering questions and suggesting specific actions. You might prompt students to consult particular references or think about their questions in new ways. Praise good efforts and encourage ongoing ones.

Scheduling process checks is a good way to promote students' progress with specific aspects of inquiry. Scheduled checks add a certain formality to your role and signal inquiry as serious business, even though you can readily maintain a facilitative collaborative demeanor. Many teachers produce sheets specifying the date for checking each stage of inquiry and the possible points for that stage. Students attach these sheets to their research folders. Stages of inquiry such as the following might be designated:

1. Research topic and essential question   10
2. Resource log   10
3. Information gathered   30
4. Organizational scheme   15
5. Representation plan   15

Scheduled checks allow you to intervene with students requiring additional support. When used to promote growth, these process checks take on a positive role.

TRY IT OUT

This section has described a number of ways to help students organize information. Select one of the strategies you have used in the past. Think about any problems you had applying the strategy and what you might have to do to make it easier for students to use.

Representing What Was Learned

Student researchers at all levels benefit from representing and sharing with others what they have learned. This step deepens the understanding both of those who did and did not conduct the inquiry.

Student researchers generally feel compelled to display all the material that they garnered during their searches. They want credit for all the information that they worked so hard to obtain and frequently have difficulty paring down the information to that which directly answers specific questions. Such reporting results in undesirably long and convoluted pieces. Inform your students that expert researchers generally know more than they include in their reports and that students should likewise not try to include every bit of information they gather.

Representing and sharing what was learned sometimes is done in an informal, casual manner. Students are assembled after spending time conducting their inquiries in order to tell what they have learned in impromptu fashion. If the class spent time in the library investigating customs of dress, then a discussion about those customs might ensue; if students were sent home with the task of asking available adults how they came to their current occupations, then the findings can be informally shared the next day.

Students should have several options for how to represent ideas. Findings can be written up in a formal report, or they might be shared through multimedia formats that embed writing in visuals and realia, as is done in most science fair

Webs provide a basis for writing well-organized reports.

projects. Students might dramatize scenes. No matter what form is used, scoring guides that describe the criteria for self-assessment and external assessment are appropriate. The following presents four ways to represent and share information.

Writing

Students typically require support transferring information from their data charts or webs into written form.

Data Chart   Reporting the information gathered onto a data chart can be quite straightforward. For example, the data chart in Figure 9.1 can be the basis for a traditional five-paragraph essay. The first paragraph is the introduction, which prepares people for the upcoming questions (e.g., "Three aspects of Hemingway's life seem to have been very important"). It may also tell why the topic is important (e.g., "Ernest Hemingway was one of the most influential and well-known American authors of the twentieth century"). The second through fourth paragraphs address the three questions, turned into topic sentences, along the top of the data chart (e.g., "Hemingway had a vigorous lifestyle," "Hemingway focused on five primary themes in his writing," and "Hemingway influenced a generation of writers"). The fifth paragraph is a summary of important findings. A data chart works especially well for short reports.

Web Turning a web into a written report follows a similar pattern. Show students how to arrange the details for each subtopic according to the desired order of presentation. Subtopic headings become topic sentences, and the bits of information become the supporting details. Be prepared to demonstrate this method of organization more than once, providing sufficient guidance when students practice it.

General Guidelines Once information has been organized, students draft and revise their written reports. Reports can be improved by having students go through the revising step of the writing process. Peer response groups work especially well; because each student has been trying to write a similar type of paper, he or she brings to the group the same knowledge of the paper's form.

At the beginning of the year in elementary school, where teachers have inexperienced students, a structured approach to sharing reports is frequently useful. For a unit on domestic animals, for example, the class would generate a series of basic questions. Questions might include these: "How does this animal help us?" "Where does it live?" "What does it eat?" and "What does it look like?" Each child selects a different domestic animal from a group students have previously called up and writes a web about the animal. When it is time to produce the written report, the children decide how many paragraphs each report should have, as well as the order of each paragraph. They might also talk about what the introductory and concluding paragraphs should include. Each student then goes off to write a short report on his or her domestic animal, using illustrations if possible. These individual reports are revised through writing conferences with the teacher and peer editing groups, and the revised reports are bound into a classroom book on domestic animals.

Speaking

Transferring information for spoken reports is slightly different from the procedures for written reports. Students giving oral reports must rely on note cards, PowerPoint frames, or some other type of reminder to help keep the order of presentation straight. Key words and apt phrases should be recorded so that students can glance at them to maintain their flow of speech. For instance, a student reporting on Connecticut might have made the following list: "Industries . . . manufacturing . . . defense products . . . ship building at Groton . . . transportation equipment . . . electrical machinery." Such telegraphic writing clearly differs from the form of a written report.

A good aid for students giving oral reports is to support their talks with visuals and realia, as presented in the next section. Props allow speakers to maintain focus by discussing the aspects illustrated by each prop. Oral reports allow immediate questioning, prompting researchers to give additional information about what they have learned. Thus, teachers should allow time for questions after an oral report.

One possibility to save class time during oral reports is for only some students actually to report to the whole class. The others can tape-record their presentations and place them with explanatory material in the classroom or school library for others to hear on their own time. One advantage of this technique is that no matter how well done the reports are, listening to thirty oral reports in a few days is bound to be boring, whereas listening to ten over several days can still be interesting.

Another time-saving device is putting students into teams to prepare a panel presentation. Each panel member could be responsible for researching an aspect of the topic. Some teachers station students with reports to give at separate locations throughout the classroom, and then have various groups of listeners rotate among the presenters. This strategy forces the presenters to repeat themselves, but repetition can be beneficial and the class routine has been varied a bit.

Multimedia Representations

Students enjoy creating illustrations, storyboards, time lines, murals, maps, collages, homemade transparencies, and models. They enjoy, too, being able to collect objects and arrange them for others. Students also enjoy using computer technology to produce multimedia representations (Kist, 2005). The term *multimedia* combines *multi*, more than one, with *media*, a means of mass communication; students combine several methods of exchange into one communication. Popular forms of media include **images** such as graphs, maps, photographs, and drawings; **texts** that range from captions to multiple paragraphs; **sounds**, such as voice recordings, music, and sound effects; and **motion**, like animation, video, and moving transitions among slides (Simkins, Cole, Tavalin, & Means, 2003). Students select the media that fits their purpose for reporting their inquiry's findings. For instance, students present the products of their inquiries in a video when they want to tell a story or demonstrate something, in a PowerPoint slide show when they want to control the user's path through their presentation, and in a web site when they want users to control their own paths.

To help these projects meet the communication expectations teachers have for inquiry reports, you could follow some of the guidelines given for science fair projects. Science fair projects need to be highly visual, self-descriptive, focused, and succinct. Communicating this to students means explaining that the display ought to be appealing, eye-catching, neat, and interesting. The question being investigated and shared ought to be clear to anyone looking at the display. The research topic being shared should be an interesting one to investigate and of a scope that is neither too large nor too picayune for the students' research capabilities.

Multimedia representations could be incorporated as part of an oral or a written sharing.

Multigenre Representations

Multigenre representations are like collages; they consist of self-contained pieces that merge into a valid whole (Allen, 2001; Allen & Swistak, 2004). They are snapshots of a single topic taken from different vantage points. More than one genre, such as poetry, exposition, drama, music, painting, photography, recorded conversation, diary entries, and so on, join with each other to provide different entry points into one topic. Representing and sharing the products of inquiry in multigenre form blur categories.

When investigating westward expansion in U.S. history, students readily could represent what they learn through multigenre means. For instance, they might design a cardboard box as a covered wagon storage bin and fill it with possible items from the trip. They might include the following:

- A handbill or newspaper column enticing settlers to head west
- Diary entries of different family members recounting the same or different events (e.g., starting out, establishing order among the travelers, family life, encountering obstacles, arriving)
- Scenic illustrations (e.g., towns, wagon trains, river crossings, hunting)
- Maps annotated with significant sites
- Time line of events
- Poems or song lyrics expressing feelings about the journey
- Letters sent home
- Tools
- Videotaped reenactment of significant events

Multigenre means certainly could represent diverse perspectives on westward expansion. Students might produce plausible artifacts from Native Americans, Chinese and Irish immigrants, congressional leaders from the eastern and western United States, and land speculators.

Computer technology is leading to rich possibilities for representing and sharing the products of inquiry through multigenre representations. Presentation software, desktop publishing programs, and multimedia creativity and authoring tools enable students at every grade level to represent ideas imaginatively. Even a cursory review of selected catalogs from vendors such as The Learning Company (www.learningcompany.com), Software Express (www.swexpress.com), Sunburst (www.sunburst.com), and Tom Snyder Productions (www.tomsnyder.com/) reveals numerous computer tools that enable students to do the following:

- Produce or transfer artwork and graphics to adorn what they write
- Stream video and audio images into original productions
- Add sound effects, animation, music, and narration to a visual display
- Present professional-quality tables, graphs, and charts
- Construct web sites

LISTEN, LOOK, AND LEARN   Briefly describe to a teacher each of the four ways to represent and share information. Ask the teacher which ones he or she has used and why. Ask the teacher to describe strengths and limitations of each of the sharing formats used. Would the teacher try any of the others you have described? Which one(s) and why?

Teaching Independent Inquiry

Students become independent when they receive support accomplishing meaningful tasks, and then the support fades away as students become proficient. This process applies to inquiry, also. When students are engaged in inquiry, teachers help them identify questions, locate information, organize information, and report information. Students as a whole class can observe how to accomplish certain strategies; then they can perform the strategies in small groups and individually as teachers gradually release their guidance. Such fading occurs throughout the school year.

In the elementary grades, teachers might walk the whole class through an inquiry unit. Teachers show students how to investigate and report a subject, with the teacher and students jointly producing a finished product. When a different unit is studied, teachers can remind students of the processes they used before. For the second unit to be researched, students might work in small groups rather than with the whole class. As students develop research skills, they are able to carry out the research task more and more independently. At the secondary level, teachers refine students' research skills. If students are already adept at locating information through an Internet search engine, teachers might show them how to use sophisticated features like advanced searching and language tools. Practically all upper-grade students benefit from attention to their note making skills. Secondary teachers also remind students of the skills they learned in earlier grades.

Avoiding Plagiarism

Students who copy reports from another source often do so out of ignorance and desperation. They are unaware of any other system for generating a written report. Several techniques can help prevent copying in your classroom (Galus, 2002). Taking students through the steps described in this chapter will model the research process for them. You might want to require checkpoints to monitor progress. These checks should not be presented as punitive; rather, make it clear that all students need feedback about how successfully they are dealing with the various stages of a report. Thus, if a student is organizing information on a data chart, check whether key words are being used, whether a variety of sources has been located, and whether sources are being identified with page numbers. This checking can be done by the inquiring student, by peers, by parents or paraprofessionals, and by teachers. Such checking, by the way, helps prevent student procrastination.

Making all initial reports oral or visual, with students not permitted to read reports but only to use notes, stresses original work. Most students are unable to memorize a long selection from the encyclopedia, so they use their own words. When you enhance their ability to speak from notes, you raise their confidence in their ability to write their own reports and present themselves to others.

In your classroom, you might monitor students at each step of the research process. Thus, students produce questions, locate sources, and produce and organize ideas before drafting and revising a report. Remember that the main concern is teaching the process of finding and sharing information on a topic; the final product, the report, reflects students' proficiencies with the process.

Assessment

Assessing student reports is an essential aspect of instruction (Stiggins, 2005). Giving students a score guide allows them to see how you weigh the different criteria, and it offers explicit guidelines for self-assessment and self-reflection. Learners can assess their own work when they know the criteria for assessment. Allow room on the list for comments for each evaluation area. Be specific with your comments. If you write nothing or only innocuous comments, such as "good job," evaluations are largely ignored, whereas more specific comments receive attention.

Journal Writing

In many classrooms, students record in a journal thoughts and reactions about their inquiries in order to clarify and self-monitor their proficiencies. Teachers occasionally set aside ten to fifteen minutes for students to conduct an inner dialogue—a metacognitive conversation—with themselves. Opportunities then are available for students to share their thoughts and reactions with partners, small groups, or the whole class. Upper-grade students might respond to prompts such as the following:

- What about inquiry is becoming clear to you?
- What inquiry skills are you developing?
- Who or what helped you the most with your current inquiry?
- What aspects of inquiry are easiest for you?
- What aspects of inquiry are most difficult for you?
- How might you overcome inquiry difficulties?
- What advice about inquiry might you give young children?
- What might you do differently with a future inquiry?

LOOKING BACK Learning the research process is more important than producing a polished report; otherwise, teachers could be satisfied with students who submitted reports

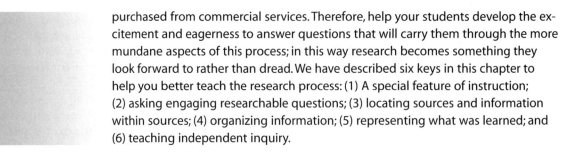

purchased from commercial services. Therefore, help your students develop the excitement and eagerness to answer questions that will carry them through the more mundane aspects of this process; in this way research becomes something they look forward to rather than dread. We have described six keys in this chapter to help you better teach the research process: (1) A special feature of instruction; (2) asking engaging researchable questions; (3) locating sources and information within sources; (4) organizing information; (5) representing what was learned; and (6) teaching independent inquiry.

ADD TO YOUR JOURNAL When involved in inquiry projects, were you introduced to strategies similar to the ones presented here? Compare the way you generated research questions in elementary and secondary school with the procedures described here. Do you consider yourself an independent researcher? Why? What can you apply from your own background to your future classroom? What kinds of research experiences will you give your students? Why? How often will your students be engaged in research activities? Why?

Additional Readings

Libraries Unlimited publishes several good references on teaching inquiry at all grade levels. Six titles describe especially worthwhile practices:

PAPPAS, M. J., & TEPE, A. E. (2002). *Pathways to knowledge and inquiry learning.* Englewood, CO: Libraries Unlimited.

RANKIN, V. (1999). *The thoughtful researcher: Teaching the research process to middle school students.* Englewood, CO: Libraries Unlimited.

STANLEY, D. B. (2000). *Practical steps to the research process for high school.* Englewood, CO: Libraries Unlimited.

STANLEY, D. B. (2000). *Practical steps to the research process for middle school.* Englewood, CO: Libraries Unlimited.

STANLEY, D. B. (2001). *Practical steps to the research process for elementary school.* Englewood, CO: Libraries Unlimited.

THOMPSON, H. M., & HENLEY, S. A. (2000). *Fostering information literacy: Connecting national standards, Goals 2000, and the SCANS report.* Englewood, CO: Libraries Unlimited.

Here is a scholarly account of how information and communication technology is affecting literacy practices:

KINZER, C. K., & LEANDER, K. (2003). Technology and the language arts: Implications of an expanded definition of literacy. In J. Flood, D. Lapp, J. R. Squire, & J. M. Jensen (Eds.), *Handbook of research on teaching the English language arts* (2nd ed.; pp. 546–565). Mahwah, NJ: Lawrence Erlbaum Associates.

These two sources have a critical edge, addressing ways to engage youth in questioning how literacy and media reflect the practices and norms of their social worlds:

ALVERMANN, D. E., & HAGOOD, M. C. (2000). Critical media literacy: Research, theory, and practice in "new times." *Journal of Educational Research, 93*, 193–205.

BEACH, R., & MYERS, J. (2001). *Inquiry-based English instruction.* New York: Teachers College Press.

Looking back more than seventy-five years to published recommendations for inquiry-based instruction provides perspective on current recommendations. Three substantial writings from the early 1900s on this topic are as follows:

GOOD, C. V. (1927). *The supplementary reading assignment.* Baltimore: Warwick & York.

KILPATRICK, W. H. (1919). *The project method.* New York: Teachers College Press.

WHIPPLE, G. M. (Ed.). (1920). *New materials of instruction* (Nineteenth Yearbook of the National Society for the Study of Education, Part I). Bloomington, IL: Public School Publishing Company.

10

Differentiating Instruction

LOOKING AHEAD   In a primary grade classroom students are working in pairs to illustrate the life cycle of a particular animal they selected. In an intermediate classroom, students had formed groups to become expert on the characteristics of a certain vertebrate (mammal, fish, reptile, or amphibian); now they are sharing their expertise with their original teams. Before reading their textbook about the basic principles of heredity, middle-grade students chose to either read silently to themselves, take turns reading aloud with a partner, or follow along with an audio-taped reading of the passage. High school students learning to describe the roles of organic and inorganic chemicals in living things have selected from a list of possibilities how they will represent their descriptions.

The content area reading, writing, and subject matter instruction in these classrooms diverges from classrooms where everyone is doing the same thing. The instruction in these classrooms is differentiated; it is modified to fit individuals. The four keys presented in this chapter on differentiating instruction are:

1. Learners deserve fair opportunities for success.
2. Differentiation begins with a climate of respect.
3. Utilize supportive people.
4. Provide structured freedom.

Differentiating instruction means addressing the needs and strengths of diverse learners. It contrasts with undifferentiated instruction that follows a one-size-fits-all approach, making no adjustments for individual differences. Differentiated instruction involves personalization, arranging classroom conditions to accommodate individual human beings. Teachers accommodate students with different academic traits by providing equal access to learning and equal opportunities to demonstrate what has been learned.

Learners Deserve Fair Opportunities for Success

Numerous factors influence student learning, so educators have developed numerous approaches to address these factors. Bilingual education and sheltered English programs are available for students who are learning English along with subject matter (Freeman, Freeman, & Mercuri, 2005). Special education programs are available for students who demonstrate extraordinary cognitive differences as well as emotional problems, physical impairments, and specific learning disabilities (Hallahan & Kauffman, 2003). Special reading programs are available for students who struggle with literacy (Rasinski & Padak, 2004). Teachers in regular classrooms adjust their instruction because they know that not everyone learns the same way, that individuals have preferred ways to process information and ideas (Denig, 2004), as well as different racial and ethnic backgrounds, career aspirations, and identities (Ladson-Billings, 2001).

Effective content area reading, writing, and subject matter teachers assume that each individual follows a different path to learning (Tomlinson, 1999). These teachers realize that some students who are learning English might benefit from working alongside another who speaks the same first language yet is slightly more proficient in English. These teachers realize that one student, who seems distracted by classroom activity, might benefit from a seat in a relatively quiet area away from distractions. They know that some students do well in discussions where individuals interrupt each other to jointly produce ideas, whereas others do well silently writing down ideas in a personal reflective journal. Effective teachers differentiate learners' experiences with the main dimensions of content area literacy and learning presented in the past six chapters (i.e., reading materials and exhibiting responses, comprehension, meaning vocabulary, writing, studying, and student inquiry).

Given today's unprecedented high-stakes educational accountability measures, differentiated instruction can be seen as a prerequisite for fair, just, and equitable treatment of students (McTighe & Brown, 2005). The U.S. commitment to excellence, to all students being proficient with high levels of literacy intensified by the No Child Left Behind legislation (see Chapter 13), means that all learners are expected to accomplish the same rigorous standards for literacy. The challenge is providing students equal opportunities to accomplish these standards. Students who start out with different levels of academic preparedness, different approaches to learning, and different interests deserve multiple instructional pathways to accomplishing uniform standards of achievement.

DO IT TOGETHER   Form groups of about three, and brainstorm ways you and your peers experienced differentiated instruction as students in your K–12 classrooms. Discuss your personal reactions to these experiences: Did they promote your literacy and subject matter learning effectively or not effectively? What did you like or not like about them?

Differentiation Begins with a Climate of Respect

Establishing a climate of respect is an important first step in differentiating instruction (Moore & Hinchman, 2003). Teachers start out establishing a climate of respect during the very first day of the class, acknowledging learners' diversities and expressing plans to honor them. These teachers affirm the values of diversity by describing everyone's inherent dignity and explaining how people with multiple perspectives and different strengths benefit society. They inform their classes that everyone will be treated like members of a club.

Forming personal connections with students is a good way to demonstrate respect. Some teachers meet and greet students at the classroom door when they enter class. These teachers sometimes shake hands and inquire politely about students' lives. Having students complete *getting to know you* cards the first day of school provides insights into students' lives outside of school. When time is available after class, these teachers talk with students about the subject at hand as well as about everyday events and personal issues. These actions demonstrate respect for students as individuals with human needs and desires as well as learners with academic requirements.

Teachers also demonstrate respect by holding high expectations for all. They do not patronize students with watered-down curriculums. These teachers state their expectations explicitly, and they regularly encourage students to put forth what it takes to achieve the expectations. Teacher who emphasize respect are sure to praise and reprimand students fairly; they do not treat any individual or group preferentially, thereby disrespecting others.

Differentiation also depends upon respect from students. As Tomlinson (2001) says about the learning environment needed for differentiation, "Mutual respect is nonnegotiable" (p. 22). Students must act courteously and acknowledge the advantages of working with others. To accomplish this, teachers assert everyone's right to be heard. They regularly provide each student opportunities to express himself or herself during whole class, group, paired, and individual situations. They do not tolerate rudeness or insults.

When assigning membership for projects and other group activities, teachers show respect by using flexible groupings. They find ways and times for students to work with various groups of classmates. Some teachers divide their classes into groups of four or five students at different levels of academic proficiency and have them remain together for several weeks. Group members put their desks together

Flexible grouping promotes differentiation.

and create a group name to promote their group identity. The members work together on projects and other tasks; they take tests and other assessments individually. Such flexible grouping encourages students to see themselves as being at liberty to interact with others, not to see themselves as restricted by the opinions and expectations of others.

Finally, teachers establish a climate of respect by helping students see themselves succeeding with academic expectations as others similar to them have done. They adorn classroom walls with positive, inclusive images of different ethnicities and regularly invite role models from various sectors of the community to speak about their successes.

In essence, establishing a climate of respect makes students feel welcome and accepted in your classroom. A climate of respect makes students feel that they belong to a community, a safe neighborhood, a caring family. They do not fear ridicule when they ask for help, express their confusion, or work with alternative materials. Students who see themselves as respected despite their learning differences are best able to benefit from different opportunities to learn.

DO IT TOGETHER Form groups of about three, and call up teachers from your pasts who effectively established climates of respect in their classrooms. Share your memories: How did those teachers establish those climates of respect? How did those teachers' classrooms compare with others not characterized by climates of respect?

Utilize Supportive People

An effective and common method for differentiating instruction involves supportive people. Teachers make themselves and others available during class to support students' literacy and learning, and they connect students with support that is available outside class.

Instructional aides, sometimes called paraprofessionals or teaching assistants, are one category of supportive people to help your learners with their content area reading, writing, and subject matter. Many schools and school districts provide aides to work with students who have language differences or special learning needs, and these people often assist other members of the class when their clients are working independently. Aides might come to your classroom every day or only a few days per week. They can assist with every dimension of content area literacy and learning. To illustrate, they might support students' literacy efforts, synthesizing information and ideas in response to a unit's essential question. They might help plan ways to produce a unit's culminating exhibit. They might assist with the graphic organizers learners use as a postreading, prewriting, or study strategy. And they might review meaning vocabulary through activities like Twenty Questions or Whatta' Ya' Know.

Groups of peers are another category of people who can support individuals' content literacy and learning. Many teachers encourage students to work with learning partners, or study buddies. Individuals are paired, then they sit beside each other in class working together on literacy and learning tasks. Although they perform academic work collaboratively, their achievement is assessed individually.

Along with learning partners, flexible groups of four or five go far to support each others' literacy and learning. A substantial amount of professional literature

Instructional aides promote differentiation.

on cooperative/collaborative learning supports the benefits of small-group practices (see, for example, Gillies & Ashman, 2003; Schmuck & Schmuck, 2001). Teachers sometimes place students in groups, and students sometimes place themselves in groups. Sometimes, class assignments are given to the groups, and sometimes the groups select their assignments.

Consider the ways small groups might address content area literacy and learning. During writing assignments, students in groups might discuss ideas and help one another plan what they will write, allow each member to write individually, then respond to what has been written and help revise the draft. When studying for a unit test, groups might collaboratively generate mnemonic devices for new vocabulary, and they might generate and answer questions they expect to encounter.

When reading novels, group collaboration is common in the form of book clubs (McMahon & Raphael, 1997) or literature circles (Daniels, 2001). For instance, all members of a group might read the same book, perhaps *The Watson's Go to Birmingham* in the intermediate grades or *Roll of Thunder, Hear My Cry* in the middle grades, and perform certain roles. The following are some of the more familiar roles enacted during literature circles (Daniels, 2001):

content connector:	relates the novel to others group members have read or to personal experiences
discussion director:	serves as the group manager; ensures all participants fulfill their roles
summary spokesperson:	summarizes each chapter
vocabulary virtuoso:	selects and explains the meanings of unfamiliar words

The set of roles listed next are time-honored, generic ones that contribute to the management of any cooperative learning situation (Kagan, 1997). You might combine these roles with the ones above—or create your own—to best serve your content literacy and learning purposes:

active participant:	contributes to group proceedings in a lively and involved manner
encourager:	promotes efforts at accomplishing the task; cheers on participants
mayor:	leads the group's efforts
record keeper:	notes the group's decisions; serves as the scribe
time keeper:	monitors the timetable for accomplishing the group's task

After reading one or a few chapters, group members gather to discuss what they read and share their task products according to their designated roles. When needed, group members help individuals refine what they produced in response to their particular task.

Tutors are another category of supportive people who help differentiate instruction. Tutors generally work one-to-one with a learner outside of the classroom. Tutors can be peers, those from the same classroom, cross-age, those from the higher grades, and mentors from the community outside the school (Berger & Shafron, 2000; Rabow, Chin, & Fahimian, 1999). The best tutoring is connected with classroom objectives so that learners are able to focus on a few outcomes at a time. Tutors can address the dimensions of content area literacy outside of class in the same way as aides and groups of peers address the dimensions inside of class.

Finally, teachers position themselves as supportive people when they make themselves available to help individuals. Circulating about the classroom when students are working independently and conferring with individuals on the fly is a common supportive practice. Many teachers schedule conferences during class to converse with individuals about their progress and intervene when appropriate. Some teachers conduct conferences about the unit-related materials individuals are reading as well as about the writing assignments and inquiry projects individuals are pursuing. Some teachers make themselves available to work with individuals before school begins, during lunch, and after school ends. They offer their services through email and web site postings, and they utilize homework hot lines and academic networked communication systems like *Blackboard*.

LISTEN, LOOK, AND LEARN   Think back to your K–12 school days as well as your classroom observations during your current teacher-preparation program. Call up the uses of supportive people you have experienced, and connect them with the categories presented here:

- aides
- pairs and groups of peers
- tutors
- making selves available inside and outside class time

Do the uses of supportive people you have observed fit the categories presented here? What other categories might you include?

Provide Structured Freedom

Structured freedom refers to a balance between classroom control and order on the one hand and student liberty and decision making on the other. Structured freedom blends teachers' plans and directions with learners' voices and choices. Classroom freedom is offered, but it is within limits. Effective classrooms combine structure and freedom, sometimes referring to it as *managed options* or *controlled choices* (Alington & Johnston, 2002; Daniels & Bizar, 2005).

Structured freedom moves according to the cycle of instruction presented in Chapter 2. Teachers and students consistently flow through the phases of planning, introducing, guiding, and culminating. A rhythm is evident as whole-class, small group, paired, and individual grouping patterns appear, disappear, and reappear. For instance, teachers and the whole class typically are together when a unit is launched, and they remain together to begin the first standards-based outcome. Once learners are prepared to work on their own, teachers begin fading out and learners fade in. Freedom is most evident during this guiding, or fading, phase of instruction as students apply, explore, and extend content area literacy and learning on their own. Teachers and the whole class frequently reconvene for brief amounts of time at regular intervals to monitor progress, share understandings, and gear up for further study. Whole class meetings typically occur when culminating instruction.

The table below, on planning structured freedom, outlines possible types of literacy choices. Two factors border the table, text and task. Text refers to the material(s) students read, and task refers to the assignment(s), or academic work, students do. When differentiating instruction by structuring students' freedom, think about offering same and different texts as well as same and different tasks.

Planning Structured Freedom

Text

		Same	Different
Task	Same	1 same text, same task	2 different texts, same task
	Different	3 same text, different tasks	4 different texts, different tasks

Same Text/Same Task

Even though the first cell in the table contains the word *same* for both text and task, several options still are available. The ways students accomplish the same text and task can be differentiated. For instance, during an upper-grade unit on survival, you might give students the identical text to read (e.g., the novel *Into Thin Air*) and the identical task (e.g., produce a response-to-reading journal, then discuss responses); however, you could have students proceed through the novel in several ways. You could have them go to different learning stations, or locations, designated in the classroom to either

(a) read silently to themselves,
(b) form a group that includes their teacher and take turns reading aloud,
(c) form a pair with their learning partner and take turns reading aloud and talking about what they have read, or
(d) read along with an audio-taped version of the novel.

Along with these choices, you could make available a listening guide, a brief outline of the text, and allow students to decide whether or not to use it. You also could establish limits, such as specifying how many words, sentences, paragraphs, or pages are the minimum and maximum for the journal entries, and have students decide what to produce within those limits.

DO IT TOGETHER Form groups of about three, and discuss ways you could use the same text and task yet vary the ways students could proceed with them. Apply this approach to differentiating instruction to units you have planned or observed.

Different Texts/Same Task

The second cell in the Planning Structured Freedom table highlights different texts with the same task. Here students all work toward the identical end product, but they use different reading materials to produce it. Book clubs (McMahon & Raphael, 1997), or literature circles (Daniels, 2001), noted earlier, commonly employ this method of planning structured freedom. For instance, you could take the upper-grade unit on *survival* mentioned in the first cell and have students read different topic-related novels individually or as members of a group. The task might still be to produce a response-to-reading journal and then participate regularly in whole-class discussions, but the reading materials could be varied. The youth might have access to *Into Thin Air* as before, but they also could have access to *survival* novels written at different levels of complexity such as *Between a Rock and a Hard Place, Endurance: Shackleton's Incredible Voyage, Hatchet,* and *The Cay.* In bilingual classrooms, students might read books written in their native languages along with simplified English-language texts.

Using different texts and the same task is common during student inquiry projects. If you present a unit on *survival* as an inquiry project, all students might work on the same culminating task (e.g., write a narrative with a theme of survival), but they could have available several different reading materials. Going beyond novels, the school media specialist could provide a text set, a collection for the class of picture books and other books of varying complexities and genres that center about the unit's topic. Students could access a launch page with links to Internet web sites such as *Five Basic Survival Skills in the Wilderness* (www .adventuresportsonline.com/5basic.htm). They could interact with commercial multimedia programs. A screenplay or a readers theater passage could be used. Again, all students would be producing a narrative, but they would be using multiple materials to gather ideas and information for the task.

DO IT TOGETHER   Form groups of about three, and discuss ways you could use different texts and the same task. Apply this approach to differentiating instruction to units you have planned or observed. Determine how it could accommodate students who are learning English or who have special learning needs.

Same Text/Different Tasks

The third cell of the Planning Structured Freedom table addresses differentiation by using the same text yet different tasks. This method involves supporting all the students in a class through the same reading material while providing substantive choices when responding to the passage. During the upper-grade unit on *survival*, you might have students read *Into Thin Air* while using a framework to generate different tasks. For instance, following a multiple intelligence framework (Gardner, 1993; Noble, 2004), you could make available choices such as the following:

Panel discussions promote interpersonal dialogues about texts.

Verbal/Linguistic:	write a speech arguing either for or against limiting access to Mount Everest
Logical/Mathematical:	prepare a chart relating climbing casualties with mountains' locations
Visual/Spatial:	produce a storyboard of key events on the mountain
Bodily/Kinesthetic:	role play a scene as climbers who want to continue their summit attempt and those who want to turn back argue with each other
Interpersonal:	conduct a panel discussion of whether or not the team leaders acted appropriately
Intrapersonal:	produce a reflective journal recounting the personal thoughts of one of the climbers
Musical:	perform a song inspired by the tragic events on Mount Everest

Taking the RAFT framework (Role, Audience, Form, and Topic) from Chapter 7, teachers and students could generate tasks in response to *Into Thin Air* such as these:

- You are Rob Hall, an expert guide who dies on Mount Everest. Recount what you were saying on your radio as you suffered from the cold and lack of oxygen.
- You are an outdoor activist speaking to the Nepalese authorities about limiting permits to climb Mount Everest. You know that some individuals pay as much as $65,000 to be led to the summit, even though many are unprepared for the rigors of the climb. What would you say?
- You are Beck Weathers, a physician who survives a freezing night exposed on Mount Everest. Explain to a friend your thoughts as you made your way to shelter.

Following a more focused, restricted framework like Reciprocal Teaching, you could have students respond to each chapter of *Into Thin Air* by choosing among four strategies:

| Summarize | Clarify |
| Question | Predict |

When employing different tasks to differentiate instruction, many teachers require learners to complete one or more assigned tasks (e.g., everyone produces a journal) along with one or more self-selected tasks (e.g., everyone completes one task from the multiple intelligence list). Task choice could be differentiated even a little more by having learners choose the sequence, or order, in which to complete them.

DO IT TOGETHER   Form groups of about three, and discuss ways you could use the same text and different tasks. Apply this approach to differentiating instruction to units you have planned or observed. Determine how it could accommodate students who are learning English or who have special learning needs.

Different Texts/Different Tasks

The final way to plan structured freedom calls for different texts and different tasks. This is the most ambitious method, one that teachers typically fade into over time. Starting out this way the first unit of the school year might overcome students who are unaccustomed to such freedom.

This method combines the different texts and tasks as presented earlier, although with some minor adjustments. When presenting the *survival* unit, you would provide different reading materials (e.g., *Into Thin Air, Between a Rock and a Hard Place, Endurance: Shackleton's Incredible Voyage, Hatchet,* and *The Cay*). You also would provide different assignments (e.g., produce a response-to-reading journal, write a narrative with a theme of survival, respond according to Reciprocal Teaching strategies). However, note that only generic stems of the multiple intelligence framework could be used, as listed here:

Verbal/Linguistic:	write a speech
Logical/Mathematical:	prepare a chart
Visual/Spatial:	produce a storyboard of key events
Bodily/Kinesthetic:	role play a conflict
Interpersonal:	conduct a panel discussion
Intrapersonal:	produce a reflective journal
Musical:	perform a song

Countless productive ways to differ texts and tasks are possible. Task Rotation is a tool for designing tasks that tap essential thinking processes. For instance, if your intermediate-grade essential question was "What are the characteristics of mammals," you might have each student choose one mammal for special analysis.

Then, each student would complete four culminating tasks that correspond to thinking processes like this:

Connect: describe personal experiences you have had either with your mammal or one very similar to it.

Organize: classify your mammal according to the groupings of kingdom, phylus, class, order, family, genus, and species.

Image: draw a picture of your designated mammal

Evaluate: construct a one-page advertising flier that promotes the characteristics of your designated mammal.

If you were guiding students through a unit on the geology of the Grand Canyon, you might have them produce their choice of at least three of the following types of patterned poetry as presented here (Moore & Hinchman, 2003).

Acrostics Spell the topic vertically, then use words, phrases, or sentences to describe the subject.

Great	**C**oursing through
River carved	**A**nd
Astonishing	**N**avigating rocky
Natural	**Y**ears
Delight	**O**f
	Nature's erosion

Copy Changes (found poems) Select words, phrases, and sentences from passages, change what you want, and arrange them in a poem.

Kaibab limestone
at the top
From the Permian Period, before dinosaurs lived.
Vishnu schist
at the bottom
Extending to unknown depths.

Repetitions Like much popular music, repeat selected terms as a refrain. Add information to the refrain as the poem progresses.

What natural wonder is in northern Arizona?
THE GRAND CANYON
What natural wonder in northern Arizona is 1 mile deep, 10 miles wide, and 271 miles long?
THE GRAND CANYON
What natural wonder in northern Arizona uncovered rocks 1,200 million years old?
THE GRAND CANYON
What natural wonder in northern Arizona has 4 life zones?
THE GRAND CANYON

Cinquain This popular form of poetry consists of five lines with specified numbers and types of words per line:

1st line: One word—noun that is the topic of the poem
2nd line: Two words—description of the topic
3rd line: Three words—*ing* words that convey the action of the topic
4th line: Four-word phrase—description of the topic that shows feeling
5th line: One word—expresses the essence of the topic

Canyon
grand magnificence
moving challenging climbing
natural deep Earth wonder
sacred

Haiku Haiku is another common yet powerful type of poem with an established pattern. It consists of three lines, each with a predetermined number of syllables, five, seven, five, to total seventeen.

Wondrous Grand Canyon
esplanade precambrian
geology now

Question-Answer Poems The title of this pattern reveals its structure, first line(s) with a question and second line with an answer. Repeat until done.

Where is the Grand Canyon?
the soul of Gaia
What's so grand about the canyon?
mass, mystery, adventure, color
What will you learn?
layer cake geology
ecology
and wonder

Wh- Poems Like question-answer poems, asking about the topic jump-starts this pattern. At least five wh- words can be used as the questions. They might be arranged as follows, although no particular order is required.

1st line: Who?
2nd line: What?
3rd line: When?
4th line: Where?
5th line: Why?

Naturalists, tourists, adventurers
Studying, experiencing, challenging
Some return often
Where the river cuts the rock
There's no comparable experience

OR

Where the river cuts the rock
There is no comparable experience
Studying, experiencing, challenging

Understandings The beginning of the poem expresses what students understand about a topic; the ending states what they find confusing, ambiguous, or unstated that they hope to learn eventually.

I understand
how the rock strata were deposited
And I understand
how the river cut the rock
But I don't understand
why the river didn't just run somewhere else

Permissions Students complete two stems. The first addresses factual exact descriptions; the second concludes with a personal statement about the topic (e.g., what it makes you think, how you feel about it, an insight).

Permit me to tell you about the Grand Canyon
It is 1 mile deep
10 miles wide
271 miles long.
The Colorado River carved it
through the Kaibab Plateau.
Water and wind deposited
what became the layers of rocks we see.
But what you should remember about the Grand Canyon
Is that natural forces made it
But people might destroy it

DO IT TOGETHER Form groups of about three, and discuss ways you could use different texts and different tasks. Apply this approach to differentiating instruction to units you have planned or observed. Determine how it could accommodate students who are learning English or who have special learning needs.

LOOKING BACK   Accommodating the strengths and needs of diverse learners requires differentiation of instruction. Teachers personalize their teaching when they arrange conditions to fit individuals. This is especially important during an era of high-stakes assessments and expectations to accomplish uniform standards of achievement. The four keys presented in this chapter are (a) learners deserve fair opportunities for success, (b) differentiation begins with a climate of respect, (c) utilize supportive people, and (d) provide structured freedom.

ADD TO YOUR JOURNAL   Reflect on your K–12 classroom experiences. How did your teachers at the different grade levels differentiate your instruction? Can you think of ways that you can adopt for your teaching that were not mentioned in this chapter? Reflect on classrooms you have experienced, with and without climates of respect. Did the teachers go beyond the ideas presented here to establish that climate? Then consider structured freedom, which is planned by mixing and matching same and different texts and tasks. Does one particular method seem most appropriate to you? Why?

Additional Readings

Two good general references on differentiating instruction across the grade levels are:

DANIELS, H., & BIZAR, M. (2005). *Teaching the best practice way: Methods that matter, K–12.* Portland, ME: Stenhouse.

TOMLINSON, C. (Ed.) (2005). Differentiated instruction [Special issue]. *Theory into Practice, 44*(3).

Here is a very pertinent companion set of references on differentiating instruction for content area reading and writing:

CHAPMAN, C., & KING, R. (2003). *Differentiated instructional strategies for writing in the content areas.* Thousand Oaks, CA: Corwin Press.

CHAPMAN, C., & KING, R. (2003). *Differentiated instructional strategies for reading in the content areas.* Thousand Oaks, CA: Corwin Press.

Compelling scientific support for a cooperative learning approach to middle school literacy is provided here:

STEVENS, R. J. (2003). Student team reading and writing: A cooperative learning approach to middle school literacy instruction. *Educational Research and Evaluation, 9*(2), 137–160.

These four books offer recommendations of differentiating instruction at the secondary-school level:

BENJAMIN, A. (2002). *Differentiated instruction: A guide for middle and high school teachers.* Larchmont, NY: Eye on Education.

Gregory, G. H., & Kuzmich, L. (2005). *Differentiated literacy strategies for student growth and achievement in grades 7–12.* Thousand Oaks, CA: Corwin Press.

Northey, S. S. (2005). *Handbook on differentiated instruction for middle and high schools.* Larchmont, NY: Eye on Education.

Strickland, C. A., & Tomlinson, C. A. (2005). *Differentiation in practice: A resource guide for differentiating curriculum, grades 9–12.* Alexandria, VA: Association for Supervision and Curriculum Development.

Here is a good source for accommodating diverse learners through a multiple intelligences framework:

Kornhaber, M. L., Fierros, E., & Vennema, S. (2004). *Multiple intelligences: Best ideas from theory and practice.* Boston: Allyn and Bacon.

11

Cases of Content Area Literacy Instruction

LOOKING AHEAD The earlier chapters of this book present content area literacy dimensions such as comprehension and writing one at a time, but life in classrooms is not so segmented. Teachers employ units of instruction to combine literature, comprehension, vocabulary, writing, studying, and inquiry within each day and across 180 school days. Teachers balance the dimensions of content area literacy so students can become proficient in all of them.

This chapter portrays teachers' efforts to balance dimensions of content area literacy during units of classroom instruction. The portrayals are in the form of fictional teachers' accounts of what they did during particular units of study. No account fully includes every dimension, because doing so would overcrowd the curriculum; dimensions of content area literacy need to be balanced across units, too.

As you read these fictional accounts, evaluate the instructional actions. The contents of this chapter are not meant to be trustworthy guides like the content of the other ones; this chapter presents problem-solving cases, opportunities for you to apply what you are learning about content area literacy instruction to specific situations. The following units of instruction, said to have been enacted at the primary, intermediate, middle, and high-school levels, are for you to judge.

Primary Level

This first account is set in a first-grade classroom, a place where teachers are entrusted with the crucial task of getting youngsters off to a good start. First-grade children typically have only rudimentary content reading and writing skills, so teachers work to launch them toward independence. This unit is said to happen during September, so it is one of the first units students encounter.

Me and My World Unit Our first social studies unit was entitled "Me and My World." The primary grades, K–3, all have this same unit, but the concepts for each vary dependent upon the grade level. I will have the three concepts for first posted along with the five for second. I will plan some joint projects, but they will also have individual projects to do dependent on grade level. I will have to model a lot of projects.

The "Me and My World" unit took all of September because we worked on it only on Tuesdays and Thursdays. The primary grades' unit builds from the individual to families to neighborhoods to the community at large to our state, nation, and world. The focus in our unit is on the uniqueness of each person as well as the many things all of us have in common. Children learned about these two ideas in myriad ways. Many literature books, both old favorites and newer ones, address both concepts. For the whole month we have been reading books like *There's a Nightmare in My Closet; Leo the Late Bloomer; Frog and Toad Together; It's Me, Hippo!; Frederick; I Have a Sister—My Sister Is Deaf;* and *The Triplets.* In addition, I brought in such concept books as *A Snake Is Totally Tail; Is It Hard? Is It Easy?; Sugaring Time; Handtalk: An ABC of Finger Spelling and Sign Language;* and *People.* I used those books both for this unit and for our first science unit on the five senses and the human body—a nice compatible set of units to work on simultaneously. These books point out the similarities among people as well as provide information about those who, due to certain handicaps, must deal with life differently. The children had all expressed curiosity about Sharon's thick glasses, asking how she could see through them since they were unable to. Jakeitha's wheelchair also was a subject of study as students learned how many things she could do as well as they could without the use of her legs.

The "Me and My World" unit was introduced by talking about alike and different. To start things off, students were asked to call up the names of types of transportation. Though the content seemed way off the topic, I wanted to use items that could be easily classified by children in a variety of ways. The various types—boats, cars, trucks, trains, planes, and so on—were listed on a chart. We talked about how all of the things on the chart were alike, with me listing, as students dictated, how the things were alike. Then students were assigned to groups and told to look for pictures or models of the different forms of transportation listed or of new ones that they discovered. In this scavenger hunt activity, I planned the groups so that each consisted both of very capable students and of those who needed more guidance. Students were able to use independent seatwork time for this activity on both Tuesday and Wednesday, as well as checking at home for pictures and models on Tuesday and Wednesday nights.

On Thursday, each group brought its pictures and models to school. I used the big bulletin board on the side of the classroom to pin up all the transportation pictures, with the models on a table underneath. I had cut apart all the names of the types of transportation from the chart, and we placed them by the appropriate pictures or models. Then I asked if they could organize or regroup them in any other way. Total silence met this question. But I waited it out. After ten seconds, Pat asked, "Do you mean by how many wheels they have?" We had quite a discussion about wheels and had to turn to several reference sources to settle the debates that arose. I find this a good way to model using references to answer questions that we have. That broke the dam, and the students realized that there were many possible ways to group the transportation pictures they had found. Next they grouped all the red pictures and models together, all the green ones, and so on, regardless of the number of wheels. Then they grouped all the forms of transportation by how many people they could carry—one, a few, or many. A fourth grouping consisted of sorting types by where they traveled—air, land, or water.

So that they would apply their new understanding of grouping to our unit of study, I gave a list of each person's name in our class, including mine, to each group and asked them to think of at least two ways of organizing that could show how people are alike and at least two ways to show how they are different. On the following Tuesday they sorted us all into diverse groups by gender, hair color, and so on. They also put Jakeitha, Sharon, Michael, Michelle, and me into a group they labeled "black people." This activity helped them to organize their world, one of the essential thinking processes.

Along with organizing, we worked on writing activities. They each compiled a book of facts about themselves, as part of my content language experience lessons. I read a number of biographies and autobiographies to them. After reading several during the Read to/Write to lessons, explicitly pointing out features as I read autobiographies and wrote my own for them, I explained that they were going to write autobiographies. They had to draw pictures of their family, home, pets, friends, favorite things to do, and so on. Under each picture, they had to tell about the picture.

After each person had completed his or her book, they all had to number each page and write in the numeral on the labeled table of contents page I had given them. They worked on this activity on the Wednesday and Thursday afternoons that I had set aside for writing conferences and groups. Within their small groups, they helped one another to copy over their sentences correctly and make sure that page numbers were in order and matched the table of contents page.

I also gave the children five questions to go home and ask their parents about, one at a time, over a three-week period. I have found that if you give children several questions at once, they frequently forget both the questions and the answers. However, if I give only one question on each day that we have social studies, students can generally remember to ask the questions. These five questions became the basis for the single paragraphs about each student, which they dictated and were then placed on the bulletin board along with their pictures. The five questions were as follows: When were you born? What was your parents' favorite thing about you when you were a baby? What did you like to do best when you were little? What was the funniest thing you did when you were little? What is the best thing about you now? Each question was turned into a statement using sentence stems again, such as "I was born . . ." and "When I was a baby . . ." The compiled statements were then written right after one another to make the autobiographical paragraph. Not all the children could read their completed paragraphs, but they surely tried! And they loved having the paragraphs read to them. I used these paragraphs frequently during reading group time throughout the month because the paragraphs were planned to use much of the same vocabulary I was trying to teach and because they were intrinsically interesting.

The number of mathematics tie-ins I could do was amazing! We had graphs all over that room—who was native to the state and who had moved from somewhere else, as well as such family facts as siblings, pets, number of family members, favorite family foods, and at-home chores. A few Venn diagrams allowed children to see how they could be part of several groupings or attributions simultaneously.

There are so many children representing various cultural groups that I have also been reading to them daily from folktales. For most of the children, I have had no problem finding folktales for their culture groups, and when I did find it difficult, I contacted parents for help. Two different parents came in to the class and told stories that had been told to them as children. It made those stories especially interesting to the class. One of the things we have noted as we discuss the stories is how themes are used over and over and how the characters experience the same feelings as we do. Children are learning to value differences as well as our shared humanity.

DO IT TOGETHER Form small groups of three, and use Table 11.1 on page 286 to rate this fictional primary-grade teachers' effectiveness with the different dimensions of content area literacy. After rating each dimension, be prepared to explain what the fictional teacher **did** to deserve your rating and what she **might have done** to be rated higher. (If you give a "very effective" rating, be prepared to explain what the fictional teacher might have done to be rated off the top of the chart.) Finally, evaluate your ratings by comparing them with others and supporting them with information from the fictional account and the corresponding chapters of this text.

Intermediate Level

The following fictional report of an astronomy unit is set in fifth grade. These preadolescents are more sophisticated than the children in first grade, but they still have much to learn. This teacher guides her students through challenging reading materials and performs several actions to further their independence.

Solar System Unit Energy and our solar system were the topics of the two science units we did this month. The students loved the energy unit because we

Table 11.1 *Dimensions of Content Area Literacy: Primary Level*

	Very Effective	*Effective*	*Ineffective*	*Very Ineffective*
Instructional units (Chapter 3)				
Reading materials and exhibiting responses (Chapter 4)				
Comprehension (Chapter 5)				
Meaning vocabulary (Chapter 6)				
Writing (Chapter 7)				
Studying (Chapter 8)				
Student inquiry (Chapter 9)				
Differentiation (Chapter 10)				

learned many of the basic concepts during P.E. We played soccer and related the energy source and energy receiver to the players. Transfer of energy was easy to understand once the students grasped that the food they ate gave them energy, which they then transferred to the ball when they kicked it.

The solar system was also fun to study. We led into it from our energy unit by beginning with the idea that all energy in our solar system originates from our sun. The most important concepts that I wanted them to learn were the following: how our planets orbit our sun, the various size and distance relationships in our solar system, and some of the distinguishing characteristics of each planet.

Before reading about planets in our science book, the students created two models of our solar system. We used reference books (*The Planets in Our Solar System, How Did We Find Out About the Universe?,* and *DK Guide to Space*) to find out each planet's size and distance from the sun. One model showed the relative size of each planet, using assorted round objects to represent size. The students were amazed to see Mercury represented by a tiny marble and Jupiter by an enormous beachball. Another model showed the distance of each planet from the sun. We had to use the hall to represent how far away Neptune and Pluto were. These two models helped the children image the size and distance represented by those huge and abstract numbers. Stunning photos from the Hubble telescope also helped generate interest in learning about space.

When looking at the science chapter in our text, I realized that the way the various planets were described fit very well into a semantic feature matrix graphic organizer. I listed the planets down one side and their major features across the top and had everyone copy this pattern into his or her science notebook.

Based on what they already knew, I told the children to put a + or − to indicate whether a planet had a particular feature. If a child was unsure about a particular feature, the space was to be left blank. "If your mind is blank, leave the space blank," I explained. See Figure 11.1 for the feature matrix that Ray filled out before

	Closer to sun than Earth	Larger than Earth	Has moon	Has rings	Orbits the sun	Inner planet	Smallest	Largest	Has life as we know it
Earth	−	−	+	−	+	+	−	−	+
Jupiter	−	+	+	−		−			−
Mars	+	−	+	−	+	+		−	−
Mercury	+	−		−	+	+			−
Neptune	−	+		−		−	−		−
Pluto	−	+		−		−	−		−
Saturn	−	+		+		−			−
Uranus	−			−		−	−		−
Venus	+	−	+	−	+			−	

Figure 11.1 Ray's Feature Matrix: Planets in Our Solar System

reading the text. As you can see, his mind was blank on many facts. I was particularly amazed to see that he was unsure whether Jupiter, Neptune, Pluto, Saturn, and Uranus orbit the sun!

Next, the children read the science text section on planets. The children were clear about their purpose for reading: to confirm or change the pluses and minuses on their feature matrix and to fill in blank spaces. As the children read, erasers were used liberally and quiet cheers and groans indicated that the children were actively comprehending rather than passively getting through the pages. When the children had finished, we performed a group task: to correctly fill out our class feature matrix. For every space, I had the children signal thumbs up if they had a plus and thumbs down if they had a minus. If I got a close-to-unanimous reply (a few are always too lazy to raise or lower their thumbs!), I put the plus or minus in the appropriate space. No response meant that we still did not know the answer, even after reading. For some spaces, there was still disagreement, so I had the children return to the text to argue their points and I again discovered the problem they have making inferences. Many children believed that the text did not say whether Pluto was larger or smaller than earth, so I had David read the sentence stating that "Pluto is probably the size of Mercury." David explained that because we know that Mercury is smaller than earth, we can figure out that Pluto is, too. While the text did not directly state that there is no life as we know it on Jupiter, the text does state this: "There is no water on Jupiter." I had to explain to the children that because life as we know it requires water, and because there is no water on Jupiter, there cannot be life as we know it on Jupiter. This "because . . . therefore" reasoning is always required for comprehension, but for many of my students, if the text doesn't say something explicitly, they don't get it! At least with this lesson and task afterward, I could see where they were not making inferences and so could lead them back to the book and explain the reasoning.

Figure 11.2 shows the feature matrix as we finally completed it. As you can see, several spaces are still blank, even after reading. Pluto is so far away that we don't know if it has a moon or rings or if it might have life as we know it. We are also not sure about life on Uranus and Neptune. Jim was disturbed by these blanks and wanted to vote on what to put there. I don't know if he was serious or just putting me on, but I tried to explain that you can't make truth by voting on it!

On Friday, we went to the library to do some more research on planets. I chose Venus and showed the students how I used the resources to find more information about Venus. I then divided them into groups for the other eight planets and helped them as they found information. Each group decided on three facts besides those we had read about in our text, and one person in each group wrote these three facts on a chart to display in our room. Of course, I had showed them how I selected three facts about Venus and wrote these on my chart. They were very proud of their charts and of their burgeoning research skills—as was I!

Finally, I used their interest in planets to do a writing lesson on how to write a paragraph. Of course, I began by modeling for them as I wrote a paragraph on Venus. First, I reviewed what I knew about Venus from our feature matrix. Then I read the three additional facts from my chart. I told them that there were many different ways to construct paragraphs but that today we were going to write paragraphs with a topic sentence, three detail sentences, and a concluding sentence. I

	Closer to sun than Earth	Larger than Earth	Has moon	Has rings	Orbits the sun	Inner planet	Smallest	Largest	Has life as we know it
Earth	−	−	+	−	+	+	−	−	+
Jupiter	−	+	+	−	+	−	−	+	−
Mars	−	−	+	−	+	+	−	−	−
Mercury	+	−	−	−	+	+	+	−	−
Neptune	−	+	+	−	+	−	−	−	
Pluto	−	−			+	−	−	−	
Saturn	−	+	+	+	+	−	−	−	−
Uranus	−	+	+	+	+	−	−	−	
Venus	+	−	−	−	+	+	−	−	−

Figure 11.2   Planets in Our Solar System

pointed to the title of our feature matrix, "Planets in Our Solar System," and explained that their paragraphs' topic sentences should get the planet into its topic—which in a feature matrix is the title. The next three sentences should describe some details about the planet from the feature matrix or chart. The final sentence could do many things; often it gave a fascinating fact or an opinion. As the children watched, I talked through my construction of a topic sentence and my selection and construction of detail and concluding sentences and wrote the following paragraph on the board:

> Venus is one of the planets in our solar system. Venus and Earth are about the same size. Venus is hotter than Earth because it is closer to the sun. Because there is no water on Venus, it can't maintain life as we know it. Venus is called the evening star and is the favorite planet of many people because it can often be seen on a clear night.

Having modeled how to write a paragraph, I had each child choose his or her favorite planet and write a paragraph about it. I reminded them to have their first sentence tell how their planet related to the larger topic of the feature matrix. Three sentences should then give specific information about their planet, based on the feature matrix, the charts, or any other information they knew. A final sentence should end the paragraph in an interesting way. "Remember, you can't include everything you know in just one paragraph. Just include what you believe is most important and interesting," I reminded them.

As the children wrote their paragraphs, the model paragraph, the feature matrix, and the charts were all available to them. When the paragraphs were written, I let several children read theirs to the class. I was amazed when Ray volunteered. His paragraph on Mars was a lot like mine in form, but it was all correct, and most important, he had volunteered to read! This was a most successful writing experience. The children actually seemed to enjoy it. I guess when you know the information, have the correctly spelled words in front of you, and have seen the form modeled, writing is not so arduous. In fact, I overheard Kazu comment, "The paragraph just wrote itself!"

I encouraged the students to read science fiction related to outer space this month. Among the most popular books were *Planet Out of the Past; The Deadly Hoax; The Doors of the Universe;* and *Another Heaven, Another Earth*.

DO IT TOGETHER Form small groups of three, and use Table 11.2 on page 290 to rate this fictional intermediate-grade teacher's effectiveness with the different dimensions of content area literacy. After rating each dimension, be prepared to explain what the fictional teacher **did** to deserve your rating and what she **might have done** to be rated higher. (If you give a "very effective" rating, be prepared to explain what the fictional teacher might have done to be rated off the top of the chart.)

Finally, evaluate your ratings by comparing them with others and supporting them with information from the fictional accounts and the corresponding chapters of this text.

Table 11.2   *Dimensions of Content Area Literacy: Intermediate Level*

	Very Effective	Effective	Ineffective	Very Ineffective
Instructional units (Chapter 3)				
Reading materials and exhibiting responses (Chapter 4)				
Comprehension (Chapter 5)				
Meaning vocabulary (Chapter 6)				
Writing (Chapter 7)				
Studying (Chapter 8)				
Student inquiry (Chapter 9)				
Differentiation (Chapter 10)				

Middle Level

The fictional teacher in this account is just beginning to teach as well as he would like. He enjoys good relationships with his young adolescent students, but his instructional proficiencies are only now beginning to develop. This report tells of his first attempt to center language arts instruction about a topic during a unit of instruction. Showing how a relatively inexperienced traditional teacher progresses toward balanced and effective content area literacy instruction can be informative.

Science Fiction Unit   In English I had felt uncomfortable with the fragmentation of doing worksheets on superlative degree in the grammar book, for instance, and reading about personal codes of conduct in the literature anthology. This fragmented way of doing things was relatively easy to manage, but it lacked the meaningfulness that I thought an English class should have. Science fiction was an upcoming unit in our anthology, so I decided to center my instruction about that topic.

With science fiction as my organizing center, I thought about a central question that would provide an overarching purpose to the unit and position the students as problem solvers. I selected "What is the value of science fiction?" thinking that this was a worthwhile and provocative issue with which students could relate. The culminating activity could be one of three: (1) give a speech, (2) produce a poster, or (3) write a movie review.

I kicked off the unit by showing brief movie clips and some action figures from *Star Wars* and *Star Trek*. The class immediately began voicing their beliefs, experiences, likes, and dislikes of these media blockbusters. After forging these links, I posed the central question, "What is the value of science fiction?" Lonnie exclaimed that making money was the obvious answer, but he became reflective when I asked for his evidence and whether or not his was the only possible answer. We brainstormed other possibilities about the value of science fiction before I explained the procedures we would be following.

The next day I read to the class a short story written by Ray Bradbury. I don't think too many male secondary-school teachers had read to these students. The story I chose was punchy and reasonably short; I reviewed it the night before I presented it, and I read it with as much force as possible. I told myself that I was at a speech contest, the students were the judges, and I intended to impress them. Well, the group attended to every word. It was a great experience! I think they were amazed at how much fun it was to form their own images while listening rather than have a filmmaker form the images for them. Again, we brainstormed possible values of such stories.

Extending my read-aloud activity to students' book projects inside and outside of class was not too difficult. I met with the school librarian to learn what science-fiction books were available. We turned up individual copies of numerous books and found a class set of *Flowers for Algernon*. I then announced to my eighth-graders that during inside-of-class book study groups they were to continue the reciprocal teaching responses they had been doing, and that they were to follow the response format I had begun on the value of science-fiction novels. Judy reacted to my news in a surprisingly negative way, "Science fiction, yucch! Why do we have to read that stuff?" I again explained the topic and informed the class that tying novels in with the short stories we would be reading made all kinds of sense—at least in terms of deepening insights into a topic. "Besides," I said, "there are some great science-fiction books. *Ender's Shadow, Regenesis*, and *Interstellar Pig* are fantastic new books, and *The Martian Chronicles, 20,000 Leagues under the Sea*, and *2001: A Space Odyssey* are classics. You'll love them! Trust me."

The students had choices of ways to respond to the novels outside of class. I divided the assignment among the "big four" literary elements—plot, setting, character, and theme—and provided alternatives for considering those elements. For instance, students could consider setting by diagramming a stage for a scene to be dramatized or by drawing a map depicting locations in the story. Students analyzed characterization by completing an adjective checklist or by justifying their choices of popular actors and actresses to portray the main characters. Once I got to thinking about it, I saw many options for eliciting responses to stories. Some examples that emerged included the following: Select a piece of representative dialogue, choose the book's most important word, describe a change that occurred in a character, explain how a situation you've been in is similar to one in the book, convince a movie producer that your book should be made into a movie, and write the book's epilogue. I tried to provide a mix between strongly academic options ("What was the theme of the story?") and more artistic ones ("Create a mobile that represents the story.").

Extending the language skills work to science fiction took more planning on my part, but it seems to have paid off. Writing informal letters and business letters was a unit objective in our language arts text, so I tied letter writing into science fiction by having students compose letters that were related to situations in the stories. For instance, as a group we read another great Ray Bradbury story about a hunter who went back in time to shoot dinosaurs. "Okay, group," I said, "we're going to write a letter to a close friend describing the trip." After detailing the topic, audience, role, and form of the assignment a bit more, I projected an overhead transparency of a model letter. I pointed out aspects such as where the date went, how to address the letter, how to sign off, and how to develop the composition. My model letter was brief, but it did have an introduction, a chronological description of the trip (which I pointed out as only one way to go), and a summarizing statement at the end. The students then went to their groups for ten minutes to brainstorm and organize what they intended to say. Finally, twenty minutes of class time was devoted to individuals writing their letters. Rather than grade the letters themselves, I gave one point to each letter written according to the form I'd presented. Students who didn't follow the form were given another chance.

Our study of science fiction culminated with student write-ups and reports. Those who presented speeches did a great job. A few even dressed up as Han Solo, Captain Picard, Captain Nemo, and others when explaining the value of reading about them. Some good insights were shared; we heard of advances predicted by science-fiction writers and of the potentials for good and bad that awaited us.

DO IT TOGETHER   Form small groups of three and use Table 11.3 on page 293 to rate this fictional middle-school language-arts teacher's effectiveness with the different dimensions of content area literacy. After rating each dimension, be prepared to explain what the fictional teacher **did** to deserve your rating and what he **might have done** to be rated higher. (If you give a "very effective" rating, be prepared to explain what the fictional teacher might have done to be rated off the top of the chart.)
Finally, evaluate your ratings by comparing them with others and supporting them with information from the fictional account and the corresponding chapters of this text.

High School Level

This final account is of a high-school biology teacher engaging the youth in her class in scientific inquiry. She sets out to deliver information efficiently as well as teach students to acquire information independently. This unit is said to occur during the end of the school year, so her older adolescents readily follow many established routines.

Inquiry Unit   In April I tried to move them into seeing themselves as potential bi-

Table 11.3 *Dimensions of Content Area Literacy: Middle Level*

	Very Effective	*Effective*	*Ineffective*	*Very Ineffective*
Instructional units (Chapter 3)				
Reading materials and exhibiting responses (Chapter 4)				
Comprehension (Chapter 5)				
Meaning vocabulary (Chapter 6)				
Writing (Chapter 7)				
Studying (Chapter 8)				
Student inquiry (Chapter 9)				
Differentiation (Chapter 10)				

ological scientists. Most of our experiments and demonstrations have been more or less prescribed. While the hands-on biology we did certainly improved learning and attitudes, the students have rarely participated in actually designing experiments to investigate hypotheses that interest them. They had been studying biology without learning how to be biologists!

Knowing how difficult this assignment would be, I began in April by telling the students to conduct and report on an original experiment investigating a particular hypothesis. Then I began the process of teaching them how to do the assignment.

First, they needed to understand what a hypothesis is and where one comes from. I asked them, what happens when you ask a question whose answer you cannot find? You must try to develop your own answer by thinking about what you know. The answer you come up with is called a hypothesis.

At this point, I wrote on the board:

Hypothesis—a possible answer to a previously unanswered question

I gave the students the opportunity to come up with hypotheses that some scientist had once developed about the same material we had studied in biology up to that point. We discussed each one, focusing the question and finding the precise wording for a possible answer. Each of these possible answers we labeled as having once been a hypothesis.

Ambrose raised an important question during these discussions, "How do you know which questions have already been answered?" I referred him back to our previous discussion of the adult and child and showed him that there are only two ways: either, know an area of biology so well that you know what is known and what is not; or, go to the library and do research until you are convinced that you are now aware of what is and isn't known.

"So that's why biologists have to go to graduate school!" remarked Terry. I strongly supported that comment.

"But we haven't been to graduate school yet!" said Ambrose in his I'm-just-about-to-give-up voice.

"No," I agreed, "but actually that will make it easier for you. You see, we really won't be able to answer questions that haven't yet been answered about biology. You don't and even I don't have the knowledge or equipment necessary to do new research in biology. You do have a lot of questions, however, that you don't have answers to. You've been asking me such questions all year! It is those questions for which you will develop first hypotheses, then experiments. Besides, even famous scientists replicate experiments in order to check results."

I had gone through the units we had studied and chosen those that could be investigated by the students. I reminded them of a unit and asked them to think of important questions they still had. We listed these on the board. Through a process of brainstorming and selection, we developed quite a list of questions across the several units I had chosen. Each student then picked a question for which he or she had to think of a possible answer (hypothesis) that could be investigated by a simple experiment.

As a group, we planned an experiment to determine whether plant leaves give off the water that the plant has taken in. I insisted that they design the experiment themselves. I kept them on task by making them vote on decisions instead of endlessly arguing about them. They had to see any weaknesses themselves and try to repair them. Once they had the basic design of the experiment, I then gave my suggestions for improvements. I am very proud of them. They were able to figure out that they had to have some way to water the plant without getting water into the air at the same time. They had also determined that the air around the plant would have to be contained so that water could not get in from any other source. Finally, they figured out that they had to have a control, a space just like that occupied by the plant, but without a plant in it.

So we obtained large plastic containers, put water in two of them, and covered them with wax paper. Then we cut a hole in one of the pieces of wax paper and inserted a small plant so that the roots went in the water in the container and the top stuck out above the wax paper. We used petroleum jelly to seal around the base of the plant so that no water could get out of the bottom of the container. We covered the two bottom containers with two top containers, turned them upside down, and sealed around where they joined with more petroleum jelly. Naturally, it wasn't long before the inside of the top container with the plant in it began to fog up with moisture, but the container without the plant remained dry just as the hypothesis would lead one to predict.

Once we had completed our class investigation, I modeled how to write up the report on a sheet I had made up for this purpose. I also had several students find books that described similar investigations, including results against which we could check our own.

They then started on their individual investigations. I required them to get an approval from me at each of three points. I had to approve of the question each chose in order to prevent unnecessary duplication and to make sure that it was not too broad. Then I had to approve of the hypothesis that each one developed. I wanted to make sure it was their own hypothesis and not one they had copied from somewhere. And I wanted the hypothesis to be one they could design an experiment to investigate. Whether it was the correct answer to their question or not made no difference to me. Finally, I had to approve the design of their experiments. Here was where I did most of my teaching this month. Reasoning with them and holding conferences about their experiments took a lot of time, but I believe they learned a lot from designing them. They met in small groups to get feedback from one another while I met with individuals. After I approved the design of an experiment, I assigned time for that student to set up the experiment in the lab. After everything was completed, I required them to report the results of their investigations on a sheet with the following entries:

Question:
Hypothesis:
Experiment:
Data:
Interpretation:

These reports were shared with their lab partners first and revised based on those comments. I read them to make comments, and they revised them again. Finally, we published these research reports in a class book called "Our Biology Experiments," which we shared with everyone who was interested and some who were not. Our librarian even put a copy in the science section of our library! We ended the month with quite a sense of accomplishment and admiration for biological scientists.

DO IT TOGETHER Form small groups of three and use Table 11.4 on page 296 to rate this fictional high-school biology teacher's effectiveness with the different dimensions of content area literacy. After rating each dimension, be prepared to explain what the fictional teacher **did** to deserve your rating and what she **might have done** to be rated higher. (If you give a "very effective" rating, be prepared to explain what the fictional teacher might have done to be rated off the top of the chart.) Finally, evaluate your ratings by comparing them with others and supporting them with information from the fictional account and the corresponding chapters of this text.

LOOKING BACK Classroom instruction is complex partly due to the challenge of balancing literature, comprehension, vocabulary, writing, studying, and inquiry in instructional units. This chapter portrays four situations where this balance is occurring. The fictional teacher in each situation approaches the challenge differently, and some accomplish it more effectively than others. Applying your new knowledge of content

Table 11.4 *Dimensions of Content Area Literacy: High School Level*

	Very Effective	Effective	Ineffective	Very Ineffective
Instructional units (Chapter 3)				
Reading materials and exhibiting responses (Chapter 4)				
Comprehension (Chapter 5)				
Meaning vocabulary (Chapter 6)				
Writing (Chapter 7)				
Studying (Chapter 8)				
Student inquiry (Chapter 9)				
Differentiation (Chapter 10)				

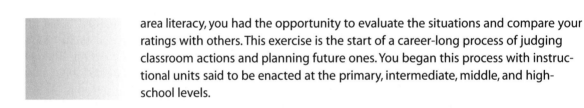

area literacy, you had the opportunity to evaluate the situations and compare your ratings with others. This exercise is the start of a career-long process of judging classroom actions and planning future ones. You began this process with instructional units said to be enacted at the primary, intermediate, middle, and high-school levels.

ADD TO YOUR JOURNAL   Reflect on this chapter's problem solving cases. What is becoming clear to you about balancing dimensions of content area literacy during units of instruction? How do you foresee employing units of instruction to combine literature, comprehension, vocabulary, writing, studying, and inquiry within each day and across 180 school days? What pitfalls do you plan to avoid, and what safeguards do you plan to promote?

Additional Reading

Additional cases of reading and writing across the curriculum are available in the following text:

STURTEVANT, E. G., & LINEK, W. M. (2004). *Content literacy: An inquiry-based case approach.* Upper Saddle River, NJ: Pearson/Merrill Prentice Hall.

12

Reading Proficiency

LOOKING AHEAD The National Assessment of Educational Progress (NAEP) consists of a series of tests and explanatory materials that offer a national perspective on the reading achievement of children and youth. NAEP states what young people are expected to do with print and then compares their expected performance with their actual performance. Due to its national scope, authoritative presentation, and sensible approach to assessment, NAEP is an excellent starting point for understanding official expectations for proficient reading.

In a manner similar to our statements about the No Child Left Behind Act in Chapter 13, we want you to know that we have mixed opinions about NAEP. We believe the NAEP literacy assessment has many positive features, but no single assessment is able to reveal the complexities of proficient reading. This chapter on reading proficiency explains the shortcomings of single assessments. It contains three key ideas:

1. NAEP expectations are sensible starting points for describing reading proficiency.
2. NAEP expectations present readers many challenges.
3. Students deserve expectations and instruction that go beyond NAEP.

NAEP Expectations Are Sensible Starting Points for Describing Reading Proficiency

The National Assessment of Educational Progress, often called the nation's report card, is a "nationally representative and continuing assessment of what America's students know and can do in various subject areas" (National Assessment of Educational Progress, n.d.). It periodically has assessed reading since 1969. The National Center for Education Statistics, which is part of the U.S. Department of Education, is responsible for conducting and reporting NAEP.

NAEP has distinguished itself over the years as a legitimate and trustworthy large-scale reading assessment, so it is a good starting point for understanding and evaluating current reading expectations. We present it in this chapter because educational policy makers use it nationally to gauge academic performance, and many state assessments are patterned after it. But to be sure, the NAEP offers only a starting point for describing state-level reading expectations because practically every state by now has produced its own set of standards and tests. (To learn what officially counts as reading proficiency in your state, you might go to your state department of education's web site through (http://nclb.ecs.org/nclb/), a resource maintained by the Education Commission of the States.) To repeat, the following expectations are from NAEP as it fulfills its charge of "providing information about the knowledge and skills of students in the nation as a whole, in each participating state, and in different demographic groupings (National Assessment of Educational Progress, n.d.). NAEP is not an exit exam used for determining who does and does not graduate, nor is it a state-level monitor of NCLB provisions.

This section describes NAEP reading expectations of youth at the fourth-, eighth-, and twelfth-grade levels. The following section then analyzes these expectations, providing perspective on the challenges they present. The final section goes beyond NAEP expectations to explain other legitimate reading goals.

NAEP Expectations

In order to assess reading performance across the United States, NAEP establishes desired academic achievement levels of all students. NAEP then compares students' desired achievement with their actual achievement. Determining what achievement levels are desired of students is a policy decision made by the National Assessment Governing Board (NAGB). The NAGB is a bipartisan committee whose members include governors, state legislators, local and state school officials, educators, business representatives, and members of the general public. The U.S. Secretary of Education appoints NAGB members, but they are independent of the Department of Education.

The NAGB so far has stipulated three reading achievement levels, basic, proficient, and advanced, for grades four, eight, and twelve. *Proficient* is what constitutes acceptable performance at the particular grade levels. Here is the general description of the proficient level reproduced from the NAEP web site:

> *Proficient.* One of the three NAEP achievement levels, representing solid academic performance for each grade assessed. Students reaching this level have demonstrated competency over challenging subject matter, including subject-matter knowledge, application of such knowledge to real-world situations, and analytical skills appropriate to the subject matter. (National Assessment of Educational Progress, n.d.)

Table 12.1   Descriptions of NAEP Proficient Reading Achievement Levels for Grades 4, 8, and 12

Grade Level	Description of Proficiency
4	Fourth-grade students performing at the Proficient level should be able to demonstrate an overall understanding of the text, providing inferential as well as literal information. When reading text appropriate to fourth grade, they should be able to extend the ideas in the text by making inferences, drawing conclusions, and making connections to their own experiences. The connection between the text and what the student infers should be clear. For example, when reading literary text, Proficient-level fourth graders should be able to summarize the story, draw conclusions about the characters or plot, and recognize relationships such as cause and effect. When reading informational text, Proficient-level students should be able to summarize the information and identify the author's intent or purpose. They should be able to draw reasonable conclusions from the text, recognize relationships such as cause and effect or similarities and differences, and identify the meaning of the selection's key concepts.
8	Eighth-grade students performing at the Proficient level should be able to show an overall understanding of the text, including inferential as well as literal information. When reading text appropriate to eighth grade, they should extend the ideas in the text by making clear inferences from it, by drawing conclusions, and by making connections to their own experiences—including other reading experiences. Proficient eighth graders should be able to identify some of the devices authors use in composing text. For example, when reading literary text, students at the Proficient level should be able to give details and examples to support themes that they identify. They should be able to use implied as well as explicit information in articulating themes; to interpret the actions, behaviors, and motives of characters; and to identify the use of literary devices such as personification and foreshadowing. When reading informative text, they should be able to summarize the text using explicit and implied information and support conclusions with inferences based on the text. When reading practical text, Proficient-level students should be able to describe its purpose and support their views with examples and details. They should be able to judge the importance of certain steps and procedures.
12	Twelfth-grade students performing at the Proficient level should be able to show an overall understanding of the text that includes inferential as well as literal information. When reading text appropriate to twelfth grade, they should be able to extend the ideas of the text by making inferences, drawing conclusions, and making connections to their own personal experiences and other readings. Connections between inferences and the text should be clear, even when implicit. These students should be able to analyze the author's use of literary devices. When reading literary text, Proficient-level twelfth graders should be able to integrate their personal experiences with ideas in the text to draw and support conclusions. They should be able to explain the author's use of literary devices such as irony or symbolism. When reading informative text, they should be able to apply text information appropriately to specific situations and integrate their background information with ideas in the text to draw and support conclusions. When reading practical texts, they should be able to apply information or directions appropriately. They should be able to use personal experiences to evaluate the usefulness of text information.

Source: National Assessment of Educational Progress, n.d.

This description of the proficient reading level provides general guidelines; however, it only hints at what actually is needed relative to reading. Table 12.1, which also comes from the NAEP web site, contains a more detailed description of the proficient reading achievement level for grades four, eight and twelve. Even though the Table 12.1 descriptions are somewhat detailed, they still do not fully illustrate what makes up reading proficiency, NAEP's expectation of acceptable reading. The descriptions found in Table 12.1 still leave too much to the imagination.

To fully understand NAEP's take on reading proficiency, you need to see (a) the passages that youth are expected to read, (b) the prompts that direct youth how to react to the passages, and (c) the written performances that are considered acceptable reactions. Such information is provided in the NAEP publication, *National Assessment of Educational Progress Achievement Levels, 1992–1998 for Reading* (Loomis & Bourque, 2001). Sections from this booklet that illustrate proficient reading are reproduced below to more fully portray NAEP's expectations. But first, due to page space constraints, note that we have reproduced from NAEP's extended passages only those particular excerpts that relate directly to the test prompts; test takers must identify these excerpts on their own.

Grade 4: Reading to Inform

Passage Excerpt:

Blue Crabs, by George W. Frame

The female blue crab mates only once but receives enough sperm to fertilize all the eggs that she will lay in her lifetime. Usually she lays eggs two or three times during the summer, and then she dies. When the eggs are fertilized and laid, they become glued to long hairs on the underside of the female's abdomen. The egg mass sometimes looks like an orange-brown sponge and contains up to two million eggs until they hatch—about nine to fourteen days later. Only one of the blue crabs that we caught last summer was carrying eggs, and we returned her to the water so her eggs could hatch.

Prompt:

Describe the appearance of a female blue crab that is carrying eggs.

Proficient Performance:

She looks like a sponge is on her belly.

Grade 4: Literary Reading

Passage Excerpt:

Sybil Sounds the Alarm, by Drollene P. Brown

Covered with mud, tired beyond belief, Sybil could barely stay on (her horse) Star's back when they rode into their yard. She had ridden more than thirty miles that night. In a daze, she saw the red sky in the east. It was the dawn. Several hundred men were milling about. She had roused them in time, and Ludington's regiment marched out to join the Connecticut militia in routing the British at Ridgefield, driving them back to their ships on Long Island Sound. Afterward, General George Washington made a personal visit to Ludington's Mills to thank Sybil for her courageous deed. Statesman Alexander Hamilton wrote her a letter of praise.

Prompt:

Sybil's ride was important mainly because

A   she rode 30 miles
B   she was exhausted when it was over
C   the British lost at Ridgefield
D   her mother allowed her to ride after all

Proficient Performance:

C   the British lost at Ridgefield

DO IT TOGETHER Gather in pairs and evaluate the sample of NAEP's Grade 4 reading expectations. Do you think the passages are suitable for this grade level? Do you think the prompts are appropriate? Do you think the models of proficient performance are appropriate? What changes, if any, might you suggest?

Grade 8: Reading to Inform

Passage Excerpt:

Dorothea Dix: Quiet Crusader, by Lucie Gerner

On her first day, she (Dorothea Dix) discovered that among the inmates were several mentally ill women. They were anxious to hear what she had to say, but she found it impossible to teach them because the room was unheated. Dix, angry at this neglect on the part of the authorities, asked noted humanitarian Samuel Howe for his help in taking the case to court. . . . Encouraged by Howe and education reformer Horace Mann, she spent two years visiting every asylum, almshouse, and jail in Massachusetts, quietly taking notes on the conditions.

Prompt:

Based on the passage, what is the most probable reason Howe and Mann encouraged Dorothea Dix to push for reforms?

Proficient Performance:

They too felt the way she did and thought it would be better to treat everyone the same.

Grade 8: Literary Reading

Passage Excerpt:

Finding a Lucky Number, by Gary Soto
One laughed with hands in his hair
And turned to ask my age.
"Twelve," I said, and he knocked
My head softly with a knuckle:
"Lucky number, Sonny." He bared
His teeth, yellow and crooked
As dominoes, and tapped the front one
With a finger. "I got twelve—see."
He opened wide until his eyes were lost
In the pouches of fat cheeks,
And I, not knowing what to do, looked in.

Prompt:

Do you think the title of the poem "Finding a Lucky Number" is a good title for the poem? Explain why or why not using evidence from the poem.

Proficient Performance:

No, because the boy is just wandering along when some old man asks him his age and then tells him it is a lucky number. But how can it be lucky when the old man only has <u>12</u> teeth!

DO IT TOGETHER Gather in pairs and evaluate the sample of NAEP's Grade 8 reading expectations. Do you think the passages are suitable for this grade level? Do you think the prompts are appropriate? Do you think the models of proficient performance are appropriate? What changes, if any, might you suggest?

Grade 12 Reading to Inform

Passage Excerpt:

The Civil War in the United States: The Battle of Shiloh

Here are two perspectives on the battle of Shiloh which was part of the American Civil War. Each of the two passages was taken from a different source; the first is from a soldier's journal and the second is from an encyclopedia. Read them and see how each passage makes a contribution to your understanding of the battle of Shiloh and the Civil War. Think about what each source tells you that is missing from the other source, as well as what each one leaves out. [Note: the journal and encyclopedia entries combine to fill about 2-1/2 pages.]

Prompt:

Each account of the battle of Shiloh gives us information that the other does not. Describe what each account includes that is omitted by the other. Does this mean that both accounts provide a distorted perspective of what happened in the battle?

Proficient Performance:

The encyclopedia gives a historical account of the battle of Shiloh. It gives all the facts but leaves out the personal experience and personal feelings of battle.

The journal entry provides the reader with the personal experience of battle and all the emotions that any one soldier might be feeling.

This does not mean that either source provides a distorted perspective on the war. It, however, forms a link between the personal and the facts to give good information on the battle of Shiloh.

Grade 12 Literary Reading

Passage Excerpt:

The Flying Machine, by Ray Bradbury

The emperor looked into the sky.

And in the sky, laughing so high that you could hardly hear him laugh, was a man; and the man was clothed in bright papers and reeds to make wings and a beautiful yellow tail, and he was soaring all about like the largest bird in a universe of birds, like a new dragon in a land of ancient dragons.

. . . "What have you done?" demanded the Emperor.

"I have flown in the sky, Your Excellency," replied the man.

"What have you done?" said the Emperor again.

"I have just told you!" cried the flier.

"You have told me nothing at all . . . I do not fear you, yourself, but I fear another man."

"What man?"

"Some other man who, seeing you, will build a thing of bright papers and bamboo like this. But the other man will have an evil face and evil heart, and the beauty will be gone. It is this man I fear."

"Why? Why?"

"Who is to say that someday just such a man, in just such an apparatus of paper and reed, might not fly in the sky and drop huge stones upon the Great Wall of China?" said the Emperor.

No one moved or said a word.

"Off with his head," said the Emperor.

Prompt:

Who does the Emperor believe should be responsible for an invention? Why does he think this?

Proficient Performance:

It is the inventor's responsibility. The Emperor felt that the inventor should have thought a little more carefully about the ramifications of such an invention.

Grade 12 Reading to Perform a Task

Passage Excerpt:

Instructions for Form 1040EZ

Use this form if:

- Your filing status is single.
- You do not claim any dependents.
- You were under 65 and not blind.
- Your taxable income (line 5) is less than $50,000.
- You had **only** wages, salaries, tips and taxable scholarships or fellowships and your taxable interest income was $400 or less. **Caution**: If you earned tips (including allocated tips) that are not included in Box 14 of your W-2, you may not be able to use Form 1040EZ. See page 23 in the booklet.

Prompt:

Name two factors that would make you ineligible to file a 1040EZ tax return.

Proficient Performance:

Two factors that would make you ineligible to file a 1040EZ tax return are you were older than 65, and blind, and your taxable income was more than $50,000.

DO IT TOGETHER Gather in pairs and evaluate the sample of NAEP's Grade 12 reading expectations. Do you think the passages are suitable for this grade level? Do you think the prompts are appropriate? Do you think the models of proficient performance are appropriate? What changes, if any, might you suggest?

NAEP Expectations Present Readers Many Challenges

If you are like many college-educated adults with whom we have worked, you might consider the NAEP expectations for fourth, eighth, and twelfth grade reading proficiency to be rather light. You might be surprised by what seem to be rather easy reading and responding tasks, and you might believe that more should be asked of upper-grade readers. However, many who have studied U.S. adolescents' NAEP performance have concluded just the opposite. Robert Linn, past president of the American Educational Research Association and the American Evaluation Association, put it this way: "The NAEP achievement levels are quite ambitious performance standards . . . the target of 100% proficient or above according to the NAEP standards appears more like wishful thinking than a realistic possibility" (2003, p. 5).

After examining the percentage of U.S. students actually reading at NAEP's proficient level or higher, Linn (2003) concluded that expecting the NAEP level of proficiency for all U.S. youth in a few years is unrealistic. He found that in 1998 only 33 percent of eighth-grade students and only 40 percent of twelfth-grade students scored at the proficient level or above. Stated the opposite way, in 1998 the majority of U.S. youth (66 percent of eighth graders and 59 percent of twelfth graders) did not read at the proficient level or higher.

Given the present NAEP findings, expecting everybody—especially the most academically challenged—to achieve reading proficiency in the near future appears to be out of reach (McCombs, Kirby, Barney, Darilek, & Magee, 2004). Many contend that U.S. educational policymakers might aspire to—or at least hope for—all youth attaining a proficient level of reading on the NAEP; however, they rightfully might expect all youth to attain at least a basic level of reading in the next few years. The reading demands exemplified by the NAEP test samples presented above are unrealistically demanding for youth who still are striving to develop their reading competence.

To understand the challenge that NAEP expectations present young readers, you need to understand what makes up reading comprehension. A workable breakdown of this proficiency is provided in the influential document, *Reading for Understanding: Toward a Research and Development Program in Reading Comprehension* (RAND Reading Study Group, 2002), often called the *Rand Report on Reading Comprehension* or just the *Rand Report* in honor of its sponsor, the Rand Corporation. The Rand Report divides reading comprehension into three elements—text, activity, and reader—and places these elements within a sociocultural setting. Understanding the elements and their setting offers good insight into expectations for proficient reading.

Text

Understanding the demands of a passage that students are expected to read is a starting point for understanding the expectations of readers. What is the reading load that youth are expected to manage?

The **vocabulary** of a text consistently influences readers' performance (Blachowicz & Fisher, 2000). For instance, words from the fourth-grade NAEP passages that can be expected to challenge some fourth-grade readers include the following:

mates	fertilize	regiment
sperm	abdomen	militia

Words from the eighth-grade NAEP passages that can be expected to challenge some eighth-grade readers are these:

inmate	dominoes
almshouse	asylum
humanitarian	bared

And here, words from the twelfth-grade NAEP passages that can be expected to challenge some twelfth-grade readers:

expediency	miniature
apparatus	executioner
annihilated	deduction

Readers must employ complicated mental operations to know these terms. For instance, knowing that *almshouse* refers to a publicly funded institution that once sheltered poor people calls for intricate intellectual efforts and resources. If the word *almshouse* were unfamiliar to readers, they might pronounce it, hoping they recognized its sound as a known word, then attaching meaning to it. They might try to figure it out by the way it is used in the context of the passage, looking for clues to its meaning in the surrounding words. They might look up *almshouses*, in a dictionary, hoping to find a meaning that makes sense with the way the word is used in the passage. And they might look at its meaningful parts, separating *alms* from *house* and examining the fit. Finally, after gaining an initial sense of this unfamiliar word's meaning, proficient readers would try to develop their understanding of it by connecting it with experiences and related words they know already.

Sentence structure, or syntax, is another aspect of text that readers are expected to control. The ways authors sequence words in sentences can place a tremendous load on readers' working memories and thinking processes. The following question on a U.S. Census questionnaire illustrates the challenge of syntax: "Approximately how many miles was it one way to the place you hunted small game most often in this state?" (RAND Reading Study Group, 2002, p. 98). You probably could figure out what this sentence was asking, but we suspect you needed to reread it, deliberately segment parts of it, and determine relationships among the parts. This is the challenge syntax often presents.

With the NAEP examples just presented, the somewhat convoluted syntax of the first sentence of the *Dorothea Dix* excerpt might challenge eighth-grade readers. The sixty-word sentence beginning with *And* in Ray Bradbury's *The Flying Machine* might challenge twelfth graders. Sentence structures like these can be especially challenging if reader's first languages are not English. Because the positions of nouns, verbs, and adjectives in sentences often vary across languages, those who are learning English require substantial syntactic knowledge to get them straight.

Genre is a third aspect of text that might challenge readers. Genre classifies passages according to how writers formalize ideas and arrange texts to portray the formalizations. Literary scholars from Plato in ancient times to Bakhtin in current times have presented countless—and often overlapping—genres such as the following:

autobiography	fantasy	online chat	teen magazine
comedy	farce	persuasion	text message
description	folklore	romance novel	western adventure
diary	graphic novel	science textbook	
drama	melodrama	slave narrative	
exposition	narration	technical manual	

Readers encountering these different genres need to understand the different purposes authors have, the different ways authors organize their writing to accomplish their purposes, and the different principles authors apply when choosing words. Knowing that drama portrays gripping human events, whereas technical manuals present mundane procedures, helps readers access these written forms.

The twelfth-grade NAEP readers face a personal journal and an encyclopedia entry in one section (*The Civil War in the United States: The Battle of Shiloh*), a folk tale in another section (*The Flying Machine*), and a procedural text in a third (*Instructions for Form 1040EZ*). Realizing how passages such as these are constructed (e.g., a chronological account), then using this knowledge to understand and remember the passage (e.g., mentally listing events chronologically) are crucial yet complicated ways to meet reading expectations.

Accessing a text's vocabulary, syntax, and genre in order to understand that text's message can be challenging. Moreover, texts challenge students at every grade level because vocabulary, syntax, and genre become more complicated at every level. Students certainly can be expected to rise to these challenges, but appropriate instructional conditions are needed.

Activity

The activity of reading is something else to examine when considering reading expectations. The activity of reading involves purpose; it is the answer to the question, "What is the reader to do with the text?" For example, youth might step into a text world for the purpose of experiencing it vicariously. Adolescents who immerse themselves in the sights, sounds, and feelings of a novel such as *The Outsiders* often do so mainly to live through it virtually, inferring the feelings and sensations of the characters. Other times youth might read for the purpose of informing themselves, grasping new ideas and information and storing them for later. Readers who spend time with informational texts like *Animals on the Trail with Lewis and Clark* often intend to understand and remember for a long time what the material has to offer.

Youth also might read somewhat brief texts for short-term use such as cooking a meal, assembling an engine, completing a work application, or running a software program. They read these materials for the purpose of performing certain actions. And youth might scrutinize what they find in print, critically examining the unstated beliefs and assumptions in a school newspaper's editorial or the implied promises of an advertisement in a magazine like *Spin*.

The NAEP reading expectations presented above involve only one particular type of activity, answering questions, and the NAEP questions are limited to a few types. Although answering certain types of test questions is a time-honored academic pursuit, it is only one of many possibilities that occur inside and outside academic circles. Other types of questions vary according to the following:

- *People who ask the questions.* In school, teachers often assign ready-made questions or generate their own, and these questions often are used to test students' comprehension. Outside of school, youth typically respond to questions from family members or friends who actually are interested in what the individual is reading and don't already know the answers to the questions. The NAEP questions are established by outsiders, people whom the youth will never meet, to test their understanding.
- *How readers answer the questions.* Some activities require youth to compose answers in their own words, and others require youth to select from the multiple choices that are provided. The NAEP reading tests generally have youth write out—rather than select—answers. Composing answers in print certainly is a worthwhile practice, although it occurs rarely outside of school and tends to complicate the assessment by connecting writing to reading.
- *How answers relate to the text.* Some activities call for youth to recover facts that are directly stated, and others call for complex reasoning and problem solving that go beyond the text. The NAEP reading activities typically go beyond the text. To illustrate, eighth-grade youth are asked about the "most probable reason" for two historical figures encouraging Dorothea Dix to push for reform. Since the reasons for encouragement are not stated explicitly in the passage, readers need to think through what the text said, connect it with what they know already, and put together a plausible response. Again, expecting readers to infer ideas and information not stated directly in the passage certainly should be encouraged, but it adds to the challenge readers face.
- *The number of texts involved.* Some reading activities involve multiple texts, while others involve a single one. For instance, the twelfth-grade section of NAEP on the Battle of Shiloh juxtaposes a personal journal with an encyclopedia account. All other passages are treated individually. Having readers synthesize what they gather from more than one text reflects real-world activity, but it also increases test complexity.

Although the NAEP has many positive features, it still requires a particular approach to print. Educators sometimes refer to this approach as *assessment literacy*, a way of reading and writing when taking tests. Many educators are concerned that overemphasizing assessment literacy shortchanges youth, focusing on a narrow aspect of reading and writing and limiting students' capacities for worthwhile inside- and outside-of-school activities. These educators advocate a balanced set of activities that go beyond writing out short answers to test questions that address brief texts. They expect readers to do things with texts, like discussing one another's interpretations, artistically representing ideas through various media, and dramatizing what they have read.

Reader

Suppose two students take the reading portion of NAEP. One student performs at the proficient level, and the other does not. What have these readers brought to the NAEP—and to other reading situations—that explains their different performances?

As presented earlier, readers bring to the page different amounts of linguistic knowledge, different understandings of vocabulary, syntax, and genre. Indeed, twelfth graders who already know the distinctions between personal journals and encyclopedia entries would not even have to read the NAEP text on the civil war to complete its corresponding activity, "Describe what each account (*personal journals and encyclopedia entries*) includes that is omitted by the other." Readers who already know that journals typically include personal experiences and encyclopedias include vast amounts of condensed information would not be challenged by this activity.

As Chapter 1 of this text pointed out, readers employ thinking processes such as connecting, organizing, and evaluating to make sense of text. The psychological literature on these processes (see, for example, Huey, 1908/1998; Stanovich, 2000) is clear that readers differ substantially in their use. Some readers organize ideas efficiently and some do not. Substantial differences are found relative to these processes even within individuals; some readers are adept at forming images but limited at applying ideas to new situations. Children and youth bring different mixes of thinking processes to what they read.

Literate identity is another quality adolescents bring to texts that affects their performance. As Chapter 1 explained, literate identity is the constellation of motivations, purposes, and perspectives individuals hold for themselves as readers and writers. Productive literate identities mean that individuals think of themselves as members of a literate community, as part of an invisible reading and writing club. They believe that they are responsible for and in control of improving their literacy performance. They expect to succeed with print, bringing a can-do attitude to texts. They seek opportunities to read and write, building literate foundations that lead to improved reading and writing. Youth who identify themselves as academic readers and writers increase their chances for proficient performance on the NAEP.

Finally, readers bring to the page different amounts of topic knowledge, different degrees of familiarity with a text's subject matter. Eighth-grade youth who already are acquainted with the topic of the mentally ill and who are already familiar with the historical figures Dorothea Dix, Samuel Howe, and Horace Mann would be expected to do better with *Dorothea Dix: Quiet Crusader* than youth who do not have this background. Twelfth-grade youth who have toured Shiloh National Military Park in Tennessee and who already know about the 24,000 killed or wounded there would be expected to read *The Civil War in the United States: The Battle of Shiloh* and do better with it than those who have not visited this site. Already knowing the ideas and information that a text presents substantially enhances readers' performances with that text.

In brief, the intellectual and motivational qualities that readers bring to a passage go far in explaining differences in their performance with that passage. Youth with well-developed linguistic knowledge, thinking processes, literate identities, and topic knowledge can be expected to read more proficiently than those impoverished in these qualities.

Sociocultural Setting

Youth take up reading and writing in part according to the beliefs, values, and norms derived from their gender, ethnicity, income, nationality, religion, and neighborhood. For instance, many boys disregard academic reading according to stereotypic masculine customs constructed through sociocultural settings rather than through biological determinations (Guzzetti, Young, Gritsavage, Fyfe, & Hardenbook, 2002). The boys' beliefs, values, and norms associated with their gender are influencing them to act a certain way toward reading. With the possible exception of some special education students, members of the NCLB subgroups (African American, Asian, Latino, limited-English proficient, low income, Native American, and White) vary in academic reading performance due to their social and cultural settings rather than through biology.

A key feature of sociocultural settings involves opportunity to learn. Stated simply, *opportunity to learn* refers to the chances individuals have to gain new knowledge. It calls attention to whether or not youth from different sociocultural settings have equitable chances to achieve in school. Distinguishing metaphors from similes and interpreting charts and graphs are fair expectations only when youth from all sociocultural settings have had adequate chances to do so. Some major aspects of opportunity to learn that account for differences in reading performance among sociocultural groups are presented in Table 12.2.

As Table 12.2 suggests, affluence is a key feature of opportunity to learn. Affluent settings increase youths' opportunities to read well. Access to plentiful print in and out of school, orderly classes with reasonable numbers of students, and regular daily attendance in school afford youth the opportunities to attain reading proficiency. Highly qualified teachers who team with parents in expecting academic excellence and who guide students through challenging experiences, thinking through texts, also go far in enhancing learning opportunities. Students of poverty, those who typically are denied such settings, predictably will struggle to meet NAEP-type reading expectations (Ancess, 2003; Chall, Jacobs, & Baldwin, 1990).

LISTEN, LOOK, AND LEARN   Visit a class and observe at least three lessons. Describe how the lessons do or do not address the NAEP reading proficiencies. What might be done to address the NAEP reading proficiencies? What might be done to go beyond the NAEP proficiencies?

Table 12.2   Opportunity to Learn

Aspect	Features
Class size	Appropriate number of students (often less than 25) according to student characteristics, subject matter, and teacher ability
Curricular rigor	Academics aligned with challenging standards and higher-order thinking; nondiscrimination policies that minimize tracking; coursework requirements for graduation that involve high levels of literacy
Language compatibility	Bridges between language spoken at home and at school; home-school connections among such things as vocabulary and social customs of speaking; translation services
Parent participation	Communication between teachers and parents; sense of welcome by the school; attendance at school functions and meetings; membership in school organizations and committees; expectations for academic success
Print accessibility	Abundant time in and out of school for reading and writing; abundant materials that students can and want to read; access to rich software and Internet sites
School community	Respectful caring relationships among students and teachers; collegial interactions; civil discourse; safe and secure facilities; orderly environment in good repair
Student attendance	Continued enrollment in a school; regular daily presence; stable classroom membership
Teacher quality	Experienced; certified; teaching within college major or minor; effectively supported with staff development; ethic of professional responsibility for student learning
Teaching practice	Gradual release of responsibility; discussion-based approaches amid high academic demands; responsiveness to formal and informal assessments

Students Deserve Instruction That Goes Beyond NAEP Expectations

This chapter so far has presented NAEP reading expectations and the challenges they present readers. This final section examines what NAEP reading expectations ignore. It addresses what policymakers' tests ignore but that deserve to be honored in classrooms and testing rooms as legitimate aspects of reading.

Youth engage in many genuine, rightful literacy activities inside and outside of school (Hull & Schultz, 2002; Mahiri, 2004). What does the NAEP ignore that deserves notice? The NAEP does not have students inquire deeply into important personal issues (e.g., What career choices do I realistically have?) or social problems (e.g., Should the U.S. allow capital punishment?). It does not include instructional communication technology either through software or online. It does not include entire novels, sets of work-related documents, or personally selected magazines. And it does not combine printed messages with spoken ones. Consequently, many youth who have difficulty with the current NAEP expectations might do better with others; conversely, many who do well with the NAEP might do worse in other reading situations.

The NAEP format reflects only a small portion of the reading many youth actually do inside and outside of school. Every day, countless adolescents log onto Internet-based texts with specialized vocabulary and presentation patterns, and they use these texts for media-based inquiries, video gaming, and instant messaging. Every day, countless adolescents digitally combine pictures and sounds with print. And every day countless adolescents read highly technical texts related to their particular passions such as animal science, automotives, cosmetology, and robotics—to name a few. Many youth who are highly proficient with these particular types of texts that fit their personal interests tend to struggle with academic texts outside those interests (O'Brien, in press).

Describing proficient reading is a complex undertaking that raises many questions. As Rothstein (2004) puts it, "Proficiency . . . is not an objective fact but a subjective judgment" (p. 88). What counts as proficient reading? What exactly does it take to be considered a proficient reader, especially by the end of high school? Is reading proficiency the same for everyone, or should it vary? Should those who plan to enter the workforce immediately after high school be expected to read like those who plan on postsecondary education? Should those who aspire to careers in the sciences be expected to acquire literary analysis skills equal to those who are entering the humanities? Should those who entered the country recently with a language other than English or those with learning handicaps be expected to read like those whose first language is English and have no handicaps?

Further, is reading proficiency the same in every situation, or should it depend on where it takes place? Should reading practices that occur online at home receive the same attention as what occurs with print in school? Should occupational reading tasks that call for immediate on-the-job problem solving receive the same attention as school-related reading tasks that involve long-term learning of abstract ideas?

An important qualification about readers' identities described in Chapter 1 pertains to their being socially situated. Youths might identify themselves as proficient readers in one situation and struggling readers in another. They might see themselves as part of an invisible literary novel reading club but not part of a popular science reading club. They might assume responsibility for their reading after school but abdicate responsibility for it during school. They might expect to do well with personal reading of religious or entertainment materials but expect to do poorly with the NAEP.

Our point in these closing words is that directing readers toward one particular type of expectation, albeit an important type, is at risk of limiting or devaluing students' proficiencies with other reading expectations. Youth certainly deserve instruction that enables them to meet educational policymakers' expectations, but they deserve instruction leading to balanced and personalized expectations, too.

LOOKING BACK   Because reading proficiency is a subjective judgment rather than an objective fact, understanding what official definitions of proficiency include—and do not include—is an important aspect of professional knowledge. Such understandings enable you to provide instruction that meets students' best interests, instruction that prepares children and youth for important tests without teaching only to the tests. This chapter contains three key ideas:

1. NAEP expectations are sensible starting points for describing reading proficiency.
2. NAEP expectations present readers many challenges.
3. Students deserve expectations and instruction that go beyond NAEP.

ADD TO YOUR JOURNAL   Reflect upon the three key ideas in this chapter and decide what you think. Are the NAEP expectations sensible starting points for describing reading proficiency? What, if anything, might be more sensible? What do you think of the challenges NAEP expectations present readers? What other challenges do they present? Are these challenges reasonable? And how far beyond NAEP-type expectations should instruction go? Should educators address outside-of-school literacies inside of school?

Additional Readings

To further examine the intricacies of assessing reading proficiency, consult the following sources.

GREDLER, M. E., & JOHNSON, R. L. (2004). *Assessment in the literacy classroom*. Boston: Allyn and Bacon.

HILL, C., & LARSEN, E. (2000). *Children and reading tests*. Stamford, CT: Ablex.

PARIS, S. G., & STAHL, S. A. (Eds.) (2005). *Children's reading comprehension and assessment*. Mahwah, NJ: Lawrence Erlbaum Associates.

13

Reading Policy

LOOKING AHEAD Since the early 1990s, state superintendents of instruction along with state and national political leaders have been deciding what students are to know and be able to do. Understanding political leaders' policies and their expectations relative to reading are crucial parts of your professional knowledge. Recognizing the strengths and limitations of reading policies informs your professional decisions.

Knowing what students are expected to accomplish enables you to direct instruction effectively. You, your colleagues, and your students can concentrate on what counts according to formal expectations. By the same token, deep understandings of reading expectations allow you to teach in a principled manner. Understanding the intended—and unintended—consequences of formal policies enables you, your colleagues, and your students to go beyond mandated expectations and fully access the wonder and power of reading.

This chapter focuses on the *No Child Left Behind Act* (NCLB), the most influential U.S. education legislation enacted in a generation. We examine NCLB here because its unprecedented accountability provisions affect the levels of reading achievement for which schools currently are responsible. Among other things, NCLB assigns serious consequences to schools that fail to move their students' reading achievement to certain levels within certain amounts of time.

In the spirit of full disclosure, we want you to know that we have mixed opinions about NCLB. On the one hand, we applaud measures that galvanize attention toward the literacy of all children and youth. On the other hand, we disapprove of overly narrow and stringent requirements for reading. As our following comments show, we believe that NCLB requirements have many positive features, but we further believe that this initiative should be modified to serve students best.

This chapter on reading policies contains two key ideas:

1. The *No Child Left Behind* Act presents reading expectations as never before.
2. The opportunity—and the challenge—of *No Child Left Behind* is to ensure that it serves students well.

The *No Child Left Behind* Act Presents Reading Expectations as Never Before

The *No Child Left Behind Act*, which President George W. Bush enacted with bipartisan congressional support on January 8, 2002, fundamentally changed the expectations of K–12 education. Although NCLB is only one part of an education reform movement that uses high-stakes testing as a policy tool (Hamilton, 2003), it is influential because of its federal origin and its emphasis on eliminating the achievement gaps displayed by traditionally underserved populations in comparison with those who are well served.

NCLB greatly expanded the federal government's role in education by placing stipulations on all fifty states that participate in its well-funded Title I program for low-income children. Educational policies officially still are reserved for the states and local school districts, but the federal government exerts its influence by withdrawing its school funding if educators do not cooperate. NCLB holds states, school districts, and schools accountable for more and more students achieving at high levels each year with the expectation that all—yes, all—U.S. students will be proficient in reading (as well as math and science) by the 2013–2014 academic year.

NCLB is a sprawling, complex piece of legislation. You can go online (www.ed.gov/policy/elsec/leg/esea02/index.html) to view the enormity of this law. Additionally, governmental authorities have been refining parts of NCLB since it was enacted. For instance, federal authorities have adjusted the academic expectations of students with significant cognitive disabilities and with limited English proficiencies. Authorities also have changed the ways teachers can comply with the requirement to be highly qualified, and they relaxed the numbers of students in particular subgroups that schools need to test. As is the case with many governmental initiatives, NCLB can be expected to change over time, so educators will need to stay abreast of its future expectations.

A dramatic indication of the commotion this legislation has stirred is the presence of 1,480,000 links we found as of this writing with an online Google search of "no child left behind." Especially timely and informative updates of NCLB issues are found at the following web sites:

Center on Education Policy	www.ctredpol.org/
Council of Chief State School Officers	www.ccsso.org/federal_programs/NCLB/index.cfm
Education Commission of the States	http://nclb2.ecs.org/Projects_Centers/index.aspx?issueid=gen&IssueName=General
The Education Trust	http://edtrust.org
National Education Association	www.nea.org/esea/
United States Department of Education	www.ed.gov/nclb/landing.jhtml

NCLB Expectations

NCLB addresses grades one to eight, although many of its provisions also affect high schools (Conley & Hinchman, 2004; Joftus & Maddux-Dolan, 2003). The federal administration has indicated plans to push the reforms of *No Child Left Behind* more deeply into high schools, albeit only those participating in the Title I program for low-income youth. Key features of the NCLB plan center about adequate yearly progress, annual achievement tests, graduation or attendance rates, subgroup monitoring, consequences, and highly qualified teachers.

Adequate Yearly Progress   NCLB expects specific percentages of students to demonstrate Adequate Yearly Progress (AYP) year by year in reading, math, and science. To establish definitions of what constitutes AYP, federal and state officials negotiate often complex formulas based on percentages of students' reaching certain scores on particular reading, math, and science tests. In addition, AYP formulas typically include test-score improvements along with rates of graduation or school attendance. AYP formulas vary from state to state with education officials from each state meeting with federal officials to determine their particular definition.

Annual Achievement Tests   Beginning with the 2005–2006 school year, all students in grades three to eight are to be tested annually in reading and math, and all students in at least one high school grade level (ten to twelve) are to be tested annually in reading and math. Science testing begins in the 2007 academic year. Individual states decide the tests to use as long as they are aligned with that state's academic standards and federal guidelines. Many states rely on national norm-referenced tests along with state-specific curriculum-referenced tests.

An important point about achievement tests involves the connections between state AYP exams and state exit exams. Exit exams are what students must pass to graduate from high school. Nineteen states had mandatory exit exams in 2003, and five states were phasing in such exams by 2008 (Gayler, Chudowsky, Kober, & Hamilton, 2003). AYP exams determine whether or not schools meet expectations; exit exams determine whether or not individuals meet expectations. AYP exams have serious consequences for schools, and exit exams have serious consequences for youths. Many states—but certainly not all—use exit exams as their NCLB-mandated measures of AYP. Our point here is that reading testing is occurring as never before. It happens frequently, and, with individual and schools' futures on the line, it carries high stakes.

Graduation or Attendance Rates   Along with achievement tests, NCLB requires schools to have an additional measure of educational progress. It calls for high schools to use graduation rates as the additional measure. It allows each state to determine its middle-school measure, and most have selected attendance rates. This stipulation is in place partly due to the disturbingly large numbers of high school dropouts, which currently is about 25 percent overall yet varies substantially when determined by subgroups.

Subgroup Monitoring   NCLB requires states, school districts, and schools to report its annual test scores broken out for the following eight student subgroups:

- African American
- Asian
- Latino
- limited-English proficient
- low income
- Native American
- special education
- White

NCLB requires states to determine a certain number of students at each grade level that is needed to constitute a viable subgroup. Some states say that twenty-five members are needed for a grade-level subgroup to exist; others say forty. Once a school identifies viable subgroups at each grade level (e.g., fifty-two low-income students are in a school's tenth grade), then at least 95 percent of that subgroup's membership must be included in the annual testing.

NCLB requires test score reports to be broken out for subgroups because their academic progress is concealed when everyone's scores are combined and reported collectively. Additionally, NCLB calls for AYP by each subgroup. If one subgroup at one grade level does not attain a certain target, then the school does not demonstrate AYP. The admonition to *leave no child behind*, which is the basis for the NCLB title, underlies this requirement. Subgroup monitoring is an explicit attempt to close the achievement gap.

Consequences   States impose consequences on schools that consistently do not demonstrate AYP. The consequences involve conventional measures such as school improvement plans and tutoring services along with bold options such as transferring students to other schools and possibly privatizing public school management. As can be seen in what follows, the consequences are incremental, moving from mild to severe across seven years.

Year one. A school goes about its business as usual.

Year two. If a school did not make AYP the previous year, then it should identify shortcomings and adjust accordingly.

Year three. If a school does not make AYP two years in a row, then it must give parents the option to use federal funds to transfer their children to higher-performing schools in the district. It also must identify shortcomings and work to remedy them with parents, teachers, and consultants.

Year four. If a school does not make AYP three years in a row, then it must provide private tutoring and other educational supplements to its low-income students.

Year five. If a school does not make AYP four years in a row, then *corrective action* is taken. Along with continuing to offer the services already instituted, a school must implement at least one of the following corrective actions: (a) replace personnel who are not contributing to AYP, (b) institute a new curriculum along with staff development, (c) decrease the school's management authority, (d) bring in an outside expert, (e) extend the school year or school day, or (f) restructure the school organizational arrangement.

Year six. If a school does not make AYP five years in a row, then *alternative governance* is begun. Along with continuing to offer the services and corrective actions already instituted, a school must implement at least one of the following alternative governance actions: (a) reopen as a public charter school, (b) replace all or most of the personnel who are not contributing to AYP, (c) contract with a private company to operate the school, (d) turn over operations to the state, or (e) implement other state-approved fundamental reforms.

Year seven. If a school does not make AYP six years in a row, then the alternative governance plan developed previously must be implemented.

Highly Qualified Teachers NCLB requires each state by the end of the 2005–2006 school year to ensure that only highly qualified middle- and high-school educators teach in the core academic subjects (i.e., English, reading or language arts, math, science, foreign language, civics and government, economics, arts, history, and geography). The criteria for teacher quality include (a) full certification by a state, which does not include certificates waived through emergency, temporary, or provisional means; (b) an undergraduate degree; (c) an academic major in the area in which the person teaches; and (d) passing an academic subject certification test in the area in which the person teaches. Teachers also can become highly qualified by participating in professional opportunities such as staff development workshops, curriculum revisions, and so on.

The criteria for highly qualified teachers are reasonable as far as they go, but they do not go far enough (Emerick, Hirsch, & Berry, 2004). These criteria focus only on teachers' subject matter knowledge, educational backgrounds, and credentials. The criteria do not include professional knowledge of teaching, demonstrations of actual classroom performance, or outcomes of teaching. Paradoxically, even though NCLB concentrates on reading proficiency, it does not require secondary-school teachers to be qualified to address reading in their core subjects.

Placing highly qualified, well prepared teachers in every classroom is a major challenge. Teacher shortages persist, especially in inner cities where low-income, limited-English students predominate. The NCLB provision for a highly qualified teacher in every classroom especially challenges those in inner cities—as well as rural areas—who frequently have limited abilities to help in the recruitment, development, and retention of teachers.

DO IT TOGETHER   NCLB is a federal law that is fundamentally affecting the education of U.S. children and youth. To determine how well informed the general public is about this law, interview about five noneducators. Ask them to describe the six key features of the NCLB plan

1. adequate yearly progress
2. annual achievement tests
3. graduation or attendance rates
4. subgroup monitoring
5. consequences
6. highly qualified teachers

Compare your findings with others in class, and—based on your limited samples—tentatively characterize public knowledge of NCLB.

The Opportunity—and the Challenge—of *No Child Left Behind* Is to Ensure That It Serves Students Well

Most educators agree with NCLB's goals of strong academic achievement for all children and closing the achievement gap. Most embrace the use of an accountability system to monitor educational effectiveness. Those who support NCLB claim that it extends a commitment to social justice, calling reading the *new civil right*. Nevertheless, educational writers have used fiery rhetoric to express passionate feelings against the specifics of NCLB. For instance, educational commentator Gerald Bracey has opposed this legislation as "a weapon of mass destruction targeted at the public schools in a campaign of shock and awe" (2003, pp. 148–149). Conversely, former U.S. Secretary of Education Rod Paige defended NCLB as a remedy to some current educational circumstances that "are not at all unlike a system of apartheid" (Robelen, 2003, ¶ 3). Another time Secretary Paige claimed (then later apologized for his claim) that the National Education Association's resistance to many NCLB provisions was like that of a "terrorist organization" (Pear, 2004, ¶ 1).

In March 2003, sixteen chief state school officers (i.e., superintendents of public instruction, commissioners of education) petitioned the Secretary of Education to allow more flexibility in the way they determine adequate yearly progress. During 2003, at least twenty Republican-controlled state legislatures passed resolutions to substantially modify NCLB's requirements or to opt out of it. And in October 2004 more than twenty education, civil rights, children's, disability, and citizens' organizations submitted to Congress a joint organizational statement of corrections needed. This statement called for a shift in NCLB's emphasis on penalizing schools to an emphasis on holding states and localities accountable for improving the conditions that affect student achievement (Joint Organizational Statement on *No Child Left Behind Act*, 2004).

While public school leaders charged with implementing NCLB generally accept the spirit of its goals, they report many obstacles achieving the goals (Public Agenda Online, 2003). One major complaint is that the law's requirements, such as annual testing of every grade, transferring students to other schools when requested, and tutoring students privately, are too costly and cumbersome. Another key objection is that the accountability requirements are too stringent.

Those who oppose NCLB claim that it places unrealistic expectations on public schools in attempts to undermine them and turn them over to private enterprise. Many political conservatives are appalled by the federal government's intrusion into educational responsibilities traditionally assumed by local and state agencies. They note that the federal government funds less than 8 percent of the nation's education program, but NCLB affects nearly all classroom activity. They are upset that the federal government's policy toward education switched from President Reagan and Congressman Newt Gingrich attempting to disband the U.S. Department of Education in the 1980s and 1990s to President George W. Bush granting it unprecedented power during the 2000s.

Many political liberals are dismayed by a NCLB's perceived overemphasis on test preparation and narrowing of the curriculum. They view the accountability measures of this law as a pathway to sterile, unproductive instruction. People from both sides of the political spectrum—especially state education officials charged with implementing NCLB—criticize its underfunded mandates. They claim the federal government provides insufficient funds to carry out its requirements to test all students annually as well as provide individual tutoring and transportation to alternative schools for students in underperforming schools.

The following provides perspective on some of the major issues relative to NCLB. Here we address four of the more challenging questions asked of this initiative.

Are the NCLB Provisions Sufficient to Close the Achievement Gap?

The subgroup monitoring element of NCLB is meant to eliminate achievement gaps. These gaps are demonstrated with findings such as the following:

- The average eighth grader who is nonwhite or who is from a low-income family reads at about three to four grade levels below those students who are white and better advantaged
- About one in seventeen youth from the nation's poorest families (those earning less than $35,377 annually) earn a bachelor's degree by the age of 24; about one in two youth from the nation's wealthiest families (those earning more than $85,000 annually) earn a bachelor's degree by the age of 24 (National Association of Secondary School Principals, n.d.).

By mandating that no child—at least no group of children—is to be left behind, NCLB is meant to compel educators to close this achievement gap. However, many educational commentators consider the reading achievement gap to be the consequence of other divisions apparent out of school. They do not see the reading achievement gap resulting just from the school practices that NCLB addresses (National Study Group for the Affirmative Development of Academic Ability, 2004).

Educators often point to the four hundred languages spoken in the United States and the prevalence of recently immigrated Spanish speakers as a big reason for achievement differences. They point to the 9 percent of the student population identified as having special needs as another reason. But perhaps the most fundamental gap that frequently is highlighted involves the comparative wealth of white, black, and Hispanic families in the United States. In 2002, the net worth of white families on average was an incredible fourteen times more than blacks and eleven times more than Hispanics (Kochhar, 2004).

Disparities in wealth affect educational achievement through home, community, and school influences (Barton, 2003, 2004; Berliner, 2005; Evans, 2005; Rothstein, 2004). Young children of affluence—unlike those of poverty—typically are born with robust birth weights then receive nutrition suitable for proper development. Children of affluence experience a great deal of rich reading in their homes, frequently being read to aloud in order to have fun and start conversations about the outside world. Children of affluence predictably are included in conversations about the adult world, developing a belief that they are entitled to solve problems collaboratively with adults and express themselves fully to adults. Children of affluence generally interact with role models who demonstrate a culture of achievement, developing expectations to excel academically, graduate from college, and enter high-status professions. Children of affluence typically have good health, missing few school days and being alert during class; they mostly live in stable neighborhoods, experiencing relatively nonviolent and orderly surroundings. By and large, these children remain in the same school, progressing through systematic programs with frequent home-school contacts. Finally, children of affluence as a rule have experienced teachers with expertise in their subjects who are present to teach every day.

Given the discrepancies among children of affluence and of poverty, reducing differences in reading achievement involves reducing differences in social and economic conditions. Social and economic improvements include assistance for struggling mothers; affordable and high-quality day care for young children; after-school and summer programs in community centers that support academics as well as cultural, athletic, and organizational experiences; and living wages and stable housing. Social improvements connected directly with schools involve high-quality early childhood education as well as fully staffed health clinics on school grounds.

Gaps in wealth also affect youths' educational achievement through the funding their schools receive (Biddle & Berliner, 2003). Funding gaps exist in places where local property taxes are used to support schools and where the local properties are poor, as in many inner cities and some rural areas, while others are prosperous. Impoverished property tax bases result in impoverished school circumstances such as the following:

- insufficient and outdated textbooks
- substandard or no libraries
- underprepared teachers
- no substitutes for absent teachers
- crowded and dilapidated classrooms
- inadequate heating, cooling, and lighting

Students of poverty—along with those of limited oral English and special learning needs—require extraordinary interventions to function academically like students of affluence with full oral English and regular learning needs. To illustrate, Pogrow (2004) offers the data-based claim that educationally disadvantaged eighth graders require thirty-five to forty minutes a day of sophisticated conversation for eighteen months to two years to develop what he calls "a sense of understanding" (p. 2), a mindset for articulating and justifying complex academic thoughts. The instructional conversations need to occur in groups of ten to twelve students led by teachers trained in Socratic techniques, using topics that intrigue students and stimulate academic thinking. Such intensive instruction comes with a cost.

A major point of contention about NCLB is the extent to which it provides resources to close the achievement gap. Many educators claim that resources are secondary to the quality of educational programs (Greene & Forster, 2004; Marshall, 2003). They assert that educators' beliefs, such as the conviction that all youth can achieve at high levels, and external standards linked to high-stakes curriculum-based tests make the difference. On the other hand, many believe that NCLB neither promises nor actually provides sufficient resources to leave no child behind. They focus on the need for resources such as reading materials, computer technology, innovative programs, additional time, adequate classrooms, and competitive salaries. They assert that a mobilization of resources similar to landing a person on the moon is needed to close the achievement gap and achieve universal proficiency in reading, math, and science by 2014. As Joftus (2003) put it, "Accountability without resources is no better than resources without accountability" (p. 13).

Another perspective on closing the racial achievement gap focuses on racism (Ogbu, 2003). While Whites frequently consider the achievement gap to be due to social class differences, many blacks assert that racism is the root cause. Even though racial accord generally seems prevalent as of this writing, institutional forces such as low expectations and lack of encouragement, placements in academically weak tracks, and inexperienced teachers are said to contribute to low academic performance (Ferguson, 2002). Minority students often come to identify with their marginal position in U.S. society. Overcoming racist beliefs and practices is said to be the first step toward closing the achievement gap.

Finally, many assert that NCLB restrictions stifle state, community, and school innovations. The federal government has intruded in the day-to-day operations of public education by mandating a particular type of achievement measure. Local sites that once were pioneers now are captives of a one-size-fits-all accountability system.

Will NCLB Narrow the Curriculum?

A major point of contention about NCLB involves whether it will focus schools' curriculums inappropriately, narrowing instruction to only what is tested (Meier, 2002; Meier & Wood, 2004). The concern is that NCLB might cause schools to resemble test preparation factories more than meaningful learning communities. Educators concerned about this danger contend that preparing youth for tests differs from preparing youth for life. They reject the brain cramming that occurs in many schools, advocating instead for debate, discussion, problem solving, critical evaluation, and creative expression. They expect youth to engage in practices that involve thinking through topics, handling different points of view, inventing new ideas, and expressing themselves in lengthy responses. Along with academic growth, they value youths' personal development, relationships with teachers and peers, and happiness and enthusiasm. They fear that NCLB will limit classrooms to timed reading and writing drills. The challenge here, of course, is to enable students to score well on tests while developing relevant lifelong reading competencies and attitudes.

Extensive research on motivation suggests that simply teaching to a test harms more than helps instruction (Alderman, 2003; Stipek, 1996; Wigfield & Eccles, 2002). The best teaching and learning occur when youths' goals are to master the topic, when they believe they will succeed after expending reasonable effort, and when they choose some of their own materials and activities. Working mainly to demonstrate superiority over others or to earn extrinsic rewards such as test scores result in inferior learning. Further, the classroom and school settings in which youth work affect their mind-sets (Roeser, Eccles, & Sameroff, 2000). An instructional environment that focuses primarily on external mandates undercuts youths' motivation to read better.

If schools overemphasize reading, math, and science, then other worthwhile subjects are at risk of being deemphasized. Especially in the lower grades, educators might focus on tested subjects at the expense of foreign languages, the arts, and physical education. This tendency might deny "our most vulnerable students the full liberal arts curriculum our most privileged youth receive almost as matter of course" (von Zastrow, 2004, p. 9). Students are denied the opportunities to find and follow their school-related passions such as journalism, sports, or theater due to misplaced attention on reading and writing proficiencies.

LISTEN, LOOK, AND LEARN   Observe about three meetings of a class. What evidence of *teaching to the test* was apparent? If you noted evidence of *teaching to the test*, how did students react to it? What might be done to remedy any negative situations?

What Aspects of NCLB Clearly Are Deplorable?

Holding students and schools accountable for high standards is like administering powerful medicine. While it can remedy certain conditions, it also can have undesirable and potentially dangerous side effects. Three aspects of NCLB that clearly are deplorable involve basing decisions on insufficient information, abandoning learners, and cheating.

Basing high-stakes decisions on only one measure of reading is unacceptable. Convincing research (Amrein & Berliner, 2003; Orfield & Kornhaber, 2001; Raudenbausch, 2004) and professional association position statements (American Educational Research Association, 2000; International Reading Association, 1999) conclude that tests can be used to identify students, teachers, and schools who need extra help, but test scores alone should not decide high-stakes educational issues. Multiple measures are needed to obtain the information required for consequential decisions about individuals and schools. Multiple opportunities to succeed with a test, along with multiple situations involving class work and homework, are indispensable for fair assessments, especially when traditionally underrepresented groups are involved (Joint Organizational Statement on *No Child Left Behind* Act, 2004).

No single test adequately reflects all the ways readers interact with print. And no single measure administered during a single test session adequately reflects growth and development over time. Restricting reading to answering questions about brief passages during one point in time exaggerates that measure and shortchanges readers. Like medical examiners assessing the health of clients, reading examiners should consult multiple measures over multiple points in time. For instance, to judge overall high school performance fully, authorities should supplement single-test information with course exit exams, Advanced Placement and International Baccalaureate tests, SAT and ACT performance, school graduation rates, percentages of graduates who enroll in as well as graduate from college or trade school, and the percentages who require remediation beyond high school.

Along the same line, basing decisions only on whether or not students perform at a certain level misses the amount of progress students make from one school year to the next. A student might enter high school speaking little English, reading English at only a primary grade level, and he or she might be antagonistic or apathetic toward schooling. If this student progresses to an intermediate-grade level in one year, then the teacher and school would deserve enormous credit, although the judgment might be *underperforming* because the student was not reading at the level specified for proficiency. Comparing reading performance before and after instruction is known as a *growth* or *value-added* measure because it tracks what schools contribute to individual students' learning over time.

Growth, or value-added, assessments are an antidote to the prevailing NCLB accountability model that focuses on getting youth to a certain level regardless of where they start (Sunderman & Kim, 2004). Before-and-after assessments work to specify the effects of teachers and schools on learning, showing the rates of growth that instruction brings about rather than the absolute levels of achievement, regardless of background characteristics like poverty. Growth, or value-added, assessments that depict school effectiveness accurately and fairly permit good teachers to remain in challenging classrooms.

Finally, decisions about youth's reading performance currently vary substantially from state to state because each state defines its own level of proficiency

Table 13.1 Percent of Eighth-Grade Students Scoring at Proficient Level

State	State Assessment	NAEP
South Carolina	21%	24%
Wyoming	39%	34%
North Carolina	86–88%	29%
Texas	86–88%	26%

(McCombs, Kirby, Barney, Darilek, & Magee, 2004). As Table 13.1 shows, equivalent numbers of South Carolina and Wyoming eighth-grade students have demonstrated proficiency on their respective state assessments and the National Assessment of Educational Progress (NAEP) (n.d.). However, discrepant numbers of North Carolina and Texas eighth graders demonstrated proficiency on the two assessments, with far more students performing well with the state's than with the NAEP's. Discrepancies like these show that states such as South Carolina and Wyoming are expecting readers to perform at higher levels than states like North Carolina and Texas. If policymakers consider youths' reading performance only on state-level assessments, then decisions about their performance will vary dramatically from state to state.

A second deplorable aspect of NCLB's high-stakes accountability system involves abandoning learners (Booher-Jennings, 2005; Settlage & Meadows, 2002). School administrators, counselors, and teachers often analyze test data to identify those students who probably (a) will pass future tests with no interventions, (b) will pass future tests if interventions are applied, and (c) will not pass future tests regardless of interventions. Using a triage mentality of saving the most promising cases, educators are at risk of focusing efforts on the middle group, those students scoring just below cut-off points, called *cusp* or *bubble* students, and allowing the higher- and lower-achieving students to coast. Moreover, in efforts to increase test scores, some schools have been known to place students in special education programs they do not need, encourage low-achieving readers to drop out and enter a General Educational Development (GED) program or alternative school (International Reading Association, 1999), or actually expel students from school.

Finally, high-stakes testing can result in cheating. In efforts to inflate test scores, educators have been known to photocopy secure tests for use in class, read off answers during a test, provide exact items or answers during test preparation sessions, disregard test administration directions (e.g., allow extra time, ignore student copying), and change students' answers or send students back to correct wrong answers (Hamilton, 2003).

Other forms of cheating involve wrongly excluding students from tests. Sometimes low-achieving students are assigned to a few days in a special protected class that excludes them from the state test, then they are reassigned to their regular classes when the test is finished. Sometimes, students who already have demonstrated proficiency are repeatedly included in later test administrations. Doing so produces higher overall test scores for the school, even though the particular students receive no academic benefit. And sometimes school administrators give faulty identification numbers to low-achieving students so their scores do not lower a school's scores. These misguided actions on the parts of teachers might be attempts to benefit students, themselves, or their schools.

What Aspects of NCLB Are Most Promising?

As indicated earlier in this chapter, we believe that many NCLB provisions affecting literacy are troublesome. As with most large-scale dramatic changes, some serious tensions are evident. Despite these strains, we think the following aspects of NCLB show promise.

One promising aspect of NCLB is that educators more and more are using assessment data to make decisions (Hamilton, 2003). Educators as never before are examining the results of instruction, determining what is and is not working, and doing something about it. Programs are being aligned and directed toward concrete results. Teaching is becoming more responsive to students' demonstrated achievement.

Another positive aspect of NCLB is the change evident in many schools toward positive expectations for struggling readers. With the notion that all youth can learn, educators seem to be focusing on struggling readers' and writers' achievement more than in the past. In many cases, these youth now are receiving multiple opportunities to learn; if one lesson is unproductive, another is tried. In addition, test results are being used to attract resources to students who are especially needy.

Third, schools, now more than ever, are articulating curricular purposes and goals that can be shared among school administrators and faculty, students, parents, and community members. Schools are focusing their efforts on clear outcomes, moving toward instructional consistency and direction. With these outcomes in mind, educators are better able to persuade one another to work collectively, engage students with what matters, and elicit support from parents and the community.

Conclusion

In general, effective educators are finding ways to work with NCLB, despite its limitations. To illustrate, Langer (2002, 2004) shows how excellent schools use assessments as opportunities to enrich curriculums rather than narrow them. Educators with this frame of mind do not focus on raising school test scores; they focus on improving youths' reading proficiencies. They consider reading test scores to be a means to the end of competent reading. When test results come in, students, teachers, and administrators interpret them in light of the goals and practices of the current curriculum. They connect test demands with course work, integrating test preparation into the ongoing curriculum rather than allocating separate time to isolated activities. They invest in schoolwide professional development devoted to literacy rather than purchase add-on reading improvement programs. In brief, they embed in schools' cultures the determination to achieve high standards through high-quality teaching.

We are convinced that bringing teachers into the conversation about NCLB and the curriculum is crucial. Doing so recognizes teachers' current professional knowledge and enhances their professional inquiry and growth (Rex & Nelson, 2004). Valuing teachers this way opens doors to reflect on their practice, explore solutions to everyday problems, and decide what best fits the situation. Closing doors to such conversations often means that the instruction occurring behind closed classroom doors continues unchanged.

We also are convinced that bringing students into the conversation is imperative. Authorizing students' perspectives on how mandated tests and course work connect with their personal, social, and cultural practices can make instruction more responsive (Cook-Sather, 2002). It permits teachers to take into account youth's experiences and perspectives relative to reading and writing. Acknowledging how young people identify themselves as readers and writers amid standards-based expectations holds great potential for adolescent literacy development.

In closing, meeting the goals of NCLB requires new ways of thinking because such goals have never been met in the past (Berliner & Biddle, 1995; Bracey, 2004; Kantor & Lowe, 2004; Rothstein, 1998). The United States has never had a golden age where all students from all walks of life obtained a high-quality intellectual education. Reports of extraordinary school and school district achievements relative to academic rigor certainly exist, but they typically were exceptions. High-achieving groups of students typically emerged in schools, but many other groups remained at limited levels. Students of poverty and of color, along with those of limited oral English and special learning needs, had especially limited expectations and opportunities to achieve academic excellence. Due to the NCLB provisions described here, attention to high levels of reading for everyone currently is at unprecedented levels. The opportunity—and the challenge—of NCLB is to ensure that this attention serves all students well.

LOOKING BACK   This chapter is meant to provide deep understandings of current governmental mandates that affect reading, teaching, and learning. It is meant to inform your professional decision making. It contains two key ideas: (1) The *No Child Left Behind* Act presents reading expectations as never before and (2) the opportunity—and the challenge—of *No Child Left Behind* is to ensure that it serves students well.

ADD TO YOUR JOURNAL Record in your class journal your reactions to this chapter. What do you think of the NCLB provisions? How might these provisions affect your teaching?

Additional Readings

Along with the numerous references listed in this chapter, the following three books provide additional context for considering the *No Child Left Behind* Act.

HESS, F. M., & FINN, C. E., Jr. (Eds.) (2004). *Leaving no child behind?: Options for kids in failing schools.* New York: Palgrave Macmillan.

POPHAM, W. J. (2004). *America's "failing" schools: How parents and teachers can cope with No Child Left Behind.* New York: RoutledgeFalmer.

SUNDERMAN, G. L., KIM, J. S., & ORFIELD, G. (2005). *NCLB meets school realities: Lessons from the field.* Thousand Oaks, CA: Corwin Press.

References

Chapter 1

Alvermann, D. E. (2001). Reading adolescents' reading identities: Looking back to see ahead. *Journal of Adolescent and Adult Literacy, 44*, 676–690.

Alvermann, D. E., Fitzgerald, J., & Simpson, M. (in press). Teaching and learning in reading. In P. Alexander & P. Winne (Eds.), *Handbook of Educational Psychology I* (2nd ed.). New York: Simon & Schuster/Macmillan.

Anderson, L. W., & Krathwohl, D. (Eds.) (2001). *A taxonomy for learning, teaching, and assessing: A revision of Bloom's taxonomy of educational objectives.* New York: Longman.

Biancarosa, F., & Snow, C. E. (2004). *Reading next—A vision for action and research in middle and high school literacy: A report to Carnegie Corporation of New York.* Washington, DC: Alliance for Excellent Education. www.all4ed.org/publications/ReadingNext/index.html.

Bransford, J. D., Brown, A. L., & Cocking, R. R. (Eds.). (1999). *How people learn: Brain, mind, experience, and school.* Washington, DC: National Academy Press.

Bruner, J. (1977). *The process of education.* Cambridge: Harvard University Press.

Colvin, C., & Schlosser, L. K. (1997). Developing academic confidence to build literacy: What teachers can do. *Journal of Adolescent and Adult Literacy, 41*(4), 272–281.

Davidson, A. L. (1996). *Making and molding identity in schools: Student narratives on race, gender, and academic identity.* Albany: State University of New York Press.

DeBlase, G. L. (2003). Missing stories, missing lives: Urban girls (re)constructing race and gender in the literacy classroom. *Urban Education, 38*, 279–329.

Dewey, J. (1910). *How we think.* Boston: D. C. Heath.

Farstrup, A. E., & Samuels, S. J. (2002). *What research has to say about reading instruction* (3rd ed.). Newark, DE: International Reading Association.

Fecho, B. (2004). *"Is this English?" Race, language, and culture in the classroom.* New York: Teachers College Press.

Gee, J. P. (2001). Identity as an analytic lens for research in education. In W. G. Secada (Ed.), *Review of Research in Education* (v. 25) (pp. 99–125). Washington, DC: American Educational Research Association.

Hagood, M. C. (2002). Critical literacy for whom? *Reading Research and Instruction, 41*, 247–266.

Holland, D., Lachicotte, W., Jr., Skinner, D., & Cain, C. (1998). *Identity and agency in cultural worlds*. Cambridge: Harvard University Press.

Jackson, D. B. (2003). Education reform as if student agency mattered: Academic microcultures and student identity. *Phi Delta Kappan, 84*, 579–585.

James, W. (1925). *Talks to teachers on psychology, and to students on some of life's ideals*. London: Longman.

Jetton, T. L., & Dole, J. A. (Eds.) (2004). *Adolescent literacy research and practice*. New York: The Guilford Press.

Jimenez, R. T. (2000). Literacy and identity development of Latina/o students. *American Educational Research Journal, 37*, 971–1000.

Knobel, M. (2001). "I'm not a pencil man": How one student challenges our notions of literacy "failure" in school. *Journal of Adolescent and Adult Literacy, 44*, 404–414.

Marzano, R. J. (2004). *Building background knowledge for academic achievement: Research on what works in schools*. Alexandria, VA: Association for Supervision and Curriculum Development.

McCarthey, S. J. (2002). *Students' identities and literacy learning*. Newark, DE: International Reading Association.

McCarthey, S. J., & Moje, E. B. (2002). Identity matters. *Reading Research Quarterly, 37*, 228–238.

McKenna, M. C., & Robinson, R. D. (1990). Content literacy: A definition and implications. *Journal of Reading, 34*, 184–186.

Mehan, H., Hubbard, L., & Villanueva, I. (1994). Forming academic identities: Accommodation without assimilation among involuntary minorities. *Anthropology and Education Quarterly, 25*, 91–117.

Moje, E. B., Ciechanowski, K. M., Kramer, K., Ellis, L., Carrillo, R., & Collazo, T. (2004). Working toward third space in content area literacy: An examination of everyday funds of knowledge and discourse. *Reading Research Quarterly, 39*, 38–70.

Moje, E. B., & Dillon, D. R. (in press). Adolescent identities as mediated by science classroom discourse communities. In D. E. Alvermann, K. A. Hinchman, D. W. Moore, S. F. Phelps, & D. R. Waff (Eds.), *Reconceptualizing the literacies in adolescents' lives* (2nd ed.) Mahwah, NJ: Lawrence Erlbaum Associates.

Moje, E. B., Young, J. P., Readence, J. E., & Moore, D. W. (2000). Reinventing adolescent literacy for new times: Perennial and millennial issues. *Journal of Adolescent and Adult Literacy, 43*(5), 400–410.

Moore, D. (2003). Adolescent literacy for all means forming academic identities. In C. Roller (Ed.), *Comprehensive reading instruction across the grade levels: A collection of papers from the Reading Research 2001 Conference* (pp. 148–160). Newark, DE: International Reading Association.

Moore, D. W., Bean, T. W., Birdyshaw, D., & Rycik, J. A., for the Commission on Adolescent Literacy of the International Reading Association. (1999). *Adolescent literacy: A position statement*. Newark, DE: International Reading Association.

Moore, D. W., Readence, J. E., & Rickelman, R. (1983). An historical exploration of content area reading instruction. *Reading Research Quarterly, 18*, 419–438.

National Reading Panel (2000). *Teaching children to read: An evidence-based assessment of the scientific research literature on reading and its implications for reading instruction: Reports of the subgroups*. Bethesda, MD: National Institute of Child Health and Human Development, National Institutes of Health.

Postman, N. (1979). *Teaching as a conserving activity*. New York: Delacorte.

RAND Reading Study Group. (2002). *Reading for understanding: Toward an R&D program in reading comprehension*. Santa Monica, CA: Science and Technology Policy Institute, RAND Education.

Reeves, A. R. (2004). *Adolescents talk about reading: Exploring resistance and engagement with text*. Newark, DE: International Reading Association.

Rogers, R. (2002). "That's what you're here for, you're suppose to tell us": Teaching and learning critical literacy. *Journal of Adolescent and Adult Literacy, 45*, 772–787.

Shearer, B. (Ed.) (2004). Multiple intelligences theory after 20 years [Special issue]. *Teachers College Record, 106*(1).

Strickland, D. S., & Alvermann, D. E. (Eds.) (2004). *Bridging the literacy achievement gap, grades 4–12*. New York. Teachers College Press.

Weinstein, C. E., & Mayer, R. E. (1985). The teaching of learning strategies. In M. C. Wittrock (Ed.), *Handbook of research on teaching* (3rd ed.) (pp. 315–327). New York: Macmillan.

Welch, O. M., & Hodges, C. R. (1997). *Standing outside on the inside: Black adolescents and the construction of academic identity*. Albany, NY: State University of New York.

Chapter 2

Bean, T. W. (2000). Reading in the content areas: Social constructivist dimensions. In M. J. Kamil, P. B. Mosenthal, P. D. Pearson, & R. Barr (Eds.), *Handbook of reading research* (vol. 3) (pp. 631–646). Mahwah, NJ: Lawrence Erlbaum Associates.

Braunger, J., Donahue, D. M., Evans, K., & Galguera, T. (2005). *Rethinking preparation for content area teaching: The reading apprentice approach*. San Francisco: Jossey Bass.

Cunningham, A. E., & Stanovich, K. E. (1998). What reading does to the mind. *American Educator, 22*(1), 8–15.

Daniels, H., & Steineke, N. (2004). *Mini-lessons for literature circles*. Portsmouth, NH: Heinemann.

Dewey, J. (1938). *Experience and education*. New York: Macmillan.

Fisher, D. (2004). Setting the "opportunity to read" standard: Resuscitating the SSR program in an urban high school. *Journal of Adolescent and Adult Literacy, 48*, 138–150.

Good, T. L., & McCaslin, M. M. (1992). Teaching effectiveness. In M. C. Alkin (Ed.), *Encyclopedia of educational research* (6th ed.) (pp. 1373–1388). New York: Macmillan.

Krashen, S. (2004). *The power of reading* (2nd ed.). Englewood, CO: Libraries Unlimited.

Langer, J. A. (2002). *Effective literacy instruction: Building successful reading and writing programs*. Urbana, IL: National Council of Teachers of English.

McMahon, S. I., & Raphael, T. E. (Eds.). (1997). *The book club connection: Literacy learning and classroom talk*. New York: Teachers College Press; Newark, DE: International Reading Association.

Moore, D. W. (1996). Contexts for literacy in secondary schools. In D. J. Leu, C. K. Kinzer, & K. A. Hinchman (Eds.), *Literacies for the 21st century: Research and practice*. Forty-fifth

Yearbook of the National Reading Conference (pp. 15–46). Chicago: National Reading Conference.

Morrow, L. M., Gambrell, L. B., & Pressley, M. (Eds.). (2003). *Best practices in literacy instruction* (2nd ed.). New York: Guilford.

Newmann, F. M., & associates. (1996). *Authentic achievement: Restructuring schools for intellectual quality*. San Francisco: Jossey-Bass.

Palincsar, A. S. (2002). Reciprocal teaching. In B. J. Guzzetti (Ed.), *Literacy in America: An encyclopedia of history, theory, and practice* (vol. 2; pp. 535–538). Santa Barbara, CA: ABC-CLIO.

Pilgreen, J. L. (2000). *The SSR handbook: How to organize and manage a sustained silent reading program*. Portsmouth, NH: Boynton/Cook.

Rex, L. A. (2001). The remaking of a high school reader. *Reading Research Quarterly, 36*, 288–314.

Schön, D. (1983). *The reflective practitioner: How professionals think in action*. New York: Basic Books.

Shepard, L., Hammerness, K., Darling-Hammond, L., & Rust, F. (2005). Assessment. In L. Darling-Hammond & J. Bransford (Eds.), *Preparing teachers for a changing world: What teachers should learn and be able to do*. San Francisco: Jossey-Bass.

Stiggins, R. J. (2005). *Student-involved assessment for learning* (4th ed.). Upper Saddle River, NJ: Pearson/Merrill-Prentice Hall.

Stone, R. (2002). *Best practices for high school classrooms: What award winning secondary school teachers do*. Thousand Oaks, CA: Corwin.

Trelease, J. (2003). *The read aloud handbook* (5th ed.). New York: Penguin.

Zemelman, S., Daniels, H., & Hyde, A. (2005). *Best practice: Today's standards for teaching and learning in America's schools* (3rd ed.). Portsmouth, NH: Heinemann.

Chapter 3

Albright, L. K. (2002). Bringing the Ice Maiden to life: Engaging adolescents in learning through picture book read-alouds in content areas. *Journal of Adolescent and Adult Literacy, 45*, 418–428.

Arter, J., & McTighe, J. (2001). *Scoring rubrics in the classroom: Using performance criteria for assessing and improving student performance*. Thousand Oaks, CA: Corwin Press.

Brown, J. L., & Wiggins, G. (2004). *Making the most of Understanding by Design*. Alexandria, VA: Association of Supervision and Curriculum Development.

Bruce, L. B. (2001). Student self-assessment: Making standards come alive. Retrieved November 20, 2004 from *Classroom Leadership*: www.ascd.org/publications/class_lead/200109/bruce.html.

Carr, E., & Ogle, D. (1987). K-W-L Plus: A strategy for comprehension and summarization. *Journal of Reading, 30*, 626–631.

Carr, K. S., Buchanan, D. L., Wentz, J. B., Weiss, M. L., & Brant, K. J. (2001). Not just for the primary grades: A bibliography of picture books for secondary content teachers. *Journal of Adolescent and Adult Literacy, 45*, 146–153.

Clark, J. H., & Agne, R. M. (1997). *Interdisciplinary high school teaching: Strategies for integrated learning.* Boston: Allyn and Bacon.

Conley, M. W. (2005). *Connecting standards and assessment through literacy.* Boston: Allyn and Bacon.

Drake, S., & Burns, R. (2004). *Meeting standards through integrated curriculum.* Alexandria, VA: Association for Supervision and Curriculum Development.

Erickson, H. L. (2002). *Concept-based curriculum and instruction: Teaching beyond the facts* (2nd ed.). Thousand Oaks, CA: Corwin.

Huffman, L. E. (2000). Spotlighting specifics by combining focus questions with K-W-L. In D. W. Moore, D. E. Alvermann, & K. A. Hinchman (Eds.), *Struggling adolescent readers: A collection of teaching strategies* (pp. 220–222). Newark, DE: International Reading Association.

Hurt, J. (2003). *Taming the standards: A commonsense approach to higher student achievement, K–12.* Portsmouth, NH: Heinemann.

Mitchell, R., Willis, M., & The Chicago Teachers Union Quest Center. (1995). *Learning in overdrive: Designing curriculum, instruction, and standards; A manual for teachers.* Golden, CO: North American Press.

Readence, J. E., Moore, D. W., & Rickelman, R. J. (2000). *Prereading activities for content area reading and learning* (3rd ed.). Newark, DE: International Reading Association.

Stiggins, R. J. (2005). *Student-involved assessment for learning* (4th ed.). Upper Saddle River, NJ: Pearson/Merrill-Prentice Hall.

Wiggins, G., & McTighe, J. (2005). *Understanding by design* (2nd ed.). Alexandria, VA: Association of Supervision and Curriculum Development.

Wood, K. E. (2001). *Interdisciplinary instruction: A practical guide for elementary and middle school teachers.* Upper Saddle River, NJ: Merrill.

Zmuda, A., & Tomaino, M. (2001). *The competent classroom: Aligning high school curriculum, standards, and assessment; A creative teaching guide.* New York: Teachers College Press.

Chapter 4

Alvermann, D. E. (1991). The Discussion Web: A graphic aid for learning across the curriculum. *The Reading Teacher, 45,* 92–99.

Applebee, A. N., Langer, J., Nystrand, M., & Gamoran, A. (2003). Discussion-based approaches to developing understanding: Classroom instruction and student performance in middle and high school English. *American Educational Research Journal, 40,* 685–730.

Benedicty, A. (1995). Reading *Shabanu,* creating multiple entry points for diverse readers. *Voices from the Middle, 2*(1), 12–17.

Boyd, F. (2003). Experiencing things not seen: Educative events centered on a study of *Shabanu. Journal of Adolescent and Adult Literacy, 46,* 460–470.

Campbell, M., & Cleland, J. V. (2003). *Readers theatre in the classroom: A manual for teachers of children and adults.* Lincoln, NE: Iuniverse.

Cunningham, A. E., & Stanovich, K. E. (1998). What reading does to the mind. *American Educator, 22*(1), 8–15.

de la Luz Reyes, M., & Halcon, J. J. (2001). *The best for our children: Critical perspectives on literacy for Latino children*. New York: Teachers College Press.

Dillon, J. T. (1988). *Questioning and teaching: A manual of practice*. New York: Teachers College Press.

Figueira, A., Hudelson, S., & Smith, K. (2002). Multicultural literacy. In B. Guzzetti (Ed.), *Literacy in America: An encyclopedia of history, theory, and practice* (pp. 364–368). Santa Barbara, CA: ABC-CLIO.

Finkelstein, N. H. (1999). *The way things never were: The truth about the "good old days."* New York: Atheneum.

Gallo, D. (Ed.) (1995). *Ultimate sports*. New York: Delacorte.

Grabe, M., & Grabe, C. (2004). *Integrating technology for meaningful learning* (4th ed.). New York: Houghton Mifflin.

Herz, S. K., & Gallo, D. R. (1996). *From Hinton to Hamlet: Building bridges between young adult literature and the classics*. Westport, CT: Greenwood Press.

Hunsader, P. D. (2004). Mathematics trade books: Establishing their value and assessing their quality. *The Reading Teacher, 57*, 618–629.

International Reading Association. (2001). *Integrating literacy and technology in the curriculum: A position statement*. Retrieved August 25, 2005 from the International Reading Association website: www.reading.org/resources/issues/positions_technology.html.

Jurstedt, R., & Koutras, M. (2000). *Teaching writing with picture books as models*. New York: Scholastic.

Kaywell, J. F. (1997). *Adolescent literature as a complement to the classics* (vol. 3). Norwood, MA: Christopher-Gordon.

Kist, W. (2005). *New literacies in action: Teaching and learning in multiple media*. New York: Teachers College Press.

Krashen, S. (2004). *The power of reading* (2nd ed.). Englewood, CO: Libraries Unlimited.

Leu, D. J., Leu, D. D., & Coiro, J. (2004). *Teaching with the Internet K–12: New literacies for new times* (4th ed.). Norwood, MA: Christopher-Gordon.

Loewen, J. W. (1996). *Lies my teacher told me: Everything your American history textbook got wrong*. New York: Touchstone.

Marlette, P. B., & Gordon, C. J. (2004). The use of alternative texts in physical education. *Journal of Adolescent and Adult Literacy, 48*, 226–237.

Miller, T. (2000). The place of picture books in middle-level classrooms. In D. W. Moore, D. E. Alvermann, & K. A. Hinchman (Eds.), *Struggling adolescent readers: A collection of teaching strategies*. Newark, DE: International Reading Association.

Moen, C. B. (2004). *Read-alouds and performance reading: A handbook of activities for the middle school classroom*. Norwood, MA: Christopher-Gordon.

O'Brien, D. G., & Bauer, E. B. (2005). New literacies and the institution of old learning. *Reading Research Quarterly, 40*, 120–131.

Parker, W. C. (2001). Classroom discussion: Models for leading seminars and deliberations. *Social Education, 65*(2), 111–115.

Ravitch, D. (2003). *The language police: How pressure groups restrict what students learn*. New York: Knopf.

Ruggieri, C. A. (2001). What about our girls? Considering gender roles in *Shabanu*. *The English Journal, 90*(3), 48–53.

Smith, J. L., & Herring, J. D. (2001). *Using drama and literature to teach middle-level content.* Portsmouth, NH: Heinemann.

Whitlin, P. (1996). *Sketching stories, stretching minds.* Portsmouth, NH: Heinemann.

Wiske, M. S. (2005). *Teaching for understanding with technology.* San Francisco: Jossey-Bass.

Worthman, C. (2002). *"Just playing the part": Engaging adolescents in drama and literacy.* New York: Teachers College Press.

Wyn, M. A., & Stegink, S. J. (2000). Role-playing mitosis. *The American Biology Teacher, 62,* 378–381.

Chapter 5

Alvermann, D. E., Fitzgerald, J., & Simpson, M. (in press). Teaching and learning in reading. In P. Alexander & P. Winne (Eds.), *Handbook of Educational Psychology* (2nd ed.). New York: Simon & Schuster/Macmillan.

Bangert-Down, R. L., Hurley, M. M., & Wilkinson, B. (2004). The effects of school-based writing-to-learn interventions on academic achievement: A meta-analysis. *Review of Educational Research, 74,* 29–58.

Beck, I. L., Mckeown, M. G., Hamilton, R. L., & Kucan, L. (1997). *Questioning the author: An approach for enhancing student engagement with text.* Newark, DE: International Reading Association.

Benedicty, A. (1995). Reading *Shabanu:* Creating multiple entry points for diverse readers. *Voices from the Middle, 2*(1), 12–17.

Block, C. C., & Pressley, M. (2003). Best practices in comprehension instruction. In L. M. Morrow, L. B. Gambrell, & M. Pressley (Eds.), *Best practices in literacy instruction* (2nd ed; pp. 111–126). New York: The Guilford Press.

Carr, E., & Ogle, D. (1987). KWL plus: A strategy for comprehension and summarization. *Journal of Reading, 30,* 626–631.

Dole, J. (2002). Comprehension strategies. In B. Guzzetti (Ed.), *Literacy in America: An encyclopedia of history, theory, and practice* (pp. 85–88). Santa Barbara, CA: ABC-CLIO.

Guthrie, J. T., & Wigfield, A. (2000). Engagement and motivation in reading. In M. J. Kamil, P. B. Mosenthal, P. D. Pearson, & R. Barr (Eds.), *Handbook of reading research* (vol. 3) (pp. 406–422). Mahwah, NJ: Lawrence Erlbaum Associates.

Hirsch, E. D., Jr. (2003). *Reading comprehension requires knowledge—of words and the world.* Retrieved August 28, 2005, from the American Educator web site. www.aft.org/pubs-reports/american_educator/spring2003/index.html.

Keene, E. O., & Zimmerman, S. (1997). *Mosaic of thought: Teaching comprehension in a reader's workshop.* Portsmouth, NH: Heinemann.

Kiewra, K. A. (2002). How classroom teachers can help students learn and teach them how to learn. *Theory into Practice, 41,* 71–80.

Kirk, R. E. (1972). Classification of ANOVA designs. In R. E. Kirk (Ed.), *Statistical issues: A reader for the behavioral sciences.* Belmont, CA: Wadsworth.

Lloyd, S. L. (2004). Using comprehension strategies as a springboard for student talk. *Journal of Adolescent and Adult Literacy, 48,* 114–124.

National Reading Panel (2000). *Teaching children to read: An evidence-based assessment of the scientific research literature on reading and its implications for reading instruction: Reports of the subgroups*. Bethesda, MD: National Institute of Child Health and Human Development, National Institutes of Health.

Ogle, D. (1986). K-W-L: A teaching model that develops active reading of expository text. *The Reading Teacher, 39*, 564–570.

Palincsar, A. S. (2002). Reciprocal teaching. In B. J. Guzzetti (Ed.), *Literacy in America: An encyclopedia of history, theory, and practice* (vol. 2; pp. 535–538). Santa Barbara, CA: ABC-CLIO.

Palincsar, A. S., & Herrenkohl, L. R. (2002). Designing collaborative learning contexts. *Theory into Practice, 41*, 26–32.

Stauffer, R. G. (1969). *Directing reading maturity as a cognitive process*. New York: Harper & Row.

Thorndike, E. L. (1917). Reading as reasoning: A study of mistakes in paragraph reading. *Journal of Educational Psychology, 8*, 276–282.

Vaughn, S., Klingner, J. K., & Bryant, D. P. (2001). Collaborative strategic reading as a means to enhance peer-mediated instruction for reading comprehension and content-area learning. *Remedial and Special Education, 22*(2), 66–74.

Vygotsky, L. (1978). *Mind in society: The development of higher psychological processes*. Cambridge, Harvard University Press.

Wood, K. D., Lapp, D., & Flood, J. (1992). *Guiding readers through text: A review of study guides*. Newark, DE: International Reading Association.

Chapter 6

Beck, I. L., McKeown, M. G., & Kucan, L. (2002). *Bringing words to life: Robust vocabulary instruction*. New York: The Guilford Press.

Blachowicz, C. L. Z., & Fisher, P. (2004). Keep the "fun" in fundamental: Encourage word awareness and incidental word learning in the classroom through word play. In J. F. Baumann & E. J. Kame'enui (Eds.), *Vocabulary instruction: Research to practice* (pp. 218–237). New York: The Guilford Press.

Brozo, W. G., Valerio, P. C., & Salazar, M. M. (1996). A walk through Gracie's garden: Literacy and cultural expectations in a Mexican American junior high school. *Journal of Adolescent and Adult Literacy, 40*(3), 164–170.

Carlo, M. S., August, D., Snow, C. E., Dressler, C., Lippman, D. N., Lively, T. J., & White, C. E. (2004). Closing the gap: Addressing the vocabulary needs of English-language learners in bilingual and mainstream classrooms. *Reading Research Quarterly, 39*, 188–215.

Cunningham, A. E., & Stanovich, K. (1998). What reading does to the mind. *American Educator, 22*(1), 8–15.

Edwards, E. C., Font, G., Baumann, J. F., & Boland, E. (2004). Unlocking word meanings: Strategies and guidelines for teaching morphemic and contextual analysis. In J. F. Baumann & E. J. Kame'enui (Eds.), *Vocabulary instruction: Research to practice* (pp. 159–176). New York: The Guilford Press.

Graves, M. F. (2000). A vocabulary program to complement and bolster a middle-grade comprehension program. In B. M. Taylor, M. F. Graves, & P. van den Broek (Eds.), *Reading for meaning: Fostering comprehension in the middle grades* (pp. 116–135). New York: Teachers College Press.

Graves, M. F., & Watts-Taffe, S. M. (2002). The place of word consciousness in a research-based vocabulary program. In A. E. Farstrup & S. J. Samuels (Eds.), *What research has to say about reading instruction* (3rd ed., pp. 140–165). Newark, DE: International Reading Association.

Harmon, J. M. (2000). Assessing and supporting independent word learning strategies of middle school students. *Journal of Adolescent and Adult Literacy, 43,* 518–527.

Harmon, J. M. (2002). Teaching independent word learning strategies to struggling readers. *Journal of Adolescent and Adult Literacy, 45,* 606–615.

Henry, M. K. (1997). The decoding/spelling curriculum: Integrated decoding and spelling instruction from pre-school to early secondary school. *Dyslexia, 3,* 178–189.

Krashen, S. (2004). *The power of reading* (2nd ed.). Englewood, CO: Libraries Unlimited.

Nagy, W., & Anderson, R. C. (1984). How many words are there in printed school English? *Reading Research Quarterly, 19,* 304–330.

National Reading Panel. (2000). *Teaching children to read: An evidence-based assessment of the scientific research literature on reading and its implications for reading instruction: Reports of the subgroups.* Bethesda, MD: National Institute of Child Health and Human Development, National Institutes of Health.

Ruddell, M., & Shearer, B. (2002). "Extraordinary," "tremendous," "exhilarating," "magnificent": Middle-school at risk students become avid word learners with the Vocabulary Self-Collection Strategy (VSS). *Journal of Adolescent and Adult Literacy, 45,* 352–363.

Scott, J. A., & Nagy, W. E. (2004). Developing word consciousness. In J. F. Baumann & E. J. Kame'enui (Eds.), *Vocabulary instruction: Research to practice* (pp. 201–217). New York: The Guilford Press.

Swanborn, M. S. L., & de Glopper, K. (1999). Incidental word learning while reading. *Review of Educational Research, 69,* 261–285.

Templeton, S. (2004). The vocabulary-spelling connection: Orthographic development and morphological knowledge at the intermediate grades and beyond. In J. F. Baumann & E. J. Kame'enui (Eds.), *Vocabulary instruction: Research to practice* (pp. 118–138). New York: The Guilford Press.

Tierney, R. J., & Pearson, P. D. (1992). Learning to learn from text: A framework for improving classroom practice. In E. K. Dishner, T. W. Bean, J. E. Readence, D. W. Moore (Eds.), *Reading in the content areas: Improving classroom instruction* (3rd ed., pp. 87–102). Dubuque, IA: Kendall/Hunt.

Venezky, R. L. (1999). *The American way of spelling: The structure and origins of American English orthography.* New York: The Guilford Press.

Chapter 7

Abrams, S. (2000). *Using journals with reluctant writers: Building portfolios for middle and high school students.* Thousand Oaks, CA: Corwin.

Bangert-Drowns, R. L., Hurley, M. M., & Wilkinson, B. (2004). The effects of school-based writing-to-learn interventions on academic achievement: A meta-analysis. *Review of Educational Research, 74,* 29–58.

Bromley, K. (1999). *Journaling: Engagement in reading, writing, and thinking.* New York: Scholastic Professional Books.

Bruce, B., & Levin, J. (2003). Roles for new technologies in language arts: Inquiry, communication, construction, and expression. In J. Flood, D. Lapp, J. R. Squire, & J. M. Jensen (Eds.), *Handbook of research on teaching the English language arts* (2nd ed.; pp. 649–657). New York: Macmillan.

Fazio, B. (1992). Students as historians—writing their school's history. *The Social Studies, 83,* 64–67.

Fisher, D., & Frey, N. (2003). Writing instruction for struggling adolescent readers: A gradual release model. *Journal of Adolescent and Adult Reading, 46,* 396–405.

Gere, A. R., Christenbury, L., & Sassi, K. (2005). *Writing on demand.* Portsmouth, NH: Heinemann.

Holston, V., & Santa, C. (1985). A method of writing across the curriculum that works. *Journal of Reading, 28,* 456–457.

Newell, G. E. (2005). Writing to learn: How alternative theories of school writing account for student performance. In C. A. MacArthur, S. Graham, & J. Fitzgerald (Eds.), *Handbook of writing research.* New York: The Guilford Press.

Readence, J. E., Bean, T. W., & Baldwin, R. S. (2000). Content area literacy: An integrated approach (7th ed.). Dubuque, IA: Kendall/Hunt.

Chapter 8

Braunger, J., Donahue, D. M., Evans, K., & Galguera, T. (2005). *Rethinking preparation for content area teaching: The reading apprenticeship approach.* San Francisco: Jossey-Bass.

Devine, T. G., & Kania, J. S. (2003). Studying: Skills, strategies, and systems. In J. Flood, D. Lapp, J. R. Squire, & J. M. Jensen (Eds.), *Handbook of research on teaching the English language arts* (2nd ed.; pp. 942–954). New York: Macmillan.

Fry, R. (2000). *How to study* (5th ed.). Franklin Lakes, NJ: Career Press.

Glynn, S., Koballa, & Coleman, D. (2003). Mnemonic methods. *The Science Teacher, 20,* 52–55.

Greene, L. J. (2005). *Study max: Improving study skills in grades 9–12.* Thousand Oaks, CA: Corwin Press.

Kiewra, K. A. (2002). How classroom teachers can help students learn and teach them how to learn. *Theory into Practice, 41,* 71–80.

Kraemer, D. J. (2005). Fighting forward: Why studying standardized tests with our students is important. *English Journal, 94,* 88–92.

Langer, J. (2000). Excellence in English in middle and high school: How teachers' professional lives support student achievement. *American Educational Research Journal, 37*(2), 397–439.

Langer, J. A. (2002). *Effective literacy instruction: Building successful reading and writing programs.* Urbana, IL: National Council of Teachers of English.

Moore, D. W., Readence, J. E., & Rickelman, R. R. (1983). An historical exploration of content area reading instruction. *Reading Research Quarterly, 18,* 419–438.

Palincsar, A. S. (2002). Reciprocal teaching. In B. J. Guzzetti (Ed.), *Literacy in America: An encyclopedia of history, theory, and practice* (vol. 2; pp. 535–538). Santa Barbara, CA: ABC-CLIO.

Pearson, J. W., & Santa, C. M. (1995). Students as researchers of their own learning. *Journal of Reading, 38,* 462–469.

Peverly, S. T., & Wood, R. (2001). The effects of adjunct questions and feedback on improving the reading comprehension skills of learning-disabled adolescents. *Contemporary Educational Psychology, 26,* 25–43.

Readence, J. E., & Moore, D. W. (1984). An investigation of current attention to the early literature on content area reading instruction. *Reading World, 23,* 299–307.

Robinson, F. P. (1941). *Diagnostic and remedial techniques for effective study.* New York: Harper & Row.

Rosenshine, B., & Meister, C. (1992). The use of scaffolds for teaching higher-level cognitive strategies. *Educational Leadership, 50,* 26–33.

Rosenshine, B., & Meister, C. (1994). Reciprocal teaching: A review of the research. *Review of Educational Research, 64,* 479–530.

Santman, D. (2002). Teaching to the test?: Test preparation in the reading workshop. *Language Arts, 79,* 203–211.

Slater, W. H., & Horstman, F. R. (2002). Teaching reading and writing to struggling middle and high school students: The case for reciprocal teaching. *Preventing School Failure, 46*(4), 163–166.

Zimmerman, B. J. (2002). Becoming a self-regulated learner: An overview. *Theory into practice, 41*(2), 64–70.

Chapter 9

Allen, C. A. (2001). *The multigenre research paper: Voice, passion, and discovery in grades 4–6.* Portsmouth, NH: Heinemann.

Allen, C. A., & Swistak, L. (2004). Multigenre research: The power of choice and interpretation. *Language Arts, 81,* 223–232.

Association of College and Research Libraries (1998). *A progress report on information literacy: An update on the American Library Association Presidential Committee on Information Literacy: Final report.* Retrieved September 15, 2005 from the Association of College & Research Libraries web site: www.ala.org/ala/acrl/acrlpubs/whitepapers/progressreport.htm.

Burke, J. (2002). *Tools for thought: Graphic organizers for your classroom.* Portsmouth, NH: Heinemann.

Callison, D. (2003). *Key words, concepts and methods for Information Age instruction: A guide to teaching information inquiry.* Englewood, CO: Libraries Unlimited.

Galus, P. (2002). Detecting and preventing plagiarism. *Science Teacher, 69,* 35–37.

Guthrie, J. T., Wigfield, A., & Perencevich, K. C. (Eds.) (2004). *Motivating reading comprehension: Concept-oriented reading instruction.* Mahwah, NJ: Lawrence Erlbaum Associates.

Kain, D. L. (2003). *Problem-based learning for teachers, grades K–8*. Boston: Allyn and Bacon.

Kellett, M. (2005). *How to develop children as researchers*. Thousand Oaks, CA: Sage.

Kist, W. (2005). *New literacies in action: Teaching and learning in multiple media*. New York: Teachers College Press.

Lambros, A. (2004). *Problem-based learning in middle and high school classrooms: A teacher's guide to implementation*. Thousand Oaks, CA: Corwin Press.

Leu, D. J., Leu, D. D., & Coiro, J. (2004). *Teaching with the Internet K–12: New literacies for new times* (4th ed.). Norwood, MA: Christopher-Gordon.

Martinello, M. L., & Cook, G. E. (2000). Interdisciplinary inquiry in teaching and learning (2nd ed.). Upper Saddle River, NJ: Merrill.

Rankin, V. (1999). *The thoughtful researcher: Teaching the research process to middle school students*. Englewood, CO: Libraries Unlimited.

Rogovin, P. (2001). *The research workshop: Bringing the world into your classroom*. Portsmouth, NH: Heinemann.

Roser, N. L., Strecker, S. K., & Ward, T. J. (1996). "What I wanna know is why Sam Houston's mom named him after a city": Moving (slowly) toward inquiry in fourth grade. In D. J. Leu, C. K. Kinzer, & K. A. Hinchman (Eds.), *Literacies for the 21st century: Research and practice*. Forty-fifth Yearbook of the National Reading Conference (pp. 134–145). Chicago: National Reading Conference.

Rossi, J. A., & Pace, C. M. (1998). Issues-centered instruction with low achieving high school students: The dilemmas of two teachers. *Theory and Research in Social Education, 26*, 380–409.

Simkins, M., Cole, K., Tavalin, F., & Means, B. (2002). *Increasing student learning through multimedia projects*. Alexandria, VA: Association for Supervision and Curriculum Development.

Stahl, S. A., Hynd, C. R., Britton, B. R., McNish, M. M., & Bosquet, D. (1996). What happens when students read multiple source documents in history? *Reading Research Quarterly, 31*, 430–456.

Stepien, W. J., Senn, O., & Stepien, W. C. (2000). *The Internet and problem-based learning: Developing solutions through the web*. Tucson, AZ: Zephyr Press.

Stiggins, R. J. (2005). *Student-involved assessment for learning* (4th ed.). Upper Saddle River, NJ: Pearson/Merrill-Prentice Hall.

Chapter 10

Allington, R. L., & Johnston, P. H. (2002). *Reading to learn: Lessons from exemplary fourth-grade classrooms*. New York: Guilford Press.

Daniels, H. (2001). *Literature circles: Voice and choice in the student-centered classroom* (2nd ed.). York, ME: Stenhouse.

Denig, S. J. (2004). Multiple intelligences and learning styles: Two complementary dimensions. *Teachers College Record, 106*, 96–111.

Freeman, Y. S., Freeman, D. E., & Mercuri, S. P. (2005). *Dual language essentials for teachers and administrators*. Portsmouth, NH: Heinemann.

Gardner, H. (1993). *Frames of mind: The theory of multiple intelligences*. New York: Basic Books.

Gillies, R. M., & Ashman, A. F. (Eds.). (2003). *Co-operative learning: The social and intellectual outcomes of learning in groups*. New York: Routledge Falmer.

Hallahan, D. P., & Kauffman, J. M. (2003). *Exceptional learners: Introduction to special education* (9th ed.). Boston: Allyn and Bacon.

Kagan, S. (1997). *Cooperative learning*. San Clemente, CA: Kagan Publishing.

Ladson-Billings, G. (2001). *Crossing over to Canaan: The journey of new teachers in diverse classrooms*. San Francisco: Jossey-Bass.

McMahon, S. I., & Raphael, T. E. (Eds.). (1997). *The book club connection: Literacy learning and classroom talk*. New York: Teachers College Press; Newark, DE: International Reading Association.

McTighe, J., & Brown, J. L. (2005). Differentiated instruction and educational standards: Is détente possible? *Theory into Practice, 44,* 234–244.

Moore, D. W., & Hinchman, K. A. (2003). *Starting out: A guide to teaching adolescents who struggle with reading*. Boston: Allyn and Bacon.

Noble, T. (2004). Integrating the revised Bloom's taxonomy with multiple intelligences: A planning tool for curriculum differentiation. *Teachers College Record, 106,* 193–211.

Rabow, J., Chin, T., & Fahimian, N. (1999). *Tutoring matters*. Philadelphia: Temple University Press.

Rasinski, T., & Padak, N. (2004). *Effective reading strategies: Teaching children who find reading difficult* (3rd ed.). Upper Saddle River, NJ: Pearson/Prentice Hall.

Schmuck, R. A., & Schmuck, P. A. (2001). *Group processes in the classroom*. Boston: McGraw Hill.

Sternberg, R. J., & Shang, L. (2005). Styles of thinking as a basis for differentiating instruction. *Theory into Practice, 44,* 245–253.

Tomlinson, C. A. (2001). *How to differentiate instruction in mixed-ability classrooms* (2nd ed.). Alexandria, VA: Association for Supervision and Curriculum Development.

Chapter 12

Ancess, J. (2003). *Beating the odds: High schools as communities of commitment*. New York: Teachers College Press.

Blachowicz, C. L. Z., & Fisher, P. J. L. (2000). Vocabulary instruction. In M. J. Kamil, P. B. Mosenthal, P. D. Pearson, & R. Barr (Eds.), *Handbook of reading research* (vol. 3) (pp. 503–523). Mahwah, NJ: Lawrence Erlbaum Associates.

Chall, J. S., Jacobs, V. A., & Baldwin, L. E. (1990). *The reading crisis: Why poor children fall behind*. Cambridge: Harvard University Press.

Guzzetti, B. J., Young, J. P., Gritsavage, M. M., Laurie M. Fyfe, L. M., & Hardenbrook, M. (2002). *Reading, writing, and talking gender in literacy learning*. Newark, DE: International Reading Association.

Huey, E. B. (1998). *The psychology and pedagogy of reading*. Bristol, UK: Thoemmes Press. (Original work published 1908.)

Hull, G., & Schultz, K. (Eds.) (2002). *School's out: Bridging out-of-school literacies with classroom practice*. New York: Teachers College Press.

Linn, R. L. (2003). 2003 Presidential Address—Accountability: Responsibility and reasonable expectations. *Educational Researcher, 32*(7), 3–13.

Loomis, S. C., & Borque, M. L. (Ed.) (2001). *National Assessment of Educational Progress Achievement Levels, 1992–1998 for Reading.* Retrieved May 16, 2003 from www.nagb.org/pubs/readingbook.pdf.

Mahiri, J. (Ed.) (2004). *What they don't learn in school: Literacy in the lives of urban youth.* New York: Peter Lang.

McCombs, J. S., Kirby, S. N., Barney, H., Darilek, H., & Magee, S. J. (2004). *Achieving state and national literacy goals: A long uphill road: A report to Carnegie Corporation of New York.* Retrieved December 18, 2004 from the Rand Corporation web site: www.rand.org/publications/TR/TR180/.

National Assessment of Educational Progress (n.d.). *Reading.* Retrieved October 7, 2005 from the National Assessment of Educational Progress web site: http://nces.ed.gov/nationsreportcard/reading/.

O'Brien, D. (in press). "Struggling" adolescents' engagement in multimediating: Countering the institutional construction of incompetence. In D. E. Alvermann, K. A. Hinchman, D. W. Moore, S. F. Phelps, & D. R. Waff (Eds.), *Reconceptualizing the literacies in adolescents' lives* (2nd ed.). Mahwah, NJ: Lawrence Erlbaum Associates.

RAND Reading Study Group (2002). *Reading for understanding: Toward a research and development program in reading comprehension.* Retrieved August 11, 2003 from the RAND Corporation web site: www.rand.org/publications/MR/MR1465/.

Rothstein, R. (2004). *Class and schools: Using social, economic, and educational reform to close the black-white achievement gap.* New York: Economic Policy Institute/Teachers College Press.

Stanovich, K. E. (2000). *Progress in understanding reading: Scientific foundations and new frontiers.* New York: Guilford Press.

Chapter 13

Alderman, M. K. (2003). *Motivation for achievement.* Mahwah, NJ: Lawrence Erlbaum Associates.

American Educational Research Association (2000). *AERA position statement concerning high-stakes testing in preK-12 education.* Retrieved October 25, 2004, from the American Educational Research Association web site: www.aera.net/about/policy/stakes.htm.

Amrein, A. L., & Berliner, D. C. (2003). The effects of high-stakes tests on student motivation and achievement. *Educational Leadership, 60*(5), 32–38.

Barton, P. E. (2003). *Parsing the achievement gap: Baselines for tracking progress.* Retrieved November 8, 2003, from the Educational Testing Service web site: www.ETS.org/research/pic.

Barton, P. E. (2004). Why does the gap persist? *Educational Leadership, 62*(3), 8–13.

Berliner, D. C. (2005). *Our impoverished view of educational reform.* Retrieved August 22, 2005, from the Teachers College Record web site: www.tcrecord.org.

Biddle, B. J., & Berliner, D. C. (2003). *What research says about unequal funding for schools in America.* Retrieved October 13, 2004, from the WestEd site: www.wested.org/online_pubs/pp-03-01.pdf.

Berliner, D. C., & Biddle, B. J. (1995). *The manufactured crisis: Myth, fraud, and the attack on America's public schools*. Reading, MA: Addison Wesley.

Booher-Jennings, J. (2005). Below the bubble: "Educational triage" and the Texas Accountability System. *American Educational Research Journal, 42*, 231–268.

Bracey, G. (2004). *Setting the record straight* (2nd ed.). Portsmouth, NH: Heinemann.

Bracey, G. W. (2003). The 13th Bracey report on the condition of public education. *Phi Delta Kappan, 85*(2), 148–164.

Conley, M. W., & Hinchman, K. A. (2004). No Child Left Behind: What it means for U.S. adolescents and what we can do about it. *Journal of Adolescent and Adult Literacy, 48*(1), 42–50.

Cook-Sather, A. (2002). Authorizing students' perspectives: Toward trust, dialogue, and change in education. *Educational Researcher, 31*, 3–14.

Emerick, S., Hirsch, E., & Berry, B. (2004). *Does highly qualified mean high-quality?* Retrieved October 28, 2004, from the Association for Supervision and Curriculum Development web site: www.ascd.org/publications/infobrief/issue39.html?reid=sb.

Evans, R. (2005). Reframing the achievement gap. *Phi Delta Kappan, 86*, 582–589.

Ferguson, R. F. (2002). *What doesn't meet the eye: Understanding and addressing racial disparities in high-achieving suburban schools*. Retrieved December 3, 2004, from the North Central Regional Educational Laboratory web site: www.ncrel.org/gap/ferg/.

Gayler, K., Chudowsky, N., Kober, N., & Hamilton, M. (2003). *State high school exams put to the test*. Washington, DC: Center on Education Policy.

Greene, J. P., & Forster, G. (2004). *The Teachability Index: Can disadvantaged students learn?* Retrieved October 25, 2005 from the Manhattan Institute for Policy Research web site: www.manhattan-institute.org/html/ewp_06.htm.

Hamilton, L. (2003). Assessment as a policy tool. In R. E. Floden (Ed.), *Review of Research in Education* (vol. 27) (pp. 25–68). Washington, DC: American Educational Research Association.

International Reading Association (1999). *High stakes testing*. Retrieved October 25, 2004, from the International Reading Association web site: www.reading.org/positions /high_stakes.html.

Joint Organizational Statement on No Child Left Behind Act (October 2004). Retrieved April 8, 2005, from the FairTest: The National Center for Fair and Open Testing web site: www.fairtest.org/.

Joftus, S. (2002, September). *Every child a graduate: A framework for an excellent education for all middle and high school students*. Retrieved June 5, 2003, from the Alliance for Excellent Education web site: www.all4ed.org/publications/EveryChildAGraduate/index.html.

Joftus, S., & Maddux-Dolan, B. (2003, April). *Left out and left behind: NCLB and the American high school*. Retrieved August 12, 2003, from the Alliance for Excellent Education web site: www.all4ed.org/publications/NCLB/index.html.

Joint organizational statement on *No Child Left Behind* act (2004, October). Retrieved January 5, 2005, from the National Education Association web site: www.nea.org /presscenter/nclbjointstatement.html.

Kantor, H., & Lowe, R. (2004). Reflections on history and quality education. *Educational Researcher, 33*(5), 6–10.

Kochhar, R. (2004). *The wealth of Hispanic households: 1996 to 2002.* Retrieved October 19, 2004, from the Pew Hispanic Center web site: www.pewhispanic.org/page.jsp?page=Reports-Reports%20Section.

Langer, J. A. (2002). *Effective literacy instruction: Building successful reading and writing programs.* Urbana, IL: National Council of Teachers of English.

Langer, J. A. (2004). *Getting to excellent: How to create better schools.* New York: Teachers College Press.

Marshall, K. (2003). A principal looks back: Standards matter. *Phi Delta Kappan, 85*(2), 105–113.

McCombs, J. S., Kirby, S. N., Barney, H., Darilek, H., & Magee, S. J. (2004). *Achieving state and national literacy goals: A long uphill road: A report to Carnegie Corporation of New York.* Retrieved December 18, 2004, from the Rand Corporation web site: www.rand.org/publications/TR/TR180/.

Meier, D. (2002). *In schools we trust: Creating communities of learning in an era of testing and standardization.* Boston: Beacon Press.

Meier, D., & Wood, G. (2004). *Many children left behind: How the No Child Left Behind Act is damaging our children and our schools.* Boston: Beacon Press.

National Assessment of Educational Progress (n.d.). *Reading.* Retrieved October 7, 2005, from the National Assessment of Educational Progress web site: http://nces.ed.gov/nationsreportcard/reading/.

National Association of Secondary School Principals (n.d.). *Advocacy Action Alert: Act now to address the needs of secondary school students!* Retrieved December 22, 2003, from the National Association of Secondary School Principals web site: http://capwiz.com/nassp/mail/oneclick_compose/?alertid=4439001.

National Study Group for the Affirmative Development of Academic Ability (2004). *All students reaching the top: Strategies for closing academic achievement gaps.* Retrieved January 13, 2005, from the North Central Regional Educational Laboratory web site: www.ncrel.org/gap/studies/thetop.htm.

Ogbu, J. U. (2003). *Black American students in an affluent suburb: A study of academic disengagement.* Mahwah, NJ: Erlbaum.

Orfield, G., & Kornhaber, M. (Eds.). (2001). *Raising standards or raising barriers? Inequality and high stakes testing in public education.* Washington, DC: Century Foundation.

Pear, R. (2004, February 24). Education chief calls union "terrorist," then recants. *The New York Times.* Retrieved February 24, 2004 from www.nytimes.com.

Pogrow, S. The missing element in reducing the learning gap: Eliminating the "blank stare." Retrieved October 13, 2004, from Teachers College Record web site: www.tcrecord.org/Content.asp?ContentID=11381.

Public Agenda Online. (2003). *Rolling up their sleeves: Superintendents and principals talk about what's needed to fix public schools.* Retrieved November 19, 2003, from the Public Agenda web site: www.publicagenda.org/specials/rollingup/rollingup.htm.

Raudenbausch, S. (2004). *Schooling, statistics, and poverty: Can we measure school improvement?* Retrieved December 16, 2004, from the Educational Testing Service web site: www.ets.org/research/pic/.

Rex, L., & Nelson, M. C. (2004). How teachers' professional identities position high-stakes test preparation in their classrooms. *Teachers College Record, 106,* 1288–1331.

Robelen, E. W. (2003, October 1). Paige: Some U.S. students face a form of "apartheid." *Education Week*. Retrieved October 3, 2003, from www.edweek.org.

Roeser, R. W., Eccles, & Sameroff, A. J. (2000). School as a context of early adolescents' academic and social-emotional development: A summary of research. *Elementary School Journal, 100*, 443–462.

Rothstein, R. (1998). *The way we were? The myths and realities of America's student achievement.* New York: Century Foundation Press.

Rothstein, R. (2004). *Class and schools: Using social, economic, and educational reform to close the black-white achievement gap.* New York: Economic Policy Institute/Teachers College Press.

Settlage, J., & Meadows, L. (2002). Standards-based reform and its unintended consequences: Implications for science education within America's schools. *Journal of Research in Science Teaching, 39*, 114–127.

Stipek, D. J. (1996). Motivation and instruction. In D. C. Berliner & R. C. Calfee (Eds.), *Handbook of educational psychology* (pp. 85–113). New York: Macmillan.

Sunderman, G. L., & Kim, J. (2004). *Inspiring vision, disappointing results: Four studies on implementing the No Child Left Behind Act.* Retrieved November 15, 2004, from The Harvard University Civil Rights Project web site: www.civilrightsproject.harvard.edu/research/esea/nclb.php.

von Zastrow, C. (2004). *Academic atrophy: The condition of the liberal arts in America's public schools.* Retrieved August 12, 2004, from the Council of Basic Education web site: www.c-b-e.org/PDF/cbe_principal_Report.pdf.

Wigfield, A., & Eccles, J. (Eds.) (2002). *Development of achievement motivation.* San Diego: Academic Press.

Name Index

Subject Index